I0104263

GOVERNANCE       JUDICIARY       PAK-ARMY

# The Living History of Pakistan

[2012-13]       Volume II

*INCLUDING*

WHY AMERICA LOST THE AFGHAN WAR

by

INAM   R   SEHRI

Grosvenor House
Publishing Limited

All rights reserved
Copyright © Inam R Sehri, 2016

(However, scholars & students are permitted
to use material of this book by quoting the exact reference)
The right of Inam R Sehri to be identified as the author of this
work has been asserted in accordance with Section 78
of the Copyright, Designs and Patents Act 1988

The book cover picture is copyright to Klenger

This book is published by
Grosvenor House Publishing Ltd
28-30 High Street, Guildford, Surrey, GU1 3EL.
www.grosvenorhousepublishing.co.uk

This book is sold subject to the conditions that it shall not, by way of
trade or otherwise, be lent, resold, hired out or otherwise circulated
without the author's or publisher's prior consent in any form of binding
or cover other than that in which it is published and
without a similar condition including this condition being imposed
on the subsequent purchaser.

A CIP record for this book
is available from the British Library

[All page with usual statements ending with]

ISBN 978-1-78148-955-0

CONTEMPORARY HISTORY IS <u>NOT</u>

THAT WHICH HAS BEEN HAPPENING AROUND?

IT IS THE <u>STATEMENT OF FACTS</u>

ABOUT WHAT THE PEOPLE

CONSIDERED SIGNIFICANT

Other Books from

# INAM  R  SEHRI

## *KHUDKUSHI*
(on Suicide)  [in Urdu] (1983)
{Details of historical perspective of 'Suicide' in various societies; &
investigation techniques differentiating in Murder & Suicides}

## *WARDI KAY ANDAR AADMI*
(Man in uniform) [in Urdu] (1984)
{Collection of short stories keeping a sensitive policeman in focus}

## *AURAT JARAIM KI DALDAL MEIN*
(on Female Criminality) [in Urdu] (1985)
{Describing various theories and cultural taboos concerning Female
Criminal Behaviour}

## *POLICE AWAM RABTAY*
(on Police Public relationship) [in Urdu] (1986)
{Essays describing importance of mutual relationships}

## *DEHSHAT GARDI*
(on Terrorism) [in Urdu] (1987)
{Various theories and essays differentiating between Freedom
Fighting & Terrorism in Middle Eastern perspective}

## *QATL*
(on Murder) [in Urdu] (1988)
{The first book written for Police students & Lawyers to explain
techniques of investigation of (difficult) Murder cases}

## *SERVICE POLICING IN PAKISTAN*
[in English] (1990)
{A dissertation type book on which basis the PM Benazir Bhutto, in
1990, had okayed the Commissionerate System of Policing in Pakistan.
Taking Karachi as the pilot project, later, it was levied for all major cities
and still going on as such}

## *SHADI*
(on Marriages)  [in Urdu]  (1998)
{A detailed exposition of Marriage explained in various religions, cultures, countries and special groups; much applauded & commented upon on PTV in 1998-99}

All the above books were published by Pakistan's number one publisher

### SANG E MEEL PUBLICATIONS,

### *25 - The Lower Mall LAHORE, Pakistan*

And are normally available with them in latest re-prints.

*Judges & Generals in Pakistan VOL-I*
[in English]  (2012)

*Judges & Generals in Pakistan VOL-II*
[in English]  (2012)

*Judges & Generals in Pakistan VOL-III*
[in English]  (2013)

*Judges & Generals in Pakistan VOL-IV*
[in English]  (2013)

*The Living History of Pakistan VOL-I*
[in English]  (2015)

{The **FOUR** volumes of *'Judges & Generals in Pakistan'* are not the stories or facts about only the honourable judges or respectable military Generals of Pakistan but also an authentic record of contemporary history.

*Living History of Pakistan* Vol-I & **Vol-II** are continuation of the same series with only a change in name of the same product. It is just for the change of taste otherwise the SCENARIOS and the PAGE NUMBERS are in the same continuity. All the above books deal with Pakistan's chequered history of massive financial & intellectual corruption, abortive rule by two political parties in succession with higher judiciary's gimmicks during 1971 onwards; Constitutional Amendments which made political parties as family businesses & apex court's nexus making the politicians more corrupt.}

Published by
*Grosvenor House Publishing Ltd*
*28-30 High Street, Guildford*
*SURREY UK GU1 3HY*

# It's me; my Lord!

## INAM R SEHRI

- Born in Lyallpur (Pakistan) in April 1948

- First Degree from Government College Lyallpur (1969)

- Studied at Government College Lahore & got first Master's Degree from Punjab University Lahore (1971);

- Attachment with AJK Education Service (1973-1976)

- Central Superior Services (CSS) Exam passed (batch 1975)

- Civil Service Academy Lahore (joined 1976)

- National Police Academy Islamabad (joined 1977)

- LLB from BUZ University Multan (1981)

- Master's Degree from Exeter University of UK (1990)

- Regular Police Service: District Admin, Police College, National Police Academy, the Intelligence Bureau (IB), Federal Investigation Agency (FIA) [1977-1998] then migrated to the UK permanently.

A part-script copied from the earlier volumes:

Just spent a normal routine life; with hundreds of mentionable memoirs allegedly of bravery & glamour as every uniformed officer keeps, some times to smile at and next moment to repent upon but taking it just normal except one or two spills.

During my tenure at IB HQ Islamabad I got chance to peep into the elite civil and military leadership of Pakistan then existing in governmental dossiers and database.

During my stay at FIA I was assigned to conduct special enquiries & investigations into some acutely sensitive matters like Motorway Scandal, sudden expansion and build-up of Sharif family's industrial empire, Sharif's accounts in foreign countries; Alleged Financial Corruptions in Pakistan's Embassies in Far-Eastern Countries; Shahnawaz

Bhutto's murder in Cannes (France); Land Scandals of CDA's Estate Directorate; Ittefaq Foundry's 'custom duty on scrap' scam, Hudaibya Engineering & Hudaibya Paper Mills enquiries, Bhindara's Murree Brewery and tens more cases like that.

> [*Through these words I want to keep it on record that during the course of the above mentioned, (and also which cannot be mentioned due to space limits) investigations or enquiries, the then Prime Minister Benazir Bhutto, or [late] Gen Naseerullah Babar the then Federal Interior Minister, or G Asghar Malik the then DG FIA, had never ever issued direct instructions or implicit directions or wished me to distort facts or to go malafide for orchestrating a political edge or other intangible gains.*
>
> *Hats off to all of them!*]

*Some top bureaucrats like Kh Zaheer, Afzal Kahoot and Saeed Mehdi twisted my arms in the name of Sharif's anger firstly sent me home then tried to imprison me – only the INTERPOL's investigations into my affairs could rescue me.*

In Ingall Hall of the Pakistan Military Academy [PMA], it is carved:

> *"It is not what happens to you that matters but how you behave while it is happening".*

I should feel proud that veracity and truthfulness of none of my enquiry or investigation could be challenged or proved false in NAB or Special Courts; yes, most of them were used to avail political compromises by Gen Musharraf's government.

That's enough, my dear countrymen.

STAYING QUIET DOESN'T ALWAYS
MEAN I'VE NOTHING TO SAY
SOMETIMES IT MEANS, PERHAPS YOU ARE NOT
READY TO HEAR MY THOUGHTS.
(Asghar Raza Gardezi PSP)

# Contents

## BITS & BOBS:

Welcome to Volume-II. Like the previous books, the chapters may not be inter-related – scenarios and pages are in continuity with the earlier volume PLUS the **FOUR** *volumes of Judges & Generals in Pakistan*; keeping it easy for references.

Each scenario is a different chapter.

*'The Living History of Pakistan'* is a collection of essays, may be irritating for some ones. No misleading intelligence story, no distracting investigative report and no concocted interview – it is simply a narration of Pakistan's contemporary history. No fiction in this book but simple unfolding of facts which most of us might have forgotten.

> *'It is the collection of tragedies and misgivings which are deliberately buried in suspicious darkness of Pakistan's power corridors. I've simply collected them, collated and placed together for those who want to keep a track of their past.'*

Most newspapers of UK *dated 12ᵗʰ December 2012* carried the news that the majority of political leaders of Pakistan failed to submit any income tax returns despite lecturing citizens on the need to improve revenue collection in a country with a yawning financial deficit.

> *"President Zardari and Rehman Malik the interior minister, were among those who did not file their tax returns in 2011 and many of those who did, paid negligible amounts.* **Pakistan has one of the lowest tax collection rates in the world, according to the World Bank, and the governments are largely reliant on loans and foreign aid for funding.**
>
> *Anyone earning more than 500,000 rupees (£3,200) a year must file electronic tax returns, but the report found only 90 of 341 members of the national assembly had done so. Only 20 of 55 cabinet ministers had filed returns, while 49 senators out of 104 paid income tax. Only 856,000 people pay income tax in the country of about 200 million people.*
>
> *They [the ruling elite] urge the masses to pay taxes, but do not become role models for them."*

The fact remains that during 2012-14, Pakistan's National Database Registration Authority [NADRA] had once chalked out a list of 3.5 million people who used to perform 3-5 foreign trips a year, live in homes of average worth Rs:90 million and keep cars of average worth Rs:40 million at home – but having NO TAX REGISTRATION. The NADRA placed that list on Federal Board of Revenue [FBR]'s record also but even then the successive two political governments could not find courage to bring them in the tax-net.

## *SERIOUS JUDICIAL GIMMICKS:*

Going back in December 1997's battle between Chief Justice and the PM, President Leghari had become an odd casualty and had to resign. New president had to be elected and sworn in within thirty days. Justice Mukhtar A Junejo was serving as acting Chief Election Commissioner [CEC] and in this capacity was also returning officer for election of the President of Pakistan scheduled for 31st December 1997. PM Nawaz Sharif's candidate was Rafiq Tarar, another retired judge.

On 18th December 1997; Justice Juenjo entertained a petition against PML[N]'s candidate Rafiq Tarar filed by PPP's former minister Aftab S Mirani. Justice Junejo rejected the nomination papers of his former colleague Justice (rtd) Rafiq Tarar stating that in view of Tarar's previous derogatory remarks about judiciary made him ineligible to be elected to the parliament and henceforth he could not be elected as president.

An appeal was immediately filed against that rejection at Lahore High Court where CJ Rashid Aziz Khan decided not to sit on bench. However, Lahore High Court suspended CEC's order the same day and allowed Rafiq Tarar to contest presidential election.

On 28th December 1997; just after 10 days of his decision, Justice Junejo was booted out and the Acting President of Pakistan Wasim Sajjad appointed Justice Abdul Qadeer Chaudhry as permanent CEC.

In 1997, Pakistan surely wrote some new chapters in judicial history. A permanent President, Farooq Leghari, appointed an acting CEC but when it became inconvenient, an Acting President Wasim Sajjad, had appointed a permanent CEC who was suitable to the then sitting government.

In above instances, the politicians did not respect judges – but what the judges used to do justice – see a few more details.

A little glance how police was humiliated at the hands of successive judiciary through the whole decade; no one else, no business tycoon, no MNA or MPA or other politically high figure, no lawyer, no media-house owner or anchor, no federal or provincial Secretary, no director of any state owned organization; no director of Steel Mills or Trading Corporation of Pakistan or PIA or Export Promotion Bureau or Rice Export Corporation or WAPDA or KESC, no Income Tax Commissioner, no Collector Customs etc etc – as all were free from vicious allegations, malpractices, corruption, mal-administration, miss-management and what more virtues like that.

*In November 1997 when PML workers headed by their MsNA & MsPA ransacked the Supreme Court Islamabad, who got punished out of the whole mess. No MNA or MPA, no worker of PML, no CSP officer either Commissioner, DC or AC of Islamabad but **IG Police Saleem Tariq Lone, SSP Altaf Ahmed, DSP & an Inspector.***

*In 2007 when the Chief Justice Iftikhar Chaudhry was brutally handled by Gen Musharraf's team then who was ultimately at loss. Neither Gen Musharraf nor any of his General, or Secretary Interior or Commissioner Islamabad; those were again considered on fault were **IG Police Iftikhar Ahmed and his team comprising of the SSP, DSP and Inspector who were declared guilty of 'contempt of court.'***

*In 2011, thrice the IG Police Punjab Tariq Saleem Dogar was called in superior courts for bullying; one DG FIA Waseem Ahmed Khan was un-ceremonially sent home, DG FIA Malik Iqbal was forced to quit his post and his successor Anwar Tehseen was showered with remarks and shouts and ultimately made to leave the organization.'*

Nowhere in the world, the judges were supposed to shout at but in Pakistan it has been a normal practice for judges hoping that it would bring headlines for leading newspapers amidst waves of *'strong judiciary syndrome'*. In all societies, the judges do not but their decisions speak – while in Pakistan the judges speak loud but their decisions *'thuss'*.

In developed democracies the things go different. In UK, during the corresponding three years the courts dealt numerous cases of corruption or public importance. Here the wrong doers got punishments irrespective of their origin or party affiliation. More MPs and less police officers were sent behind the bars.

*Five MPs and one Lord were sentenced for claiming benefits which were not justified for their ranks. The financial involvement in each case was less than twelve thousand pounds but all they got jails.*

No shouting in courts, no media glamour for judges. The people even do not know the names of judges who wrote those decisions in routine.

Similar happened with UK's media lords on *2011's famous 'hacking scandals'* case in which an empire of *179 years old newspaper 'News of the World'* had to stumble down their circulation. The newspaper finished, paper's chief had to face interrogations; careers of many ended up in jail, press closed and hang over continued to haunt many.

Referring to **Saad Rasool's** essay appeared in *'Pakistan Today' dated 4th November 2012*:

*'In fact, since restoration [of Judiciary in March 2009], dissent has all but vanished from the courts (barring a few exceptions, e.g. Justice Nasir-ul Mulk in the Mukhtara Mai case). It begs the question: do all the judges, on all the benches, in all the courts, in all the cases, agree on all the points of law?*

*The answer, in all likelihood, is 'no'! In Pakistan it has been happening since decades especially in CJP Chaudhry's era – pick up any file of fat people, you'll be amused.*

*These are troubling times. And the judiciary today stands in the gaze of history. Many (and measurable) advances have been made over the past 5 years, towards the turning of a new leaf in our constitutional history. But let's not kid ourselves: there is need for a lot more – and a jurisprudence of DISSENT too.'*

## SERIOUS POLITICAL GIMMICKS:

*On 14th April 2010,* as many as 736 prisoners undergoing jail terms in various prisons of the Punjab were freed while 3,238 convicts benefited from the special remission granted by President Zardari to celebrate the success of the 18th Amendment. In Rawalpindi region only, 215 convicts were freed while 610 were benefited, 167 prisoners were released from Adiala Jail only - including Ahmad Riaz Sheikh, former Additional DG FIA.

The media anchors of that day held in most TV live shows that:

*'Mr Zardari wanted to get his friend Ahmed Riaz Sh out of the prison so he rightly used the excuse of celebrations of 18th Amendment; good it was that others got benefited too.*

*The whole lot of freed and benefited prisoners were thankful to Mr Sheikh and not President Zardari.'*

The main provision for celebration of the passing of 18th Amendment for the Pakistan's Constitution was that *'the political parties are not bound to hold elections within'*; meaning thereby that the future prime ministers in Pakistan would not go out of Zardari – Bhutto, Sharifs, Chaudhrys of Gujrat and JUI's Rehman families. President Zardari was delighted more but it suited most of the party leaders in Pakistan.

Meanwhile, a petition was filed by one Azhar Siddique Advocate in the Lahore High Court [LHC] the same day against the Punjab government for non-implementation of presidential order regarding remission in sentences of convicted prisoners – but of no avail.

**Another Picture here:**

Referring to *'the News'* dated **30th September 2010;** in a PPP parliamentary party meeting held at the Presidency during the last week of September 2010, *President Zardari had confessed that he was betrayed and trapped by top players of the game in the NRO case.*

Mr Zardari had said so in the presence of his big media team comprising top professionals like Farhatullah Babar, Faouzia Wahab, Farrah Ishphani, Jamil Soomro, Qamar Zaman Kaira and dozens of PPP ministers. However, amongst the politicians, Maulana Fazalur Rehman had advised Mr Zardari NOT to bring the NRO issue in the Parliament; *'Aaj News'* of *7th November 2009* is referred.

Mr Zardari was given certain assurances in exchange for not defending it before the Supreme Court but the *"players of the game"* did not execute their promise and cases against him were reopened. Amidst fiery speeches by his party men, Zardari told them in his firm style though he was betrayed and trapped but he would not take any "dictation" from any one.

During that parliamentary party meeting Senators Dr Safdar Abbasi and Babar Awan were admittedly hailed because these two were the only high voices which had argued rather agitated that NRO should be defended in the SC by all means but their voices were ignored because some "top guns" had given Mr Zardari authentic assurances on the basis of which he decided not to defend the NRO in the SC.

Reportedly a Karachi-based former judge who enjoyed good reputation and was considered to be a credible person had visited the Presidency and secretly met Asif Ali Zardari advising that he should not worry about the Swiss cases, as they were closed transaction. All the assurances went futile and Mr Zardari was shocked when he heard that all the 17 judges of the SC had given decision against him.

See another situation:

Referring to the daily *'Pakistan today'* dated **17th November 2012;** according to calculations performed by Transparency International, Pakistan lost an unbelievably high amount, more than Rs:8.5 trillion (US $94 billion), in corruption, tax evasion and bad governance during the last four years . An adviser of Transparency International acknowledged that:

> *"Pakistan does not need even a single penny from the outside world if it effectively checks the menace of corruption and ensures good governance".*

The Transparency International also noted that the four years of the then [PPP] regime had been the worst in terms of corruption and bad governance in the country's history.

Pakistan was passing through a difficult condition due to Terrorism. Its economy was facing fluctuations day by day. At the time of independence, Pakistan had very low resources and capital, so the processes of progress were very slow. Unfortunately the politicians of Pakistan were all not well aware of modern global system and the required needs of the country. Due to bad policies, Pakistan was facing a lot of problems at all world forums.

Even today; the major problem in the country is poverty, caused by un-equal distribution of wealth, which is becoming the grounds of crime and social disorder through all regions and in all walks of life.

**Moreover;** referring to *media reports dated 30th September 2013;* a massive amount of Rs:2.4 billion was spent from the meagre resources of Pakistan's national exchequer by former president Asif Ali Zardari and former prime ministers Syed Yusuf Raza Gilani and Raja Pervaiz Ashraf on their *133 foreign tours in five years of the PPP government.*

According to details from the Foreign Ministry, Rs; 2.4 billion were spent on foreign tours during PPP regime. Raja Pervez Ashraf during his short nine month tenure made eight foreign tours. *The president made seven foreign visits in 2008, 20 in 2009, 14 in 2010, 22 in 2011, 23 in 2012 and six in 2013 including 16 private visits to Dubai that cost the national exchequer an aggregate of Rs:1.31 billion.* Former PM Yusuf Raza Gilani went abroad for 51 visits, including two private visits to Britain, which cost Pakistan about one billion rupees.

**In March 2013,** just a few days before departing of the PPP government, the then Interior Minister Rehman Malik had told the Senate [while replying certain questions on Karachi situation] that *'during 5 years rule of the PPP, he has issued 69473 arms licenses of prohibited bore including sub-machine guns'.*

Mostly, arms licenses were issued to the members of Sindh provincial assembly and parliamentarians; thus each Sindh Assembly member got about 200 arms licenses on average – some might have got more some less {*Irfan Siddiqui's Naqsh e Khayal* of *1st November 2013 is referred*}

## PAKISTANI LEADERSHIP:

Referring to the *daily 'Jang' dated 8th April 2012*; before partition of 1947, only 20,000 Muslims were killed by extremist Hindus in undivided India in forty years; about 20,000 Muslims were killed in Hindu - Muslim clashes of India during forty years after partition *but more than 40,000 Muslims have been killed by their own Muslim brothers in last 25 years in Pakistan*; why so.

Most probably; because the so called WOT [war on terror] had been pushed into Pakistan due to the short sightedness of our successive rulers during 2001-14; military and the political elite both.

**On 4th November 2015;** while addressing the second Pakistan Investment Conference, Prime Minister Nawaz Sharif stated: *"Our democratic and economic journey has not been without setbacks. But the Pakistani nation has once and for all decided that its future lies in a liberal and democratic country, where the private sector thrives and no one is left behind."*

Former Ameer of Jama'at e Islami [JI] Syed Munawwar Hasan had immediately condemned PM's statement saying that *'the liberals should enlist themselves as a minority in Pakistan'.* Only two days earlier then Ameer of JI Syed Sirajul Haq had shared his pearls of wisdom while saying '**... had Quaid-i-Azam and Allama Iqbal been alive, they would have been in Islami Jamiat-i-Talba**'.

During late 1960s, the JI leaders had condemned Zulfikar Ali Bhutto and the Pakistan People's Party [PPP] for adopting the slogan '**Socialism is our economy**', surprisingly, the JI was soft on 'Capitalism' & the West in general. In 'Liberalism', the JI leaders could only see something obscene or related to sexual freedom; whereas, Liberalism as a political philosophy stands for democracy, pluralism, tolerance and fundamental rights plus similar virtues.

Economic liberalism, as pointed out by the PM Sharif, had to support free market with least interference by the government. If some societies of West had, in the past, tolerated sexual permissiveness, that did not mean that each society of the world would include that vulgarity into the political theme of 'Liberalism' – Pakistan has its own social fabric and its own cultural beliefs. There was no justification in rejecting the concept in totality.

In any case, PM Sharif was speaking with reference to political system and economic development as he had added: *"I can confidently say that our direction is set, and we are now implementing our nation's economic and democratic agenda."* But the JI leaders had a prejudicial mind-set and a blurred vision of their own.

*On 11th November 2015*; various politicians spoke openly on the Parliamentary floor including one Mahmood Achakzai who busted out against the Pak-Army on the issue of ISPR's press release. He concluded his remarks with the saying:

> *"..... if the time demanded sacrifice from us, from the Baloch nation; we'll stand with civilian Sharif of Lahore – meaning thereby that we'll be with PM Nawaz Sharif instead of standing by Gen Raheel Sharif – we will stand with the democracy."*

Basically Mr Achakzai was feeling his own *'democracy at home'* in danger because at the time of speech:

- He himself, **Mr Mahmood Achakzai,** was an MNA and ADVISOR to the Prime Minister on Balochistan Affairs.

- His first brother **Mohammad Khan Achakzai** was GOVERNOR of Balochistan.

- His second brother, **Majeed Khan Achakzai** was an MPA in the Balochistan Assembly.

- His third brother, **Hameed Khan Achakzai** was an MPA in the Balochistan Assembly.

- His sister in law, **Naseema Khan Achakzai** was an MNA in National Assebmly on women seats quota.

- His first brother in Law, **Qazi Maqbool** was Manager Quetta Airport.

- His second brother in law, **Khan Hassan Manzoor** was DIG Motorways Pakistan

- Sister in law of his wife, **Spozemai Khan** was an MPA in Balochistan Assembly.

- Wife's nephew Salaar Khan, Lecturer in Balochistan University.

- Wife's cousin Qazi Jamal, registrar in Balochistan University.

Thus it was fact that had the democracy gone with the Army's interference; Mahmood Achakzai's whole family would have gone home if assemblies dissolved.

## ZARDARI vs PAK-ARMY:

Referring to a **'White Paper' issued by the Central Command of PPP,** on the completion of fourth anniversary of Gen Musharraf's military rule, it had been held that:

> '.....since the military take over [in October 1999], the unanimously adopted 1973 Constitution had not been restored fully, though the Army Chief had dared to incorporate in it a plethora of constitutional amendments through an ever - controversial Legal Framework Order, which carried the General's personal agenda..........

> As far as the situation on the judicial front was concerned, all the Bar Associations and elected bodies of the lawyers had declared their no confidence in the government for its unconstitutional and illegal steps.

> For the first time in the country's 56-year history, the bar and the bench had developed some serious differences and the situation had worsened

*to an extent that demands were raised by the lawyers' community for the removal of puppet Chief Justices in the Centre and in the Punjab who were dancing to the tunes of their khaki masters.'*

*About FIVE years later:*

It is abundantly available on media record that the differences of the PPP with military establishment had taken start when Mr Zardari [then in the capacity of PPP's Chief only] triggered the trouble in *May 2008*, only a few weeks after the change of government, at a briefing arranged for him and the new prime minister Mr Gilani at the ISI headquarters. There at ISI HO:

*Mr Zardari had lectured the military leadership on strategic issues and delivered his action plan to deal with problems concerning India and Afghanistan.*

Mr Zardari tried to give a practical shape to that plan when in ending July 2008 the Prime Minister's office issued orders to place the entire administrative, financial and operational control of the ISI under the Federal Ministry of Interior [of Rahman Malik].

*This had invited an immediate response from the Army and the notification was withdrawn within three hours.*

Mr Zardari made another stunning move when he invited Afghan President Karzai, without consulting the security establishment, to join him in the maiden press conference Zardari held after taking oath as the president of Pakistan in September 2008. In the same press conference:

*Mr Zardari shocked the civil and military leadership alike by making astonishing statement of a major breakthrough on Kashmir within a month.*

Neither the prime minister nor his cabinet, nor the Army elite was aware of any such development.

*President Zardari's interview with the Wall Street Journal in October 2008 where he described the Kashmiri Mujahideen as terrorists* and mocked Gen Musharraf for calling them "freedom fighters" was considered 'unwanted' statement by the GHQ at least.

*On 26th November 2008,* in the wake of terrorist attack on Mumbai, President Zardari, without any consultations with national security establishment, instantly agreed to the demand of the Indian PM Manmohan Singh to send the ISI Chief to New Delhi, a move that was later back-peddled on PM Gilani's intervention.

President Zardari's relations with the military received another blow when the 'New York Times' broke the story in the last week of *August 2009 about US diplomat Zalmay Khalilzad's secret contacts with Zardari* in his bid for Afghan presidency. Khalilzad was on warpath with Pakistan's establishment during his tenure as the US ambassador to Kabul and revelations of his secret contacts with Zardari was disturbing news for the GHQ.

Later, the then army leadership got disturbed where the GHQ noticed with shock that the Presidency saw no problems with the controversial clauses of the Kerry-Lugar Bill that was declared *having mistakes* even by the United States ambassador in Islamabad. This KL Bill gave an impetus to serious differences of perception between President Zardari and the Pak-Army on issues of national security.

All the above moves were being played by President Zardari on the instructions of Islamabad based US Ambassador in Pakistan. He was bound to take that dictation because the US admin had educated and trained Mr Zardari to act like that during his stay in America during 2004-08.

**Brig Imtiaz's Fate:** During the last week of August 2009, Brig Imtiaz appeared on electronic media [in Rauf Klasra's live TV program] with full passion and fervour to unearth the details about the 1992 Karachi operation; termed by media *'as the sudden reawakening of his zameer'* [conscience]. He had been convicted in various NRO cases, imprisoned on corruption charges and had been in prison. *In 2008, when he was suddenly freed by the Islamabad High Court [IHC], his illegally acquired property and assets were restored to him.*

Brig (rtd) Imtiaz Ahmed served as Director in charge Internal Security ISI for several years in Islamabad and later as DG Intelligence Bureau (IB) in the first government of Nawaz Sharif. The next Prime Minister Benazir Bhutto had put him in jail for about three years on charges of being part of the operation to oust her in 1989 during her first government.

Later, Gen Musharraf also kept him in jail for four years till his acquittal by the High Court. He was the only spymaster of Pakistan who was jailed for eight years, after serving 15 years in the ISI and the IB.

How *Pakistan's 'best' spymaster, Brig Imtiaz,* got so rich – might be through selling sensitive information he was taking care of, or extortion of big politicians, or coercion or through *'secret funds at his disposal'*; but no one is allowed to think so loudly in Pakistan.

## *FINANCIAL GIMMICKS:*

Daily *TELEGRAPH* on *30th August 2010* mentioned that:

> *'Asif Zardari, who chose to flaunt his wealth while the country he is supposed to rule was flooded...... In a book Pakistan – Eye of the Storm, the former BBC correspondent Owen Bennett-Jones wrote:*
>
> *"Between 1947 and 1959 up to 73 per cent of Pakistan's total government spending was devoted to defence. The average for the later period was 60 per cent."*
>
> *And nothing had changed by the end of 2005. The British High Commission then estimated that Pakistan's military, including the ISI, took 70 per cent of government spending for itself.'*

It was not the whole truth – rather whole fabricated hearsay. Details about this myth have been countered in the last chapter of this book, **Scenario 129**, with actual figures from Pakistan's budgets and strong *'msn News'*.

**This total bluff, based on hearsay – without any analysis of actual figures on record,** is also encountered here. A very recent analysis of mid 2015 titled as '<u>Pakistan - Defense Spending</u>', given by world known American sponsored media site www.globalsecurity.org is placed below;

> *'Pakistan announced on 5th June 2015 that it would increase its military spending by 11% for fiscal year 2015-16 - from Rs:700 billion [US$ 7 billion] to Rs:780 billion [US$ 7.8 billion].*
>
> *As per the budget document, Rs:700 billion were allocated for Defence Affairs and Services constituting 16.27% of the total budget and is quite less than the much propagated and misperceived notion of 80% or 70%. It has been so for many years; during the financial year 2013-14, share of defence budget was 15.74%, while it was 17.79% during 2012-13.*
>
> *The myth that allocation for defence is the single largest component in Pakistan's budget is also not true. For the year 2014-15, Rs:1,325 billion*

*were kept for the debt servicing and Rs:1,175 billion for Public Sector Development [PSDP]; the first and 2nd largest chunks respectively.*

*The argument that Pakistan spends a very high percentage of GDP on defence is no longer true. During the year 2013-14, the defence spending was 2.7% of GDP, which has been so, for many years.*

*From 1958 until 1973, the published defense budget accounted for between 50-60% of total government expenses. After that, the proportions were much lower, falling to even 30% levels and ranging between 5-7% of GNP. The defense budget for fiscal year (FY) 1993 was set at Rs:94 billion or US$3.3 billion, representing 27% of government spending and almost 9% of the GDP.*

*In real terms, Pakistan's defence allocations remained more or less capped since early 2000-01 despite the traditional security challenges vis-à-vis India on the eastern front and the new unprecedented internal security threat in the form of the Al Qaeda, and allied foreign and local militants.*

*According to the latest Economic Survey of Pakistan, all through the 2000s, Pakistan defence budget remained pegged at 3.1% of the GDP, compared with 5.6% during the decade of 1990s and 6.5% during the 1980s. The pattern of this downward slide in defence spending started during Gen Musharraf's rule, who slashed it to 3.9% of the GDP during early years in power and later to 3.3%.*

*According to World Bank figures for 1988 to 2003, Pakistan's military expenditures represented 25–29% of state expenditures and 6–7% of gross national income. In fiscal year (FY) 2004, military expenditures constituted just 18% of government expenditures.'*

## Other drastic scenes:
Referring to the *daily TELEGRAPH dated 23rd September 2012*, Graham Hand, Chairman of a UK government sponsored meeting on *'Fighting Global Poverty'* addressed his colleagues:

*"There's lots of money. We've all got money! We signed treaties so they have to give out the money! Welcome to the world of 'aid-funded businesses. Look how rich some people have become from fighting global poverty.*

*Britain's Department for International Development [DFID], paid out almost half a billion pounds last year to battalions of mostly British consultants, many of them on six or seven - figure personal incomes paid in large measure by the aid budget."*

UK's new Development Secretary, Justine Greening, had ordered an immediate internal review, yet hardly realising how deeply embedded in her Government the *"poverty barons"* had become.

Again: *the TELEGRAPH of 1ˢᵗ April 2013:* British people were upset when their government bestowed £300m of its taxpayers' money to a controversial programme of cash handouts in Pakistan [*Benazir Income Support Program*] which was accused of bankrolling the re-election campaign of Pakistan Peoples Party [PPP].

As per report mentioned above, in evidence to UK's parliamentary inquiry, it surfaced that the said Programme [BISP] was being used to buy support for President Zardari, and his party. The report mentioned that:

*'Britain's Department for International Development (DFID) was pouring money into a scheme driven by "clientelism". It is not stolen to the extent to which previous cash transfers were stolen, but this is the mechanism - which is funded partly by DFID - to make friends and influence people.*

*This is the re-election campaign of Mr Zardari, which is funded by DFID - well done.*

**Pakistan has one of the smallest tax bases in the world and two-thirds of its politicians pay no income tax at all,** *yet the country can still afford to give them aid to expand nuclear arsenal.'*

The report was replete with repeated allegations of corruption and claims that officials from the PPP – later led by Bilawal himself – had obtained lists of beneficiaries for follow-up visits in which families were to be told to remember from where the cash was flowing in. PPP's opposition parties roared in media that BISP was nothing more than a scam to "buy votes" in the then forthcoming elections of 11ᵗʰ May 2013.

The irony of fate with Pakistani nation remaind that PML(N) once vowed to overhaul the scheme and rename it as *'National Support Programme'* to avoid the taint of politicking. In a dossier of allegations, it concluded the programme was riddled with *"rampant corruption, nepotism and embezzlement"*.

But when the PML(N) itself came in power after the said elections, they preferred to keep the whole scheme in tact with the allocation of hefty Rs:75 billion in the budget announced for 2013-14. The corruption went manifold in BISP – both PPP & the PML[N] behaved similar loot and plunder while dealing with that poor people fund.

At the latest stage the whole BISP was being run and managed by a 'LOTA' lady politician named Marvi Memon.

# Scenario 112

## SC's JUDGMENT IN RPPs CASE:

> *Before going through these deliberations, kindly see the*
> *following figures to dispel away a general perception*
> *that 'Pakistan has no power supply'. It was not*
> *the whole truth nor is it now.*

## *STATISTICS & CAUSE OF ACTION:*

As per statistics available from the Federal Ministry of Water & Power, Pakistan gets electricity from three main sources; Hydral, Thermal (Gas or Furnace Oil or Steam) and Nuclear. Four major power producers in Pakistan are Water & Power Development Authority (WAPDA), Karachi Electric Supply Company (KESC), Independent Power Producers (IPPs) and Pakistan Atomic Energy Commission (PAEC). When the PPP took over the reigns of the country in 2008, they inherited the following installed capacity of power generation; mostly in working order. The details were:

**WAPDA HYDAL:**

Terbela 3478 MW; Mangla 1000 MW; Ghazi-Brotha 1450 MW; Warsak 243 MW; Chashma 184 MW; Dargai 20 MW; Rasul 22 MW; Shadi-Waal 18 MW; NandiPur 14 MW; Kurram Garhi 4 MW; Renala 1 MW; Chitral 1 MW; Jagran (AK) 30 MW: **Total Hydal = 6461 MW.**

**WAPDA THERMAL:**

Gas Turbine Power Station Shadra 59 MW; Steam Power Station Faisalabad 132 MW; Gas Turbine Power Station Faisalabad 244 MW; Gas Power Station Multan 195 MW; Thermal Power Station Muzaffargarh 1350 MW; Thermal Power Station Guddu 1655 MW; Gas Turbine Power Station Kotri 174 MW; Thermal Power Station Jamshoro 850 MW; Thermal Power Station Larkana 150 MW; Thermal Power Station Quetta 35 MW; Gas Turbine Power Station Panjgur 39 MW; Thermal Power Station Pasni 17 MW: **Total Thermal = 4811 MW**

**WAPDA's Total Hydal + Thermal capacity was = 11272 MW**

**Karachi Electric Supply Company (KESC):**

Thermal Power Station Korengi 316 MW; Gas Turbine Power Station Korengi 80 MW; Gas Turbine Power Station SITE 100 MW; Thermal Power Station Bin Qasim 1260 MW: **Total (KESC) = 1756 MW**

**Independent Power Producers (IPPs):**

Hub Power Project 1292 MW; AES Lalpir Ltd Mahmood Kot MuzaffarGarh 362 MW; AES Pak Gen Mahmood Kot MuzaffarGarh 365 MW; Altern Energy Ltd Attock 29 MW; Fauji KabirWala Power Company Khanewal 157 MW; Gul Ahmad Energy Ltd Korengi 136 MW; Habibullah Coastal Power Ltd 140 MW; Japan Power Generation Lahore 120 MW; Koh e Noor Energy Ltd Lahore 131 MW; Liberty Power Limited Ghotki 232 MW; Rousch Power Khanewal 412 MW; Saba Power Company Sheikhpura 114 MW; Southern Electric Power Company Ltd Raiwind 135 MW; Tapal Energy Limited Karachi 126 MW; Uch Power Ltd Dera Murad Jamali 586 MW; Attock Gen Ltd Morgah Rawalpindi 165 MW; Atlas Power Sheikhupura 225 MW; Kot Addu Power Co Ltd 1638 MW: **Total (IPPs) = 6365 MW**

**Pakistan Atomic Energy Commission (PAEC):**

KANUPP 137 MW; CHASNUPP-1 325 MW; **Total (Nuclear) = 462 MW**

Electricity generated through hydal means has been the sole domain of WAPDA and the production varied between minimum of 2414 MW and maximum of 6761 MW depending upon the river flow, rains on the mountains and quantity of water released from dams during the four seasons.

Total Power Generation Capacity of Pakistan (including all sources) was 19855 MW in early 2008 and the electricity demand in mid 2010 was only 14500 MW. The problem cropped up because the PEPCO was generating about 10000 MW only due to political gimmicks allegedly causing determined loss to Punjab for its industrial shut down because of the rivalry between two governments; PML(N) in Punjab and PPP in Islamabad.

Obviously up to 20 hrs power shutdowns in the country, especially in industrial hubs like Faisalabad were not because of the lack of generation capacity but either because of IMF/World Bank policies imposed by the government or due to lust & ill intentions of power players. The Power

Generation companies were not buying Furnace Oil from PSO saying they don't have money for it but the government was paying for Electricity that was generated by the RPPs from the same Furnace Oil. Pakistan's refineries like PRL continued operating at 40% capacities; allegedly, IMF/World Bank/US had imposed conditions on Pakistan to reduce budget deficit by importing less crude oil [*verification remained in question*].

Faisal Saleh Hayat, the then Federal Minister for Housing & Works, through a widely publicised press statement in early September 2009, had urged the Supreme Court to take action in respect of Rental Power Projects (RPPs) which, according to him, was just another name of corruption. He had raised the issue of corruption in the award of RPPs' contracts before every forum, including the National Assembly, but his voice was not attended to. The people involved in this massive scam of US$5 billion could have been questioned – but none bothered.

Syed Faisal S Hayat then moved the Supreme Court of Pakistan through a detailed application **on 26th September 2009,** wherein reiterating the allegations of corruption, he relied upon certain documents of the PEPCO, WAPDA and Ministry of Water & Power to prove his assertions. In para-wise comments of the respondents, all stakeholders denied the allegations of corruption quoting reliance over the approval No: ECC 135/9/2006 dated 16th August 2006; a decision of the Cabinet meeting.

When the petition was pending for hearing, another MNA Khwaja Asif belonging to PML(N), vide CMA No.3100/2010, joined the proceedings w.e.f. 21st October 2010.

## WHY RENTAL POWER PROJECTS (RPPs):

In Pakistan, during the last decade zero MW of electricity had been added to the national grid. The new housing schemes, expanding industrial production and other electricity needs kept on rising over the years and as a result the short fall increased to 7500 MW till 2006 which had lead to an excuse for the then military government to indulge in the RPP plans allegedly brewing benefits for their own – but nothing proved on record. Faisal Saleh Hayat himself was the Minister Power.

[Later, for the 19 RPPs, the Auditor General of Pakistan [AGP] noted in its *Annual Audit report for the fiscal year ending 30th June 2011,* that the government had paid Rs:16.6 billion to RPPs in advance payments and had created a liability of $1.7 billion for itself through the contracts. Thus the AGP recommended cancelling the contracts of RPPs by saying:

*'The RPPs had failed to achieve their commercial operation date [the contracts obligated date by which the RPPs were required to begin supplying power to the grid]; four contracts were never signed and six were dropped due to violations of contracts by power companies. Eight contracts are currently active but have yet to achieve commercial operation status.*

*... Who in the government was responsible for awarding rental power contracts without screening the capabilities and track records of companies bidding for the projects? Many power projects have installed old equipment that has a very low efficiency rate when it comes to power production. No feasibility study was carried out and the policy was adopted in haste.'*

An earlier press statement should also be kept in sight where [referring to the *'Express News'* dated 19th March 2010] Iranian Ambassador in Islamabad Mashallah Shakree had astonishingly told the media that:

*'Iran is offering 2200 MW power to Pakistan on much cheaper price. We can double the quantity if Pakistan wants it. We can negotiate the payment schedule also as we have that power as surplus. We are already supplying power to Turkey and Armenia successfully. Why Pakistan is after rental powers, the most expensive item in the world market.'*

There was nobody to tell Iran that though Pakistan's economy was crippled by power shut downs, but our most corrupt political elite, ministers and bureaucracy wanted their shares and commissions, nothing else.

*On 22nd June 2010,* the issue of corruption in RPPs sparked a heated debate between Minister for Water and Power Raja Pervaiz Ashraf and Makhdoom Faisal Saleh Hayat in the National Assembly, both of them sticking to their stance and challenging each other. The matter went so fiery that even the speaker had to expunge certain remarks of Raja P Ashraf against Mr Hayat. The debate was based on purchase of flats worth four million Pounds in London by Raja Pervaiz Ashraf but the minister said in the National Assembly: *'I swear to God that I and my family do not own a single penny property in any foreign state.'*

During SC proceedings in this case of corruption over the RPPs, much panic was seen in the government quarters. The CJP Iftikhar

M Chaudhry sought details of how much electricity the rental power plants were supposed to provide, how much they were producing and what the government had paid them so far. PML(Q)'s Faisal Saleh Hayat accused the government of running the rental power projects for the sole purpose of money making urging that the **Asian Development Bank (ADB) had also pointed out corruption in the scheme.**

In fact the Asian Bank's report was a charge sheet against the Federal Minister Raja Pervaiz Ashraf. The CJP enquired as to why no action was taken if the ADB report had made them responsible for loss. The SC constituted a one-man commission to investigate the corruption charges and state negligence in RPPs and nominated Justice (rtd) Rehmat H Jaffri as commission.

**On 2nd October 2011,** just days before the final hearing date, a fresh summary was drafted to be placed before the federal cabinet, seeking replacement of the earlier 7-14 per cent advance payment with Fuel Payment Letter of Credit (FPLC) or with fortnightly advance payments for fuel purchases. The said summary was to accommodate **70MW Kamoki Energy** and **65MW Sialkot Energy** RPPs which were being paid Rs:1.493 billion before production of their single unit. The two projects were among the six RPPs which the Asian Development Bank (ADB) had said should be reviewed before any further action on them. The Federal Ministry of Water and Power [MoW&P] subsequently reviewed the contracts of the six firms and cleared four of them.

See some more gimmicks. Referring to the *'Dunya News' dated 30th June 2011:*

> *'Karkey [of Turkey] Rental Power Project has become a white elephant as govt has to pay $9 million every month. According to the Central Power Purchase Agency (CPPA), we have to pay Rs:41 per unit and in case of non-operation; the government still has to pay Rs:26 per unit. It has capacity to generate 231 MW while only 10 MWs are generated at present. The CPPA maintains that no bank is ready to assist open LC for the aforesaid power plant.'*

The other **201MW Reshma Power Plant** was the second most expensive plant (costing 4.97 Cent per unit) after Karachi's ship - mounted Karkey of Turkey (5.98 cents per unit), excluding oil price. The contractual terms between Pepco and the Reshma Power clearly provided all the four options in the contract; slapping liquidated damages (LDs), reducing term of rental contract by a year, re-negotiating the tariff and even cancelling the entire contract. The plant had to be online by the end of 2009 but it was not fully operational till June 2011 at least. According to the contract, Pepco was bound to take charge of the situation; people wondered how and why.

The haste with which the Power Minister Raja Parvaiz Ashraf went to inaugurate Reshma 201MW plant could be gauged from the fact that it had only one machine [out of four (50MW each)] and that too on a test run.

The plant, like the afore-mentioned 'Karkey', had not achieved even 10 per cent of generation capacity till then. Reshma Power came out of the bidding in late 2008 and the PPIB approved it on 9th April 2009. <u>The MoW&P had directed Pepco to change the terms and double (making it 14%) the advance payment — amounting to $55.26 million (Rs:4.576bn) — and it was done accordingly.</u>

Whereas the agreement signed in September 2009 contained:

*"In case the seller (RPP) fails to complete the project within cure (stipulated) period of 30 days after the targeted COD and thereafter, the seller will be charged at the rate of $191 per day per megawatt up to a maximum amount equivalent to $17,190 per megawatt for a delay of up to three months after cure period.*

*Such amount will be charged from first rental payment of the monthly rental service fee. If achievement of commercial operations date (COD) is further delayed due to the seller, the buyer shall have the right to re-negotiate the contract."*

However, instead of renegotiating the project which had failed to achieve COD for nearly a year, and till much after, the ministry and Pepco landed in an "accommodating mode" on the pretext that *'rental plants got delayed for third party audit by the Asian Development Bank, that were beyond their control. Reshma Power is no exception.'*

Some sane voices in the PPP had told the PM in writing that the contracts of the said RPPs should be abolished at once which had pushed the four years of the PPP rule in vain. Referring to the *'Dawn' of 21st November 2011,* four leaders of the PPP told PM Gilani through a written letter calling for scrapping of the government's rental power policy and urged him to take action against former minister Raja Pervaiz Ashraf and other persons whose conduct was being scrutinised by the Supreme Court.

The said letter signed by Haider Ali Khan, member of PPP Punjab Council and son of former PPP information minister Khalid Kharal, Chaudhry Khizar Abbas, Rao Iqbal Ahmed Khan and Rana Iftikhar Khan said:

> *'We as candidates of Pakistan People's Party urge you to abolish the rental power policy, cancel all corruption - infested agreements with rental companies and take strong action against Raja Pervaiz Ashraf and all secretaries and Pepco officials who have played havoc with the party and the people of Pakistan. We suggest the prime minister to take action against irregularities in rental power schemes otherwise it will be taken by the Supreme Court and the credit will go to them.*
>
> *We believe that a few people in the government are working for their own interests, instead of the party, and they must be thrown out. There is strong resentment among party leaders and workers over some controversial decisions taken by the government.'*

The SC on various occasions had pointed out that the rental power policy was a failed strategy of Gen Musharraf and the PPP's ruling regime. As per aspirations of the millions of Pakistanis, the government had no reason to continue with such a failed policy. At that moment the people were forced to buy electricity at an exorbitant rate of Rs:52 per unit from one such rental power plant.

The party workers asked the high-ups that why the whole party and country should suffer because of the greed and lust for money of few individuals. The four PPP leaders particularly questioned the wisdom behind the continuation of such policies which were though once started during the rule of Gen Musharraf but they had abondened the same shortly after.

## *SUPREME COURT'S VERDICT:*

*On 30th March 2012,* announcing the verdict of the Rental Power Projects case, a two-member bench of the Supreme Court (SC) headed by Chief Justice Iftikhar M Chaudhry said that all the RPPs should be dissolved. The hearing of the case was completed in ending 2011 and **on 14th December 2011, the judgment was written but reserved.** Declaring all rental power project contracts 'illegal', the CJP said legal proceedings should be carried out against all those involved in the corruption; adding:

> *'Pakistan Electric Power Company (Pepco), Water and Power Development Authority (Wapda), National Electric Power Regulatory*

*Authority (Nepra) and the federal government are [collectively] responsible for the corruption of billions of rupees'.*

The petitioners, former Federal Minister for Housing and Works Faisal Saleh Hayat and MNA Khwaja Asif appeared in person while the PPP government departments, sponsors and owners of the rental power plants were represented by their counsels. 90-pages judgment was authored by the CJP Iftikhar M Chaudhry himself.

The SC observed that the policy of the rental power projects was not defined on a transparent basis; rather than overcoming circular debt, the authorities endorsed more contracts. It was ordered by name that legal proceedings should be carried out against the former Federal Minister for Water & Power Raja Pervaiz Ashraf and the then Federal Secretary responsible for releasing finances; also noted that the mark-up should be charged in addition to the retrieval of money. The judgment said:

*'The government of the day, under Article 29 read with Article 2A of the constitution, is bound to formulate policies for the promotion of social and economic well being of the people, which includes provision of facilities to citizens for work and adequate livelihood with a reasonable rest and leisure, etc.*

*Government/Executive, being the custodian of the national resources on behalf of the nation, is bound to preserve and protect the same by strictly adhering to the relevant laws, conventions, experiences and have no authority to compromise with the resources, which fall within the definition of property in terms of constitutional provisions, belonging to general masses falling within the ambit of Article 24 of the Constitution.*

*In the cases of Bank of Punjab vs Haris Steel Industries AND Liaqat Hussain vs The Federation of Pakistan... Article 9 has been interpreted and its scope has been enlarged to each and every aspect of human life. Therefore, whenever a policy is framed with reference to uplifting the socio - economic conditions of the citizens, object should be to ensure enforcement of their fundamental rights.'*

The apex court pointed out that in 2006, when the then military government had decided to adopt the phenomenon of rental power project, no feasibility study [*based on the input of the experts on the subject to determine whether or not the implementation of the project was advisable*] was carried out which was crucial. The feasibility study, based on the extensive research to ascertain that what would be the impact of such a project in terms of costs of the project, its results, future prospects, operational implications, advantages and disadvantages, should have been there first and then to proceed further.

Further that NEPRA did not play its due role in the process of RPPs; firstly for the reason, that bids were invited on the basis of reference tariff of the fuel; secondly, the NEPRA was directed to follow the guidelines already issued in respect of IPPs, but NEPRA failed miserably to perform its due functions in many respects.

> [*The ECC of Gen Musharraf's era had approved a plan to introduce rental power into the national electricity grid during a meeting on 12th August 2006, and approved two unsolicited projects: the 136MW plant at Bhiki and a 150MW plant at Sharqpur in Sheikhupura district of Punjab – but those projects were not catered for during the Army regime – PPP blew air in those balloons when they came in power in 2008.*
>
> *Some shrewd bureaucrats on 15th February 2008, just three days before general elections sensing the PPP's victory, decided to allow the Pakistan Electric Power Company (Pepco) to install rental power plans with higher capacities of between 800MW and 1,200MW; blindly following the footprints of corruption.*
>
> *The PPP government continued the policy and awarded contracts for even bigger rental power projects at an ECC meeting on 10th September 2008, making commitment to buy rental power upto 2,700MW depending on similar concocted documents.*
>
> **The PPP government paid Rs:16.6 billion in advance and created a liability of $1.7 billion which was payable as rental charges to the RPPs on delivery of energy. Till the SC's verdict of 12th March 2012, only 120MW was produced as against 2700 MW contracts.**]

Supreme Court of Pakistan had announced the reserved judgment in Human Rights Case No. 7734-G/2009 & 1003-G/2010 (Alleged Corruption in Rental Power Plants) and other connected Human Rights Case No. 56712/2010 (Fraud in payment of RPPs detected by NEPRA).

The main crux of the judgment was as under:-

> '....... The binding force of the Constitution commands them [the executive & PPP government] to ensure well being and prosperity

*of Pakistan, so whenever they feel threat to the well being of the people for any reason, they [the apex judiciary] are bound to preserve the same.'*

## HOW CORRUPTION ESCALATED:

In 1994 [during Benazir Bhutto's 2nd spill of government], the Private Power and Infrastructure Board (PPIB) was created as "One Window Facilitator", *interalia,* with a view to promote private sector participation in the power sector of Pakistan and to facilitate investors in establishing private power projects and related infrastructure, execute implementation agreements with project sponsors and issue sovereign guarantees on behalf of Government of Pakistan.

On 16Th December 1997, the Regulation of Generation, Transmission and Distribution of Power Act, 1997 (hereinafter referred to as the "the Act, 1997") was promulgated by the then PML(N) government.

In 1998, Pakistan Electric Power Company (PEPCO) was incorporated under the Companies Ordinance 1984 with a view to improve the efficiency of the power sector, to meet customers' electric energy requirements on a sustainable and environmental friendly basis, to stop load shedding, to construct new grid stations, to reduce line losses, to minimize tripping and theft control, to revamp generation units and to improve customer services, and develop an integrated automated power planning system for generation, transmission and distribution to ensure system stability, fault isolation and upgrade relying, metering and tripping system at the level of National Transmission and Distribution Company (NTDC) as well as Distribution Companies [DISCOs].

During the initial years of the PPP regime [2009-10], the amounts paid to sponsors by way of 7% + 7% = 14% became another alarming issue. Since there were lot of complaints of corruption in awarding contracts of RPPs, against all concerned individually and collectively, therefore, Ministry of Finance went for 3rd Party Evaluation/Audit and to achieve the object, ADB was appointed to do the needful. The ADB report revealed that enhancement of down payment from 7% to 14% was not to be allowed without inviting fresh biddings and changing the terms of the contract with a view to ensuring fair competition amongst the bidders.

The petitioners were agitating that there were illegalities committed by Government in making payment of 14% advance to the bidders, particularly, when there was no commitment/agreement at the time of notifying the bids. After much discussion, the said ADB report was accepted and in pursuance thereof, 9 RPPs were allowed to continue and that 14% advance amount paid to the bidders on the basis of reference value went into billions of rupees.

The petitioners contended that a meagre amount of electricity was being generated through the RPPs, although billions of rupees were spent on those projects. Admittedly; after spending billions of rupees in the shape of 7% to 14% down payment; plus exemption from payment of customs duty [@6%]; plus withholding tax, against average cost of Rs:24 per unit kWh, *only 120 MW electricity was being generated* by the RPPs.

Moreover, the power cost was very high and was not in accordance with the provisions of section 7 of the Act, 1997 whereby NEPRA was required to protect the interests of the consumers. Further, **this cost was not final; it was subject to fuel cost component and other charges** of overhead transmission payable to NTDC.

Therefore, RPPs' were proved a total failure and incapable of filling the gap in the demand and supply on a short term basis. The SC was right to point out that peculiar mode of massive corruption under the garb of technicalities; see the details:

- Bhikki RPP was paid Rs:8,698.46 million against supply of only 811.605 mkWh electricity.

- Sharaqpur RPP was paid Rs:13,941.82 million against generation of 1520.420 mkWh electricity.

- Out of nine RPPs set up after 2008 to whom advance payments were made, six RPPs, namely, Techno Sahuwal, Guddu, Reshma, Young Gen, Naudero-II and Techno Samundri had returned the advance payments in pursuance of orders passed by the SC from time to time.

- Advance payments made to Karkey, Gulf and Naudero-I were not returned till SC's decision at least.

- Karkey was generating 48.33 MW against capacity of 231 MW; Naudero-I was generating 9.16 MW against capacity of 51 MW whereas, Gulf was generating 50.08 MW against its capacity of 62 MW; as per their contractual generation pledge.

- Pakistan Power Resources (Piranghaib Power near Multan) did not generate electricity at all although down payment of US$14.58 million was made to it, which had not been returned.

- Though Reshma Project returned the down payment, according to learned counsel, yet it was still functioning and generating 15 MW only against pledged capacity of 201.3 MW.

- Per unit cost of electricity produced by the RPPs remained on very high side, e.g., Karkey was ranging from Rs:35 to Rs:50; Gulf from Rs:18 to Rs:19 and Naudero-I from Rs:12 to Rs:19 whereas as per decision of the ECC dated 10th September 2008, efforts were to be made that the tariff of the RPPs should be lower than that of the IPPs based on similar technology for their first 10 years. Thus, in this manner, the decisions of the ECC were also violated blatantly.

- While awarding contracts to RPPs, particularly Gulf, Karkey, Reshma, Naudero-I, Naudero-II, Bhikki and Sharaqpur; grave illegalities and irregularities were committed, and procedural lapses and deviations were made from mandatory legal requirements and the same were entered in a non-transparent manner.

Immediately after Supreme Court's order dated **18th November 2012**, the sponsors of Reshma Rental Power Plant reimbursed Rs:4.5billion mobilisation advance it received for generating electricity under Rental Power agreement. However, the payment was not made in dollars nor did it include the two-year mark-up, in violation of the court's directive. Mockery was that Reshma Power Plant had earned interest for two years on the mobilisation advance while it had generated only 5 MW power.

In total, a sum of Rs:8.69 billion could only be recovered from certain RPPs on account of advance payments and interest, whereas, proceedings for recovery of interest amounting to Rs:445.5 million from Young Gen and Reshma, were pending when judgment was announced.

The SC made certain serious observations reflecting lack of control of the government over very serious issue of 'load shedding' since about five years. It was held that:

- Prior to the introduction of RPPs, the system of generation of electricity under the control and management of MoW&P, WAPDA, PEPCO, etc, had sufficient potential to produce more electricity, but instead of taking curative steps for its improvement, including clearance of circular debt of the IPPs or resorting to other means of generation of electricity, billions of rupees were spent on BHIKKI and SHARAQPUR RPPs, which proved complete failure because the object was not achieved as the shortage of electricity persistently continued, and yet more RPPs were installed for ulterior motives.

*[As emphasised in the SC judgment that annulled all the 19 RPPs, Pakistan had installed capacity of 21,000MW, but electricity was not being produced up to that achievable level just to make money in the RPPs.*

*Meaning thereby that acute load shedding had deliberately been aggravated by the PPP government simply to provide a justification for the RPPs tainted with monumental corruption; but still there was no worthwhile raise in the power generation capacity.*

*While the PPP government continued to spend in projects like the Benazir Income Support Programme (BISP), averaging Rs:95 billion a year, and protection of its top leaders in Pakistan and abroad, it has avoided sparing just Rs:300b to get rid of the vicious circular debt then which rose to Rs:503 billion till their last day in power (March 2013). The PML(N) government paid it all in one go when assumed power on 1st June 2013.]*

- The Federal Government, WAPDA, PEPCO, etc had failed to control pilferage of electricity from the system because of bad governance and failure of the relevant authorities to enforce the writ of the Government. The SC observed that *'the Government is required to improve the existing system of generation and transmission of electricity, by taking all necessary steps, including clearing of circular debt, etc, so that electricity can be generated to the maximum capacity and on priority basis.'*

The SC in its judgment had asked the NAB to get criminal cases registered against the ministers and bureaucrats, advisors and other power players to unearth the conspiracy against the whole nation. The expected detailed investigations were aiming at the glaring irregularities and criminal intentions of the contract signatories especially a cogent factor written and highlighted in most of the contracts that *'the litigations would be settled in UK'*. Why it was admitted or allowed to be incorporated in the terms; the future moments would reveal.

## CONTRACTS WITHOUT TRANSPARENCY:

Referring to an essay penned down by one *Zulqurnain Javed* available on webpages, Sindh is the most feasible region for wind power, having the production capacity for setting up wind mills, and generating up to 35000 MW which is more than sufficient for upcoming 25 year needs for Pakistan's growing economy.

Secondly; talking of the fossil fuel, Pakistan keeps one of the largest coal reserves at Thar to produce cheap electricity. 2% of Pakistan's energy was being produced from nuclear which could be raised to 10-20 times. Yet what the PPP government opted for was rental power projects; an ambiguous and ill-intentioned decision it was. Zul Javed held that:

*'Lack of transparency is the biggest hurdle in development of alternative energy. In one report, NEPRA did not allow setting up of wind mills in Sindh as the power companies demanded 8 cents per unit and NEPRA was adamant to pay 7.5 cents per unit. This was back in 2007. Now in 2011, NEPRA is willing to pay 16 cents per unit, to the same companies, how ironical?'*

The summary of the whole some Rental Power misappropriation or LOOT and the judgment of the apex court on it be viewed as under:

- The contracts of all the RPPs - solicited and unsolicited, signed off or operational, right from BHIKKI & SHARAQPUR up to PIRANGHAIB, NAUDERO-I & NAUDERO-II were entered into in contravention of law & Rules, which, besides suffering from other irregularities, violated the principles of transparency and fair & open competition, therefore, the same were declared illegal and void *ab initio*. The contracts of RPPs were ordered to be rescinded forthwith and all the persons responsible for the same were liable to be dealt with for civil and criminal action in accordance with law.

- On accepting the ADB's Audit Report, 9 out of 19 RPPs were allowed to operate; subsequently, 6 out of 9 RPPs were discontinued either having been signed off or having failed to achieve the target whereas remaining 3 RPPs, i.e., KARKEY, NAUDERO-I and GULF were functioning, but they were producing electricity much less than their generation capacity, except GULF. Piranghaib of Multan had not generated any electricity at all, although down payment was made to it, which was not returned. BHIKKI and SHARAQPUR were paid exorbitant rentals in billions of rupees, but generation of electricity was much below the agreed or the pledged capacity.

- The Ministry of Finance, WAPDA, PEPCO as well as GENCOs were declared responsible for causing huge losses to the public exchequer, which run into billions of rupees by making 7% to 14% down payments to the RPPs. Recovery of the amounts with mark up outstanding against the RPPs in terms of the performance guarantees was ordered by the SC.

- The RPPs proved to be a total failure and incapable of meeting the demand of electricity on a short term basis. In terms of Constitution and aforementioned Act of 1997, the NEPRA was mandated to safeguard the interests of the consumers, but the concerned officials of NEPRA failed to perform their duties diligently.

All the Government functionaries, including the respective Ministers for Water & Power holding charge in 2006 and onwards during whose tenure the RPPs were approved and set up, the functionaries of PEPCO, GENCOs, PPIB and NEPRA along with sponsors (successful bidders) who had derived financial benefits from the RPPs contracts and Secretaries Finance holding the charge when the down payment was increased from 7% to 14% had prima facie, violated the principle of transparency under Articles 9 & 24 of the Constitution and section 7 of the said Act of 1997, therefore, their involvement in getting financial benefits out of the same by indulging in corruption and corrupt practices was not to be overruled.

RPPs on the whole portrayed that Pakistan's political elite was least interested in making decisions in the public interest and all they cared about was their kick-backs and commissions. Going through the contracts undertaken with the companies, one could find disgusting conditions like *'all litigations would be dealt in UK'*. The strategy adopted was simple; first to portray RPPs as a solution to load shedding, sign contracts, get the commissions and later leave the public to pay the high costs hoping that no one would remember the fraud after a few years.

God bless the media and then the SC who had taken notice of the mega scandal at appropriate time in the public interest. Astonishingly, the government continued to claim having no funds for buying the furnace oil for already installed power plants but 'willingly paid' extra bugs to RPPs and then supplying them with the same furnace oil for which there were insufficient funds.

Daily *'the Nation' dated 1st April 2012* had pointed out that:

> 'To understand the true scale of their crime, the larger consequences of PPP's anti-people RPP policy and corrupt actions must also be factored in. It would be difficult to put a price on the millions of work hours lost due to load shedding, the mental anguish of millions of citizens, the loss to industries and businesses, the laid off labour, the dark streets of our cities, the dry tube wells in our fields.

*It is not just a case of some corrupt government functionaries making
millions on the side, but one that shows a complete disconnect with
their constitutional obligations and their insensitivity to the hardship
and torture visited upon the people they govern due to their actions.'*

Punjab province appeared as the worst victim of power failures owing
very little to the Pakistan Electric Power Company (Pepco) compared to
other provinces and the federal government, the statistics revealed. The
industry went completely crippled in that province, rendering hundreds of
thousands of daily wage earners jobless. Punjab owed Rs:4 billion to
the Pepco whereas a dispute was going on between the Punjab government and the Pepco for some time over an outstanding payment of Rs:1.5
billion, which was later settled; as it was related to excessive billing.

On the other hand, the Sindh government owed about Rs:49 billion
to the Pepco; the Karachi Electric Supply Company (KESC) being the
major defaulter. Balochistan owed Rs:13 billion; the Khyber-PK owed
Rs:1.6 billion but the sword was placed on the Punjab's throat due to
Sharifs in power.

## SELF CREATED CIRCULAR DEBT:

Though the Supreme Court had completed the hearing of the said RPPs
case in mid December 2011 but till announcement of judgment on the
30th March 2012, so much more material had been pouring in to give the
insight knowledge to the honourable judges. For instance, the Economic
Survey of Pakistan for 2010-11 indicated that due to high energy prices,
there was a shift from expensive imported furnace oil to indigenous gas,
creating a huge gap between demand and supply and compelling the
government to tackle this with load management strategy, along with
increase in prices.

The fact remains that most IPPs were operating well below their generating capacity because they were not made payment of energy produced.
The installed capacity of power generation in the country was then
19,855 MW, which was not being tapped due to the complicated circular
debt in the energy sector. Most of the IPPs had to obtain oil on credit
from Pakistan State Oil, as they had not enough cash because of power
theft, transmission losses, and non-payment of electricity bills by large
industrial & business consumers, and even government departments.

In April 2009, the circular debt of RPPs was Rs:104 billion only. They
sharply slipped into the grave sand of inter-corporate circular debt then;

till Dec 2011 it was Rs:275 billion indicating an increase of 147%. PEPCO owed money to independent power producers (IPPs), who in turn owed money to oil companies. The PPP government had not been able to resolve the crisis in four years. Receivables stood at Rs:775.2 billion and payables at Rs:516.7 billion. Out of Rs:258.5 billion, net receivables of PSO stood at Rs:51 billion, SSGCL Rs:7.1 billion, PEPCO Rs:2.7 billion, OGDCL Rs:115.5 billion, PARCO Rs:37.5 billion, KESC Rs:27.5 billion, GHPL Rs:9.6 billion and PPL Rs:22.2 billion.

On the other hand, SNGPL had net payables of Rs:13.4 billion and the Karachi Water and Supply Board Rs:1.2 billion. Pakistan's energy production relied heavily on expensive furnace oil and gas. With interruption in supply of oil and gas, it became impossible for energy generation to continue at the required pace. According to industrialists, the pattern of electricity production on any day was such that gas was supplied to highly inefficient public sector power plants, while over 200 percent more efficient private sector power plants remain closed. These plants could produce double the electricity from the same quantity of gas used by inefficient power plants. The cheapest source of electricity remained hydro power generation.

It may not be out of place to mention here that the government of Pakistan made a written commitment with the IMF in November 2008 that *'the circular debt would be ended till March 2009 definitely'* but subsequently neither the government had seriously tried to remove the causes of circular debt nor moved forward to overcome the debt. Even after the SC's judgment, the matter was expected to bring uproars because the government of Pakistan was going to be dragged in the UK's courts for arbitration; another floodgate of corruption was ready for opening.

The government continued to state that long-term projects, which would take four to five years to start, to enhance power generation were in place but no progress report till today. It was unfortunate that in our national grid the share of power generation through hydro petroleum sources remained at 34 per cent only; the rest was availed by the IPPs and other expensive producers. In that situation, the RPPs jugglers jumped in to fill the electricity gap and, instead of generated power, they brought bags of heavy kickbacks for the corrupt players in the government; politicians and bureaucrats both and at all levels.

On 30th March 2012, the apex court had directed the NAB to proceed against those who were responsible for the stated chaos since 2006 till then. As a result, on 20th April, NAB had issued arrest warrants for 33 persons, including Liaquat Jatoi, Shaukat Tareen the then Finance Minister and Raja Ashraf, the then Federal Minister and later the prime minister but the progress remained nil.

During the 3rd week of April 2012, the Supreme Court declined to approve the NAB Chairman's proposal for reutilization of existing rental power plants [RPPs] through a transparent bidding process to address prevailing energy crisis in the country. A 3-member bench headed by the CJP Iftikhar M Chaudhry expressed dismay over non-implementation of the court's verdict of 30th March in letter and spirit, in which it had rescinded all the RPP contracts by declaring them illegal and non-transparent besides asking the NAB to proceed against all persons, including former power minister Raja Pervez Ashraf.

NAB Chairman Fasih Bokhari had tried to seek approval of the apex court relating to suggestion that he intended to ask the government to put up for bidding all rental power plants for generation of electricity in Pakistan. The Supreme Court brutally reprimanded the Chairman and his team that why the looted wealth of the nation could not be recovered; not a single arrest made.

Till 15th May 2012, NAB could recover only Rs.1772 millions from the RPPs.

## DACOITS' FIGHT ON LOOT-DIVIDENDS:

In police organizations a general wisdom prevails that *'thieves & dacoits are mostly caught when they fight over the division of looted & plundered money'*; could RPP's issue be viewed in that context.

The key figure MNA of RPPs Raja Pervaiz Ashraf maintained that the policy of RPPs in Pakistan was first adopted by Gen Musharraf's government in 2006 [*it has been discussed in detail in above para-graphs*] by employing two RPPs. The PPP regime simply accelerated that policy to overcome the load shedding problem on quick basis. Raja cried that **Faisal Saleh Hayat was the minister in that militarised cabinet which had passed policy on RPPs in 2006** and he had signed that summary too.

PPP's stalwarts maintained that it was not the 'national cause' or the extreme love with the people of Pakistan that brought Mr F S Hayat to the apex court but *'might be some left over share from the old deals of 2006'.* However, their cries were ignored by the apex court on the reasons;

- If there was any irregularity in the deals of 2006, it should have been brought before the court or any other forum.

- Then there were two projects in 2006; why raised to 19 in 2008 by the PPP regime.

- The democratic set up of 2008 should have examined the outcome and benefits of 2 RPPs of 2006. If they had not delivered anything positive in two years then PPP should have got them closed. Instead the PPP went for another 17 projects to loot the country hastily using the old footprints.

Bureaucracy in Pakistan is also known for its character throughout the history that some left behind officer from the MoW&P had provided the whole set of documents having 'dubious deals' to Mr Faisal S Hayat. In the case, the recovered money from the RPPs had not been taken out from Raja Pervaiz Ashraf but from the concerned 'Directors' and mostly from the top bureaucrats but no body would dare to ask them; even the SC.

The Transparency International, **on 1st November 2012,** reported a mega corruption scandal to the prime minister in which the NAB allegedly cleared one of the Rental Power Project [RPP] without recovering $220 million from it. Allegedly, this huge embezzlement was done in connivance with the NAB where M/s Karkey RPP was allowed to leave Pakistan without paying the recoverable money. [*Interestingly, the name of PM Pervaiz Ashraf was among the accused persons in that RPP case too.*]

According to the judgment of the Supreme Court announced **on 30th March 2012** in the RPP case, besides other actions, the court directed the government to take the following action to recover all payments made to the RPPs with mark-up, who had failed to achieve CoD within the stipulated time. Some of the details have already been given in earlier paragraphs but see another snippet below:

*"Para 38: Mr Kamal Anwar, ASC assisted the court as Amicus Curiae. He submitted that advance payment was made to 9 RPPs, namely, Karkey, Gulf Rental Power, Reshma Power, Techo Sammundri Road Faisalabad, Techno Sahuwal Sialkot, Guddu, Young Gen, Naudero-I and Naudero-II, details whereof have been given hereinabove. None of them could achieve COD within time, on account of which their contracts were signed off.*

*Statedly, the bank guarantees furnished on behalf of all the bidders have also been en-cashed. ...... However, Karkey (231.8 MW), Gulf (62 MW), Naudero-I (51 MW) and Reshma (201 MW), which are still functioning, had achieved delayed COD."*

'Accordingly, recovery from Karkey RPP which failed to achieve COD within the stipulated time, works out to be approximately $220.76 million. Karkey was paid 14% advance $79.05 million; $7.654 million per month from April 2011 to March 2012 ($91.84 million); Total to be repaid by Karkey is $170.89 Million; Bank interest for 3-1/2 years on $79.05 million is about $45 million, and for 1 year on $91.84 million is $12.87 million so the total recoverable amount from Karkey Power Plant was therefore $220.76 million'. Though the power plant failed to supply 232 megawatts, its administration was all set to leave Pakistan by paying less then 20 million dollars. *GEO TV's* live program *of 30th October 2012* is referred.

In view of above, the Supreme Court had to direct the National Accountability Bureau (NAB) on immediate basis to assure the court that the Turkish ship-mounted rental power plant Karkey would not be allowed to leave till the company cleared its arrears. PML(Q)'s MNA Faisal Saleh Hayat, the complainant of RPPs corruption had told the apex court that the NAB was trying to resolve the matter in *'its own way'*. Karkey Company was being pardoned Rs:22 billion and was being told to leave; it was alleged by Makhdoom Faisal S Hayat in a letter signed and sent by him to the apex court in October 2012.

The CJP remarked *'how such matters could be resolved outside the court'*; the country was being deprived off with billions of rupees through NAB's ill intentions in the name of plea-bargaining with Karkey.

During November 2012 the cases pertaining to *Chichoki Mallian* and *Nandi Pur* were also fixed. In an earlier hearing, the court had given NAB 24 hours to submit a report over allegations of an underhand deal of the bureau with Karkey. After four days, the NAB's prosecutor, in person, had rejected the allegations and affirmed that Karkey would not be moved.

## SC ORDERS FOR PM's ARREST:

On 15th January 2013, Supreme Court ordered the Federal Investigation Agency [FIA] that the sitting Prime Minister of Pakistan, Raja Pervaiz Ashraf, former Federal Minister of Power, should immediately be arrested by the NAB along with other sixteen accomplices [including Naveed Qamar, Waqar Masood etc] in Rental Power Case and within 24 hours. The apex court ordered that:

> '.... All concerned, regardless of their rank, who have been booked in the case be arrested and if someone leaves the country, then Chairman NAB will be held responsible along with his investigating team'.

FIA's Immigration desks at all the 24 airports of the country were told to place the accused persons on the Exit Control List [ECL] but even then nothing happened; not a single arrest – it was Pakistan.

The Supreme Court's order came at a time when Allama Tahirul Qadri was delivering speech to *'millions people Dharna'* after leading a 38 hours long march from Lahore to Islamabad to demand electoral reforms. Participants of the march celebrated while chanting *"Long Live Supreme Court"* when Allama Qadri mentioned the court's decision during his speech.

**On 18th January 2013,** NAB told the SC that *'it does not have enough evidence to arrest Prime Minister Raja Pervaiz Ashraf and 15 other accused in the rental power plants (RPPs) case.'*

NAB's additional prosecutor general presented a progress report in the court which stated the NAB Chairman as saying that *"the investigation and inquiries are not yet complete."* NAB Chairman Admiral Fasih Bukhari and Prosecutor Gen KK Agha had contended that the Supreme Court was overstepping its jurisdiction because it had nothing to do with the investigation. A three-member bench headed by Chief Justice Iftikhar M Chaudhry had expressed dissatisfaction over the NAB report relating to the implementation of its judgment of 30th March 2012.

Three days earlier, the apex court had directed that investigation reports be submitted to the authorities concerned and references against the accused people be approved for their arrest. The NAB Chief told the court that before framing criminal charges against anyone they had to go through the different records and collect evidence to substantiate the allegations. Till then two reports in respect of Piraghaib and Techno Sahuwal prepared by NAB's Rawalpindi office was ready to be considered by the executive board for a final decision.

The fact remains that during the course of year's long proceedings before the apex Court, enough material and facts surfaced that could point towards corrupt practices involving billions of the poor nation in the Rental Power Projects. However, no conviction has taken place yet and believably no conviction would be there. Pakistan's whole history, from the murder of PM Liaquat Ali Khan in October 1951 till today is the witness. No investigations; and if there are investigations – no convictions; salute to Pakistan's 'perfect' judicial practices.

Not even a single conviction of any corrupt politician, top bureaucrat, or high ranking General or towering Pir or god-fathered *jageerdar* [big landlord] or industrialist *Mian or Chaudhry* in Pakistan's 66 years history. All investigations were always faulty or the 'legal & procedural requirements' or 'due process of law' were not fulfilled so all the courts were always helpless. What a continuing coincidence since birth of this country. The only two quotable convictions, of Z A Butto in 1979 & of Nawaz Sharif in 2000 were not on the basis of their actual sins [*for some more than the punishments articulated*].

Here, in the RPPs Case, the Supreme Court deliberated a 3-page order saying that:

- Chairman NAB was asked for removal of the DG NAB Rawalpindi and two IOs associated with the investigation of the RPP cases.

- The SC observed that the IOs were not allowed to ensure the implementation of the court's judgment.

- The SC directed the Additional Prosecutor General NAB, Rana Zahid Mehmood, to [firstly] submit Investigation Reports to the concerned authorities, [secondly] to get approved the final reports/references against the accused and [thirdly] to cause arrest of all the accused including the PM Raja Pervaiz Ashraf.

That was another point that in the NAB Ordinance the Additional Prosecutor General had no powers to accomplish the said tasks of the apex court.

[*Section 8 of the NAB Ordinance appoints a Prosecutor General whose mandate is to "give advice to the Chairman NAB upon... legal matters" & perform other "duties of legal character" and the PG MAY appoint Additional PG "to institute or defend cases".*]

In effect, the Additional PG was one of the lawyers of NAB, and possessed no legal mandate in terms of administrative work – especially not without the express directions of the Chairman.

Similarly Section 18 of the NAB Ordinance empowers the Chairman or an officer authorized by him to initiate proceedings, inquire, investigate, and/or arrest the accused. It is a mandatory requirement that before ordering an arrest, it is the Chairman who must be satisfied. The Additional PG does not figure into this equation at any place.

Thus for many people it was surprising that why the SC had asked the Additional PG to make arrests of the accused persons involved. The reasons were obvious; the apex court had categorically shown 'distrust' over the intentions of Chairman NAB Adml Fasih Bokhari.

Nothing would happen as per Pakistan's history, the accused persons were given the benefits of a known & golden principle of jurisprudence [innocent till proven guilty]; in that country the ruling elite can never be proved guilty – come what may, see the history.

Then where the Rs:84 billion of RPP gone; no answer with any one; no one amongst those sitting ministers and secretaries was proved guilty; case went untraced. Dr Tahirul Qadri had also left his *Dharna* midway with no apparent result; the people have short memories in Pakistan.

Four years back, PM Raja Pervaiz Ashraf was given the title of *Raja Rental* after he was accused of receiving kickbacks in the dubious rental power deals. He had been defending himself in the Supreme Court but the judges were never convinced.

## *THE ULTIMATE FATE:*

On 5th **December 2013,** the National Accountability Bureau [NAB] Executive Board authorised two more investigations against former PM Raja P Ashraf and officials of the Ministry of Water and Power in multi-billion RRP scam. The first investigation was authorised against officials and government functionaries in the case of Rental Power Plant installed at Summandari (Faisalabad), involving alleged corruption worth Rs:2.8 billion.

The second investigation was authorised in the case of Walters Power International & Naudero-I Larkana involving corruption worth $28.423 million. Besides Ex PM Raja Pervaiz, former Water and Power Secretary Shahid Rafi, Additional Secretary Zarar Aslam and WAPDA General Manger Rana Amjad were also made accused in the case. Till then, RPP Naudero-II case was being heard in the Accountability Court, Islamabad, in which Raja Pervaiz was the main accused in addition to nine others.

**On 3rd June 2014,** an Accountability Court in Islamabad indicted former PM Raja Pervez Ashraf and 11 others in an RRP case. Former Finance Minister Shaukat Tareen, former Federal Secretaries Ismail Qureshi and Shahid Rafi were also among those charged in the case of alleged corruption in the Sahuwal and Piranghaib rental power projects. The AC judge Muhammad Bashir dismissed pleas filed by Mr Tareen and Mr Qureshi requesting their names be dropped from the case.

NAB had been investigating 12 RPPs cases in which nine firms reportedly received more than Rs:22 billion as mobilisation advance from the government to commission the projects, but most of them were accused of failing to set up plants. The bureau had already recovered Rs:13 billion in various RRP cases till then.

**On 31st July 2015,** the National Accountability Bureau [NAB] during an Executive Board Meeting ultimately decided, consequent upon the observations of December 2013, to file a corruption reference against former PM Raja P Ashraf in a case pertaining to rental power project Naudero-I. Former Secretary Water & Power Fayyaz Elahi, former MD Private Power and Infrastructure Board [PPIB] Fayyaz Ahmed Khan and ex-MD of Pakistan Electric Power Company (Pepco) Tahir Basharat Cheema were named as co-accused.

In the said case, the accused allegedly awarded RPP contracts of 51 megawatts without open competitive bidding in violation of RRP rules, National Electric Power Regulatory Authority (Nepra) Act and Rental Services Contract (RSC) to favour sponsors at the cost of state exchequer.

# Scenario 113

## PAKISTAN DISGRACED BY AMERICA:

### *PM GILANI PRICED IN LONDON:*

*On 1ˢᵗ May 2012,* Secretary Hilary Clinton threatened that drone attacks would not be contained rather may be launched excessively. In her speeches at Delhi and Dacca she openly blamed Pakistan that *'Aiman ul Zawahiri is hiding in Pakistan so another attack would be there'*. American Congress passed amendments to curtail foreign aid for Pakistan. The Presidency and the GHQ both went upset and the Parliamentary unanimous resolution was once again buried under compromises.

Additionally, **on 2ⁿᵈ May 2012,** during President Obama's visit to Kabul, President Hamid Karzai was offered $4 billion dollar per year to be finally stamped at Chicago Conference on 20ᵗʰ instant. Strategic partnership treaty was also signed then – as has been detailed earlier.

In the *2ⁿᵈ week of May 2012,* the convicted prime minister of Pakistan, Mr Gilani, paid a sudden visit to London with his entourage of about 70 people, mostly belonging to media and office bearers of selected Union Councils from his constituency in Multan, to hit two targets with one bullet.

*PM Gilani was called to London to have a 'nice' but bullying message and Pakistan immediately opted to work on the same pay & allowances.* Look at the ultimate deal:

- Mr Zardari would be called to join NATO Conference in Chicago on 20ᵗʰ May 2012 [*which was on original agenda*].

- NATO supply would be opened but containers would not be allowed to take arms & ammunition.

- Foreign security establishment would be reduced.

- Pakistan would be paid $1500 for each consignment **entered in Afghanistan.**

[*Why NOT while un-loaded at Karachi port – one could feel the difference – indicating that some containers would be deliberately declared lost in the way to Afghan borders*].

The agenda was clear. *PM Gilani was summoned by the British PM David Cameron to convey the US stern orders for opening of NATO supply routs in Pakistan against some dollar bags,* mostly in the name of military & civil aid, which was happily 'negotiated'.

On his return after 5 days hilarious stay in London with his electioneering team, the PM Gilani immediately called Cabinet Defence Committee's meeting in Islamabad and *decided to open the supply routs declaring the deal beneficial for Pakistan* which was blocked on 26th November 2011 after *Salala* Check Post episode.

If the Pakistan government was serious in having restored its lost honour of 2001-10, it could have taken a concrete decision within a week or two based on hard facts and national interests. The regime remained constrained to issuing the press statements only. Once an All Parties Conference was called; once the Parliamentary Committee on Defence was agitated; the longest joint parliamentary meeting in the history of Pakistan was held on 13th May 2011 to get another joint resolution passed. Drone attacks were condemned, *Salala* event damned and the US was asked to come with apology but then - *'tain tain fish'*.

The disqualified PM Gilani cooked up astonishing logic for taking the said decision. They tried to hoodwink the Pakistan's populace and media by saying that NATO supplies were being opened because:

- *Pakistan's friend Turkey was in NATO so how could Pakistan block their supplies* [as if it was not known to them earlier].

- *About 48 countries were included in NATO so how Pakistan could make all of them angry* [again, as if it was not known to them earlier].

But who would reveal that how many bags of Sterling Pounds were annexed with these carefully [& cunningly] coined hints.

Soon after, Mr Gilani packed up and left the PM House for good.

While taking this one sided decision alone by pushing the parliamentary resolution under the carpet, the Cabinet's Defence Committee forgot that when the Americans had started their direct negotiations with Taliban they had not even consulted either Pakistan or Afghanistan. The US had reverted back to these two affected countries only after getting diplomatic defeat in *'Qatar Process of 2011'*; US Ambassador Mark Grossman's open confession was on the record.

Secondly, the American elites were trying to win scores for 2012's US elections and as the time passed the Afghan issue subdued slowly and gradually; perhaps automatically too.

Pakistan's Defence Committee also failed to bear in mind that America was going to formally announce for *'Taliban's Office'* in **Doha** during December 2011's Bonn Conference but could not do so because US - Taliban deals were in doldrums due to internal friction amongst the Taliban's Command on the question of negotiations and certain agenda items with the US.

The so called strategy of *'confidence building measures'* between the two factions, the US & the Taliban, had miserably failed and the US were going furious day by day **as the world's only super power was being defeated even on the negotiation table.** Till March 2012 there was a complete deadlock; mud slinging on each other and was noticed by all.

[*The US-Taliban failure got momentum when in January 2012 Taliban asked the US to release their five companions, including Taliban's former Governor & Interior Minister named Khairullah, from Guantanamo Camp and bring them to Qatar.*

*As a process, the US Congress needed to be served a 30-days notice for each release from the Camp. The Americans delayed it because they wanted a worldly announcement from Taliban to shun terrorism and opening of meaningful dialogue with Karzai government. Both sides refrained thus their negotiation process halted.*]

Pakistan's Cabinet Defence Committee also disregarded the then prevailing facts about smuggling of high spec arms from Helmand province into Quetta and Karachi which had raised Pak-army's suspicions; CIA and British MI-6 had no answer for those known transactions. These arms included 8mm and 9mm calibre pistols of the US make, which were primarily under the CIA supervision, [made] stolen during Helmand Operation of 2010, launched by the British troops, but transported to Pakistan through Afghan security officials.

Those US-made used [not new or packed] arms were available in all over Pakistan but abundantly in the local markets of Karachi and Quetta to be used by the alleged Baloch dissidents, Lyari's law breakers, and some of the misguided sectarian groups. The small arms of the European make had also found sale outlets in other areas of Pakistan which were mostly been sent there through Afghani Taliban.

Security analysts knew that the US-NATO forces were intentionally going ignorant about that dirty game to destabilise Pakistan under a settled conspiracy program. At the same time, one should admit that the PPP government and the Parliament both were impotent. They knew the above facts but were not able to launch offensive hand on those sale points nor could they amend the laws to give exemplary punishments to the stockists. Those were probably the Lyari gangsters backed by Parliamentarians themselves.

## *OBAMA's AGREEMENT WITH KABUL:*

To mark Osama Bin Laden's first anniversary, the US President Obama paid a surprise visit to Kabul *on 2nd May 2012*. There he signed a *'Strategic Partnership Agreement'* with Afghan Chief Executive Hamid Karzai thus entered perhaps the most complicated phase of its decade - long war in Afghanistan. Beating the [practically non-existing] dead horse again at a military base near Kabul, President Obama said that:

> 'We have a clear path to fulfil our mission in Afghanistan. The goal that I set, **to defeat Al Qaeda and deny it the chance to rebuild,** is now within our reach. **Our goal is to destroy Al Qaeda,** and we are on a path to do exactly that.'

Then President Obama, during that speech had not laid down any detailed timetable for withdrawal of the US forces from the region. President Obama had earlier announced his new program for Afghanistan *on 1st December 2009* in New York Army Centre. As per plans, Chicago Conference of 20th May 2012 was expected to be the final round. The players were there but the participants were having different goals in their minds.

On the other hand, President Obama's new agreement with Afghanistan dated *2nd May 2012* ensuring the presence of American 'experts' even after **NATO leaving by the end of 2014,** blinked to another suspicious scenario. The US bases at Bagram, Kandahar and Kabul would remain operational much beyond 2014. When historians pondered beyond 2014 plans those days, they could imagine the well trumpeted:

*"...geography of the new South Asian region, a part of the new world order game - comprising Tribal areas of Pakistan, the adjoining areas of Afghanistan, the territory of southern Bahawalpur till Gwadar and the Indian Ocean."*

All bits & bobs were pointed out as linked to the US plans for WOT.

President Obama's visit to Kabul was retaliated just hours after Obama left the capital. On the same day of 2nd **May 2012** the Afghan Taliban launched an attack [detonating a car bomb, allowing four assailants disguised in *burqas* and armed with hand grenades] on Green Village in Kabul's outskirts killing seven civilians and wounding about twelve - a clear message to Obama not to think about permanent bases in Afghanistan.

As per Afghan-US agreement, 'some' US troops were to remain in Afghanistan to pursue the essential missions: train, advise and assist Afghan forces, help Kabul defend its sovereignty, and conduct counter - terror operations in the region, **especially against Pakistan.**

Obama's message to the Afghan people was that *'as you stand up, you will not stand alone.'* Perhaps the Americans learnt a lesson from the history that they had to fight the longest war of the US history here because after Soviet's expulsion from the region in 1980s, they had left Pakistan alone to suffer the after effects and miseries of war. Recalling the catastrophe of Pakistan, Obama had to assert that:

*'I am confident that the Afghan people will understand that the United States will stand by them.'*

The later developments denied even that second promise.

Obama's new Afghan accord became a big challenge for the Taliban and Pakistan, which assumed that time & tune was on their side and that Karzai regime would collapse around 2014 or earlier. Obama also knew that Afghanistan's sovereignty would continue to depend upon cooperation from Pakistan; which was not available to them in those particular days.

As against the original American plans of withdrawal from the South Asian Region [*announced in West Point Academy address on 1st December 2009*], this accord pledged enhanced US financial and military support beyond 2014, overtly displaying to the world that it owed no intentions to quit Afghanistan for another decade at least. During the next one year both governments worked out exact features of a long-term military partnership keeping Iraq agreement in sight but Karzai expected more than that. Although in his speech, Obama made it clear that:

*'The US will not seek permanent military bases in Afghanistan. We will not build permanent bases in this country, nor will we be patrolling its cities and mountains.'*

At this moment, Afghanistan's Strategic Partnership Agreement with India, signed in October 2011 at New Delhi should be kept in mind; also that on 20th May 2012, the Chicago Conference to reinforce Obama's commitments for Afghan security. Given the inability of Afghanistan to support a large armed force, the US and its allies were expected to pledge an annual payment of nearly $4 billion to Afghanistan. In July same year [2012], the world powers again assembled in Tokyo and made financial pledges to Afghanistan's development in the coming years.

Pakistan, however, could not ignore US envoy in Afghanistan Mr Crocker's policy statement that '*... if we or Afghanistan are threatened or attacked by countries outside of Afghanistan, we have the right of self-defence.*' Taliban's attack events were of course included in that scenario too. Pak-Army took a serious note of it as the statement was openly directed towards Pakistan.

Both Afghan and US officials celebrated that 2nd May 2012's US-Afghan Accord calling it a historic bilateral commitment; a new beginning in the US-Afghan relationship but for Afghan people it was not a point of jubilation because, as per White House's fact sheet, *'the Strategic Partnership Agreement itself does not commit the United States to any specific troop levels or levels of funding in the future',* thus the actual decision was with the US Congress; like Kerry Lugar Bill.

Simultaneously, Karzai was quick to remind his Interior Ministry that *'if you have any doubt about any US intelligence report, do not conduct any operation based on it,'* reminding of Karzai's vision of a sovereign Afghanistan. Afghan government had already blocked NATO's notorious night operations and had also demanded control of the sole US military prison including its detainees. The US officials had expressed concern about both prospects.

The same like fears were felt by the American intelligentsia; see *Anthony Cordesman's* essay published at website of *Centre for Strategic and International Studies Washington',* saying that:

*'None of the tensions between the US and the Karzai government have gone away. The broader problems with Afghan governance and corruption are not diminishing. Progress in creating effective Afghan forces is increasingly questionable, the insurgents are clearly committed to going on with the fight, and relations with Pakistan seem to take two steps backward for every apparent step forward.'*

A wide gulf of mistrust prevailed amongst the two; one could recall the events of burning of the Holy Qura'an at Bagram Air Base in February 2012; murder of 16 men, women and children by an American sergeant in southern Afghanistan in March 2012; killings of Westerners by rogue Afghan security forces and sharp rise of Taliban infiltrators accounting for 20% of NATO casualties that year.

The fact remained that the US & NATO had operated in the Afghan region under United Nations Security provisions but then Kabul sought to negotiate a '**Status of Forces Agreement**' with Washington defining legal terms and conditions under which the US forces wanted to operate further. Nearly 50% of the country had already become the responsibility of Afghan security forces but Afghan government aspired to take the full charge by 2013; though Obama had another one year in mind while saying that:

*'Our troops will be coming home. Last year, we removed 10,000 US troops from Afghanistan. Another 23,000 will leave by the end of the summer [2012]. After that, reductions will continue at a steady pace, with more of our troops coming home. And as our coalition agreed, by the end of 2014 the Afghans will be fully responsible for the security of their country.'*

For many in America, it was the start of presidential campaign from Obama. Afghanistan was also heading towards a new presidential election; but looking for a suitable moment. The American military drawdown was highlighted for the forthcoming election scenario in both countries. Ponder about Obama's key deliberations trumpeted high everywhere in media, local & foreign, then:

*'I recognize that many Americans are tired of war but we must finish the job we started in Afghanistan, and end this war responsibly. The goals are limited. **To build a country in America's image or to eradicate every vestige of the Taliban would require many more years, many more dollars, and most importantly, many more American lives.**'*

President Obama had aspired to kill two birds with one cartridge.

But this bonanza of relationship could not last more than a year. See *'Foreign Policy' [FP]'s* <u>Situation Report</u> dated 9<sup>th</sup> July 2013:

> *"......Frustration, accusations, and a bad VTC - the US may accelerate the drawdown of forces in Afghanistan in part due to the souring relationship between President Hamid Karzai and President Obama. The NYT reports this morning that Obama has become increasingly annoyed, especially after the prospect of peace talks stumbled out of the gate last month.*
>
> *A video teleconference between the two, aimed to defuse tensions, only worsened them. Now the "zero option" for a residual force, long thought to be a negotiating tactic, is back on the table.*
>
> *The idea of a complete military exit similar to the American military pullout from Iraq has gone from being considered the worst-case. The officials cautioned that no decisions had been made on the pace of the pullout and exactly how many American troops to leave behind in Afghanistan. ......but the hardening of negotiating stances on both sides could result in a repeat of what happened in Iraq."*

## PAKISTAN HUMILIATED MORE:

However, Obama's visit to Kabul and signing of an accord in May 2012 was an adequate answer to Pakistani and Afghani Taliban which thought that the Americans were leaving the region much before than 2014; apparently they, or some of them, were going to stay for another decade at least.

While signing that *'Strategic Partnership Agreement'* on 2<sup>nd</sup> May 2012, instead of thanking Pakistan that day, the US preferred to launch another drone attack in FATA killing ten civilians and leaving about the same number injured. Additionally the US Secretary of State Hilary Clinton paid a 'deep tribute' to Pakistan by revising his determination that *'the US would increase drone attacks on Pakistan side of Afghan border to keep Kabul safe'*.

Why this anger, hatred and humiliation from a strategic partner; the US, for whom Pakistan slipped into the so-called 'war on terror' in which the later lost its 42,000 civilian lives and about 5000 of its army troops in addition to sustaining $67.925 billion [as per GoP's official declaration] loss of economy during WOT years. Due to NATO's supply vehicles Pakistan's 4046 kilometre roads were severely damaged and Pakistan's National Highway Authority (NHA) made a demand of Rs:123 billion in 2011 just for minimum repair of that infrastructure back but the US & Pakistani governments both refused.

Both partners were okay till **January 2011** when the issue of Raymond Davis suddenly cropped up. The Pakistani people felt that issuance of more than 6000 visas to Americans without scrutiny and security clearance during 2009-10 had in fact brought a secret brigade of CIA's army in the country. Then Osama's episode of 2nd **May 2011** occurred which the US SEALS accomplished single handedly which made most Pakistanis more critical of the US. The two countries moved apart. The last strike on their mutual relations was seen when the *US attack on Salala,* on 26th **November 2011,** caused death of 24 Pak-army troops including officers.

No compensation, even no regret or remorse from the US, so the temperature of Pakistani people continued rising. The US drone attacks went on increase instead. Army stood by the general sentiments. The PPP regime was not in a position to make angry any of the two. The NATO supply routs were blocked in November 2011 but the Parliament remained in doldrums to take any decision thus America went more furious, too.

The US exit strategy from Afghanistan could not go smooth either. Direct US negotiations with Taliban in Qatar failed; joint efforts of Pak - US - Afghan Commission could not bring Taliban on negotiation table in Kabul thus direct attacks on the capital increased day by day.

US wanted to follow its December 2009 exit plan but had to announce on 2nd May 2012 through Obama - Karzai pact that US would stay in the region for another one decade. Contrarily, there was enormous pressure from the American public for *'calling back of troops'* and Obama also wanted to avoid this pit fall in [then] up-coming US elections but had to make an open announcement that *'Afghanistan would not be left alone'.*

Pakistan's policy makers were fantastic. Two years back, the US asked Pakistan to help them bring Taliban on negotiation table. Immediate conclusions were drawn that the US got defeated and so would quit soon; thanks to TV live analysis made by celebrity anchors on defence and foreign affairs. The Pakistan could not come up with facts; it could have dissociated itself from the whole game.

When the disappointed America had opted for direct talks with Taliban to get a way out, Pakistan could have stayed aloof; arresting Mulla Brother and putting him in the jail was misinterpreted on both sides.

That was the reason the US ultimately decided not to include Pakistan or Taliban in the negotiation and thus the Obama - Karzai pact of 2nd May 2012 [**Strategic Partnership Agreement**] was signed; exit plans were simply extended for another decade.

Very cogent questions emerged; what the US would do here even if it stayed here beyond 2014. What had the US achieved in eleven years war so far; what progress had it made in achieving its objectives – zero. The US had plundered its wisdom, budget, honour, its military's morale, and popular will of its public up till that moment and lost more with time.

During the year 2012, two odd events took place in Afghanistan; firstly of *burning the Holy Qura'an* in Bagram Cantonment and secondly of *killing of 16 Afghan civilians* by an American Officer on duty. The US government offered formal apology to Karzai government for both events but refused to show similar behaviour for Salala Post killings despite Pakistan's repeated 'requests'.

On 20th May 2012, US and its allies assembled in Chicago and announced $4 billion yearly aid for 'rehabilitation & development of Afghanistan' but what *they had given to Pakistan [recall $1.5 billion of Kerry Lugar Bill]* and what they allocated for Pakistan's development; not a penny.

Earlier, another most important event in Afghanistan; *Taliban attacks of 15th April 2012* had almost shaken the country. Seven bomb blasts simultaneously at the Afghan Parliament & NATO HQ campus; the American, British, German and Russian embassies and high ranking hotels rocked Kabul. In Jalalabad, suicide bombers attacked the airport building. In Gardez, the Police HQ building was brought to trashes. In Logar province, the Governor's office was taken hostage.

In Hamid Karzai's Presidential palace, the on going negotiation sessions with *Hizb e Islami* were shifted to a safe house. The delegation of Pakistan's lady Parliamentarians had to hide in Pakistan Embassy. Six attacking Taliban were killed and dozens got injured.

What did the whole scenario speak; that the Afghan Taliban had not gone weak despite the American's war strategy to crush them. Ultimately, the US again resorted to sit on negotiation table with Taliban but with a changed agenda. The Taliban were also secretly induced to launch a forceful fight with Anti - Taliban groups in Northern Afghanistan. Again the same old tactics of 'divide & rule'; but did not work well this time.

Despite such hostile situations in the region, the US & Pakistan expected normalcy in their mutual relationship; an astonishing phenomenon. Both had the parallel demands. Pakistan wanted that:

- *The US should end Drone attacks unless Pak-Army consulted first for each attack.*

- *The US should include Pashtun Afghan Taliban in the negotiation process. It was because the Eastern and Southern Afghanistan parts were controlled by Pashtun Taliban and Karzai government had no writ there.*

The US at the same time demanded that:

- *Pakistan should open NATO supply rout immediately and without any prior condition.*

- *Pakistan should use its influence to bring Afghan Taliban on negotiation table in Kabul.*

The civil & military heads in Pakistan wanted to perform the said functions on their part without hitch but this time both were looking at the public anger in Pakistan. The PPP government did not want to take risk at the moment but ultimately bowed its head to seek dollars in aid. To please the general populace, the leadership started releasing 'secret news' that Osama's killing operation was done by the US *'with cogent help from Pakistan's civil & military bosses'*; Defence Minister Ahmed Mukhtar's media interview of those days is referred in that context.

Intelligence guided media reports kept on building general public opinion in Pakistan that *'the US would bow down within a month if NATO supplies blocked'* but then six months passed. Neither the US offered apology for *Salala* attacks nor the drone attacks could be subsided. Estimations went wrong; future assumptions in Pakistan and media's hue & cry both were taken as mockery.

Another development on internal front took place in Pakistan.

The Rangers and security forces, in pursuit of criminal gangs and ammunition in Lyari, Karachi, got 3 police officers killed & 58 injured during those few days. Earlier the army's security dons were unaware of terrorist's attack plans on Dargai [Malakand] & GHQ and got senior officers hostages.

Simultaneously, the Khyber PK police were ignorant of buses full of armed men breaking the Bannu jail and got 382 convicts escaped. Even the media guru reporters could not find clues of such big events but they knew well about plans of the US & Taliban and were able to discuss their minds in their daily talk shows. The general populace was frustrated, in short.

What could Pakistan do then; *simply to stick to the nationalist approach* - to concentrate on the security of Pakistan's own people especially in border regions, their welfare and rebuild. A big NO to the American plans should have appeared on cards; however, Pakistan's political elite did no think so; they forgot what was happening in Afghanistan; Afghan Taliban and Karzai and the US were making out their own way.

The Pakistani military and political leadership were advised that:

> *'Let the dust settle down. Old philosophies of by-gone Generals [that there should be pro-Pakistani rule in Afghanistan] have outdated now; we have already suffered a lot on this count.*

> *Let the Afghan people decide their fate; the world community laughs when we try to be 'their guides'; on what basis – while their own country Pakistan was burning and falling into rocks due to those old myths.'*

It was the need of the time to ponder into the assertions seriously then.

## CHICAGO CONFERENCE OF 2012:

A two-day NATO summit kicked off in Chicago [USA] on the future of Afghanistan *on 20th May 2012*. It was the 25th NATO summit, the largest-ever, with participation from 61 countries, and the first hosted by the US since 1999. It was intended to discuss the strategy agreed upon in Lisbon in 2010 which had called for:

- *renewed commitment to fight in Afghanistan;*
- *a robust agreement on missile defence; and*
- *more integral cooperation in emerging threats like cyber security.*

The next conference was planned in Tokyo to firm up financial commitments for the $4.1 billions annual budget for NATO's presence in Afghanistan till 2024 and Afghan development projects. The two issues which dominated the talks were:

- *Reopening of NATO's supply route through Pakistan, and*

- *New French President's upholding his election pledge of withdrawal from Afghanistan by the end of 2012.*

On NATO's supply routes through Pakistan, the Americans were visibly irritated at not being successful in arm - twisting Pakistan after months of engagement in negotiations; especially when Colin Powel could do this with just one phone call [*how badly Pakistanis were treated in the past*].

Everyone in Chicago Conference termed Pakistan distasteful describing *Salala* attack on Pak-Army as an accident – *which was a blatant lie*. No one was there to tell the participants that it was a pre-mediated, unprovoked and well planned murder of 24 Pakistani soldiers, spread over two hours where each one of them was picked and targeted.

In a spirited show outside the venue, the anti-war crowd dubbed NATO as militarised extension of the global expansionism; some termed it *'US sponsored terrorism'*. The US administration had signed a multibillion - dollar drone contract with Northrop Grumman; but was disliked by 99% of the "Wall Street investors". A group of Afghanistan and Iraq war veterans also attended the rally to return their medals; a gesture signifying how deeply disenchanted the Americans were with the war.

Russia had declined the invitation to attend that Conference as its relations with NATO were tempered by US plans to deploy anti-missile equipment in Romania & Poland region. The major cause of summit's shallowness was the financial crunch all over the Europe and in America itself. During UN-backed operations in Libya, only eight out of 28 members participated. The US had itself planned to cut down defence expenditure; by over $800 millions for that year.

All the above indicators added up in NATO's weakness of political, financial and military stamina for any Iraq - style re-intervention, should the Taliban appear to recapture political power in Kabul. If NATO had any contingency plans for such an eventuality, the said aspects of war were not discussed in Chicago, at least not for the public.

President Zardari was the only participant to state at the summit that *'there can be no military solution to the war in Afghanistan'*; sadly, no other leader took this theme seriously. Zardari knew that Pakistan was not in a position to take another wave of millions of refugees. One Taj Khatak, referring to an essay available at media *on 24ᵗʰ May 2012*, opined that:

'The US should know that there can be no stability, progress or peace in any country where over 40 percent of its population is sidelined and considered an enemy, and Afghanistan is no exception to such historical situations.

The problem gets complicated as **Pakhtuns** have been in power in Afghanistan since decades, **Tajiks** dominated army, cabinet occupied by **non-Pakhtun** and major population [Taliban] declared as enemy; how the outsiders could bring peace there.'

## PEACE TALKS AMIDST ALLEGATIONS:

During the *2ⁿᵈ week of May 2012*, legislation was introduced in the US Congress that would deduct $50 million from the aid to Islamabad for every American killed by terrorists operating from the safe heavens in Pakistan; given the name *'Pakistan Terrorism Accountability Act of 2012'*. The said deducted amounts were to be reserved for *'the victim's family'*. Rohrabacher, Chairman of the House Foreign Affairs Oversight and Investigations Sub-Committee said that:

'For too long America has funded the Pakistani government, giving it free money, while elements of the ISI and Pakistan's military operated radical Islamic groups that are actively murdering Americans. Americans will not accept this.

Pakistan helped to create the Taliban and Pakistan's intelligence service hid Osama bin Laden from the US for years. Today, one of the most dangerous and sophisticated groups killing American troops in Afghanistan is the Haqqani Network, which is closely operated by the Pakistani government through its ISI.'

Pakistan's army commanders and the PPP government were aware that earlier former Chairman of the Joint Chiefs of Staff, Admiral Mike Mullen, had also maligned Pakistan's ISI by saying that:

*'It [ISI] had directed the Haqqani network to plan and conduct assault on our embassy (in Kabul in September 2011) ... We also have credible*

*evidence that they were behind the June 28th attack against the Inter-Continental Hotel in Kabul. The Haqqani network acts as a veritable arm of Pakistan's Inter-Services Intelligence agency.'*

During the first week of February 2013, the British PM David Cameron held talks with Afghan President Hamid Karzai and Asif Zardari, Pakistan's President. After a few sessions spread over two days at Chequers, the British PM hoped that Afghan presidential and parliamentary elections in April 2014 would draw moderate elements of Taliban into the democratic process before the departure of NATO troops.

The discussions, the third between the countries to be hosted by the UK, felt the dire needs for closer co-operation between the two governments as indispensable in preventing a collapse of Afghan authority after NATO & American's exit.

Historically, the Afghans used to accuse the Pakistani security services of backing the Taliban but this time the two leaders had agreed "an unprecedented level of co-operation", including a new strategic partnership in the autumn. The dynamics between the two had visibly improved. The most concrete outcome of the talks was that the two sides had agreed to the opening of an office in Qatar's capital, Doha, for negotiations between the Taliban and the Afghan High Peace Council.

*[The Council is assigned to handle the Taliban and is chaired by Salahuddin Rabbani. He replaced his father, the former Afghan president Burhanuddin Rabbani, who was assassinated in September 2011 by a suicide bomber.]*

Earlier, in December 2012, PM David Cameron had announced to withdraw 3,800 of the country's 9,000 troops from Afghanistan during 2013. Before the talks, Karzai had desired to call the *'external elements involved in creating instability and fighting in his country'* to join the peace talks. In an interview with *'the guardian'* in London on *3rd February 2013'*, Karzai said that:

- *'The exit of foreign forces [referring to NATO, Americans & others] will not bring more violence for them to perpetrate against their own people, but a serious, strong, good reduction in violence will occur.'*

- *..... whether western troops were "fighting in the wrong place" during their decade - long mission in Afghanistan, saying **security*** *was better in southern Helmand province before the arrival of British forces; so they should discontinue doing that and leave Afghanistan.*

- *...... the greatest long-term threat to the country was not the insurgents but meddling by foreign powers.*

- *..... the neighbouring country, has provided sanctuaries for the Taliban for years, and [he accused] Islamabad's military intelligence of manipulating the insurgents.*

- *The trilateral meetings follow moves by Pakistan to build confidence ... which would be almost impossible without Pakistani support.*

- *As a pullout for the Nato-led mission draws closer, the focus on peace talks is gaining ground.*

- *Afghans were not concerned whether the west felt it had succeeded or failed in their country; because they were focused on trying to recover from 30 years of war. He expects fighting to diminish after most foreign troops have gone.*

- *In 2002 through 2006, Afghanistan had a lot better security; when we had our own presence there, with very little foreign troops, schools were open in Helmand and life was more secure.*

- *I don't want to be interpreted as saying that the arrival of foreign troops brought less security or worsened security for us. Whatever happened was the past; now we are looking forward to the future.*

Daily *'the guardian'* observed that <u>President Karzai had shown strong nationalist sentiment then</u>, forged through years fighting the Soviets and then the Taliban, which brought him into conflict with western countries supporting his government financially and with troops; .......and Karzai earned a reputation as erratic, emotional and prone to believing paranoid conspiracy theories, according to leaked US diplomatic cables.

Afghan vs West ties were perhaps irretrievably damaged during the 2009's Afghan elections, which were marred by allegations of massive fraud, when Karzai felt western allies were trying to remove him from power.

Karzai's critics described him as an obstructive protector of corrupt relatives and cronies, pointing to his one brother in the southern city of Kandahar who, before he was assassinated, was alleged to have links with drug traffickers, and another who was a shareholder in a bank that nearly collapsed under $900m (£560m) of bad loans. Karzai's wife was a doctor who once worked in Afghan refugee camps in Pakistan.

Afghanistan in 1989 was a simpler proposition but in 2013 was transformed into a place infinitely more complicated and dangerous... not just for itself but for its neighbours, too. In 1989, it was a country contained within its borders but 24 years later, it stretched across the Durand Line. Two simple propositions:

- *The Taliban based in FATA of Pakistan went more loyal to Mullah Omar than to Pakistan.*

- *North Waziristan, in real terms, became more loyal to Afghanistan geographically though being a part of Pakistan.*

**The Afghan 'mujahideen' in 1989 rejoiced over the circumstances that they had defeated a superpower [Russia]; in 2013 they were able to lay claim to a far bigger victory.**

The Americans, out of utter degradation and dishonour, tried to make hell of the situation through buying of Taliban, both on Pak-Afghan border and within Pakistan. **The US made life difficult for all by coming to Afghanistan in 2001, even more knotty and thorny by leaving the job half-done or just less than that.**

The PML(N), JUI & JI or other stalwarts amongst politicians proposing talks with the Taliban were not apprising the likely settlement. No one could spell the expected goal or outcome. If they were so blank, thinking not beyond the slogans, then they should not have encouraged the Taliban and confuse the Pak-Army contingents risking their lives in the killing fields of Tribal Area.

*Taliban had rejected both Imran Khan and Maulana Fazalur Rehman as mediators; lollipops were pushed far away, rather thrown out.*

Nevertheless, there were elements in Pakistani society next to friendly with the Taliban; no shortage of sympathies for them but the Taliban kept confusion in that regard. Like Swat was under Mullah Fazlullah in 2007, their support network in the form of *'madrassas'* and friendly religious parties were available to them throughout the country.

The MQM had started crying well in time that spreading areas of Karachi had gone Taliban - dominated, with their own *jirgas* to settle local disputes. Allegedly, the Taliban had set their stepping into the shoes of the Awami National Party [ANP], and the MQM was seen much disturbed; their decade's old monopoly and monarchy was at stake, too.

Ayaz Amir, in *'the News' of 15<sup>th</sup> February 2013* rightly commented that:

> *'Afghanistan is only living up to its reputation of being the graveyard of empires. **But who told us [the Pakistanis] to play with fire there? Now it's just not our fingers that are being burnt but much more.***
>
> *......through our folly we are reversing 200 years of history. Our military commanders talk strangely of training Afghan troops. **Our own house in disorder, we have the hubris to offer free advice to others.***
>
> *And as the Americans prepare to leave...the Taliban are dreaming of duplicating in Pakistan their victory that side of the Durand Line.'*

Thus, Pakistan continued to remain in dilemma. Internally the government writ stayed at constant stake since long. On external affairs it did not know that how the US or Afghanistan would behave in the coming years. Pakistan's Military was constantly facing hardships both financially and on technical grounds; some vital spares of jet fighters and artillery's arsenal had gone out of stock, for instance.

Let us try to read the message on the wall, if not learning from history.

> *[Parts of this essay were published at pakspectator.com on 27<sup>th</sup> October 2011; on 13<sup>th</sup> May 2012, on 15<sup>th</sup> May 2012 and on 16<sup>th</sup> May 2012]*

**The Tail piece:** In fact, the end game in Afghanistan had taken start in 2008 after Gen Musharraf's loud [& denouncing] deliberations but it continued with little ifs & buts. Gen Musharraf had suffered on that count because in August 2008, he was ousted from the Presidency and Mr Zardari sworn in. In America, President Bush also departed and Obama was welcome in White House. In both the countries, the rulers changed but the war on terror continued as before.

Then it was going to be the second stint of President Obama there in America [2012]. In Pakistan, the PPP regime was also near end; the next elections were to be held a year after [2013].

# Scenario 114

## DRONE ATTACKS DILEMMA-I:

Pakistani people came to know about [the American] drone attacks on 18th June 2004, the first known on record at least, a strike which killed 5–8 people including Nek Muhammad Wazir [*a Pashtun military leader*] and two children, near Wana in South Waziristan. Pak-Army initially claimed that the attack was done by them.

The second known drone attack was launched about a year later; on 14th May 2005 two persons were killed including *Haitham al-Yemeni* in a strike near the Pak-Afghan border in North Waziristan. The success in achieving their targets without any loss brought a chain of such strikes. On 5th November 2005, a strike destroyed the house of Al-Qaeda's 3rd in command, Abu Hamza Rabia killing his wife, three children and four others. Rabia himself was not there but on 30th November 2005, in another attack in Asoray, near Miran Shah of North Waziristan, Abu Hamza Rabia was also killed along with 4 other militants.

> [Some sources maintained that Hamza Rabia was not killed on that day of 30th November 2005 but the event had taken place on 4th December 2005 - the rest of the details were same.]

The above missile strike was seen and picked up by one Hayatullah Khan, a journalist from Waziristan **attached with GEO TV**. It proved to be his last assignment in North Waziristan. Khan had filed photos and story showing that US missile killing senior al Qaeda's figure Hamza Rabia. The story had also appeared in an **Urdu daily Ausaf**. His story had contradicted the state's official stance that Rabia had died in a blast caused by explosives located inside the house — the same sort of questions that surrounded the death of Baitullah Mehsud later.

The next day, Khan was abducted and after six months, **on 16th June 2006**, his dead body was found near the market in Miran Shah. The corpse was thin and dirty, in the same clothes Khan had been wearing when he was abducted. Sailab Mehsud, then president of the Tribal Union of Journalists, told the CPJ:

> "*We know that the government had a hand in this. A message has been sent that we should stop doing our work. For us, the post - Hayat period will only be more dangerous.*"

Mehsud was right about future risks. Since Hayatullah Khan's death, at least 13 more Pakistani journalists had been killed on duty, five of them murdered. Hayatullah Khan's younger brother was also killed in late 2006, while his wife was killed in a bomb attack in 2007 just to eliminate the possible evidence of Hayatullah's brutal murder.

The unrest amongst the whole Pakistani nation was seen **on 13ᵗʰ January 2006** when an airstrike killed 18 civilians, in Damadola area of Bajaur agency but allegedly missed Ayman al-Zawahri; five women, eight men, and five children were amongst the dead.

After about nine months, on **30ᵗʰ October 2006** another air strike through an armed helicopter was aimed at Chenagai to target Ayman al-Zawahri but destroyed a *madrassa* [religious school] in Bajaur killing 84 children. Pak-Army once again claimed it their own activity urging that the militants were providing weaponry training to the youngsters of Al Qaeda & Taliban there.

Khyber PK's one provincial minister Sirajul Haq [*later elected as Ameer Jamat e Islami* ] got furious declaring it '*an open American aggression*' as they were innocent school children. In all major cities of Pakistan, thousands took part in protests against Pakistan's alliance with the US, chanting "Death to Bush" and burning American flags.

On **24ᵗʰ February 2007**; a document – *"Killing of journalists"* – was made public after a meeting between Interior Secretary Syed Kamal Shah and a delegation of the International Federation of Journalists in Islamabad. It was, interalia, managed by Syed Kamal Shah as a pack of lies, given in that report that '*the government believed the high profile murder of tribal journalist Hayatullah Khan was the result of a monetary dispute.*'

[*Interior Secretary Kamal Shah was openly declared* '**Liar of the first order**' *then by the media while his person was widely discussed in those days' live TV talks. He was blamed for extending threats to the journalists on various counts.*]

Pakistan repeatedly protested drone attacks as an infringement of its sovereignty and because civilian deaths were having been resulted, including women and children, which had further angered Pakistan's new PPP government and people.

On **4ᵗʰ October 2008**; *the Washington Post* reported that there was a secret deal between the US and Pakistan allowing these drone attacks –

as those were flown from a Pakistani base. Though Pakistani foreign minister Shah Mehmood Qureshi had denied it but <u>the news was based on facts; Jacobabad and Shamsi Airbase, 190 miles (310 km) southwest of Quetta and 30 miles (48 km) from the Afghan border were earmarked for drones.</u>

The drone attacks continued, despite repeated requests made by Pakistani government through different channels. TTP's Baitullah Mehsud, while claiming responsibility for the 2009 Lahore Police School attacks, stated that it was in retaliation for the drone attacks. Then, Pakistani intelligence had agreed to secretly provide information to the US on Baitullah Mehsud's whereabouts while publicly the Pakistan's PPP government continued to condemn the attacks.

The India - friendly senior US officials were pushing President Obama for extending the strikes into Quetta in Balochistan against the Quetta *Shura*. Mike Mullen had told the media that in an effort to strengthen trust with Pakistan US was sharing drone surveillance data with Pakistan and the US defense budget for 2011 asked for a 75% increase in 'drone funds' to enhance the drone operations. The media had noted that:

> *"During the Bush administration, there was drone attack in Pakistan every 43 days; during the first two years of the Obama admin, there was a drone strike every four days."*

The US sources confirmed that President Obama had broadened the base of drone attacks to include targets seeking to destabilize Pakistani civilian government; thus the attacks of 14th – 16th February 2009 were against training camps run by Baitullah Mehsud. **On 25th February 2009** Leon Panetta, Director CIA, reiterated that the strikes would continue.

*The Washington Times* of 4th March 2009 confirmed that the drones were targeting Baitullah Mehsud and *President Obama had given green signal expanding the drone strikes to include Balochistan.* The US officials had briefed their President that the drone strikes had killed nine of al Qaeda's 20 top commanders. Further, that many top Taliban and al Qaeda leaders, as a result of the strikes, had fled to Quetta or even further to Karachi.

Till May 2009, there was no doubt left that the US was sharing drone intelligence with Pakistan and that was why Leon Panetta had once more reiterated **on 19th May 2009** that the US intended to continue the drone attacks – and with more intensity.

In December 2009 expansion of the drone attacks was authorized by the US President to parallel the decision to send 30,000 more American troops to Afghanistan. From Pakistan there was also a green signal for that in the back drop of Taliban's siege & attack on GHQ **on 10th October 2009.**

## FATA PEOPLE WELCOME DRONES?

**On 28th April 2009;** President Zardari, through Pakistan's Consul General to the US, Aqil Nadeem, had asked the US '*....to hand over control of its drones in Pakistan to his government. If the US government insists on our true cooperation, then they should also be helping us in fighting those terrorists.*'

But the suggestion was rejected by the US who were worried that Pakistanis would leak information about targets to militants.

In an analysis published in *Daily Times* on 2nd **January 2010;** Farhat Taj challenged the view that the local people of Waziristan were against the drone attacks – rather they supported the attacks and see the drones as their 'liberators' from the clutches of Taliban. She wrote:

> '*The people of Waziristan are suffering a brutal kind of occupation under the Taliban and al Qaeda. It is in this context that they would welcome anyone, Americans, Israelis, Indians or even the devil, to rid them of the Taliban and al Qaeda.*'

The world ultimately got known that '*...they are not going to advertise that, but that's what they are doing.*' A study called '**The Year of the Drone**' published in February 2010 by the New America Foundation found that from a total of 114 drone strikes in Pakistan between 2004 and early 2010, approximately between 834 and 1,216 individuals had been killed. About two thirds of whom were thought to be militants and one third were civilians.

**On 25th March 2010,** the US State Department legal advisor Harold Koh came with surprising statement that:

> '*The drone strikes are legal because of the right to self-defense; the US is involved in an armed conflict with al Qaeda, the Taliban, and their affiliates and therefore may use force consistent with self-defense under international law.*'

It remains a fact that till early 2011 the US used to fax notifications to the ISI detailing the dates and general areas of future drone attack operations. The ISI used to send a return fax acknowledging receipt, but not approving the operation. Pakistan used to clear the airspace over the area and on the dates designated in the US fax.

However, after the 2nd May 2011 raid that killed bin Laden, the ISI ceased acknowledging the US faxes, but continued clearing the airspace in the areas where US drones were scheduled to be operating. Perhaps, the US sent the faxes primarily to support legal justification for the drone attacks.

In **March 2011**; the GOC 7th Division of Pak-Army, Maj Gen Ghayur Mehmood delivered a briefing *"Myths and rumours about US predator strikes"* in Miranshah. He said that:

> '......*most of those who were killed by the drone strikes were Al Qaeda and Taliban terrorists. Military's official paper on the attacks till 7th March 2011 said that between 2007 and 2011 about 164 predator strikes had been carried out and over 964 terrorists had been killed. Those killed included 793 locals and 171 foreigners. The foreigners included Arabs, Uzbeks, Tajiks, Chechens, Filipinos and Moroccans.'*

On **28th April 2011**, Gen David Petraeus was made Director <u>CIA</u> overseeing the drone attacks – another factor to further inflame relations between the two nations. As per information available from ***Washington Post's record as of September 2011***, around 30 Predator and Reaper drones were operating under CIA for Pak-Afghan area of operations. The CIA drones operated under the CIA's Counter - Terrorism Center (CTC), based at CIA's HQ in Langley, Virginia with about 2,000 people on staff at that time.

Till ending 2011, the circumstances were changed. On **9th December 2011**, Pak-Army Chief Gen Kayani issued a directive to shoot down US drones – *"any object entering into our air space, including US drones, will be treated as hostile and be shot down."*

However, in January 2012, the then ISI Chief Gen Pasha secretly negotiated and signed a pact with Director CIA Gen Petraeus in Qatar to '<u>re-admit the attacks of guided airplanes on Pakistani soil. He had also agreed to enlarge the CIA presence in Shahbaz air base, near the city of Abbottabad, where Al-Qaeda chief Osama bin Laden was killed in May 2011</u>.'

On the other side; as per report, published in 2012 from **Stanford and New York University Law School**; US drone strikes were extremely unpopular in Pakistan.

Whereas, the 2012 poll by the **Pew Research Center's Global Attitude Project** found that only 17% of Pakistanis supported drone strikes; and remarkably, among those who professed to know a lot or a little about drones, 97% considered drone strikes a bad policy.

Civilians in Waziristan interviewed for the report believed *"that the US actively seeks to kill them simply for being Muslims, viewing the drone campaign as a part of a religious crusade against Islam."*

Many professionals working in Waziristan believed that drone strikes encouraged terrorism. The report reflected similar conclusions reached by reporters for *Der Spiegel*, *The New York Times* and CNN.

The *Los Angeles Times* once reported that in North Waziristan a militant group called *Khorasan Mujahedin* targeted people suspected of being informants. According to the report, the group kidnapped people from an area suspected of selling information that led to the drone strikes; tortured and killed them, and their videotapes of killings were sold or distributed in markets as warnings to others.

In October 2013, *'The Economist'* continued to find support among locals for the drone attacks as protection against the militants, claiming no civilians were killed this year.

## AMERICA's CONFLICTING DATA:

The *information, released through & confirmed by Pak-Army* to a parliamentary question, said that no civilian had been killed since January 2012 till October 2013. The drone strategy went successful because 2,160 foreign intruders called as Islamic force were killed since 2008.

The claim caused widespread surprise in the country where the remote controlled aircraft had been widely hated because of the popular belief that they killed tens of civilians in each strike. It also puzzled analysts, media men and human activist organizations many of whom had long assumed Pakistan was helpless in drone attacks strategy of US and its NATO allies.

In fact, it was an interesting turn in the wholesome debate on drones playing havoc with all those anti-drone campaigners who have been arguing that drones kill civilians thus must be stopped. Basic information about the number of civilians and militants killed by drones always remained controversial and highly politicised in Pakistan.

On 14th July 2009, Daniel L. Byman of the **Brookings Institution** stated that *'although accurate data on the results of drone strikes is difficult to obtain, it seemed that ten civilians had died in the drone attacks for every militant killed.'* He suggested that the real answer to halting al-Qaeda's activity in Pakistan would be long-term support of Pakistan's counter - insurgency efforts.

According to a report of the Islamabad based **Conflict Monitoring Center** (CMC), as of 2011, more than 2000 persons were killed, and most of those deaths were of civilians. The CMC termed the CIA drone strikes as an *"assassination campaign turning out to be revenge campaign"*, and showed that 2010 was the deadliest year till then regarding casualties resulting from drone attacks, with 134 strikes inflicting over 900 deaths.

According to the **Long War Journal,** as of mid-2011, the drone strikes in Pakistan since 2006 had killed 2,018 militants and 138 civilians. **The New America Foundation** stated in mid-2011 that since 2004 2,551 people were killed in the strikes, with 80% of those militants. The Foundation stated that 95% of those killed in 2010 were militants. As of 2012, 15% of the total people killed by drone strikes were either civilians or unknown. The foundation also stated that in 2012 the rate of civilian and unknown casualties was 2%, whereas the **Bureau of Investigative Journalism** said the rate of civilian casualties for 2012 was 9%.

The **CIA's official figures** claimed that the strikes conducted between May 2010 and August 2011 killed over 600 militants and did not result in any civilian fatalities; this assessment was criticized by Bill Roggio from the **Long War Journal** and other commentators as being unrealistic. An essay in *New York Times* claimed that, as of August 2011, the drone campaign had killed over 2,000 militants and about 50 civilians.

In **February 2012 Associated Press Investigation** found that militants were the main victims of drone strikes in North Waziristan contrary to the "widespread perception in Pakistan that civilians... are the principal victims." The AP studied 10 drone strikes. Their reporters who spoke to about 80 villagers in North Waziristan were told that at least 194 people died in the ten attacks. According to the villagers 56 of those were either civilians or tribal police and 138 were militants, with 38 of the civilians dying in a miscalculated attack which took place on 17 March 2011.

*[Villagers stated that one way to tell if civilians were killed was to observe how many funerals took place after a strike; the bodies of*

*militants were usually taken elsewhere for burial, while civilians were usually buried immediately and locally.]*

According to the report, compiled in 2012, of the __Columbia Human Rights Clinic__, despite their strong efforts, two of the tracking organizations, *the Long War Journal* and *New America Foundation*, significantly and consistently under-estimated the potential number of civilians killed in Pakistan during the year 2011.

According to the London based __Bureau of Investigative Journalism__, at least 300 civilians had been killed by drones since 2008. Distinguishing civilians from those engaged in hostilities was also found difficult. Invariably after each drone strike Pakistan lodged forthright public complaints with the US, despite substantial evidence that the country had secretly co-operated with the CIA through intelligence sharing.

Referring to a __Columbia Law School__'s later report *"Counting Drone Strikes Deaths" dated 30ᵗʰ September 2012* analysed by Alice K Ross [published in the US media on *5ᵗʰ October 2012*] of __Bureau of investigative Journalism__:

> *'President Obama's personal involvement in selecting the targets of covert drone strikes means he risks handing a "loaded gun". If Obama leaves, he's leaving a loaded gun: he's set up a programme where the greatest constraint is his personal prerogative. There's no legal oversight, no courtroom that can make [the drone programme] stop.'*

President **Obama** *'personally approved every military target'* in **Yemen and Somalia** and around a third of targets in Pakistan but nothing given in writing, the report said. The remainder of strikes in Pakistan were decided by the CIA; no one was there to justify the drone campaigns and their targets under international law. However, the fact remains that the CIA has no institutional history of complying with international law or setting up procedures for civilian deaths. The report observed:

> *'It was a covert spy agency; it wasn't set up for this. We don't know how prepared they are to monitor civilian deaths or how concerned they are'.*

To this day, the CIA has never officially acknowledged its campaign though it was supposed to be accountable to Congress. The report also called for a task force to examine what measures were in place to protect civilians. The main cause of concern for law-abiding Americans was that the drone strikes had prompted retaliatory attacks from militants on those they believe were US spies, and stirred anti-US sentiment and violence among civilians in Yemen and Pakistan.

The said report compared the **Bureau of Investigative Journalism**'s estimates of drone deaths in Pakistan to similar projects by the **Long War Journal, the New America Foundation and the Pakistan Institute of Peace Studies**, noting that:

> *"They consistently point to significantly higher civilian casualties than those suggested by the US government's statements. The problem remained that the very terms 'civilian' and 'militant' are ambiguous, controversial, and susceptible to manipulation."*

The truth was revealed by the *'New York Times'* dated 29th May 2012 that all *'military-aged males are held to be militants'*.

White House always placed its focus on the extent to which drones could protect American lives while the impact on Pakistani lives went ignored. So much trust was placed in technology that policymakers mostly failed to consider whether drone attacks were wreaking havoc on human beings of the same kind but living on the other part of the globe.

**Columbia Law School's Human Rights Clinic** found the Long War Journal and New America Foundation both *'significantly undercount'* civilian deaths caused by the drone attacks in Pakistan and elsewhere. Those under-estimates provided false justification to policymakers who wanted to expand un-manned drone strikes to new locations or against new groups. Exclusive or heavy reliance on the casualty counts of those two organisations was not appropriate because of the significant methodological errors.

Each drone strike reported in 2011 was examined and compared the datasets of each organisation with the available media reports. The *HR Clinic* found that between 72 and 155 civilians were credibly killed by drone strikes in 2011. *The New America Foundation*, which is widely cited by many US media organisations, reported only that between three and nine civilians had been killed; *the Long War Journal* counted 30 civilians lost their lives. By contrast the Bureau's minimum estimate of 68 civilian deaths was significantly closer.

What result; that the counts provided by the **Bureau of Investigative Journalism** and similar organisations were *'estimates only, not actual* *body counts'*. Citing a cogent illustration for the drone event of 30ᵗʰ October 2011 [cited elsewhere in these pages] in which the missiles hit a vehicle and a house in Dattakhel, North Waziristan. There came up THREE stories for the same one attack; one that the dead were all militants, second version insisted they were civilians - that four of them were chromites miners while the third contention was of a mixture of two aforesaid versions.

In March 2012 *the New York Times* published an investigation claiming the second story as correct - they were chromite miners.

Chris Woods, who was leading the Bureau's drones investigation team, welcomed the Columbia Law School's findings; US monitoring groups had been significantly under reporting credible counts of civilian deaths in Pakistan.

The US government had launched those attacks on targets in Pak-Afghan border areas of Pakistan using drones [unmanned aerial vehicles] controlled by the American CIA's Special Activities Division [SAD]. The strikes were initially ordered by President George Bush and had increased substantially under President Obama. Various surveys had shown that the strikes were deeply unpopular in Pakistan and had contributed to a negative perception of the US; the figures for US liking dropped from 58% in 2001 to 87 % in 2013.

## DRONES DECLARED ILLEGAL:

In May 2013; the Peshawar **High Court** ruled that *'the attacks are illegal, inhumane, violate the UN charter on human rights and constitute a war crime'*. However, the Obama administration disagreed, stating that *'the attacks do not violate international law, and that the method of attack is precise and effective'*.

Pakistan's PPP government publicly condemned the drone attacks. However, it had allowed the drones to operate from Shamsi Airfield in Pakistan until 21ˢᵗ **April 2011**. According to secret diplomatic cables leaked by *Wikileaks, Pakistan's Army Chief Gen Kayani not only tacitly agreed to the drone flights, but in 2008 requested the Americans to increase them.*

An **International Crisis Group** report concluded that drone strikes were an "ineffective" way of combating militants in Pakistan. Towards ending 2013, the Pakistani Taliban [TTP] withdrew an offer of peace talks after a drone strike killed their deputy leader. The Pakistani Taliban's threats were already on record to "teach a lesson" to the US and Pakistan. Earlier, the TTP had killed 10 foreign mountain climbers near K2 peak. In another mis-targeted bomb killed fourteen civilians, including four children instead of security forces in Peshawar at the end of June 2013.

In early June, the **CIA itself admitted** that they did not even know who it was killing in some drone strikes. Few days later, PM Nawaz Sharif, again called for an end to drone strikes in Pakistan. Even that call was not given weight and a US strike killed another nine people, an act that prompted Sharif to summon the US Ambassador in protest and to demand, an *'immediate halt'* to the drone attacks.

When in July 2013—a drone strike killed another 17 people in Waziristan, the findings of US **Center for Naval Analyses**, based on classified US military documents, declared that: *'American drones strikes were 10 times more likely to cause innocent casualties than bombs or missiles launched from planes.'*

In July 2013, the US had drastically scaled back drone attacks because the Pakistani military had started planning to end American *"airspace violations"*. The CIA was instructed to be more "cautious" and limit the drone strikes to high-value targets. In an interview in October 2013, one former drone operator said that children killed during strikes were reported as slain dogs.

The military record told that drone strikes were halted after 26th November 2011 since NATO forces killed 24 Pakistani soldiers in the Salala incident. Shamsi Airfield was got evacuated of Americans in December 2011. The incident had prompted a stop to the drone strikes for about two months *but again resumed on 10th January 2012.*

In March 2013, Ben Emmerson, the UN Special Reporter led a UN team that looked into civilian casualties from the US drone attacks, and stated that the attacks were violation of the sovereignty of Pakistan. He confirmed that Pakistan did not agree to the drone attacks, which was contradicted by US officials without citing any reason.

The **Bureau of Investigative Journalism** [BIJ]'s estimated cumulative statistics about US drone strikes till July 2013 told that of all the drone attack victims since 2004, more than 76% of the dead fall in the legal grey zone, 22% were confirmed civilians (included 5% minors) and only the remaining *1.5% were high-profile targets.* The statistics was:

- Total reported killed: 2,548 - 3,549

- Civilians reported killed: 411 - 890

- Children reported killed: 168 - 197

- Total reported injured: 1,177 - 1,480

- Total strikes: 370

  o Strikes under the Bush Administration: 52

  o Strikes under the Obama Administration: 318

Amnesty International published *Will I Be Next? US Drone Strikes in Pakistan*, a 75-page examination of drone strikes [*Amnesty also termed it 'not comprehensive'*]. It was a field research into nine of 45 reported strikes that occurred between January 2012 and August 2013 in the Northern Waziristan region of Pakistan. Among the stories it told:

> 'On 6th July 2012, 18 male labourers, including one boy, were killed in a series of US drone strikes in the remote village of Zowi Sidgi. Missiles first struck a tent in which some men had gathered for an evening meal and then struck those who came to help the injured from the first strike.
>
> On 24th October 2012, 68-year-old Mamana Bibi, mother of four local high school teachers - eldest named Rafiqur Rehman, was killed in a targeted drone strike; she was gathering vegetables in the family fields in Ghundi Kala village [of North Waziristan]. Her five grandchildren were also wounded.'

The Pakistan government publicly opposed drone attacks as too many civilians were killed in addition to their intended target - Islamist militants. The precise extent of human loss on the ground always remained unclear because the media people had only limited access to the affected regions. In North Waziristan, allegedly many *jihadi* fighters were eliminated, but neither the Pakistani government nor the US authorities ever released full details. The London - based Amnesty researchers mentioned in their report:

> "People who are clearly no imminent threat to the US are being killed. The US has to come clean publicly with the justifications for these killings."

Much earlier, the Western powers had reached the conclusion that:

> 'Pakistani Taliban [TTP] effectively control North Waziristan, and offer safe havens to al Qaeda and the Afghan Taliban who are fighting NATO troops across the border while logistic support of some locals are also available abundantly'.

The US maintained that they never infringed on Pakistan's territorial sovereignty as Pakistan had surrendered the area to militants long ago where most drone strikes occur.

As per available record with **Bureau of Investigative Journalism**, the US carried out 376 drone strikes in Pakistan since 2004, with the death toll given in an earlier paragraph. As per local media reports, about 926 of the dead were civilians whereas the Pakistani government officials frequently quoted that *'militant groups have killed about 42,000 Pakistanis, adding about 5200 security personnel since 2001'*.

## WHITE HOUSE JUSTIFICATION:

US President Barack Obama said the strikes targeted *'people who are on a list of active terrorists'* but the US did not routinely speak publicly about drone operations, which had killed hundreds in those years of WOT. *Mr Obama made his comments during an hour-long video "hangout" on Google's social network.*

More than 130,000 questions were submitted before the hangout began, and six people were invited to join the president online for the event. They were able to ask questions and seek follow-up answers from Mr Obama – was a good gesture in fact. Replying a question, Obama said that:

> "For us to be able to get them [Al Qaeda warriors] in another way would involve probably a lot more intrusive military action than the ones we're already engaging in. Drones have not caused a huge number of civilian casualties - important for everybody to understand that this thing is kept on a very tight leash".

An Amnesty International statement demanded:

> ".......a detailed explanation of how these strikes are lawful and what is being done to monitor civilian casualties and ensure proper accountability. What are the rules of engagement? While the president's

*confirmation of the use of drones in Pakistan is a welcome first step*
*towards transparency, these and other questions need to be answered."*

In one incident in March 2011 at least 40 people were killed in North
Waziristan - all were civilians attending a tribal meeting – in fact it was
a *jirga* of nationalist tribal leaders to gain a consensus that how the
*'foreigner Taliban'* be pushed out from their areas. The drone took it
as Taliban's gathering and killed most of them – the rest went seriously
injured.

Drone attacks fuelled anti-American feeling in Pakistan. Country's
foreign ministry responded to Mr Obama's remarks by saying: *"Our*
*position on drone strikes is clear and based on principles. Drone attacks*
*are unlawful, counterproductive and hence unacceptable. We cannot*
*condone violation of our sovereignty."* But *the BBC*, referred to its
release dated **31st January 2012**, held that despite Pakistan's public condemnation of drone strikes, however, the country's civilian and military
leaders privately supported them till mid 2011 at least.

Referring to the *BBC dated 6th June 2012*: The US increased the intensity
of launching drone attacks; eight attacks during the previous two weeks.
Before that increase in strikes, there had only been 11 such attacks in the
preceding six months.

The BBC held that there was a sense in Islamabad that this increase in
frequency of attacks was a means of putting pressure on - even punishing
- the country at a time when it had refused to re-open supply routes
to NATO troops in Afghanistan unless certain demands were met.
Though Pakistani PM Gilani had already bowed his head before the
British PM Mr Cameron during his visit to London during early May
2012 assuring him, and through extension to the US, that NATO routes
would be opened within the same month.

Abu Yahya al-Libi's death, along with his 14 companions, was confirmed
during one of the attacks then - Washington felt justified, but it did not
appease a large section of Pakistani society, for whom US drone attacks
had become a source of considerable resentment.

The BBC's correspondent added the details of deaths of important
militant leadership as: **June 2012** - Senior al Qaeda leader Abu Yahya
al-Libi; **February 2012** – Al Qaeda commander Badar Mansoor; **August
2011** – Al Qaeda commander Atiyah Abd al-Rahman; **June 2011** -
Senior al-Qaeda fighter Ilyas Kashmiri; **August 2009** - Taliban leader
Baitullah Mehsud.

49 year old Libyan Al-Libi was 2$^{nd}$ in command to Ayman al-Zawahiri, who was named al-Qaeda leader after Osama Bin Laden's death a year earlier. Libi, also known as Hasan Qayid, and Yunis al-Sahrawi, was member of the Libyan Islamic Fighting Group before he allied himself to Osama Bin Laden. He was considered by the organisation to be a daring and inspirational figure - a convincing speaker with strong religious credentials.

Libyan Al-Libi was captured by Pakistani forces in 2002 and sent to the US military airbase at Bagram in Afghanistan, from where he escaped [or made to escape] in July 2005 along with three other al Qaeda members. Reportedly, his American and Afghan guards were heavily paid from outside for his release.

## STORY OF A DRONE OPERATOR:

[**Brandon Bryant** *was a former sensor operator for the US Air Force Predator program who manned the camera on the unmanned aerial vehicles, commonly known as drones. After he left the active-duty Air Force in 2011, he was presented with a certificate that credited his squadron for 1,626 kills.*]

Air Force pilot Brandon Bryant served as a sensor operator for the Predator program from 2007 to 2011, manning the camera on the unmanned aerial vehicles that carried out attacks overseas. In a documentary cum live interview titled as **A Drone Warrior's Torment: Ex-Air Force Pilot Brandon Bryant on His Trauma from Remote Killings,** he spoke his heart.

On 25$^{th}$ October 2013, live on air [or replayed] for 50.20 minutes at *American TV channel 'Democracy'*, Bryant explained how the United States used drones, and their impact. He described the grisly scenes he watched unfold on his monitor as an Air Force drone operator in **an article in GQ magazine, "Confessions of a Drone Warrior".**

About his first strike, Bryant told that it was roughly around **26$^{th}$ January 2007,** I got on shift [in Nevada] as a multi-aircraft control qualified sensor operator, which is where a pilot controls multiple drones, and then a sensor operator controls one drone.

From the darkness of a box in the Nevada desert, he watched as three men trudged down a dirt road in Afghanistan. On his console, the image showed the midwinter landscape of eastern Afghanistan's Kunar

Province. He zoomed the camera in on the suspected insurgents, each dressed in traditional *shalwar kameez;* he knew nothing about them: not their names nor their thoughts.

He was told that they were carrying rifles on their shoulders, but they were shepherd's staffs. A directive from somewhere above, a mysterious chain of command that led straight to his headset, was clear: confirmed weapons. He switched from the visible spectrum; a safety observer loomed behind him to make sure the "weapon release". His targeting laser locked on the two men walking in front; a countdown started as three...two...one...then the flat delivery of the phrase "missile off the rail."

Seventy-five hundred miles away, a hellfire flared to life, detached from its mount, and reached supersonic speed in seconds. As he watched the men walk, they had fallen behind; then bright and silent as a camera flash, the screen lit up with white flame. When the smoke cleared there was blood around the three dead bodies.

That was Brandon Bryant's first shot; it was early 2007 - a few weeks after his 21st birthday.

As a sensor, Bryant's job was to work in tandem with the drone's pilot, who sat in the chair next to him. While the pilot controlled the drone's flight manoeuvres, Bryant acted as the Predator's eyes, focusing its array of cameras and aiming its targeting laser. When a Hellfire was launched, it was a joint operation: the pilot pulled a trigger, and Bryant was responsible for the missile's "terminal guidance".

In the words of President Obama *'with enormous potential growth and expenditures, drones will be a centre of our policy for the foreseeable future.'* By 2025, drones will be an $82 billion business, employing an additional 100,000 workers. Most Americans—61% in the Pew survey of 2013—supported the idea of drones, a projection of American power that won't risk American lives.

Transparency has not been the defining feature of US drone policy over the last decade; a parallel and clandestine war was being waged in places like Pakistan, Yemen and Somalia. Since 2004, the CIA carried out hundreds of strikes in Pakistani territory, cutting secret deals with Pakistani intelligence to operate a covert assassination program. Another covert CIA drone base was operated from Saudi Arabia to launch strikes in interior of Yemen.

By the spring of 2011, almost six years after he'd signed on, Senior Airman Brandon Bryant left the Air Force, turning down a $109,000 bonus to keep flying. He was presented with a sort of scorecard covering his missions; total enemies killed were 1,626. However, one night, on his drive home, he started sobbing; pulled over and called his mother and told her *'I killed someone, I killed people, and I don't feel good about it'*.

Other members of his squadron had different reactions to their work. One sensor operator, whenever he made a kill, went home and chugged an entire bottle of whiskey. A female operator, after her first shot, refused to fire again even under the threat of court martial. Another pilot had nightmares after watching two headless bodies float down the Tigris.

Bryant himself would have bizarre dreams where the characters from his favourite game, *'World of War craft'*, appeared in infrared. By mid-2011, Bryant was back home feeling angry, isolated, depressed; finally went to see a therapist. After a few sessions, he just broke down:

> *"I told her I wanted to be a hero, but I don't feel like a hero - just wasted the last six years of my life."*

She diagnosed him with post-traumatic stress disorder. A year after, he was walking with a cane, had headaches and memory lapses, and fell into a black depression.

On his facebook page, Bryant wrote:

> *'.......I'm ashamed to have called any of you ...... brothers in arms...... Combat is combat. Killing is killing. This isn't a video game. How many of you have killed a group of people, watched as their bodies are picked up, watched the funeral, then killed them too?*
>
> *Yeah, it's not the same as being on the ground. So what? Until you know what it is like and can make an intelligent meaningful assessment, shut your goddamn mouths before somebody shuts them for you.'*

# Scenario 115

## DRONE ATTACKS DILEMMA-II

### *WIKILEAKS PLAYED AGAIN:*

In 2010, the controversial whistle blowing site **Wikileaks** released numerous documents relating to Pakistan which showed the Pakistani military and other arms of the government had *"quietly acquiesced"* with drone strikes even though they had publicly condemned them. In August 2008 the then PM Yousuf Raza Gilani reportedly said: "*I don't care if they do it as long as they get the right people. We'll protest in the National Assembly and then ignore it*."

That latest cache included documents which appeared to refer to a direct Pakistani role in the selection of targets, with the newspaper referring to one 2010 entry describing hitting a location *"at the request of your government"*. There was also a reference to a *"network of locations associated with a joint CIA-ISI targeting effort"*.

With Bob Woodward's name in the byline, it was assumed that it was a case of an official leak in exchange for services rendered - in the form of the headline: *"Secret memos reveal explicit nature of US - Pakistan agreement on drones."*

This leak of files was deliberately done to 'the Washington Post' by the CIA in those particular days to push back PM Nawaz Sharif's demand that '*the US needs to respect Pakistan's sovereignty and territorial integrity and end drone strikes.*' The purpose of the CIA in leaking those memos was to show that drone strikes were being conducted with the Pakistani government's cooperation. But.....that *cooperation* was more like '*a mafia earns through a protection racket*'.

One could recall a CIA's note sent to Pakistani envoy Hussain Haqqani in Washington before the notorious memo-gate originated in May 2011, signed by an official listed as the country's Director General for America with forwarding note that:

> *"Kindly find enclosed a list of 36 US citizens who are [believed] to be CIA special agents and would be visiting Pakistan for some special task -Kindly do not repeat – visas not issued."*

The said CIA's report made no mention of January 2011's event that seriously ruptured US-Pakistani relations, revealing the threat the CIA posed far beyond North Waziristan. Raymond Davis, a 36 year old former *'special forces soldier'* employed by the CIA, was arrested after he shot two youngsters labeling them *'suspected armed robbers'* in Lahore. Shortly after the killings, *the guardian* had reported:

> *'Pakistani prosecutors accuse the spy of excessive force, saying he fired 10 shots and got out of his car to shoot one man twice in the back as he fled. The man's body was found 30 feet from his motorbike......by what explanation it was a self defense – [only Rehman Malik knew the background knowledge].'*

The Pakistani government was aware of Davis's CIA status yet kept quiet in the face of immense American pressure to free him under the Vienna Convention. President Obama described Davis as "our diplomat" – a blatant lie it was, and dispatched his chief diplomat, Senator John Kerry, to Islamabad. Kerry returned home empty handed; though CIA's installed agent in Pakistan, the then Interior Minister Rehman Malik got him rescued later.

Most Pakistanis were outraged at an armed American rampaging through their docile population called *Lahorites*.

**SIGNATURE STRIKES** - CIA's another blunder: The documents also revealed a major shift in the CIA's strategy in Pakistan as it broadened the campaign beyond *"high-value"* targets and started firing missiles at gatherings of low-level fighters. CIA's that practice was known as *"signature strikes"* approving targets based on patterns of suspicious behavior detected from drone surveillance cameras and ordering strikes even when the identities of those to be killed were not known. At times, the evidence seemed circumstantial.

On 14th January 2010, a gathering of 17 people at a suspected Taliban training camp was struck after the men were observed conducting *"assassination training, sparring, push-ups and running."* The compound was termed as linked to an al Qaeda facility hit three years earlier.

On 23rd March 2010, the CIA launched missiles at a "person of interest" in a suspected al Qaeda compound. The man caught the agency's attention after he had *"held two in-car meetings, and swapped vehicles three times along the way."*

On 11th May 2010, 12 men were targeted and killed who were *"probably" involved in cross border attacks* against the US military in Afghanistan.

Although often uncertain about the identities of its targets, the CIA expressed remarkable confidence in its accuracy, repeatedly ruling out the possibility that any civilians were killed. One table estimated that as many as 152 "combatants" were killed and 26 were injured during the first six months of 2011. No details that who were they – and columns for 'civilian deaths or injuries' contained mention of NIL.

The CIA targeting 'someone' by a missile strike could be described as a "person of interest" was strange for even Americans who knew that a *person of interest* should be someone that authorities were investigating — someone who might end up being arrested. Here 'persons of interest' turned out to be those who caught the CIA's attention on their Radar drones machine in Nevada - they formed an impression that a person was of military aged height and stature so killed him — just to be safe.

## US CHANGED DRONE POLICY 2013:

Referring to the '*New York Times*' dated 22nd May 2013; when President Obama had embraced drone strikes with open arms in his first term; the targeted killing of suspected terrorists were defined well his presidency.

'..... *But lost in the contentious debate over the legality, morality and effectiveness of a novel weapon is the fact that the number of strikes has actually been in decline. Strikes in Pakistan peaked in 2010 and have fallen sharply since then; their pace in Yemen has slowed to half of last year's rate; and no strike has been reported in Somalia for more than a year.*'

The statistics then available had shown that decline as the number of drone attacks on Pakistan and Yemen were: in 2008 – 35; 2009 – 53; 2010 – 117; 2011 – 64; 2012 – 46 and in 2013 – 13 [*source: NYT dated 22nd July 2013*].

The reasons of the said decline were the reports of innocent civilians killed by drones — whether real or, as American officials often asserted, exaggerated — had shaken the claims of precise targeting. The strikes had become a staple of Al Qaeda propaganda, citing that the US was at war with Islam - described by convicted terrorists as a motivation for their crimes, including the failed attack on a Detroit-bound airliner in 2009 and the attempted car bombing at Times Square in 2010.

Notably, a growing list of former senior Bush and Obama administration security officials had also expressed concern over the US drone policy; amongst them Michael V. Hayden - CIA Director in 2008, Gen Stanley A McChrystal - who commanded American forces in Afghanistan; James E. Cartwright - the former Vice Chairman of the Joint Chiefs of Staff; and Dennis C. Blair, the former Director of National Intelligence were found as very vocal voices.

One of Mr Obama's ambitions on assuming presidency in 2008 was to build more positive American image in the Muslim world - but the drone strikes pushed the US to be more negative. As per **NYT** cited above:

> '.....In Pakistan, for instance, 19 percent of those surveyed by the Pew Research Centre had a positive view of the United States in the last year of George W. Bush's presidency. By last year, the approval rating had fallen to 12 percent.'

Globally these operations were hated; it was the face of American foreign policy, and it was an ugly face. This decline could also be correlated with shifting political conditions in Pakistan. For instance, the CIA had cut back on strikes as relations had grown strained after the arrest of the CIA contractor, Raymond Davis, in January 2011 Lahore; the incursion of a US SEAL team to kill Osama B L alone in May 2011 in Abbotabad and finally due to *Salala event* of November 2011 in which NATO bombing killed 24 Pak-Army soldiers. The major factor was the *'growing awareness of the cost of drone strikes in US - Pakistan relations'*.

Within Pakistan, the problem stood multiplied. The Al Qaeda or Taliban – the alleged target of those attacks – being unable to shoot-down or stop the drones, had taken out their frustration and vengeance through a series of terrorist attacks in the heart of Karachi, Lahore, Quetta and Peshawar, targeting civilian and state personnel alike. Neither the drone-attacks stopped nor had the retaliatory aggression and violence subsided. And this spiral of violence, in addition to weakening the State and making Pakistan one of the most precarious nations in the world, had resulted in the loss of thousands of innocent lives over the past decade. The statistics are abundantly available.

As the vicious cycle of violence continued, the American President, while addressing the National Defence University, **on 23rd May 2013,** acknowledged that:

*'Drone attacks cannot be used as a long-term and effective weapon to counter terrorism in porous border region between Pakistan and Afghanistan'.*

During that remorseful address, President Obama opened a new phase in the terrorism linked struggle by **restricting the use of drone strikes and shifting control of them away from the CIA to the military; might not be in a formal way.**

The US administration that day had formally acknowledged for the first time that it had killed four American citizens in drone strikes outside the battlefields of Afghanistan and Iraq. The new shift virtually ended the *"signature strikes"* - attacks on groups of unknown men based only on their presumed status as members of Al Qaeda. Pentagon had suggested them last week that the current conflict in Pak-Afghan region could continue for 10 to 20 years. Thus Obama had to admit that:

*".......for me, and those in my chain of command, these deaths will haunt us as long as we live......there must be near-certainty that no civilians will be killed or injured".*

The salient features of a new policy, in terms of the drone attacks, stipulated that:

- *'A drone strike will not be ordered if a target can be captured, either by the US or by a foreign government.*

- *A strike can be launched only against a target posing an "imminent" threat.*

- *Preference shall be given to the military to control the drone program, although the CIA will continue to control the attacks in Pakistan and Yemen.'*

Those were those days when the PML[N] had swept the general elections in Pakistan. Across Pakistan, a party that had long-standing ties with many religious organizations and religious political parties, had surfaced. There was little hope of a push towards negating the *madrassa* culture during the next parliamentary term - the talks of entering into 'peaceful negotiations' with the Taliban were already on their finger tips.

The strategy of winning the 'hearts and minds' of people was being trumpeted but at the same time seemed lost because the drone attacks were still on. Khyber PK was being targeted the most.

Negotiations with Taliban were not at all the correct choice but, in the circumstances, the PML[N] had decided in its favour just to keep their streets safe and children alive. Pushed against the wall, they had chosen to open dialogue with the beast, and sent a message to the whole world that the US drone attacks had forced Pakistan to go by that way.

## LATIFULLAH MEHSUD CAPTURED [?]:

*On 11th October 2013*, the Afghan government revealed that TTP's 2nd in-command Latifullah Mehsud was in the custody of US troops, who was apprehended a week earlier. It was be a major blow to the TTP, which had waged a decade-long insurgency from sanctuaries along the Afghan border; also helped the Afghan Taliban in their war against US-led NATO troops in Afghanistan.

Latifullah Mehsud *[believed to be around 30 years-old, once served as Hakimullah Mehsud's driver but eventually worked his way up the ranks to become a trusted deputy]* was arrested by American forces as he was driving along a main highway through the eastern Logar province; Logar's Governor Arsallah Jamal told the media. Mehsud served as a senior deputy to Pakistani Taliban leader Hakimullah Mehsud too.

Governor Jamal said Latifullah Mehsud was in a car with two or three other men when the US military arrested him. However, the much trumpeted hue & cry by the Karzai government moved the analysts to conclude that '*the Americans had in fact snatched Latifullah from the Afghan Intelligence through coercion; while in eastern Afghanistan and taken to the Bagram base near Kabul'*.

TTP had confirmed Latifullah Mehsud's capture amidst claims that he was actually seized by the Afghan army at the Ghulam Khan border crossing in the Khost province **on 5th October 2013** while returning from a meeting to discuss swapping Afghan prisoners for money.

A spokesman for President Hamid Karzai, Aimal Faizi, told **the 'Washington Post'**:

> *"The Americans forcibly removed him and took him to Bagram; he had only agreed to meet Afghan operatives after months of negotiations. Mr Karzai, who was then holding talks with visiting US Secretary of State John Kerry, was furious about that US operation."*

As per **BBC dated 12th October 2013**, Latifullah Mehsud was also named for the attempted bombing of Times Square in New York in

2010, as well as attacks on US diplomats in Pakistan and many Pakistani civilians. In retaliation, TTP had vowed to attack the US homeland again. However, there were strong indications that the Afghans were trying to recruit him as a go-between for peace talks. He had recently become the right-hand man of Hakimullah Mehsud, acting as a negotiator for him in talks with other militia leaders.

Though the Pentagon said Latifullah Mehsud was captured in a US military operation in Afghanistan, but the Washington Post newspaper reported correctly that he was forcibly snatched from an Afghan government convoy in Logar province several weeks ago as Afghan officials were trying to recruit him to launch peace talks.

Referring to *Al-Jazeera's Jane Ferguson*, reporting from Baghlan province, [*12th October 2013's* report is referred];

> *"It is believed that [Latifullah] Mehsud was in the custody of Afghan intelligence officials because they were hoping to be able to use him to help negotiate peace talks between the Afghan government, the Taliban and the Pakistani government.*
>
> *Afghan authorities were not happy about the Mehsud being snatched from the custody of Afghan intelligence officials and that it directly affected the sovereignty of the government on its own soil."*

The US Foreign Office had declared that the US would like to capture people alive for interrogation purposes; *"Capturing them alive means avoiding civilian casualties."* President Obama preferred to focus on targeted strikes and increased the use of drones but with the amount of casualties, he pulled him back, planned to use special forces, and capturing [suspects] alive so they could be interrogated.

## N SHARIF's AGENDA ON DRONES:

As per world media reports of mid October 2013, a United Nations investigation had till then identified 33 drone strikes around the world that had resulted in civilian casualties; thus violated international humanitarian law.

The 22-page report by the UN's special reporter on human rights and counter-terrorism, Ben Emmerson QC, called on the US to declassify information about operations co-ordinated by the CIA in Afghanistan, Yemen, Iraq, Libya, Somalia & Pakistan and to clarify its position on the legality of drone strikes. QC Emmerson had travelled to Islamabad for his investigation and procured records of as many as 330 drone strikes in Pak-Afghan border regions since 2004 in which up to 2,200 people were reportedly killed – of whom at least 400 were civilians.

[*Astonishingly, the UK had reported only one civilian casualty incident, in which four civilians were killed and two civilians injured in a drone strike by its Royal Air Force in Afghanistan on 25th March 2011.*]

However, QC Emmerson criticised the CIA's involvement in US drone strikes for creating *"an almost insurmountable obstacle to transparency"*. It failed to reveal its own data on the level of civilian casualties inflicted through the drone attacks in Pakistan and elsewhere in the world.

Thus when the Pakistani PM Nawaz Sharif went to see the American President Obama [scheduled on 23rd October 2013], there was a lot of pressure on him from the vibrant media of Pakistan and his coalition parties in the Parliament to press upon the US government to shun its policy of drone attacks in Pakistan's tribal areas.

Referring to the *Guardian dated 23rd October 2013;* Pakistan's PM Nawaz Sharif did mention of drone problem but could not convince or pressurize President Obama to even minimize the number of attacks or civilian killings because the US drone policy was directly related with the American security concerns. So much the humiliation for Pakistan's visiting leadership was that the 2500-word joint statement issued by the White House after their one-on-one meeting in Washington did not even mention drone attacks.

Contrarily Pakistan was *"directed to do more to ensure respect for mutual sovereignty and territorial integrity by curbing cross-border terrorism"* from within Pakistan – should have been responded adequately.

Pakistani criticism of the US drone program cogently irritated many in US defence circles, who knew that many of the attacks were secretly sanctioned or even assisted by Pakistan's military and civil elite; thus declared Pakistani leaders' public condemnation as hypocritical. There prevailed a general understanding that there was no likelihood of any changes in American drones program untill the superpower's own wish prevailed. Karl Inderfurth, a former Assistant US Secretary of State openly opined that:

*"There are always overlapping thoughts on drones policy behind the closed doors. The real question is whether there is some private*

*understanding about the need to curb the attacks. The numbers have come down since Obama's speech to the National Defense University in May [2013], but not to zero."*

Speaking after his meeting with Obama, PM Nawaz Sharif said that *'let there be no doubt about our commitment for a peaceful and stable Afghanistan. This result remains unwavering.'* The US acknowledged Pakistan's efforts to support an inclusive reconciliation process in which Afghans were to determine the future of their country; both Leaders called on the Taliban to join the political process and enter into dialogue with the Afghan government.

Indian media, at the same time, left no stone unturned to make the world believe that Pakistan and US were not able to survive as successful partners because Pakistan had no solution for the global terrorism; as Pakistan's civil leadership would not like to stand by the US in Afghanistan any more because of their military restraints.

From India's viewpoint the interests and objectives of Pakistan and US in Afghanistan were diametrically opposed to each other and often conflicting. The Indian apprehensions could only be bought had the analysts talked about the circumstances of some years earlier but not in 2013. No doubt that a decade and half before Pak-Army used to perform seeing the Afghan Taliban in power but then the situation on ground changed drastically.

At last Pakistan's military and civil elite both reached the conclusion that Afghanistan should be left to Afghans with no interference or spon-sorship from outer world – neither from Pakistan nor from India-US coalition. The gambling time was over for all in Afghanistan. Pakistan's army chief Gen Kayani had already surrendered his ambition of staying in; he was retiring in ending November that year [2013]. Though Indian media lobbies were constantly propagating that:

*'.....then there will be another chief running the Pak-Army.... they are all chips of the same old block. Ayub, Yahya, Tikka, Niazi, Zia, Musharraf, Kayani – in what way was any of them different from the usual pattern - all were prepared to gamble everything on the chance'.*

BUT there were bitter replies from Pakistani opinion makers too; published on the same media pages saying that:

*'Pakistan in fact is being destroyed by the Taliban who are actually the CIA agents – they get weapons and dollars from CIA & India.... They*

*are not 'Muslims', they are not followers of 'Islam', they use name of Islam to fulfil their ulterior motives of bloodshed and chaos; and they are the relics of anti-soviet CIA agents left behind since Russia's withdrawal from Afghanistan'.*

One contributor opined: the laughable claim that the Taliban had anything to do with Islam only worked on those who had no clue about the religion and culture.

How come 'terrorists' started to 'originate' in Pakistan only after 2001? Was there any instance before then? The reason the terrorists were planted in Pakistan was to destroy it's economy and to extend the American influence into the region. The US was not able to attack Pakistan directly because it was a nuclear power - it was not Saddam Hussain's Iraq.

Amnesty International had released a report that week based on investigations of nine drone strikes in Pakistan between May 2012 and July 2013. After interviewing survivors and assembling other evidence, AI concluded that at least 30 civilians were killed in the attacks.

Amnesty had mounted a major effort to investigate those nine of the many attacks, including one that killed 18 labourers in North Waziristan [detailed earlier] as they waited to eat dinner in an area of heavy Taliban influence in July 2012. All those interviewed by Amnesty strongly denied any of the men had been involved in militancy. Even if they were members of a banned group, that would not be enough to justify killing them.

*On 21ˢᵗ October 2013*, Amnesty International [AI] Report highlighted the case of a grandmother who was killed while she was picking vegetables in from her fields North Waziristan; details given earlier. Some other incidents which could have broken international laws designed to protect civilians were also mentioned with details. AI demanded that the US officials responsible for the secret CIA drone campaign against suspected terrorists in Pakistan had committed war crimes and should stand trial.

PM Nawaz Sharif had urged the US President Obama in open and in the meeting that drone attacks on Pakistan be ended. When the PM was there, all the western press, especially the BBC, Washington Post and the Telegraph made it a point to repeat the old stories that the drone attacks had the tacit approval of the successive army and political elite in the past. They cited the CIA's 'discretely' leaked reports, Hilary Clinton's meeting accounts, Pakistan's Foreign Office notes for issuance of visas to the CIA workers etc.

Nawaz Sharif did not feel embarrassed over those press clippings while there in US rather boldly told them that: "*__Whatever understandings there may or may not have been in the past, the present government has been very clear regarding its policy on the issue__*." The Pakistani Foreign Ministry had also a press statement in that regard. Conveying a clear message that: "......*__we regard such strikes as violation of our sovereignty as well as international law - they were also counterproductive__*."

The stories repeated in the Washington Post told nothing; the subject experts already knew about the American drone programme and Pakistani complicity - but the gun was seen spreading smoke at that belated stage. Significantly, the details came out when PM Nawaz Sharif was making a populist appeal for an end to the programme, which many believed was the centrepiece of American counter - terrorism strategy. The revelation had no doubt taken some of the wind out of Nawaz Sharif's sails but he boldly prevailed.

Earlier **in April 2013**, Pakistan's former military ruler, Gen Musharraf, admitted in an interview that his government had signed off on drone strikes, albeit *"only on a few occasions"*.

In the Pakistani tribal areas, details of casualties in drone strikes were invariably provided to the media by intelligence agents posted there. They often displayed considerable knowledge about the targeted buildings, and gave precise numbers and identities of some of the people killed. In the early days of the drone programme, when such strikes were practically unheard of, these agents actively prevented local journalists from publicising evidence about the attacks or the casualties or about the nature of the people killed or wounded.

But who could ask America and especially its CIA.

Then the American and Western media tried to knock down PM Nawaz Sharif. An article titled __*WAR in CONTEXT*__ dated **24th October 2013** appeared in the '*Washington Post*':

> '......*despite repeatedly denouncing the CIA's drone campaign, top officials in Pakistan's government have for years secretly endorsed the program and routinely received classified briefings on strikes and casualty counts, according to top-secret CIA documents and Pakistani diplomatic memos obtained by The Washington Post.*'

The files described dozens of drone attacks in Pakistan's tribal region and included maps as well as *'before and after'* aerial photos of targeted compounds over a four year stretch from late 2007 to late 2011 in which the campaign had intensified dramatically. Markings on the documents indicated that many of them were prepared by the CIA's Counter-Terrorism Center specifically to be shared with Pakistan's government. They hyped the success of strikes that killed dozens of alleged al Qaeda operatives and asserted repeatedly that no civilians were harmed.

The documents obtained by that *'Washington Post'* focussed on at least 65 drone strikes in Pakistan over the last few years and were labelled as *"talking points"* for regular CIA briefings. Although they were marked *"top secret"* but they were cleared for release to Pakistan. The newspaper said the documents provided a detailed timeline of the CIA drone programme:

> "......*tracing its evolution from a campaign aimed at a relatively short list of senior al-Qaeda operatives into a broader aerial assault against militant groups with no connection to the 11 September 2001 attacks*".

The report told that the files exposed the explicit nature of the arrange-ment between the two countries in the period when neither any drone programme even existed nor acknowledged.

*On 30th October 2013*; Pakistan's Ministry of Defence sent an official reply to a question to be placed before the Senate first time divulging that the number of civilian fatalities in drone strikes amounted to just 3% of the total number of people killed; [only] 67 civilians were killed in 317 US drone strikes since 2008 till ending 2013. The said figure of 3% was strikingly lower than tallies compiled by organisations that tracked drone attacks through media reports, which claimed hundreds of civilians were killed.

Referring to a live TV show *'AAJ' dated 30th October 2013*; the US House of Representatives Foreign Affairs Committee member & Congressman Alan Grayson said during a media talk that **drone strikes in Pakistan could stop in a day had Pakistan seriously wanted it**. BBC Urdu quoted Alan Grayson as saying that:

> *'Had Pakistan wanted and stopped facilitating the US drone attacks on its territory it "could end tomorrow." Pakistan's armed forces were capable of tackling militants and that in such a situation, the US should not have blood on its hands. He had received no evidence from the Obama administration to suggest that there would be a drop in drone strikes carried out in Pakistan by the end of this year.*

*Pakistan has a strong air force which has the power to impose a restriction on its borders whenever it chooses to; such attacks were not possible without the consent of the country struck. Take the example of Iraq - the war in the Middle Eastern country ended only after the host government had asked the US troops to leave its soil.*

*There were only a handful of militants in Pakistan, whose numbers hardly run into hundreds, whereas the strength of Pakistan's military was more than a million; if the Pak - Army wanted, they could control the situation and ease the lives of thousands of citizens.'*

Referring to UK's *'Telegraph' daily of 31ˢᵗ October 2013*:

*'The US president, Barack Obama, held a White House meeting with Pakistani PM Nawaz Sharif, last week. Despite Sharif's claim that he would raise the drone issue, there was no mention of it in the two leaders' joint statement. Senior officials, however, hinted that an understanding has been reached with the US which will see drone strikes come to an end in the near future.'*

## HAKIMULLAH MEHSUD KILLED:

Referring to Reuters report of the day, the head of the Pakistani Taliban [TTP] Hakimullah Mehsud was killed by a US drone strike *on 1ˢᵗ November 2013*; he was believed to be in his mid-30s and had been reported dead several times before. Later several intelligence, army and militant sources across Pakistan confirmed he had [actually] been killed in the drone strike in North Waziristan region on that day.

Hakimullah Mehsud's TTP had been considered an umbrella for militant groups allied to the Afghan Taliban. Among the dead were Hakimullah's personal bodyguard Tariq Mehsud and his driver Abdullah Mehsud. One intelligence source added that at least 25 people were killed in the strike because TTP's commanders conference was being convened at Hakimullah's residence under attack.

Hakimullah Mehsud had taken over the TTP in August 2009 after a drone strike killed its former leader Baitullah Mehsud. The regional sources had confirmed that drones had fired four missiles at a compound in Danda Darpa Khel, a village about 5 km from the regional capital of North Waziristan, Miran Shah.

Earlier, the US had placed $5 million reward for Mehsud's capture after he appeared in a farewell video with the Jordanian suicide bomber [named Khalil Abu Malal Al Bilavi] who killed seven CIA employees at a base in Afghanistan in 2009. US prosecutors had charged him with involvement in the attack. Hakimullah Mahsud was also found linked and on the back of one Faisal Shahzad who was responsible for a failed car bomb blast in Time Square of New York on 1st May 2010.

Very few people knew that the Chief of Lashkar e Jhangvi [LeJ] named Qari Hussain was also a cousin of Hakeemullah Mahsud. LeJ was responsible, as per their own claims, for numerous known massacres of Hazara Town Quetta in which hundreds of Shia sect Muslims were killed in suicide bomb blasts. Similar episodes of Karachi and Gilgit were also bravely claimed by that faction of LeJ.

A similar drone strike in May 2013 had killed Mehsud's number two and one of his most trusted lieutenants was captured in Afghanistan four weeks earlier. This drone strike and Hakimullah's death followed months of debate over potential peace talks between the TTP and the new government of Pakistani PM Nawaz Sharif. The Federal Interior Minister had termed this drone strike a *'purposeful effort'* to frustrate and thwart the peace negotiations between the TTP and the ruling regime.

A 3 member's Pakistani government delegation, which was going for negotiations with the TTP **on 2nd November 2013**, was stopped after reports that their chief Hakimullah Mehsud had been killed in a US drone attack.

Blaming the Pakistan government for the killing of Hakimullah Mehsud in the US drone attack, the TTP *on 3rd November 2013* announced they would not hold any peace talks with the government and threatened to avenge the killing of their leader. It had been unanimously decided by all factions of the Taliban declaring that *"it's a puppet government of the US and it deceived us in the name of peace talks."*

The TTP's spokesman Shahidullah held that the PML[N] government was neither sincere nor serious in peace negotiations; he termed it playing a double game with the TTP.

*On 7th November 2013;* the TTP finally and formally rejected dialogue with the Pakistan government following the appointment of their new chief Mullah Fazlullah; Taliban spokesman Shahidullah Shahid added that Mullah Fazlullah had always voted against negotiations with Pakistani government.

The decision to appoint Mullah Fazlullah as the new TTP Chief and Sheikh Khalid Haqqani its deputy chief was taken by the TTP Shura on the same day [7th Nov 2013]. Though the Interior Minister Ch Nisar Ali Khan had trumpeted that the drone strike was *"not just the killing of one person, it's the death of all peace efforts"* but even then the new commander of TTP refused to continue with the talk drama of Pakistani politicians.

During mutual discussions, three names of senior Taliban commanders were presented at the TTP's Shura meeting. They were Maulana Fazlullah, Hafiz Said Khan and Maulana Gul Zaman.

Hafiz Said Khan was the TTP leader in Orakzai Agency belonging to the Orakzai tribe hailing from the Mamozai area. Among the militant circles, he was known as one of the most hard-line and dangerous militant commanders. Besides his native Orakzai Agency, he had organised dozens of deadly attacks on key installations in major cities of the country, including the US Consulate in Peshawar through four suicide bombers, the Peshawar airport, military checkpoints, mourning processions of the Shiite community and worship places of Ahmadis.

It was Said Khan who had organised a suicide car blast on the tribal *jirga* in Orakzai Agency on 10th October 2008 killing over 50 people. He proudly claimed the recent suicide car attack on the compound of Mulla Nabi Hanafi in Orakzai Agency. Like Maulana Fazlullah, he too had two wives and was father of three children.

The third militant commander was Maulana Gul Zaman, belonging to the same Orakzai Agency but was the TTP Ameer in the Khyber Agency.

After a week's thread-bare discussions in TTP's ruling council to reach a decision, the announcement of the new leader was made by the TTP's caretaker leader Asmatullah Shaheen [amidst heavy cerebral gunfire] at a news conference at an undisclosed location near Miranshah. *"Peace talks with the government are not possible as Pakistan is not an authority and is under US slavery,"* added Asmatullah Shaheen.

Mullah Fazlullah was a hard-line commander, who had ordered to fire at Malala Yousafzai in October 2012; had resisted the Pak-Army Operation of 2008-09 in Swat and had pioneered a violent campaign against polio vaccination. The Taliban immediately announced on Fazalullah's selection that TTP wanted revenge for the killing of Hakimullah Mehsud.

Since his eviction from Swat in the said army operation, Mullah Fazlullah moved to the *velayat* of Nooristan in Kunar province of Afghanistan, from where he launched several attacks against the Pakistani military, including one in September 2013 that killed Maj Gen Niazi.

Mullah Fazlullah is known for enforcing hard-line Islamic law, burning the girls schools, public floggings and beheadings. The analysts viewed Fazalullah's selection as the new Chief with two major disadvantages - he was not based in Pakistan and he was not a native of the Waziristan tribal region, the main militant sanctuary. First time the militant's command had moved into non-Mehsud people from Waziristan.

Mullah Fazlullah was known for his radio broadcasts calling for strict Islamic laws and earning him the nickname *"Mullah Radio"*. He imposed strict Islamic law on the residents and tasked his men to burn down music shops and prevent barbers from cutting beards. On his radio, he used to announce the names of men ordered to be beheaded for breaking the Taliban's strict rules.

*'The guardian'* dated *7th November 2013* observed that:

> '.....Perhaps most alarming for Pakistan is Fazlullah's success in setting up a base of operations in Kunar and Nuristan, provinces in eastern Afghanistan where the Kabul government has minimal control. If he stays in Afghanistan he will remain even further out of the reach of the Pakistani military than [Hakimullah] Mehsud, who ran the TTP from North Waziristan.'

The decision to appoint Fazlullah surprised some analysts who assumed the leadership would remain in the hands of members from the Mehsud tribe, which had controlled the loose alliance of militant groups since it was created in 2007. Authentic source told that 46 out of 60 senior TTP figures who met on 2nd-5th November 2013 voted for Khan Said Sajna, a member of the Mehsud tribe *"but Fazlullah ultimately won because other commanders opposed Sajna's soft corner for the [Pakistani] government"*.

Khan Said Sajna was considered more inclined to consider peace talks with the Pakistani government but perhaps was killed in another drone attack during November 2015.

Two reasons for Mullah Fazlullah selection; One, he was considered very hard-line and secondly for his expected non-interference with operations of the multiple groups in the TTP franchise; see the details of the two military operations in Swat: in 2007 and, the more decisive one, in 2009.

Mulla Fazlullah, a Gujjar from Swat, was not a Pakhtun by blood; thus replacing a Mehsud, especially when the TTP core comprised mainly of Mehsud tribe highlanders, was unusual. While Fazalullah headed his own faction of the Taliban, he was not close to the former TTP Chief Hakimullah Mehsud – yes Khan Said Sajna was but he could not succeed.

Tribal affiliations should have been on play though the TTP claimed to control the Punjabi Taliban and fighters from Chechnya, Uzbekistan, China, Middle East and what else. Mehsuds were known highlanders - considering themselves martially superior since old British times. The analysts wondered how the FATA northerners accepted someone from the Lower Swat Valley as their leader; more so that Fazalullah was not operating from Waziristan. How could he manage central control over TTP operations, given the difficulty of communication, especially electronic communication?

Mulla Fazlullah was close to some of the Punjabi Taliban groups that also provided fighting cadres to him during the second military operation in 2009. This included **Jundallah,** the group responsible for the attack on the All Saints Church in Peshawar in October 2013.

Then the main question; why Hakeemullah Mehsud agreed on talks with Pakistan government. Simple answer - the objective for which they played had already been achieved. They wanted to ensure that the Pakistan Army stayed away from North Waziristan for some weeks or months at least. Winter of 2013 had already started and during cold seasons the guerrilla warfare normally slows down.

The fighting season was almost over and the next spill was expected in March or April 2014. **On 5th April 2014,** Afghanistan was to hold the first round of its presidential elections amidst the withdrawal of NATO forces from the region. TTP wanted to keep the Pak-army away from North Waziristan till then at least.

After spring 2014, even if the Pak-Army went into North Waziristan, the TTP could have gained strategic depth in the *Loya Paktia* region of Afghanistan. The Afghan Intelligence was already providing funds and sanctuaries to Mulla Fazlullah and his men. The scenario in the region was much changed with Obama's 2nd stint in the White House to see continuity with his 1st December 2009's speech in New York's military school - the TTP groups were clandestinely siding with the Afghan army and police in their fight against the Afghan Taliban.

Mulla Fazlullah, while in Nuristan, was also linked to the *Salafi Taliban* who operated independently of the mainstream TTP. His wounded men were being treated in Jalalabad; Afghan Taliban were not able to operate against him. Like other TTP groups, Fazlullah's was also close to the remaining Al Qaeda elements while a number of alliances were also continuing in between because of local politics there.

The political elite in Islamabad were helpless except to wait for the TTP's fresh attacks in the wake of false slogans of talks and negotiations – what else they could do to betray the innocent Pakistani populace.

A widely quoted fact remained that:

> *"If you look at the history of successive heads of the TTP, each time they elected a more hardliner leader."*

# Scenario 116

## HOW & WHY AMERICA DEFEATED:

The poor people of both countries, Pakistan & Afghanistan, were being crushed; human blood was – so cheap here.

Pakistan's Northern Areas, especially regions around Peshawar, have been under operations of one kind or the other since 2008. Adam Khel, Khyber, Mohmand and Orakzai Agenies are specially referred where a series of un-ending operation were being launched but without any success. One of the normal episodes of those days:

> 'During the Sunday night of **14th October 2012,** Pakistan's Taliban attacked two check posts of Mattani police station on the outskirts of Peshawar and killed five security personnel, including Superintendent of Police (SP) Rural Khurshid Khan, while 10 police and Frontier Constabulary (FC) men were injured. It was a surprise attack on the Ghaziabad and Frontier Road check posts at around 10pm and the militants were equipped with RPG-7 rockets and heavy machine guns; the exchange of gun fire continued for almost 45 minutes.
>
> The militants over ran the Ghaziabad check post building and torched it completely. This was the second such attack in the past 12 hours. Earlier in the morning an FC constable was killed in a sniper attack on the Frontier Road in Sheikhan in the jurisdiction of Badabher police station.'

What did it speak and what was needed; a consensus in national patriotic approach which were missing those days. Policies in the Foreign Office and GHQ were coined with opposite directions. The PPP's political leadership had pushed the Pak-Army in sand grave of uncertainty; sometimes Swat Operation became priority and the other moment they were expected to make search of Taliban in the Tribal belt.

In the Capital, all the three major institutions, the judiciary, army & executive, were at dagger drawn with each other; all they wanted to paste 'failure labels' on each other. When the three did not find a way out they dragged 'media people' from their collars and made them stand in the middle to get stoned.

In general public, a question kept on volleying: Are the TPP & Afghan Taliban same?

There were very strong beliefs and evidences that the Taliban in both the countries, Pakistan & Afghanistan, were one and the same; or at least there command level was interlinked. Once CIA Centre at Khost in Afghanistan was stormed by a suicide bomber in which at least seven CIA officers were killed. The suicide bomber was later identified as one Abu Dijana of Jordan who was trained, instructed and sent by Hakimullah Mahsood.

Referring to *daily 'Jang' of 20th October 2012*, Saleem Saafi, the veteran columnist had seen the related video in person. Nek Mohammad was once the Incharge Kargha Camp in Afghanistan when the country used to be under Mulla Umar's Taliban government. Baitullah Mahsood, before being the head of Pakistani Taliban, was the 2nd in Command with Mulla Dadullah, the known Afghan Taliban leader.

Abdulla Mehsud, another Pakistani Taliban leader, was actually arrested in Afghanistan while fighting Americans there and was taken to Guantanomo Bay from where he was released after years to be welcome by Pakistani Taliban as their Amir. He was purposefully sent back with 'proper' briefing and future strategy to weaken Pakistan.

Most of the Taliban in Swat, who were later handled by the Pak-Army in 2007-09, were the same persons who had accompanied Maulana Soofi Mohammad to Afghanistan after Nine-Eleven episodes. Still Mulla Fazalullah of Swat [son in law of Maulana Soofi Mohammad] is in Afghanistan with his comrades with his HQ in Nuristan.

The above spills indicated that the Taliban on both sides of Pak-Afghan border were inter-related; their targets might not be chosen by one command; their activities might not be overseen by one centralised body but they knew each other's mode of activity when the operations were launched in Afghanistan or Pakistan. In Afghanistan, the US and NATO forces were attacked because they were considered as foreign intruders and in Pakistan the security personnel were targeted because the Pakistani government was, for long, considered America's ally.

But the America was equally suffering by its follies from within. The Afghan War had gone expanded as against its initial estimates. Obama had already signed pacts with President Karzai and plans were chalked out to quit the Afghan lands till ending 2014.

In 2001, America thought that their troops would simply walk into the Afghan soils, the Pak-Army would be there to aid them and Afghanistan would be a new American colony in Asia. The facts were other way round. America got badly beaten on the Afghan soils by guerrilla Afghan Taliban AND the US got defeated on internal front in its own country; see few narrations here.

Referring to a British Report: 'Afghanistan an Un-winnable War' appeared in the electronic media, *Antiwar.com* dated **14th March 2013** is referred:

> *'An internal report from the British Defence Ministry has concluded that the ongoing occupation of Afghanistan is un-winnable in military terms, ruling that the NATO goals have largely failed and the survival of the Karzai government cannot be guaranteed. ..... Whenever international troops leave, they will be leaving Afghanistan with a very weak economic base and NATO will be on the hook for "large-scale support" of the government for many years.'*

Comparing with the NATO occupation for Afghanistan to the previous attempt by the Soviet Union, there were *'an extraordinary number of similar factors'* surrounding the two wars, and that commanders could have learnt the lessons of the Soviet war.

Elaborating; both wars aimed at imposing *"an ideology alien to the Afghan people"* and that both eventually abandoned it in favour trying to secure relative support for their respective propped-up governments as the only alternative to the *mujahedin*, adding that the historical estimate of the NATO war would be, as with the Soviets, linked entirely to how long the government survived after they leave.

The UK's Defence Ministry downplayed the importance of that research report, insisting that the determination that *'the war is un-winnable'*, would not change the official government position - that continuing the war was vital to British national security.

## DEADLY INSIDER ATTACKS:

Referring to the *BBC of 11th March 2013*; one of the reasons of US quit from the Afghan region could be described as *Deadly insider attacks* which had become one of the defining features of the later phase of conflict. The killings had undermined NATO's ambition to fight "shoulder to shoulder", against the Taliban. But what were the factors behind those incidents? BBC News examined the complex web of reasons that lead Afghan soldiers to turn their guns on their allies.

In Afghanistan's scenario of those days, it was difficult to develop a clear picture of why this happened as few *"rogue"* soldiers were taken alive - most were shot dead and several escaped. Meanwhile, the Taliban claimed responsibility for almost every instance of an Afghan soldier in uniform gunning down his NATO ally. Few believed such claims as credible.

In August 2012, NATO officials **estimated that about 25% of those attacks** were the result of Taliban infiltration into the security forces - previously the official record had figures of 10% of the attacks linked with insurgents. They were quick to point out that Afghan forces also turn their weapons on other Afghan soldiers. **'General Notes on Afghan War'** written by Commander *Gen John R. Allen* of the Marine Corps, appeared in *'New York Times dated 23rd August 2012* is referred here.

Gen John had held a video news conference a day after Afghan officials blamed foreign intelligence services for being behind most of the insider killings. Gen John had not seen the information that prompted the said claim, but sought to clarify that why Afghan forces had resorted to kill their American colleagues in increasing numbers. The General tried to sort out roughly 15% additional attacks – which could be caused by Taliban coercion of soldiers or police officers, either directly or through family members. He also noted that more Afghans than Western troops had been killed by such insider attacks.

Such attacks had raised concerns about the mission to train Afghan forces in order to hand over security control to them by 2014 - Western troop withdrawal deadline then announced. Even then, Gen John insisted that the NATO countries should remain committed to the strategy of working with the Afghans as trainers and advisers despite the intensified insider attacks. *"The closer the relationship with them — indeed the more we can foster a relationship of brotherhood — the more secure we are,"* he asserted.

Even so, American and allied troops had to be "more watchful" because *40 NATO service members were killed by insider attacks within seven months* of that year, already more than last year's total, and with at least 9 of the deaths coming over the past two weeks. Gen john Allen thought it as the pressure of fighting through the Ramadan fasting which could be responsible for that surge.

The general opinion of the intelligentsia was that the things could have been better in Afghanistan had the US not launched new adventure in Iraq. One remarked that:

'**When you can't trust the people you're training and working with side-by-side each day or tell which side is friend or foe, it's time to quit now.**'

A day earlier, President Karzai had asserted *for the first time* '*Afghan officials believed that foreign spy agencies were behind most of the attacks, putting it directly at odds with NATO's assessment of the crisis*'. The Afghan authorities were studying every known insider attack, also known as *green on blue attacks*. Based on interrogations of attackers who had been detained and other evidence like letters and records of phone calls, the government had concluded that *it could be the job of the foreigners*. Karzai did not name them, but the government frequently accused **Pakistan** and **Iran** of meddling.

Till that moment, however, Gen Allen did not believe Karzai's stance. The American General had determined that *most of the "green on blue attacks" stemmed from "disagreements and animosities" as well as "personal grievance & social difficulties."*

On the other hand, Afghan officials believed that the *figure of 25% had underestimated* the true level of Taliban infiltration or influence.

The BBC's correspondent in Kabul, Bilal Sarwary, had examined a number of insider attack cases, and discovered that a disproportionate number of the soldiers came from two remote districts in Afghanistan's eastern Nangarhar province - the areas where Taliban militants wielded influence over local populations and the writ of central government was weak. Further; many of the cases involved fake recruitment files and Afghan intelligence officials had no cogent explanations for rogue soldiers whose recruitment files had serious flaws.

The yearly figures for attacks and killings therein, given by the BBC, were that in 2007 - 2 attacks, 2 Isaf soldiers dead; 2008 - 2 attacks, 2 dead; 2009 - 6 attacks, 10 dead; 2010 - 6 attacks, 20 dead; 2011 - 21 attacks, 35 dead; 2012 - 46 attacks, 60 dead;

*Source: International Security Assistance Force (ISAF). Some attacks in 2012 and 2013 were still under investigation and not included above.*

In those remote districts, mobile phone ring tones contained Taliban chants. Even if the Taliban had not actively recruited the rogue soldiers, the influence they exercised on vulnerable soldiers was not to be taken lightly, intelligence officials argued.

One commander for the Afghan local police in Kunar - who used to be a Taliban fighter - told BBC that: *"Two years ago [in 2010] there was a decision taken by Taliban leadership to focus more on infiltration and rogue soldiers instead of suicide attacks, and other attacks."* Many analysts believed they were rooted in underlying, even subconscious resentments that were prone to flare up and with deadly consequences.

[History]: *During the last century, the British on India's north-west frontier worked with Pashtun militias and it was not uncommon for units with a good combat record to turn and shoot their own British advisers - simply think about cultural misunderstandings.*

*Pashtun culture is governed by strict codes. The main pillar of the Pashtun code is called '**Pashtunwali**' and Afghans will do anything to protect this. It means they are very sensitive to anything perceived to insult their traditions, religion and values.*

*It has been called **"motivation by rage rather than ideology"** and perceived personal, cultural and religious transgressions can prompt such rage - sometimes seemingly innocent, but many security personnel come from conservative and rural areas where such codes are impor-tant. When American soldiers raise their hand, it is generally a signal to stop. In Afghanistan, it is simply a greeting.*

*US soldiers are often accused of appearing arrogant and superior - such perceived attitudes can be deeply hurtful. Quite often foreign forces have no idea they have just insulted their colleagues.]*

More serious:

In Afghanistan the desecration - albeit accidental - of the Islamic holy book Qura'an [or Koran], or American soldiers urinating on the bodies of dead Taliban fighters or posing for photographs with body parts have all caused anger. One such soldier had **killed three British soldiers in 2010** when they killed a young girl: *"Was she a Taliban? You didn't even know her name,"* the British soldiers had no answer so were fired and killed. The British Authorities had later rejected their claims too.

Night raids and raids on homes of suspected fighters were necessary military operations for NATO soldiers, but Afghans believe the home is a sanctuary.

The list keeps growing and each incident reminds the soldier of all the previous indignities.

Under the *Pashtun* code called **Melmastya,** which means hospitality, Afghans will protect a guest at any cost. But their guests' conduct must also remain within certain parameters. If they fail to respect the values of their host, they cross the line. Many of the soldiers killed by their Afghan colleagues - sometimes without even knowing - would have crossed the line.

Many more little things; some soldiers joined hads with the US because they got rice and meat twice a day. Those were the kind of luxuries they could not afford in their communities. Some had been brought up by stepmothers and joined the police because they were not well looked after. Another soldier's only love in life was having a gun and firing it - that was why he joined the army.

Some Afghan soldiers had stresses and strains of violent postings; for some food was terrible, some were exhausted and could not get enough leave, their pay used to arrive late and some when fell ill, were given poor medical care. More Afghan recruit soldiers had complaints of violence and sometimes even abuse.

When a young Afghan man in uniform, posted to an area with a particularly brutal insurgency, would face with such pressures, the results could be anything but unpredictable.

## *BURNING OF QURA'AN:*

The American and the NATO commanders were not educated that the family, village culture and tribal ties are the glue of Afghan society. One of the angry protests against the inadvertent burning of copies of the Qura'an by NATO soldiers took place at *Khogyani Base,* in the eastern province of Nangarhar early that year. Local villagers came to the base and the protest turned ugly. One of the Afghan soldiers at that base was from the same village and when he saw locals from his home village up against troops at the base he picked up his gun and killed two US soldiers.

The Afghan army had not allowed soldiers to serve in their home villages but, in that case, the village came to the base and that soldier could not contain his anger.

Moreover; a number of policemen and soldiers were having family members affiliated to the Taliban - such was the intricate web of Afghan family and clan networks. Authorities knew that the vast majority of Afghan soldiers were professional and knew their duties - but circumstances could conspire to test their loyalties.

At a ceremony then at *Bagram* base, one Afghan commander told TV crew where to start filming - he pointed out politically sensitive locations. A US soldier harshly shouted at his commander and asked him to avoid such mistake.

The commander turned towards the US soldier via his translator and said: *"If I had a gun, I would empty an entire magazine in your stomach."*

Afghan War could be compared with a marriage. Marriages start great, the initial years are a honeymoon, the middle years get a little grinding. Sometime in the later years things fall apart – and that situation was cropping up in Afghanistan.

Gen John can be cited here again: his guess was perfect as a lot of people in Afghanistan, 10 years ago, loved the fact that the West was there. A decade later they were just tired of it. They were tired of their *'fumbles and bumbles and mistakes'*. They were tired of the enemy [Taliban] that had no shortage of blood and bold attacks.

*A US SOLDIER - MAJOR BENJAMIN TUPPER* accounted for:

> '..... *I also know the Americans and British and Romanians and Polish I served with in Afghanistan, we had good intentions. We went in there with the highest degree of respect and camaraderie that we could display towards our Afghan soldier and police peers as well as civilians.*
>
> *Even with those good intentions, we have to be honest that __we have left a track record of mistakes.__ Some of them have been literal mistakes such as bombing the wrong compound.*
>
> *I always point to the example of the sergeant who went out in the middle of the night and killed Afghan women and children. While we discount them and say that sergeant had mental problems, Afghans see a guy in US army uniform!*
>
> *Even though 99.9% of us go in with good intentions and professional standards... some Afghans have gone from loving the West to wondering what our true intentions are.....[in fact we were moving towards the ending game].'*

Major Benjamin Tupper, interviewed for *BBC Radio 4's PM programme
dated 11ᵗʰ March 2013* is referred. He is the author of *Greetings From
Afghanistan, Send More Ammo:* Dispatches from Taliban Country.

## COST OF IRAQ & AFGHAN WARS:

During the 2ⁿᵈ **week of September 2013**, the Harvard University's
Kennedy School of Government [United States] published a report that
the decade-long American wars in Iraq and Afghanistan [till then] ended
up costing as much as $6 trillion, the equivalent of $75,000 for every
American household. The Afghan War was not over yet because, as per
Obama's program, the American forces were to stay till ending 2014 and
some contingents even beyond that.

A point to ponder that when President George Bush's National Economic
Council Director, Lawrence Lindsey, had told the 'The Wall Street
Journal' [WSJ] that the war would cost between $100 billion and $200
billion, he had found himself under intense fire from his colleagues who
claimed that this was a gross overestimation. Thus Lawrence Lindsey
was forced to resign and quit.

One may recall that the Bush administration had claimed at the very
outset that *'the Iraq war would finance itself out of Iraqi oil revenues'*,
but Washington DC had instead ended up borrowing about $2 trillion to
finance the two wars, the bulk of it was borrowed from foreign lenders
like China; thus adding nearly 20% to the US national debt between
2001 and 2012.

Till mid 2013, the US had already paid $260 billion in interest on the
war debt; a profound impact on the federal government's fiscal and
budgetary crises over a protracted period was an additional phenomenon.
Care and compensation for thousands of troops left physically and
psychologically damaged by the two wars being estimated in detail by
other sister organisations to add misery for the Americans.

The report stated that:

> *"The Iraq and Afghanistan conflicts, taken together, will be the most
> expensive wars in US history—totalling somewhere between $4 trillion
> and $6 trillion. This includes long-term medical care and disability
> compensation for service members, veterans and families, military
> replenishment and social and economic costs. The largest portion of
> that bill is yet to be paid.*

*Another major share of the long-term costs of the wars comes from paying off billions of dollars in debt incurred as the US government failed to include their cost in annual budgets and simultaneously implemented sweeping tax cuts for the rich.*

*In addition, huge expenditures are being made to replace military equipment used in the two wars. The improvements in military pay and benefits made in 2004 to counter declining recruitment rates as casualties rose in the Iraq war."*

The fact remains that till mid 2013:

- 1.56 million US troops—56% of all Afghanistan and Iraq veterans—were receiving medical treatment and were entitled for 'special **benefits for the rest of their lives'.**

- Exactly half of the veterans from Iraq and Afghanistan had applied for permanent disability benefits till then; about 50,000 American troops were declared **"wounded in action".**

- One-third of returning veterans were diagnosed with mental health issues—suffering from **anxiety, depression, and/or Post-Traumatic Stress Disorder (PTSD).**

- Over a quarter of a million troops had suffered **Traumatic Brain Injuries (TBI)** mostly combined with PTSD, posing greater problems in treatment and recovery.

- The suicide rate for US Army personnel, with many who attempted suicide suffering serious injuries, was almost doubled.

- The *Veterans Administration's budget* had to be doubled over the past decade, from **$61.4 billion in 2001 to $140.3 billion in 2013.**

- Among the most severely wounded were 6,476 soldiers and Marines who had suffered **"severe penetrating brain injury",** and another **1,715** who had **one or more limbs amputated.**

- Over 30,000 veterans were listed as suffering 100% service-related disabilities, while another 145,000 were listed as **70 to 90 percent disabled.**

- The Walter Reed Medical Centre, US Army's flagship hospital at Washington DC, treated hundreds of amputees and severe casualties;

this facility had received 100 amputees for treatment **during 2010; 170 amputees in 2011; and 107 amputees in 2012.** Mostly such living was considered worse than death.

Soaring medical costs for veterans was attributed to several factors. Among them was that soldiers in Iraq and Afghanistan had survived wounds that would have cost their lives in earlier war periods. While the US government had till then spent $134 billion on medical care and *disability benefits for Iraq and Afghanistan veterans, this figure was estimated at $836 billion* over the coming decade. The worst of those casualties took place under the Obama administration as a result of the so-called surge that the Democratic president ordered in Afghanistan.

Even then, massive direct spending on the two imperialist interventions continued. With over 60,000 US troops remaining in Afghanistan till ending 2013, it was estimated that the cost of deploying one American soldier for one year in the Afghan war amounted to $1 million. Those troops continued suffering casualties with every passing day.

The US has been maintaining a vast diplomatic presence in Iraq, including at least 10,000 private contractors providing support in security, IT, engineering and other occupations; as well as logistics support and payments for leased facilities in Kuwait. The US think tanks had been able to dispel illusions that ending wars in Iraq and Afghanistan would produce any "peace dividend" that could help restructure or improve conditions of poverty, unemployment and living standards for common US populace, but unfortunately, the decisions were mostly made by the *'Defence Experts' in Pentagon and 'Strategic Planners' at CIA HQ* who used to dictate the political elite in one way or the other – so the all fuss.

Another treat on the 'Cost of War' is available at *TomDispatch.com*

*The last time I saw American soldiers in Afghanistan, they were silent. Knocked out by gunfire and explosions that left them grievously injured, as well as drugs administered by medics in the field, they were carried from mede-vac helicopters into a base hospital to be plugged into machines that would measure how much life they had left to save. They were bloody. They were missing pieces of themselves. They were quiet.*

*The time I spent in trauma hospitals among the wounded and the dying and the dead - it was almost as if they had fled their own bodies, abandoning that bloodied flesh upon the gurneys to surgeons ready to have a go at salvation. Later, sometimes much later, they might return to inhabit whatever the doctors had managed to salvage. They might take up those bodies or what was left of them and make them walk again, or run, or even ski. They might dress themselves, get a job, or conceive a child. But what I remember is the first days when they were swept up and dropped into the hospital so deathly still.*

*..... I was in the north, at the historic Dasht e Shadian stadium near the city of Mazar e Sharif, the stadium was famous for a day during the Soviet occupation of Afghanistan when local people invited 50 Soviet soldiers to enjoy their traditional sport event and slaughtered them on the spot.*

*What had happened to those boys who had been there at breakfast in the DFAC? Dead or torn up by a sniper or a roadside bomb, they had been whisked off by helicopters and then... what?*

*...... I asked to follow casualties from that high desert "battle space" to the trauma hospital at Bagram Air Base, onto a C-17 with the medical teams that accompanied the wounded soldiers to Landstuhl Regional Medical Centre in Germany – the biggest American hospital outside the United States – then back onto a C-17 to Walter Reed Army Medical Center in Washington, and in some cases, all the way home.*

*Over the years, more and more of America's kids made that Mede vac journey back to the States; 106,000 Americans wounded in Iraq and Afghanistan or evacuated from those war zones because of accident or disease. Witness the fact that, as of June 2012, 247,000 veterans of Afghanistan and Iraq had been diagnosed by the VA with post-traumatic stress disorder, and as of May 31, 2012, more than 745,000 veterans of those wars had filed disability claims with the Veterans Administration (VA). Taxpayers have already spent $135 billion on medical and disability payments for the veterans of Afghanistan and Iraq, and the long-term medical and disability costs are expected to peak at about mid-century, at an estimated $754 billion.*

*Then there were the "fallen", the dead, shipped to Dover Air Base in metal "transfer cases" aboard standard cargo planes. They were transferred to the official military mortuary in ceremonies from which the media, and thus the public, were until 2009 excluded – at least 6,656 of them from Iraq and Afghanistan by February of this year. At least 3,000 private contractors have also been killed in both wars. Add to this list the toll of post-deployment suicides, and soldiers or veterans hooked on addictive opioids pushed by Big Pharma and prescribed by military doctors or VA psychiatrists either to keep them on the job or, after they break down, to "cure" them of their war experiences.*

*The first veterans of the wars in Afghanistan and Iraq returned to the United States 10 years ago in 2003, yet I've never spoken to a damaged soldier or a soldier's family members who thought the care he or she received from the Veterans Administration was anything like appropriate or enough. By the VA's own admission, the time it takes to reach a decision on a veteran's benefits, or simply to offer an appointment, is so long that some vets die in waiting.*

*So it is that, since their return, untold numbers of soldiers have been looked after by their parents. I visited a home on the Great Plains where a veteran has lain in his childhood bed, in his mother's care, for most of the last decade, and another home in New England where a veteran spent the last evening before he took his own life sitting on his father's lap.*

*As I followed the sad trail of damaged veterans to write my new book, I came to see how much they and their families have suffered, like Afghans, from the delusions of this nation's leaders – many running counter to international law – and of other influential Americans, in and out of the military, more powerful and less accountable than themselves.*

*Like the soldiers, the country has changed. Now, in Afghanistan as in Iraq, Washington scrambles to make the exit look less like a defeat – or worse, pointless waste. Most Americans no longer ask what the wars were for.*

**Another scenario** on the upper side: One angry career officer told:

"They only follow orders. **It's the other 1% at the top who are served by war,** the great American engine that powers the transfer of wealth from the public treasury upward and into their pockets. Following that money trail reveals the real point of the chosen conflicts. **The wars have made those profiteers 'monu-fuckin - mentally rich.' It's the soldiers and their families who lost out.**"

*For more details: 'They Were Soldiers: How the Wounded Return From America's Wars – the Untold Story' at tomdispatch.com is referred.*

An essay by *Ernesto Londoño* appeared in the *'Washington Post'* dated *28th March 2013* is also referred.

## AMERICA's ZERO OPTION:

On 16th January 2014, the White House convened a meeting of top national - security officials to discuss the Afghan war and future of the US troop presence. Mr Biden lost previous debates on Afghanistan, but his arguments for a smaller force [*likely of 2,000 to 3,000 troops*] gained more footing within administration.

On the other hand, Mr Karzai refused to sign a security agreement allowing American forces to remain in small numbers after the NATO's departure that year. Some US officials advocated for 9,000 - 12,000 troops in post-2014 scenario suggesting that a full pullout would make more military sense instead of going by Joe Biden's minimal presence.

A US military official told the *'Wall Street Journal'* [WSJ] that *'we are coming to grips with the potential for zero'*. The WSJ further held [*its essay on Afghanistan dated 16th January 2014 is referred*] that the resumption of debate and the push by Mr Biden and his allies in the administration block for a limited force in fact prompted Mr Karzai to refuse to sign the security agreement and thus President Obama to withdraw all US forces. The **US Institute of Peace's Andrew Wilder** commented that*:*

> *'Pulling the rug out from under Afghanistan really risks collapse... We're in the endgame with Karzai, hopefully, by announcing a **Zero Option** based on our frustrations amid negotiating with a president who should soon be gone.'*

The US government had sent a message to Karzai through the new fiscal bill of 2014 [passed by the Senate just a night earlier] making 50% cut in the civilian assistance for Afghanistan, from $2.1 billion to $1.12 billion. Many feared that the US was going to break its promises to Afghanistan; in fact denying honouring its financial commitments made in Tokyo. That was why Mr Karzai had refused to sign on the Bilateral Security Agreement [BSA].

As per **the International Crisis Group's Graeme Smith [writing for the NYT also]:**

> *'The Taliban are still here [in South East Afghanistan] and those people are anxious about 2014 because the US & NATO troops are leaving.*

*Sales of medication for anxiety, depression, and insomnia increased 30-fold. Fear of Taliban resurgence is so widespread that it is hurting property prices and the value of Afghanistan's currency, scaring investors away, and impelling Afghans to seek foreign asylum.*

*Worries about the year ahead are a kind of pathology here. Afghans are too scared about the withdrawal of American troops but the US government seems satisfied. In its latest report to Congress, the Pentagon said that fighting had eased in 2013, reporting a 12% drop in security incidents over the previous summer.'*

The above debate becomes more alarming when the US Army, already reeling upon cuts from its peak of 570,000 to about 490,000, was just told that those cuts figure be taken through serious planning to limit the force unto 420,000 only – austerity drive? The writing was on the wall.

With Iraq now a distant memory and Afghanistan winding down by the end of 2014, the US Army had to cut its size. Eyebrows were up - speaking before a December budget deal, Army Chief of Staff Gen Ray Odierno had also attempted to make his case while saying that:

*"If Congress does not act to mitigate the magnitude, method and speed of the reductions under the Budget Control Act with sequestration, the Army will be forced to make significant reductions in force structure and end strength - such reductions will not allow us to execute the 2012 Defence Strategic Guidance."*

**Maren Leed,** a former **senior adviser,** however, held that: *"I go back to Trotsky: We may be done with war, but war may not be done with us."*

**National Guard Bureau's Gen Frank Grass** told that: 'as the Army completes its force structure review, it is extremely important to note that final troop levels will be decided by Congress.' It may be kept in mind that US Army's annual cost to maintain readiness for a regular infantry brigade combat team is $277 million; the cost to prepare the unit for deployment is $8 million - for a total cost of $285 million.

Now turn the page please; referring to former **Defence Secretary Robert Gates'** new memoir titled as **_Duty_:**

'Each time he visited US troops in Afghanistan, he [Robert Gates] found himself **enveloped by a sense of misery and danger and loss.** American policy has become perilously over-militarized; **the use of force [is] too easy for presidents.**

*But viewed up close – far from the 'antiseptic offices' of the White House or the CIA – war is never anything but "bloody and horrible," and its costs are measured in **lives ruined and lives lost.'***

Robert Gates was repelled by what he saw as the White House's **aggressive, suspicious, and sometimes condescending and insulting** attitude toward the uniformed military. Leaving aside his focus on tortured state of civil - military relations, his critique of the president's inner circle in fact went far deeper.

However, President Obama did not hire Robert Gates any more – no way. Whether the Zero Option gained momentum or not, let us wait for the historians' analysis in detail.

A well-known British DM Report: **'Afghanistan an Un-winnable War'** had said:

*'Afghanistan is not called "Graveyard of Empires" for no good reason. Alexander, Genghis, Mughals, Persians, Brits, Russians all occupiers failed there. Now US/NATO warriors are facing historic defeat. If they had brains, they would learn from history.*

*Afghanistan has not been and never will be conquered, and will never surrender to anyone. Afghans are a very freedom-loving and proud people.'*

Total withdrawal of US troops was wishful thinking. History tells us no army had withdrawn from Afghanistan except through disgrace and utter defeat. The US war in Afghanistan was a complete failure by all military benchmarks. **The US top decision makers wanted to define "success" as the rapid growth of opium poppies and its value, which proved explosive under US and NATO occupation; <u>more money was there for CIA's black operatives – but what the US earned as government.</u>**

For Yankees, famous quote by Alexander could have been the guidance note: *"Afghanistan is easy to march into but hard to march out of".*

Pakistan's general populace remained concerned that, why their government and the army had been wasting their resources and time to remain studious ally of US **'war on terror'**? They had been playing the role of rented mercenaries, conducting military operations at the behest of outsiders knowing about the Alexander's historical remarks and the British reports in abundance.

Where did Pakistan stand after twelve years of war? Forty seven thousand dead, foreign debts tripled, killing and more of the same. But the then civilian and that military leadership were pleasantly repeating the same follies and yet expecting different results.

Pakistan needed to draw a comparison from history especially the US Civil War, what it led to for over a hundred years [*and what chaos goes on in this country*]. Everything that Pakistan's previous leaderships have been ham-fistedly doing on American dictates, was just sowing the seeds of much worse blow back that would haunt them for hundred of years.

*[Published at www.pakspectators.com as*
*Lead Story on 19th January 2014]*

# Scenario 117

## THE GREAT US RETREAT:

One could recall those summer days of 2005-06, when some reprobate groups, bearing the flag of Balochistan Liberation Army [BLA] and purporting their origin from Bugti tribe started scaring the Chinese engineers working in Baloch areas and taking them away for ransom.

Once those rebellious criminals had scuttled the Chinese President Hu Jintao's planned visit to Gwadar; just few months after the formal launch of the port city. Gwadar was the height of Sino - Pakistani strategic cooperation then - aiming to make it modern port city; supposed to link Central Asia, western China, and Pakistan with markets in Middle East and Africa.

The American media, however, had accused Pakistan of building a naval base in the guise of a commercial seaport directly overlooking international oil shipping lanes. *Had it true, the US should have been happy if Pakistan was their strategic partner in South Asia.*

The Indians and some other regional actors were also not comfortable with the Gwadar project because they could feel it as commercial competition or possibly taking big chunk of Gulf trade by Pakistan and China. The Baloch dissidents were being used by many regional and international supporters who never wanted Pakistan moving firmly and strongly to develop the Baloch areas. No doubt, some short sighted Baloch leaders were also helping the rebels to create hindrances in the Pak-China joint projects because their own tribal *'sardari'* was at stake through numerous angles.

## *WHY PAKISTAN TURNED EYES:*

Sardar Akbar Bugti died **on 26th August 2006**; some said that the security forces had launched an operation whereas there are reports to suggest that the mud-cave had come down due to blast triggered from inside. The fair investigation report has not been made open yet despite lapse of nearly a decade. US intelligence and their Indian advisors could not cultivate an immediate replacement for Mr Bugti - so they launched an alternate plan.

The US & Indian alliance chose another battlefield and started supporting Abdullah Mehsud, a Pakistani Taliban fighter held for five years in Guantanamo Bay, and then handed over back to the Afghan government, to whom the first *'test assignment'* was allocated to kidnap Chinese engineers working in Balochistan. Mehsud performed that job vigilantly and kidnapped two Chinese engineers; one of whom was eventually killed during a rescue operation launched by the Pakistani security forces.

Abdullah Mehsud had done his leadership well with the help of TTP's that faction which remained associated with Al Qaeda on one side while taking dictations from the Afghan Taliban leadership, too. In early 2007, Abdullah was eliminated in an operation while secretly returning from Afghanistan after meeting his handlers there. A chapter soon closed and the TTP's command was transferred to Baitullah Mehsud.

Referring to Ahmed Quraishi's essay on media dated 19th November 2007:

> *'This is where Pakistani political and military officials finally started smelling a rat. All of this was an indication of a bigger problem. There were growing indications that, ever since Islamabad joined Washington's regional plans, Pakistan was gradually turning into a* ***'besieged-nation'***, *heavily targeted by the American media while being subjected to strategic sabotage and espionage from Afghanistan.'*

From Pakistan side; that was the beginning of *'ending strategic partnership with the US'* in fact – and, near many analysts the start of **'Retreat of US'** from the whole region, too. Afghanistan, under America's watch, had turned into a vast staging ground for sophisticated psychological and military operations to destabilize neighbouring Pakistan. During the years 2005-07, the heat against Pakistan and its military had started emanating; concentrating on Pakistan's western regions in an un-ending demand of *'do more'*:

Historians may write it other way but the fact remained that Sardar Bugti's death brought an immense blow to the BLA but the shadowy group's backing states didn't repent. His grandson, Brahmdagh Bugti, was welcome to enjoy a safe shelter in the Afghan capital Kabul, from where he continued to guide his dissident men allegedly on the plans and dictations of RAW through Afghan Intelligence.

Saboteurs trained by the RAW in Afghanistan were inserted into Pakistan to aggravate extremist passions here; sometimes using the name of

BLA and sometimes the religious seminaries against Shiite community. Chinese engineers and workers continued to be targeted by individuals pretending to be Islamists or nationalists and whatever the name suited to them. *Some of them were using encrypted communication equipment far superior to what the Pakistani military owned then.*

Another phase was also seen those days when the most modern arsenal, communication equipment and bags of dollars were fed into the religious movements and al Qaeda remnants in all the B areas of Balochistan. Exploiting the situation, some members of Pakistani media started promoting the disinformation campaign that the Pak-Army was killing its own people.

The rest of the unsuspecting media quickly picked up that message. Some failed joint Pak-US operations against Al Qaeda were given more importance and coverage whereas civilian deaths caused by US drone attacks were also pasted on the foreheads of Pak-Army during that media campaign – the general populace of course demonstrated their panic.

The western block of US + NATO, the UK was also a part of that, found it as the perfect timing to launch a book *Military Inc. Inside Pakistan's Military Economy*, a book authored by Dr Ayesha Siddiqa, a correspondent for *'Jane's Defence Weekly'*, a private intelligence service – some say it a subsidiary of MI-6. The said book was launched in Pakistan in early 2007 which had portrayed the Pakistani military as an institution that was doing more business and less defence job. [*The US, NATO & India should have been delighted over Pak-Army's that sort of engagement – far away from their military professionalism*]

Citing the same article of <u>Ahmed Quraishi referred</u> above; the *insiders believed that the said book was sponsored jointly by Indian & American security establishments.* Originally from 1988 to 2001, Dr Siddiqa worked in the Military Accounts department and then received a year long fellowship in the United States. Allegedly, the final manuscript of her book was vetted at a publishing office NOT in UK or Pakistan. Some of the juicy details of this campaign included:

> "The American media persistently insisted on handing over Dr A Q Khan to the US to fetch a final conviction against the Pakistani military. Benazir Bhutto demanded after returning to Pakistan in 2007 that the ISI be restructured. Bhutto's opponents compared her attitude with that of July 1999 when an unsigned full page advertisement had

*appeared in major American newspapers with the headline:* **A Modern Rogue Army - with its Finger on the Nuclear Button.**"

Strangely, just a few days before Benazir Bhutto's statement about restructuring the ISI, an **American** magazine '**The Weekly Standard**' published an interview saying:

> "*A large number of ISI agents who are responsible for helping the Taliban and al Qaeda should be thrown in jail or killed. What I think we should do in Pakistan is a parallel version of what Iran has run against us in Iraq: giving money [and] empowering actors.*" (Steve Schippert, <u>Weekly Standard, Nov 2007</u>)

Newsweek came up with an entire cover story with a single storyline: '**Pakistan is a more dangerous place than Iraq**'. Senior American politicians, Republican and Democrat, had argued that <u>'Pakistan is more dangerous than Iran and merits similar treatment'</u>.

**On 20th October 2007,** Senator Joe Biden told ABC News that:

> "*We should be in there. We should be supplying tens of millions of dollars to build new schools to compete with the madrassas. We should be in there building democratic institutions. We should be in there, and get the rest of the world in there, giving some structure to the emergence of, hopefully, the re-emergence of a democratic process.*"

Two years later, **in September 2009,** the US tried to implement that planning through *Kerry Lugar Bill* but it was tied with so humiliating terms & conditions that Pakistan Army had to refuse it.

The International Crisis Group (ICG), during the same days, recommended gradual sanctions on Pakistan similar to those imposed on Iran including seizing Pakistani military assets abroad. It was all regarding Pakistan's nuclear assets and to '*secure*' them depicting Pakistan as a

nation incapable of protecting its nuclear installations. Astonishing explanation it was that a nation [Pakistan] knows how to make a nuclear weapon but does not know where to keep it safe and how to protect it.

**On 22nd October 2007,** Jane Harman from the US House Intelligence panel gave statement that:

> "*I think the U.S. would be wise – and I trust we are doing this – to have contingency plans [to seize Pakistan's nuclear assets], especially because should Gen Musharraf fall, there are nuclear weapons there.*"

The whole above scenario was developed about the possibility of Pakistan breaking up and the possibility of new states of *'Balochistan' & 'Pashtunistan'* being carved out of it. [*Details are available in Scenario 111 of* **'Living History of Pakistan Vol-I'**] Interestingly, it had taken start from Swat where the *Maulana Sufi* was instructed to take down the Pakistani flag from the top of state buildings and replacing them with his own party flag at an appropriate time; but the Pak-Army handled the situation quite in time. For full details about Swat Operation, book **'Judges & Generals in Pakistan Vol-II'**; Scenario 55 Pages 694-710 is referred.

Then the whole American media was deployed to float theories about how Gen Musharraf might *"disappear" or be "removed"* from the scene; it was an attempt to prepare the public opinion for his possible assassination. Already the Pakistanis were made to believe that Benazir Bhutto had the US backing as the next leader of the country.

Americans knew it well that such signals from them and their actions were enough to invite potential assassins to target Benazir Bhutto. Now it is a historical fact that Benazir was ultimately killed in the same way as planned. A dress rehearsal of this scenario had already taken place on **18th October 2007** in Karachi and the UN Security Council had to ask the western forces to 'assist' the investigations into the assassination attempt on Benazir Bhutto.

Why the Americans were very serious this time about Pakistan; simply because they had been kicked out of Uzbekistan a year earlier, where they were maintaining bases. They were in trouble in Afghanistan and Iraq. Iran continued to be a mess for them and Russia and China were much above the US economy. Pakistan must be 'secured' at all costs; it was the apparent US motto then.

This is why the US ambassador in Islamabad Anne Patterson had added one more address to her other most frequently visited address in Karachi, Bilawal House. Bryan Hunt, the US Consul General in Lahore had started wearing the national Pakistani dress, the long shirt and baggy trousers, and was moving around issuing tough warnings to Islamabad to end emergency rule, to resign as army chief and give Benazir Bhutto access to power.

What were the options open for Pakistan then.

To begin with, Islamabad simply ignored John Negroponte, the no: 2 man in the US State Department, who had come to Pakistan those days "to deliver a tough message" to Gen Musharraf, who flatly told him *'he won't end emergency rule until all objectives are achieved.'*

Might not be true but Gen Musharraf's objectives included mainly the cleaning up northern and western Pak - Afghan borders. Gen Musharraf had also told Washington publicly that *"Pakistan is more important than democracy or the constitution"*, a bold position he had taken then.

Pakistani officials had already enraged till then that how Afghanistan had turned into a staging ground for sabotage in Pakistan. Islamabad did not want to see Washington acting as a bully any more either; so cutting off oil supplies to US military in Afghanistan and denying the United States use of Pakistani soil and air space were under serious consideration.

In the developed scenario of ending 2007, Pakistan needed reviewing its role in the war on terror [WOT]. Islamabad needed to fight terrorists on its border with Afghanistan but different methods were to be applied for domestic extremists. That was *the moment when Islamabad started parting ways with Washington.*

The Americans were telling the world media that they had paid Pakistan $10.65 billion over the past five years but it did not mean that they had got right to decide Pakistan's destiny. What they didn't tell the world was how Pakistan's help secured for them their biggest footprint ever in energy - rich Central Asia.

## EPIC CENTRE OF TERRORISM 2012-13:

Five Years Later: Originally; Pakistan's political elite never concentrated on the real threat from terrorist activities within the country nor they ever paid attention to the fatal events occurred on its Pak-Afghan border areas. The Pakistan peoples Party [PPP], though in saddles since early 2008 could not exhibit its acumen of understanding the real problem not its political opposition PML[N] ever apprised them of the threats.

Of and on army operations to fight against terrorism and extremism were launched since about fiver years, but neither the political leadership nor the Pak-Army had truly formulated a comprehensive policy and action plan to combat militancy.

The PPP government essentially relied on the army leadership to invent and execute policy and the Pak-Army did not want to drag itself in civil natured activity. In this vacuum, many political leaders, especially from the religious parties, including Imran Khan, had come out with their policy prescriptions based on *the idea that militancy would vanish if the US forces roll back from the Afghan soils.*

It was true that the foreign occupation of Afghanistan had given rise to strong nationalist impulse that nurtured militancy in Federally Administered Tribal Areas [FATA], but there were other factors too. Overlooking other main reasons that had pushed Pakistan into the *'epicentre of terrorism'* could be taken as short sightedness of both civil and army leaderships.

Once an attempt by the Khyber PK government was made to devise a strategy to combat militancy, albeit delayed; it was an admirable initiative but the federal government of PM Gilani did not stand by it by heart. Result was that tens of tribal *jirga* leaders of FATA areas who were sympathetic to Pakistan were either bombarded or assassinated. Blemished and inconsistent external and internal policies pursued over decades had brought Pakistan at the verge of 'failed state'.

The maximum threats came from the Tehreek e Taliban Pakistan [TTP] and *jihadi* elements but the sectarian and ethnic militants also posed a serious menace. Although the army's selective operations in FATA brought about limited success, the TTP remained a compelling hazard. Attacks were launched at major military installations, intelligence bases and places of worship where different radical groups acted independently or in union with other groups. Poor governance, weak state structures and flawed national policies facilitated the rising power and influence of these groups.

The writ of the state was not seen anywhere and the leaderships, both political and military, went bewildered and puzzled. Illiteracy, unemployment, the elitist character of our society, endless lust for dollars and persistent corruption also contributed to extremism. There was no strategy seen with the government to neutralise the sectarian and radical organisations; they continued to advocate violence and mobilize bloodshed.

Till 2008, the people had started raising voices that nine years military rule had contributed towards militancy. When the PPP government took over, they thought that it would herald well for combating terrorism but it did not prove its ability nor had the acumen. Referring to *'The Express Tribune' dated 31ˢᵗ May, 2012:*

*'......but the verdict of the people against military rule and their rejection of religious parties were regrettably not channelled usefully against extremist forces. To clean the swamp of militants required*

*economic development and political integration of FATA into the mainstream, along with a host of other measures.*

*Terrorism could be beaten when political elite mobilise themselves to isolate and defeat its perpetrators, but by remaining a silent majority they allowed a free hand to militants. The TTP and other militant groups have become media savvy and are putting across their narrative effectively.'*

The Interior Ministry of the PPP government totally failed in its objectives; no militant organisation was banned; no watch on their activities was laid; no intelligence was attempted to get to the roots of such groups; their motivation level could not be ascertained; no source of their funding was identified and their patrons could not be located.

The Interior Ministry remained busy in delivering speeches against their opponents and kept on transporting the looted money bags to Dubai and London. Issuing of Blue Passports to the sons, daughters and parents of their beloved ones, and stamping gratis visas for the CIA agents and XE employees remained the priority jobs for whole hierarchy of the ministry.

The TTP, on the other hand, kept on paying its cadres from earnings acquired from criminal activity, drug trade, charities and collecting extortion money called *'bhattas'*. Their financial inflows had to be squeezed; had to coin special laws try-able in summary courts with specially enhanced powers for the judges.

There was a large internal displacement of people during military operations, nearly 300,000 in South Waziristan alone. No suitable rehabilitation plan was available with federal or provincial government except photo sessions of the local political figures. They were in turn exploited by the militants. With 70-80% of the population unemployed, a female literacy rate of 3-5%, and a large number of people under the age of 30, the government's highest priority in FATA should have been focussed on employment and education coupled with provision of material basic necessities

Militancy and extremism can nowhere be defeated piecemeal; a comprehensive policy and a serious action plan was needed – the nation, though having nuclear capabilities within, but was being drifted into a dangerously downward spiral by the militants – sometimes seemingly connived with the ruling PPP stalwarts in Karachi and PML[N] elite in Punjab.

## PAK-ARMY's NEW DOCTRINE:

During ending weeks of 2012, a new chapter was added to the Pakistan's Army Doctrine that also included threats posed by sub-conventional warfare. In was a conspicuous and visible paradigm shift in its decades-old policy; Pak-Army first time openly described home - grown militancy as the "biggest threat" to national security. Even the outsiders had noted that:

> "Pakistan's armed forces were trained for conventional warfare but the current security situation necessitated the change. Forces fighting on the front-line in the tribal regions were put to immediate and vigorous training as per requirements of sub-conventional warfare".

The foreign media, with distinguished presence in Pakistan like BBC, CNN, Herald Tribune and allied foreign inspired press like the Daily Times and Dawn celebrated that **New Military Doctrine in Green book 2102**. The news & reports openly indicated that the Pakistan Army had felt the "internal threat" as a bigger challenge than the external one. The ISPR and the media, however, moved their steps very cautiously due to its sensitivity.

According to the new Military Doctrine, ongoing activities of Taliban militants in the restive tribal regions and unabated terrorist attacks on government installations in major cities were posing a real threat to Pakistan's security. The said Doctrine dealt with operational prepared-ness and was to be reviewed on and off. For decades, the army consid-ered India as its No 1 enemy but growing extremism in the country compelled the military authorities to review its strategy keeping in view the both fronts.

A senior military official confirmed to the media that preparation of the new doctrine started a year ago and was then put into full operation. Director General [DG] ISPR Maj Gen Asim Saleem Bajwa told the media that:

> '....the development is definitely there. Army prepares for all forms of threats. Sub-conventional threat is a reality and is a part of threat matrix faced by our country. But it doesn't mean that the conventional threat has receded.'

According to the BBC, the new Army Doctrine talked about unidentified militant groups and their role to create unrest in the country. It also mentioned that Pakistani militants had found refuge across the Durand Line in Afghanistan; mostly on reciprocal basis.

The Doctrine also mentioned about the *'foreign proxies'* for creating unrest in some parts of the country; although it did not name any country but obviously the pointing was towards India and Afghanistan with, of course, the US at the back of both. India's proven role in creating disturbances in Balochistan, in the backdrop of deadly separatist insurrection since 2004 could be cited as reference.

Pakistan never pre-empted the US raid in Abbottabad on 2$^{nd}$ May 2011 alone because of lack of threat perception from western borders [Afghanistan] and Pak-Army's whole attention remained focussed on Eastern Border strategies but, as Lt Gen (rtd) Talat Masood told the BBC:

> *"It's a fact that before the new army doctrine, India was Pakistan's No 1 enemy. All military resources were focused on India. For the first time it has been realised that Pakistan faces the real threat from within – a threat which is concentrated in areas along western borders."*

The new strategy also stressed that formulation of the defence policy was not the responsibility of the army alone. Other organs of the states would play their respective roles, too. In an effort to elicit public support against violent extremism, the army made public its new doctrine which was adequately adored, admired and respected.

It was abundantly available on record that throughout his tenure, Gen Kayani, the Army Chief, had been falsely blamed to deflect US pressure for Pakistani action against *jihadi* groups operating from the tribal areas along the border with Afghanistan. The world media have been forgetting that Pakistan had also been facing similar threats and killing activities from the splinter groups having refuge in Afghan territorial limits. *Pakistan was burning in its own way;* the domestic challenges included acute violence in two of its major cities, Karachi and Peshawar; growing Sunni - Shia conflict; and a chronic electrical power crisis that was more of a threat to stability than terrorism.

Scepticism and disbelief prevailed on both sides; the US & Pakistan. The US had given a practical demonstration to the whole world, by launching a direct attack in Abbotabad; declaring open that it did not believe in Pakistan any more. That event was the parting of ways in fact.

During the same days of 2011, Pakistan was planning to launch offensive cleansing operation in Waziristan as per US-Pak commitments. After the

US operation in Abbotabad Pakistan was no more bound to honour its part of 'moral commitment'. Then *Salala* event of 26<sup>th</sup> November 2011, killing 24 Pakistani army-men played a vital role. The US in fact tried to frighten Pakistan through that bombing – but the US move got them into its own neck.

Pakistan not only delayed the Waziristan Operation but also blocked the US and NATO transportation through the Pak-soils. Pakistan had to wait for its operations till the US forces started packing up from the Afghan soils though the NATO routes were opened in mid 2012.

So these were two litmus tests for analysing the value of that pronounced doctrinal change, both of which entailed fundamental departures in well-established security calculations which ultimately ended with the US un-ceremonial departure from Afghan lands.

Due to routine shifting within the army planning portals, Pakistan might have tolerated the Taliban for some years, depending upon the geo-political situations around and especially versus India - out of fears of Indian strategic encirclement. However, when the Taliban's organization splinted into factions, adopted structural changes within themselves, when the Taliban went multidirectional under various leaderships within, when Taliban themselves divided into more than twenty groups, when Taliban's some groups started joining hands with Al Qaeda – the change in Pakistan Army's policy documents was inevitable.

Every state on globe wants to keep its borders silent but keeping its safety first – so was the Pakistan Army's desire. They never felt any possibility of aggression from Afghanistan; neither sponsored by the Afghan government nor from the independent non state actors near Pak-Afghan borders. As the domestic militants, mostly the sectarian promoters, started waging war against the Pakistani state, Pak-Army had to move its horses as per demand of the situation.

Pakistan wanted to help the US to become involved in reconciliation process between the Taliban and the Kabul government, including releasing a number of jailed Taliban leaders as a goodwill gesture, as well as offering other diplomatic services to bring diversified chiefs of various tribal leaders on negotiation table; one US Commander [Gen Mc Chrystal in early 2009] did not consider it worth. Mc Chrystal tried its best for about a year to ride on solo flights but the Taliban continued to dither about on one pretext or the other.

After eight months the next US commander Gen Paetrus especially requested the Pakistan Army again to go with the earlier offer. The core item on the agenda remained that *'Afghanistan has to bear his burden at his own'*.

A Reuters report correctly conveyed the message to the US, reflecting the Pakistan military's resolve, saying: *'...... we just want them to be masters of themselves so we concentrate on our own problems'*. The outcome brought significant implications not only for Pakistan itself but the larger region as well.

The more talked about apprehension; whether the doctrinal revisions would bring about a more relaxed nuclear posture towards India. Pakistan might have rapidly expanded its nuclear stockpile [*it is Pakistan's prerogative being a free and independent nation*], especially in tactical nuclear weapons. Many were worried that South Asia was on the verge of a destabilizing nuclear arms competition – but Pakistan's stance was clear and logical.

Gen Kayani justified the need for battlefield nuclear options by pointing to the threat posed by the Indian army's Cold Strategic Doctrine which had miss-interpreted and thus un-necessarily out-blown the threat of Pakistan's nuclear development and demanded sanctions on it in order to deter Pakistan's alleged adventurism.

The polarised world kept on crying but there were no signs that Pakistan's military establishment was reversing its objectives, though PPP leadership, on the instigation of their US counterparts, sometimes asked tougher questions about the direction of the nuclear program. After Gen Kayani's scheduled retirement during ending 2013, the resolve has gone more strong with the new PML[N] government in saddles along with the new army Chief Gen Raheel Sharif.

## *NEW DOCTRINE vs EASTERN BORDERS:*

On 30th December 2012, COAS Gen Kayani used a term *'amorphous enemy'* in his speech at the 98th Midshipmen Commissioning term and 7th SSC Officer's class in Karachi. In a significant revision to the Green book, Gen Kayani had enshrined another dimension in the threat matrix and declared the **'internal threat'** as the biggest threat to the security of the country. The ISPR had told the media then that:

*'Though the army's new doctrine of focusing on Strategic as well on sub-conventional warfare was put into practice in May 2012. It has*

*already created waves with its reporting in the international media.*
*A professional army like of the Pakistan Army has to review its doctrine*
*with adding of new subjects/matters, as in the present case.'*

**Till January 2013;** the new doctrine was just out; the general populace
in Pakistan was worried if the Pakistan Army was moving away from the
threat on the Eastern border. The fact remained that the *Pak-Army had*
*the same old policy with a few additional chapters added*. Gen Kayani
and his commanders started focussing on the internal threat then, though
the army should have planned that strategy a decade ago. An Anti-Terror
Division could have been created in the post Nine Eleven era.

The Green book, which the Pak-Army announced as new blue print then
discussed, published and circulated amongst their decision making
officers and staff like each year's routine with special strategic papers
written by professional soldiers; given with their possible solutions and
suggestions on numerous subjects. 2012-13's Green Book had papers
focusing on internal terror threats. The international media made a big
deal about this. That year, the Green books were made available to the
public think tanks too.

The much-discussed *'strategic depth'* doctrine of the military also
remained fully intact - which clarified that *a peaceful, secure and friendly*
*Afghanistan meant that our western borders are safe*. Hence the Pakistani
military could fully concentrate on the eastern borders.

The intelligentsia had genuine reservations that why Pak-Army finally
talked about this new strategy when the writing had been on the wall
since a decade at least. Gen Kayani, had left all of the Pakistan Army's
major installations naked and defence-less. Normal contingency plans
were definitely in place to safeguard each military installation like
**Dargai** SSG Training Centre, GHQ, **Kamra** Air Base, Karachi Naval
Base and many others but Pak-Army officers, retired and serving both,
raised fingers on the competency of Gen Kayani.

Gen Kayani, as Army Chief, witnessed attack after attack on its vital
installations. Gen Kayani could not even defend his own office - GHQ
in Rawalpindi. It took a few idiots with Kalashnikovs to keep the
sixth largest army's base hostage for more than a day. How could goons
attack the Mehran Airbase or Kamra - how could a fly transgress into
these key-bases? The Pakistani nation had been so confident in their
army – that how could a mosquito cross the boundary walls into
such huge installations - what to speak of RAW's paid some *'mir-jafars*
*or mir-sadiqs'* in Pak-Army?

During 2009-10, the Interior Ministry had facilitated more than 6000 US spy-agents, by issuing them Pakistani visas without ISI's clearance, issued from Washington and Dubai Consulates by keeping open their offices on Sundays & Fridays respectively, many of them with address in Pakistan written as *President House Islamabad* – all of them were Black Water & XE's undercover security personnel. Gen Shuja Pasha's team failed to keep their track. In short – Gen Kayani and Gen Pasha both faced colossal failures in their tenures and Pakistan and its army itself suffered a lot then.

Gen Kayani & Gen Pasha's teams, sorry to say, were unable to infiltrate and extinguish the TTP, and they failed to prevent the massive inflow of foreign fighters and spies into Pakistan. Pakistan's western borders remained loose and it has not been able to use the Afghan war to country's advantage. Why did it take so long for the army to recognize existence of foreign agencies in Pakistan?

Pak-Army's retired Generals, the old strategists, maintained that the *'foreign agency infested'* Wakhan Corridor should have been targeted much earlier when the Pak-Army had noticed the first anti-Pakistan activity there. Gen Kayani should have taken notice of the intentions of the then political leadership who were keen to award an MFN status to India – while they never wanted it in open.

The whole Pakistan was devastated with India & US made arsenal, explosive mines, communication gadgets, bomb making devices and dangerous chemicals – did Gen Kayani or Gen Pasha's teams ever called the record of off - loaded containers at Karachi terminal to compare with the actually left *Chaman* or *Torkham* borders then.

The corruption stories of officers and men deployed by Pakistan Customs Directorates on the entry & exit points were printed in the western and American media – which indicated that Pak-Army had not kept track of those containers and the 'business' flourished day by day involving billions of dollars for American sellers, transporters, security agencies and Pakistan Customs; and it continued for years.

Dr Shoaib Suddle's Inquiry report into *'Lost ISAF Containers'* was never called by Gen Kayani or Gen Pasha's team to know the real background facts. A detailed perspective on ISAF Containers is available in Scenario 94 of **'Living History of Pakistan Vol-I'**.

No doubt, the Pak-Army remained alert against the threat matrix - mainly composed of external threats, nuclear threats, and conventional warfare - there was no or little attention given to the internal threats, whatsoever. Till ending 2012, Pakistan had gone late and the non-state actors had gone too strong and organized. After the loss of nearly 47,000 Pakistani lives, the Pakistani decision makers felt they were facing a well funded and foreign supported terrorist groups spread all over Pakistan.

By this pace, Pakistan would take one more decade for its army to recognize the extant of cyber terror.

Pak-Army's activity, however, remained confined up to planning and documentation that whole year of 2013 till Gen Raheel Sharif stepped in and an action plan announced. Gen Kayani had chaired the meeting. It was resolved then that:

> *".....the threat matrix of conventional and now sub-conventional threat will be addressed simultaneously and no one has forgotten to counter the conventional threat being faced by the country"*

What took so long Gen Kayani to recognize the obvious?

## CIVIL INTERNAL FACTORS:

During the same month on the civil side, Prime Minister Raja Pervez Ashraf said that Pakistan would have to redefine its military doctrine to comprehensively tackle terrorism – in other words the political elite had also given green signal to the army for shaping the said new doctrine. Some of the public statements at different occasions were:

- *"We need to work on a strategy which can comprehensively tackle terrorism. We have to redesign and redefine our military doctrine to achieve this objective.*

- *The forces of doom and gloom thrive in an environment of chaos, uncertainty and instability. We need to guard against all such forces, which are out to derail the system so assiduously put in place after a protracted struggle.*

- *Threats to Pakistan's national security stem from mainly non-state actors who are targeting state's symbols and institutions in a bid to impose their agenda. This is an enemy which is nameless and faceless.*

- *While highlighting the sacrifices of the security forces, law enforcement agencies and citizens in the war against terrorism, we need to redefine the military doctrine.*

- *Our national security institutions must improve intelligence gathering and establish effective coordination among civil and military institutions to attain optimum results."*

All bull-shit political statements – not a single phrase that the government would change 170 years old legal procedures, standards of evidence and summary courts procedures to dispose off the cases within days not years.

The military's desire to combat terrorism had always been thwarted by weak laws and flawed prosecution process. Belatedly a strong anti-terrorism law was introduced in the National Assembly but could not bring any fruit.

The army was bitter about the Swat experience where it successfully flushed out the terrorists back in 2007-08 - but it had to continue holding Swat without the civilian administration developing the capability to take over. Not a single person, that the military nabbed in the once peaceful valley, had been convicted.

The new chapter in Pakistan Army's Doctrine blamed *foreign proxies* from unnamed countries for creating unrest in some parts of the country. It was obvious that the army was referring to India's role in creating disturbances in Balochistan, which had been plagued by a deadly terrorist activity since 2004 through unidentified militant groups [TTP, BLA]. It also mentioned that Pakistani militants had found refuge across the Durand Line in Afghanistan. The ISPR explained that:

*"Pakistan's armed forces were trained for conventional warfare but the current security situation necessitated the change...Forces fighting on the front-line in the tribal regions are now being trained according to the requirements of sub-conventional warfare."*

But; it only took 10 years to realize this.

The *Express Tribune dated 29ᵗʰ January 2013*, ended an essay with:

*'We wish Gen Kayani a fond farewell. His term of office will be remembered for his failures, not his successes. Perhaps the next general will stop the drones, and create an army which can face future and present threats.'*

*In 2011-13,* Pakistan was preoccupied with rising violence in Karachi and Quetta and then in general elections, the paradigm shift in the US policy on Afghanistan was not taken much note of. The Pak-Army had placed a plan before America, as far as in 2010, to cope with the the then prevailing situations within Afghanistan and across the borders. That doctrine was built on three advisory but friendly propositions based on the factual foresight that American troops had to be withdrawn from Afghanistan – sooner or later.

The three step strategy suggested by Pak-Army was firstly – ISI would be ready to put in efforts for reconciliation among Afghan factions – perhaps it might not be possible otherwise; secondly - Jalalabad – Torkham - Karachi route would be made open, being the most viable, for withdrawing American forces; and lastly - India would not be allowed to play any role during implementation of the said plans.

Recalling the little history; in 2009, Gen McChrystal, Commander ISAF and of US Forces in Afghanistan (USFOR-A), had asked the US government for a 'troop surge' which inducted 30,000 - 40,000 additional troops into Afghanistan. In 2010, 101st Combat Aviation Brigade, 502nd Infantry Regiment, 187th Infantry Regiment, 1st Brigade Combat Team and the 101st Sustainment Brigade were deployed to Afghanistan. *'the News' dated 3rd March 2013* is referred.

The year of 2010, Gen Petraeus, the new commander ISAF and USFOR-A, instead of considering the Pakistan's offers seriously and preferred to implement his **"Comprehensive Counter - Insurgency (COIN) strategy"**. Gen Petraeus' COIN had his own four way solution of the Afghan War based on firstly by securing and serving the population; secondly by understanding local circumstances; thirdly by separating hard core from reconcilable; and lastly by living among the people.

By 2011, for America the cost of war in Afghanistan reached a colossal $500 billion mark and the US had suffered 1,814 fatalities. By that time, Petraeus' four way strategy of COIN had started falling flat – one by one. America could no longer sustain the war in Afghanistan – neither politically nor financially. Finally, President Obama, in a prime time speech, indicated to follow Pak-Army suggestions by announcing a troop drawdown schedule.

That was the background that **on 2nd December 2012,** US Secretary of State Hillary Clinton had to initiate talks with Pakistan's COAS Gen Kayani.

**On 17th December 2012,** the Federal Court in New York was officially told by the White House that:

*"In the view of the United States, the Inter-Services Intelligence (ISI)
is entitled to immunity because it is part of a foreign state within the
meaning of the FSIA (Foreign Sovereign Immunities Act)."*

This was an implicit acceptance of the ISI's indispensability by the US
elite in the Afghan endgame. It was a great win for Pak-Army and its ISI.

**On 29th December 2012,** Pakistan received $688 million as Coalition
Support Fund (CSF). According to the Ministry of Finance, "*from May
2010 onwards Pakistan had asked for $2.5 billion under the CSF but
only $1.9 billion have been reimbursed.*"

**On 10th February 2013,** two convoys each hauling 25 shipping containers from Afghanistan entered Pakistan at the Chaman and Torkham
borders heading back to where they came from. To be certain, those
convoys were in fact taking back around 750,000 major military
items, mainly communication gadgets and heavy arsenal, valued at about
$40 billion.

It was known to the world media that the British government had acted
as the intermediaries in that latest US - Pakistan negotiations and that
Turkey, Qatar and Saudi Arabia were also involved in talks. Pakistan
had once again become the key player in the Afghan endgame. In fact;
India's plans of encompassing Pakistan had evaporated till then.

So far as elections 2013 were concerned, the ISPR had rightly clarified
that:

'*The Army supports timely elections and the military has no favourites.
Whoever wins the elections fair and square and forms a government is
acceptable to it. Hence Nawaz Sharif has nothing to fear that powers
that be have any desire to block him.*'

In that context, the military leadership considered it an insult to its
intelligence to be accused of backing Tahirul Qadri. Totally rejecting the
then popular public perception that '..... **non-state political actors
looking at the GHQ for support**' to scuttle the election process in the
name of accountability was not only discredited but abandoned as well.

Once it was perceived that the APC called by Maulana Fazlur Rehman
had the unspoken backing of the military. Maulana was keen that the
civilian leadership should collectively hold talks with the Tehreek e
Taliban Pakistan [TTP]. Talks were settled to take place with a position
of strength rather than weakness. Similarly any agreement was to be

strictly within the ambit of the constitution, law and writ of the Pakistan government.

The military was extremely worried about internal instability, terrorism and a weakening economy in Pakistan. The military supported intra-Afghan dialogue with the belief that political process should be in the lead. Within the parameters of its strategic doctrine the military desired a stable and peaceful Afghanistan. It was no longer keen to foist a government of its choice in Kabul. However, it firmly believed that once the US troops left the Afghan soils, Pakistan should not be left in the wrong corner as it was done after the Soviet troops had left Afghanistan in 1980s.

# Scenario 118

## AMERICA QUITS AFGHANISTAN

### *AMERICA's OWN DISORDERS PLAYED:*

America's own war analysts said that they lost war due to their own miss-management.

On 7ᵗʰ October 2010; a Senate report was issued for the media stating that US funds for private security contractors in Afghanistan had flowed to warlords and Taliban insurgents, undermining the war effort and fuelling corruption. The investigation by the Senate Armed Services Committee found that the government had failed to vet or manage those hired to provide security under contracts worth billions of dollars, with disastrous results. Carl Levin, Chairman of the Committee held that:

> *"Our reliance on private security contractors in Afghanistan has too often empowered local warlords and powerbrokers who operate outside the Afghan government's control and act against coalition interests. This situation threatens the security of our troops and puts the success of our mission at risk."*

The report further said that under one US Air Force subcontract for an Afghan air base, Armour Group — a subsidiary of the British based firm G4S — used Afghan warlords to recruit security guards. The warlords included *"Taliban supporters"*. While the contract was in force, one of the warlords was killed in a US-Afghan military raid *"on a Taliban meeting being held at his house"*.

In a review of more than 125 Pentagon security contracts from 2007 to 2009, the committee found *"systemic failures, including security contractors' failures to vet personnel or to ensure that their armed personnel received adequate training."*

The report endorsed efforts by the US and Nato commander in Afghanistan, General David Petraeus, who had ordered a reform of security contracting and warned that spending large amounts of money without enough oversight could unintentionally feed corruption and the insurgency.

The US Defence Secretary Robert Gates also acknowledged the problem and in a letter to Levin, said the Pentagon had dramatically expanded oversight of contracts and had created task forces to overhaul contract work. **Richard Fontaine,** a senior fellow at the Centre for a **New American Security** said that:

> *"The Senate report is yet another wake-up call for the Pentagon, and I think they will have to address the problem. But the military faced a difficult dilemma.*
>
> *In some cases, it appears that the choice is stark — allow subcontractors to pay the Taliban protection money — and essentially fund the enemy with taxpayer dollars — or bar protection payments and absorb a higher degree of risk of attack.*
>
> *This choice is made even more difficult given that we rely on contractors and not military personnel to carry out a variety of security tasks, including convoy protection."*

The Afghan government had condemned the role of private security contractors and formally banned eight foreign firms, including the controversial company formerly called *Blackwater.* Kabul had given security firms working in Afghanistan four months [two months had already gone till then] to cease operations, which could present a major headache for Nato-led troops and international organizations which rely on the contractors employing thousands of Afghan nationals; both from for and against the Karzai regime.

*Another Aspect:* For some, the end game in Afghanistan had started in the backdrop of President Obama's program announced **on 1st December 2009** in New York Army Centre; considering that **Chicago Conference of 20th May 2012** was the final round. The players were there but the reps were having different goals in their minds. Think about the two odd deliberations, which had already been discussed in detail but reiterating again:

> '*One,* Hillary Clinton said that Ayman el Zawahiri is likely to be hiding in Pakistan; *two,* the US Senators are coming up with fresh demands to bind Pakistan's security set up for routing out the Haqqani net work'.

That was why the relations between the USA and Pakistan were seen at their lowest ebb. Moreover, after **Salala check post attack,** there was uproar against America throughout the country; the military administration was more disturbed.

The US Defence Department officially declared that Pakistan refused to be part of a joint investigation into the 26th **November 2011**'s NATO attack on Pakistani check post in Salala of Mohmand tribal area. The decision was one of the several that Pakistan's military and civil authorities had taken in its protest against the said attack in which 24 army personnel including one major and one captain were killed.

**On 29th November 2011;** the Press Secretary US Defence, George Little, had confirmed Pak-Army's refusal in his briefing to the media. Pakistan's Director General Military Operations (DGMO) Major Gen Ashfaq Nadeem had already ruled out the possibility of a joint probe, saying that earlier joint investigations carried out after similar attacks were unable to produce any results. Pakistan's military elite had decided to go by their independent decision.

Meanwhile, Pakistan's Parliament held a joint session to discuss the attack and the senate passed a **unanimous resolution** opposing the attacks. The cogent question was that would the senate's resolution and the parliament's impending joint session be able to form a concrete strategy against such attacks? And if formed, will such a strategy be followed in future?

**On 14th April 2012,** a unanimous adoption of the revised recommenda-tions of the Parliamentary Committee on National Security (PCNS) was agreed as a civilian approach to Pakistan's foreign policy though very little was different to what went before. Details were:

- *The NATO convoys would be allowed but without arms and ammunition; [the Americans held that they never despatched arms through containers] however, Pakistan's security were permitted to peep into the containers.*

- *Pakistan would seek (note 'seek' and not 'demand or else') a cessation of the drone strikes. [Hillary Clinton had made crystal clear just a week before that* **'America will continue its drone strikes whether we seek their cessation or not'**].

- *There would be no foreign bases on Pakistani soil; since the closure of the 'so called secret' Shamsi airbase in Balochistan.*

- *Contractors or operatives would not be allowed; meaning thereby that the Americans should go more careful about covert operatives not to repeat Raymond Davis episodes again.*

- *Strict monitoring of all goods in transit at entry and exit points would be launched for tax and transit fees though Pakistani tax teams were known world over for their bargain skills in any odd situation.*

- *Pakistan would seek (but again not demand) an apology for the Salala incident which triggered this wave of tension; already settled that America would offer a 'regret to restore our national pride and dignity' though the US had flatly refused it.*

- *New protocols would be adopted but it would be an update of existing Standard Operating Procedures.*

- *Hot pursuit would not be permitted for Americans [but on rare occasions would be tolerated or ignored as before].*

- *There would be no more unwritten and secret agreements, between Pakistan and America; allegedly Gen Pasha was not given more extension on the issue that he had bargained secret pact with the US Commander for drone attacks in FATA [February 2012] perhaps without approval of the Army Chief Gen Kayani.*

- *The oil and gas pipeline projects with Iran and Turkmenistan would be actively pursued and Pakistan would continue a results oriented dialogue with India. It was not at all related with American role in War on Terror.*

The Pakistani intelligentsia and media analysts concluded that '*it was an impressive wish-list and a cautious statement of intent, but hardly a policy document and the nature of our relationship with the US remains a work in progress.*'

The above agreement though conveyed green signal for the US and NATO to use Pakistani corridor for their transportation but had also suggested pointedly that '*the US should start packing his luggage to leave that South Asian region*'.

On the other hand, President <u>Obama's new agreement with Afghanistan</u> dated **2nd May 2012** ensuring the presence of American 'experts' even after NATO leaves by the end of 2014, had given rise to another suspicious scenario. The US bases at Bagram, Kandahar and Kabul were to remain operational much beyond 2014.

When one pondered beyond 2014, the well trumpeted geography of new region, a part of the new world order game, comprising of Tribal Areas of Pakistan, the adjoining areas of Afghanistan, the territory of southern Bahawalpur till Gwader and the Indian Ocean all seemed to be linked to the US plans of Afghanistan's War on Terror.

Referring to Usman Khalid's analysis [at Rifah Party's website dated **21st May 2012**]:

> 'The re-opening of the supply line to Afghanistan is no longer an issue. It is in Pakistan's interest to facilitate the withdrawal of NATO forces by the end of 2014 and logistic support until then. However, **Pakistan cannot support the overall design of USA which is now being made in consultation with India.** Pakistan - US relations will move along a rough and bumpy road.'

The two miscalculations made by Pakistan and the US had caused thorns to grow on both sides of written history: Pakistani intelligentsia made the people believe that the NATO troops in Afghanistan would not be able to sustain this blockade for more than a month and the US would come running begging forgiveness for *Salala killings* and drone attacks etc.

The CIA & Pentagon also miscalculated the response of Pakistan by taking it for granted that Islamabad would not be able to survive beyond a month without US-aid. Then both, the Pakistan and USA corrected the wrongs by taking a cautious stance on NATO supply route; hats off to the **Chicago Summit**, the roughness had toned down on both sides. A concrete set of measures were required to solve the Afghan problem. Throughout the journey from Bonn to Chicago, a potent question remained alive that:

*'Can Pakistan be ignored with its unique connectivity matrix in this part of the world?'*

## US & IRANI DOLLAR BAGS IN WOT:

According to a report published in *'New York Times' dated 28th April 2013*:

> 'For more than a decade, wads of **American dollars packed into suitcases, backpacks and, on occasion, plastic shopping bags have been dropped off every month** or so at the offices of Afghanistan's president — courtesy of the Central Intelligence Agency [CIA].'

Some American officials said the cash had fuelled corruption and empowered warlords, undermining Washington's exit strategy from Afghanistan. One official openly admitted that:

> *"The biggest source of corruption in Afghanistan was the United States itself. The US was not alone in delivering cash to the president Karzai; the later had acknowledged a few years ago that **Iran regularly gave bags of cash** to one of his top aides."*

American officials knew that CIA kept on providing cash to maintain access to Mr Karzai to guarantee its influence at the presidential palace, which wields tremendous power in Afghanistan's highly centralized government. **Whether the US got what it paid for – not sure; Karzai seemingly remained unable to be bought.** Karzai was seeking control over the Afghan militias raised by the CIA to target operatives of Al Qaeda and insurgent commanders and the CIA continued to pay.

Tens of millions of dollars were flown from the CIA to the office of President Hamid Karzai. Mr Karzai's Deputy Chief of Staff from 2002 until 2005 named Khalil Roman sarcastically confirmed it saying: **"...we called it 'ghost money, it came in secret and it left in secret."**

The CIA, which declined to comment on it, had long been known to support Ahmed Wali Karzai, brother of the Afghan president and a suspected player in the country's booming illegal opium trade, who managed to get regular payments since past eight years.

**On 12ᵗʰ July 2011,** Ahmed Wali Karzai, was assassinated by one of his own trusted aide in Kabul. The agency paid the Karzai family for a variety of services, including helping to recruit an Afghan paramilitary force that operated at the CIS's direction in and around the southern city of Kandahar, Afghan President's home town.

The US special considerations with Mr Karzai created deep divisions within the Obama administration. The CIA's practices also suggested that the US was not doing enough to stamp out the lucrative Afghan drug trade, a major source of revenue for the Taliban. Some American officials argued that the reliance on Karzai's brother undermined the American push to develop an effective central government that could maintain law and order and eventually allow the US to withdraw.

Maj Gen Michael T Flynn, the senior American military intelligence official in Afghanistan had rightly held that *'.... we are perceived as backing thugs, and we are just undermining ourselves.'*

Ahmed Wali Karzai had once told in an interview that he cooperated with American civilian and military officials, but did not engage in the drug trade and did not receive payments from the CIA. He used to operate a paramilitary group, *the Kandahar Strike Force*, which was used for raids against suspected insurgents and terrorists.

Ahmed Wali Karzai, was being paid for allowing the CIA and American Special Operations troops to rent a large compound outside the city — the *former home of Mullah Mohammed Omar*, the Taliban's founder. The same compound was also the base of the Kandahar Strike Force. In a way Mulla Omar was CIA's landlord - the senior American officials knew it.

Wali Karzai had also helped the CIA communicate and sometimes meet with Afghans loyal to the Taliban; his role as a coordinator between the Americans and the Taliban was then regarded as valuable placing a greater focus on encouraging Taliban leaders to change sides. Some American officials considered that the allegations of Wali Karzai's role in the drug trade were not substantiated as nothing that could stand up in court.

The fact remained that in the beginning of the Afghan war, just after the Nine Eleven episode, the US officials paid warlords with dubious backgrounds to help topple the Taliban and maintain order because there were few American troops in Afghanistan. But as the Taliban became resurgent and the war went intensified, the US needed a strong central government in Kabul to check the Taliban's moves. As the US committed more troops, more officials went frustrated with President Karzai.

Later, Wali Karzai's suspected role in the drug trade, as well as what the White House then described as the mafia-like way that he commanded over southern Afghanistan, made him a malicious figure. The US military and political officials held the circumstantial evidence that Wali Karzai got enriched himself by helping the illegal trade in poppy and opium to flourish. The senior officials in the Bush administration had also held the same views – it was on record that:

*"Hundreds of millions of dollars in drug money are flowing through the southern region, and nothing happens in southern Afghanistan without the regional leadership knowing about it. If it looks like a duck, and it quacks like a duck, it's probably a duck. Our assumption is that he's benefiting from the drug trade."*

The US officials held that Afghan opium trade, the largest in the world, directly threatened the stability of the Afghan state, by providing enough money the Taliban needed for their operations. The Obama administration repeatedly vowed to crack down on the drug lords who were believed to be very near to the President Karzai but could not move so for unknown reasons. White House pressed President Karzai twice to move his brother out of southern Afghanistan, but he had flatly refused to do so.

In an interview in mid 2010, Ahmed Wali Karzai denied his role in the drug trade or taking money from the CIA, though admitted receiving regular payments from his brother, the president, for 'expenses,' but said he did not know where the money came from. Among other things, he introduced Americans to insurgents considering changing sides and also given the Americans the needed intelligence though he was not adequately compensated for that dangerous job. He said '....*it was my duty as an Afghan.*'

## FORMER CIA OFFICER SPEAKS:

A former CIA officer who had served in Afghanistan opined in the 'New York Times' dated 27th October 2009:

> '...*the [CIA] agency relied heavily on Ahmed Wali Karzai, and often based covert operatives at compounds he owned. Karzai might have the drug trade but it mattered little to CIA officers focused on counterterrorism missions.*
>
> *Virtually every significant Afghan figure has had brushes with the drug trade. If you are looking for Mother Teresa, she doesn't live in Afghanistan.*"

For years, first the Bush administration and then the Obama administration held that the Taliban availed benefits from the drug trade, and the US military once expanded its target list to include drug traffickers with ties to the insurgency. The military had generated a list of 50 top drug traffickers tied to the Taliban who were to be killed or captured.

Senior Afghan investigators knew plenty about Karzai's involvement in the drug business. A top former Afghan Interior Ministry official familiar with Afghan anti-narcotics operations told that a major source of Karzai's influence over the drug trade was his control over *key bridges crossing the Helmand River on the route between the opium growing regions of Helmand Province and Kandahar.* Karzai used to charge huge fees to drug traffickers to allow their drug - laden trucks to cross the bridges.

However, it remained impossible for Afghan anti-narcotics officials to investigate Karzai family for that because *"....this government has become a factory for the production of Taliban because of corruption and injustice."* Americans believed that Karzai had expanded his influence over the drug trade, thanks in part to the US efforts to single out other drug lords.

The American officials believed that the cash dollars from the CIA coupled with Karzai's own drug money had fuelled corruption and empowered most Afghan warlords, undermining Washington's exit strategy from Afghanistan. American officials themselves held that *"....the biggest source of corruption in Afghanistan was the United States."*

The US was not alone in delivering cash to the President Karzai; he had acknowledged in person in 2010 that Iran regularly gave bags of cash to one of his top aides.

The US officials jumped on the payments as evidence of an aggressive Iranian campaign to buy influence and poison Afghanistan's relations with the US. What they did not say was that the CIA was also plying the presidential palace with cash — and unlike the Iranians, it continued for long.

American and Afghan officials familiar with the payments said the agency's main goal in providing the cash was to maintain access to Mr Karzai and his inner circle and to guarantee the agency's influence at the presidential palace, which wielded tremendous power in Afghan government.

[*It was not clear that the US was getting what it paid for. Mr. Karzai could defy the US and the Iranians because much cash had piled up in the palace 'unnecessarily' - Karzai was seemingly unable to be bought.*]

It was that strategy over which *President Obama had signed a 'Strategic Partnership Deal with Afghanistan on 2ⁿᵈ May 2012,* directly leading the Iranians to halt their payments. Like the Iranian cash, much of the CIA's money went to paying off warlords and politicians, many of whom had ties to the drug trade and, in some cases, the Taliban. Interestingly, the cash from Tehran was being handled with greater transparency than the dollars from the CIA.

Much of the money went to keep old warlords in line. One Abdul Rashid Dostum, an ethnic Uzbek whose militia served as a CIA proxy force in 2001, used to receive $100,000 a month from the palace to serve as Mr Karzai's emissary in northern Afghanistan. *"I asked for a year up front in cash so that I could build my dream house,"* he was quoted as saying in a 2009 interview with <u>Time</u> magazine.

When word of the Iranian cash leaked out in October 2010, Mr Karzai told reporters that *"....he was grateful for it. The US is doing the same thing. They are providing cash to some of our offices."* No one used to mention the agency's money at cabinet meetings; it was handled by a small clique at the Afghan National Security Council.

At a farewell cocktail party in the *third week of April 2013* hosted by the departing French Ambassador to Kabul: <u>Bernard Bajolet</u>, who was leaving to head France's Direction Génerale de la Sécurité Extérieure, its foreign intelligence service; spilled the beans saying:

> *".... French troops are still fighting in Afghanistan we can claim to have done its part. We lost more troops than all but three other countries before withdrawing its last combat forces in the fall.*
>
> *That the Afghan project is on thin ice and that, collectively, the West was responsible for a chunk of what went wrong, though much of the rest the Afghans were responsible for. The <u>West had done a good job of fighting terrorism, but that most of that was done on Pakistani soil, not on the Afghan side</u> of the border."*

His tone was neither shrill nor reproachful. It was matter-of-fact. Mr Bajolet continued with his comments.

> *"I still cannot understand how we, the international community, and the Afghan government have managed to arrive at a situation in which everything is coming together in 2014 — elections, new president, economic transition, military transition and all this — whereas the negotiations for the peace process have not yet started."*

Mr Bajolet was echoing a point shared privately by other diplomats –:

> *"Afghanistan; a country that depends almost entirely on the international community for the salaries of its soldiers and policemen, for*

*most of its investments and partly for its current civil expenditure, cannot be really independent.*"

On one side this wholesome game of dollars award was going on and on the opposite the US was on the move for opening talks with the Taliban. See a little report.

Referring to Husain Haqqani's essay printed in US media **on 27th June 2013**, the US was still looking for peace talks with the Taliban in Qatar, despite the fact that the group had attacked the presidential palace and a CIA office in Kabul earlier that week. In Haqqani's opinion, negotiating with the Taliban was going to be a grievous mistake.

Unlike most states or political groups, the Taliban were not amenable to a pragmatic deal. They were a movement with an extreme ideology not to compromise easily on their deeply held beliefs. Before committing the blunder of negotiating with them again, American diplomats were not able to study the history of Washington's engagement with Taliban during Bill Clinton's regime.

The said talks were arranged through the good offices of Pak-Army Chief Gen Kayani and the US had opened a Taliban office in Qatar for that very purpose. Taliban officials immediately portrayed the American concession as a victory. They flew the Taliban flag, played the Taliban anthem and called their new workplace the office of the *"Islamic Emirate of Afghanistan"* — the name of the state they ran in the 1990s before being dislodged from power after 9/11. An intentional move it was - which reflected the Taliban's view of the talks as beginning of the restoration of their emirate. Though there was no sign that the Taliban were ready for political accommodation.

The fact remained that Pakistan did not want to become a party between that two party talks. Pakistan might had contacts in the far past with Taliban but it had no control over them especially during the PPP regime. For the Taliban, direct dialogue with the US was a source of international legitimacy and an opportunity to regroup. They were most likely playing for time while waiting for American troops to withdraw in 2014.

A latest interview [dated 13th September 2015] of a former CIA officer named Michael Scheuer is available at X99TV and most media pages. Mr Michael remained in interaction with ISI for most time in his twenty years career. In a frank interview available on media he admitted that the

US should not have stepped in Afghanistan without having a thorough study of the area, their cultural traits and traditions. He categorically stated that:

*'ISI is also an intelligence agency just likes of America or Australia and* **'the job of intelligence agencies anywhere is never to help the other countries; its job is to take care of his own state interests'.**

*For ISI the world over perception prevails that it is 'a rude horse' but my twenty years experience in intelligence tells that 'ISI is the most disciplined and professional service; it works for its own country'.* [....quite opposite to its politicians]

*The US has to quit that region one day but ISI will remain there after all. ISI prefers to have an Islamic government in Afghanistan and that is in Pakistan's favour. The US itself is responsible for loose moves in Afghanistan.*

*The Americans were made to understand that Osama is dead so their problems have gone. But the US state functionaries have done so badly there in that region that it is in their neck now.* **In 2001, Al Qaeda was operating from one platform – now they are fighting from SIX operational platforms.**

*I also admit that we Americans are not 'behaving manly'; its enemy sacrifices hundreds of lives every week and we Americans are beating our heads and chests over 160 deaths in fifteen years - whereas we are superpower with 300 million population.*

*Every American in Washington says today* **that Pakistan is no good friend.** *My contention is that there is no friend of America* **who had got a decade long civil war in his country for the US** *– neither India nor Israel.* **Pakistan did so for us.** *We Americans were wrong – we did not understand the pitfalls in Afghanistan – so we suffered.'*

## US WAS WARNED TO RESIST WAR:

When Bush administration had decided to conquer Afghanistan after Nine - Eleven episodes, the historians of America went worrying that what the US government was going to do. The then recent past of Afghanistan and the humiliating defeat, the Russians had suffered on that land, was still being talked and discussed in the US print media. The general populace might not be remembering the world events or geo-political changes around but the intelligentsia and the academics were really concerned about their government's abrupt decisions.

**A 256 pages book titled:** *Fear's Empire: War, Terrorism, and Democracy* **written by** Benjamin R. Barber **and released in** *October 2004* had timely warned the **US decision makers sitting in Pentagon and White House** that what mistakenly judgment their president Mr Bush had done.

In Afghanistan, it happened the same way with the US forces what Benjamin had warned in 2004; the US political elite and army commanders found themselves trapped and since 2010 they had been planning to come out of that strategic sand grave through various pacts and negotiations – but could not avoid its defeat.

The Americans used usual cosmetic phrase *'...we have a duty to rebuild and defend that country, until it is strong enough to defend itself.'* But the intentions were wrong – from some countries the US planned to snatch oil reserves [think Iraq & Libya] – from some countries Opium and Hashish [think Afghanistan].

Why the American Generals and commanding army officers have gone billionaires during the Afghan war – some body will dig it out some time.

Now see an American blog by one *Moein Daqiq* says: **July 23, 2013 at 10:18 am:**

> *"I will say US and NATO were not very honest to Afghanistan in the recent decade. They know all the causes and roots of problems and they didn't address it at all. Instead they killed innocent people in the afghan villages.*
>
> *US is here for the region and for Americans not for Afghans. Everybody is playing the bloody game in my country for their own interest. If the author is aware of all these things who believes that CIA is not. The other factor that contributes to this matter is the Afghanistan corrupt government, which is established and supported by USA and the credits go to them."*

One *Hekmat Sial* **July 23, 2013 at 12:21 am** on the same website// **pubrecord.org**

> *"I agree to some extent with the article published by Barber. However, if Pakistan and Afghanistan two countries in the South-east Asia do not work out their issue themselves peace will never come to their home.*

*Both countries are in the best geo-strategic located countries which are paramount for the global economy to boost up particularly for China. These two countries are significant for the countries in the central Asia as well. ...... the history is going to repeat for sure; no matter what that could be."*

I leave the rest for my readers to draw conclusions – let us go straight.

Citing again the American Brave Advisor Mr Riedel who feared that the forces unleashed in 10 years of war may yet come to haunt the whole world:

*"There is probably no worse nightmare, for America, for Europe, for the world, in the 21st Century than if Pakistan gets out of control under the influence of extremist Islamic forces, armed with nuclear weapons...The stakes here are huge."*

That was an indirect tribute to the Pak-Army and its ISI once again – where the world's no: 1 super power stood amazed and feared through a personal experience of decade long war which ended with mix feelings of shame and humiliation.

Now see **Tom Engelhardt's** sarcastic and cynical remarks
about **AMERICA** appeared in media through
**TomDispatch.com & commondreams.org** on 29th January 2013
*'The Setting Sun and the American Empire'*

*'That was the nature of the great Afghan drawdown. The words "retreat," "loss," "defeat," "disaster," and their siblings and cousins won't be allowed on the premises.*

*But make no mistake, the country that, only years ago, liked to call itself the globe's "sole superpower" or even "hyper-power," whose leaders dreamed of a Pax Americana across the Greater Middle East, if not the rest of the globe is... not to put too fine a point on it, packing its bags, throwing in the towel, **quietly admitting—in actions, if not in words — to mission unaccomplished,** and heading if not exactly home, **at least boot by boot off** the Eurasian landmass.*

*Washington has, in a word, had enough. Too much, in fact. It's lost its appetite for invasions and occupations of Eurasia, though special operations raids, drone wars, and cyber-wars still look deceptively cheap and easy as a means to control... well, whatever.*

*As a result, the Afghan drawdown of 2013-14, that implicit acknowledgement of yet **another lost war**, should set the curtain falling on the American Century as we've known it. It should be recognized as a landmark, the moment in history when the sun truly began to set on a great empire. Here in the United States, though, one thing is just about guaranteed: not many are going to be paying the slightest attention.*

*No one even thinks to ask the question: **In the mighty battle lost, who exactly beat us? Where exactly is the triumphant enemy?** Perhaps we should be relieved that the question is not being raised, because it's a hard one to answer. Could it really have been the scattered jihadis of al-Qaeda and its wannabes? Or the various modestly armed Sunni and Shiite minority insurgencies in Iraq, or their Pashtun equivalents in Afghanistan with their suicide bombers and low-tech roadside bombs? Or was it something more basic, something having to do with a planet no longer amenable to imperial expeditions?*

*Did the local and global body politic simply and mysteriously spit us out as the distasteful thing we had become? Or is it even possible, as Pogo once suggested that in those distant, unwelcoming lands, we met the enemy and he was us? Did we in some bizarre fashion fight ourselves and lose?*

*After all, last year, <u>more American servicemen died from suicide than on the battlefield in Afghanistan</u>; and a <u>startling number of Americans were killed in "green on blue"</u> or <u>"insider" attacks by Afghan "allies"</u> rather than by that fragmented movement we still call the Taliban.*

*Whoever or whatever was responsible; our Afghan disaster was remarkably foreseeable. In fact, anyone who, from 2006 on, read <u>Ann Jones's Afghan reports</u> at **TomDispatch** wouldn't have had a doubt about the outcome of the war. Her first piece, after all, was prophetically entitled **"Why It's Not Working in Afghanistan."** (The answer is a threefold failure: no peace, no democracy, and no reconstruction.)*

*From Western private – contractors – cum - looters making a figurative killing off the "reconstruction" of the country to an Afghan army that was largely a figment of the American imagination to up-armoured US soldiers on well - guarded bases whose high-tech equipment and comforts of home blinded them to the nature of the enemy, hers has long been a tale of impending failure.*

*Now, that war seems headed for its predictable end, not for the Afghans who, as Jones indicates in her latest sweeping report from Kabul, may face terrible years ahead, but for the US.*

**After more than 11 years, the war that is often labelled the longest in American history is slowly winding down and that's no small thing."**

So leave the mystery to the historians that why America – the superpower was beaten and defeated - but mark the moment please; it's historic.

# Scenario 119

## CONST'L ARTICLES 62 & 63 VIOLATED:

The fundamental moral edge of parliamentary democracy over other forms of political governance is that the parliamentary system is based on the precise ethical standards of personal and collective conduct of the political leadership that comes into power by virtue of a public mandate. When the said public mandate is violated in any shape or form, the accountability of political leadership becomes a necessity, in collective as well as of the individual capacity whenever a breach of public trust occurs.

If a cabinet member is accused of an unlawful act or a political action or personal conduct that is detrimental to national interests, violates public trust, or breaches the constitutional pledge, the Prime Minister immediately asks the accused Minister to resign; a time-honoured convention it remains. Political history is full of instances where an elected government is voted out through *'no confidence move'* if and when it fails in its public mandate, accused of incompetence, mismanagement, corruption, inefficiency and personal or collective loss or violation of public trust.

## *DR QADRI SPEAKS LOUD:*

*On 17ᵗʰ January 2013,* virtually the entire political opposition - worried at Dr Tahirul Qadri's popular uprising - joined hands and gathered in Lahore to pass a counter resolution against him. The height of hypocrisy was that they all had themselves been highly critical of the government's performance and their NRO brand of rapprochement. In fact they were un-consciously favouring the status quo, aimed at another innings of unaccounted loot and plunder.

President Asif Zardari had once again manoeuvred the opposition - that had not only been gunning for each other's throats, but also the ruling political elite - to fall into his lap by declaring to save the system; a system that had brought nothing but misery and despondency to the masses. Imran Khan's PTI, however, distanced itself from the lot; he also stayed away from Dr Qadri's march, though agreeing, in principle, with his demands for 'change'.

On the rejection of Dr Qadri's petition for reconstitution of the Election Commission, the whole nation was assured of thorough vetting of the candidates in 30 days time by the ECP. Moreover, Federal Board of Revenue [FBR], State Bank of Pakistan [SBP], NADRA, NAB and other relevant institutions were asked to extend all possible help to the Election Commission. The ECP and its Chief Election Commissioner [CEC] Fakhru Bhai were declared *'dishonest'* by the masses and media when they finally gave only seven days for that process in the final schedule of elections 2013.

The general populace was hopeful that tax evaders, loan defaulters and those who got their loans written off, did not pay their dues: in short all cheats and fraudsters would not be able to avail a smooth-sailing like in the past, and would be obstructed; but later, the ECP's nefarious and wicked designs brought utter disappointment for all. Keeping all the critics and reservations about Dr Qadri's person aside, he did his job well as the nation would not enter the next elections in the same half-asleep manner with asymmetrical minds like before.

Referring to *'the Nation' of 7th February 2013*; Mr Zardari, being the democratic head of state, should have terminated his party secretary Jehangir Badar for being named as 'helping hand' in OGRA's Rs:82 billion scam; should have ended the NAB Chairman's services for politicising his office in an ugly row with the Supreme Court. Let the Pakistanis wait for a bleak tomorrow and the days that follow a political irrationality of such kind if such rogue practice continued.

Dr Tahirul Qadri of Pakistan Awami Tehreek [PAT]'s aggressive intervention in that dark political arena was considered a hope. He demanded that:

- *The massive developmental funds given to parliamentarians must be made illegal [then being used to pre-rig the coming elections of 2013] and should be used to subsidise gas, power, petrol and other daily consumable items for the public.*

- *To ensure free & fair elections, all the four members of the Election Commission of Pakistan [ECP] should immediately be removed; these members were appointees of two vested regimes in power.*

- *To immediately freeze the discretionary funds of the Prime Minister and Chief Ministers; these funds were being used to influence voters amounting to pre-poll rigging again.*

The two ruling political parties opposed Dr Qadri labelling him as a *'foreign agent'* or *'a clergyman backed by the army'* but indeed, his points served as the real **catalyst for 'change'**; the politicians should have thanked him for waking them up from a deep slumber. He had successfully addressed the country's middle and lower middle class to an unprecedented show of resilience and discipline. He had successfully sent out a loud and clear message - locally and internationally – that:

> *'Pakistan is a peace-loving and disciplined state, and if given a clean, trustworthy and inspiring leadership, its people can play a crucial role in conflict prevention and peace building worldwide.'*

Articles 62 and 63 of Pakistan's constitution were meaningfully reinvented for the constitution by much-reviled Gen Ziaul Haq [*the original clauses of Articles 62-63 were there in ZA Bhutto's Constitution of 1973 which contained almost the same words but Gen Ziaul Haq had added 10-15% momentous stuff in it*] but the post-Musharraf democratic order under Pakistan's most liberal political party PPP found no difficulty in retaining the two clauses intact; hence, the embarrassment for status quo gurus was there.

> [*These articles were part of the 1973 Constitution, subsequently amended in 1974 and made harsher in 1985. Article 62 deals with the qualifications for becoming a Member of Parliament and Article 63 deals with grounds or basis for disqualification from the membership. Gen Musharraf also amended some clauses in a positive direction to clean the muddle and mess.*]

In *'the News' of 14th April 2013*, an essay pointed out that *'the moral standards, incorporated in the said articles have been interpreted by the honourable higher courts in numerous judgments, including **Shahid Nabi Malik v. Muhammad Ishaq Dar** (1996 MLD 295), that the moral and subjective qualifications are not self-executing'*, and thus could not be used as a sword to disqualify candidates on mere allegations or popular belief.

Under this judicial restraint, the *'mischief'* of Gen Ziaul Haq's constitutional intervention remained under check; though the successive so called democratic parliaments, since 1989 till today, should have found time to reconsider or reframe these provisions. The politicians wanted to do it much earlier but each time the compromises and constraints prevailed.

However, starting with the NRO case and continuing with the disqualification of former PM Mr Gilani in 2012, Articles 62 and 63 made a comeback into Pakistani jurisprudence. Though in the said later situation too, the intelligentsia believed that it was President Zardari's studious and scholarly plan to get rid of his prime minister without roars from PPP's workers.

Then a phase of disqualifications of certain parliamentarians on the basis of their dual nationalities and fake degrees was seen. These actions at the hands of the superior court, though taken after much care of due process of law, generated intense debates all around in the print and electronic media, making Pakistan a laughing stock in the name of Articles 62 & 63.

That was the moment when Dr Qadri entered the scene with an entire agenda of electoral reforms, focused primarily on capricious application of Articles 62 and 63. Dr Qadri's long march and *dharna*, initiating a cogent debate about the partisanship and bias role of the Election Commission of Pakistan [ECP] ended with loud voices and high expectations of weeding out the corrupt politicians from the electoral process; but astonishingly the SC emerged as thick shield for them all.

Taking strength from the apex court's mood, the ECP played a dubious role through the judicial officers, in their capacity as Returning Officers — grilling the prospective candidates about reciting *Dua-e-Qunoot* and the fourth *Kalima*, and ascertained their loyalty to the 'ideology of Pakistan' by asking if they knew who wrote the national anthem. All fundamental rights were pushed into *'backseat to this witch-hunt, culminating perhaps most manifestly in the disqualification of one Ayaz Amir from Chakwal for exercising freedom of speech and expression'*.

Intelligentsia also opined that application of Article 63, relating to loan defaults and criminal liabilities, required a conviction by court of competent jurisdiction, as held in judgment *BoP v. ACRO Spinning* (2012 CLD 1819) following the due process of law. The judicious application of this clause was not possible within few days, before the deadline of 17th April whatsoever; the date the final list of candidates displayed for elections 2013.

It was widely felt that the ECP and its Returning Officers used the provisions of said Articles 62 and 63 as a blanket license to embarrass, weed-out [and thus defame] prospective candidates, in a subjective and arbitrary manner. As a result the Election Tribunals had to face with a plethora of appeals, which were not at all decided within the given timeframe of six days and established standards of natural justice could not be applied. Before the Election Tribunal of Multan, comprising of two LHC judges, exactly *200 appeals were launched on 10th April 2013; in one day only.*

So, coming back and keeping in view the five-year performance of the democratically elected PPP government, during which several amendments were made in the constitution to suit the needs of the corrupt, uneducated and tax-evading politicians, Dr Qadri had rightly demanded the realistic and truthful implementation of constitutional provisions like Article 62 & 63 in letter and spirit, which could bar the defaulters from contesting elections.

Earlier during ending March 2013, the ECP announced for adding a vacant space in the ballot paper to be marked by the voter if he considered none of the candidate deserving. ECP announced for holding re-elections in constituencies where 51% of electorate would tick the *'vote for none'* option on the ballot paper; meaning thereby rejection of the whole lot of candidates.

But astonishingly, the ECP itself avoided to implement its own announcement and preferred to conduct elections as per routine gimmicks.

The Returning Officers (ROs) were asking meaningless questions about religious rituals instead of screening the character of the candidates; making a mockery of the whole process. The PAT had also demanded 30 days time in order to enable all relevant organizations to help the ECP in conducting fair, strict and meaningful scrutiny; but all wishes in vain at last.

The ROs were not sufficiently briefed by the ECP except that a questionnaire containing 40 phrases was sent to them as their curriculum. There were only three tangible criteria that were actually required to find out the suitability of aspirants to the public offices:

- *Firstly; if they had a criminal record;*

- *Secondly; if they defaulted on loans or have evaded taxes given their assets and declared properties;*

- *Thirdly; if they have been charged for forgery or cheating on account of possessing counterfeit educational degrees that they may have submitted to qualify for a member of the legislature.*

The FIA, SBP, NAB, FBR and the respective courts could easily determine a candidate's suitability to seek nomination but, due to ECP's utter bad intentions and lack of fore-sightedness, the ROs confined themselves up to *kalmas* and *duas* and nothing beyond. Uproar was natural and expected then.

The ECP during the first week of April 2013 rejected the nomination papers of **Nawaz Sharif, Shahbaz Sharif** and **Imran Khan** on the basis of discrepancies in the statements of their debts, assets, and sources of income and tax payments. These accusations, as ECP claimed, had been supported by the NAB's record. *The NAB immediately issued statement that there were no unpaid debts on accounts of both the Sharif brothers*; their nomination papers were instantly approved.

It is on record that the papers of **Musarrat Shaheen**, a veteran film actress, were approved because she had successfully recited the 2nd Kalma before the Returning Officer when asked. The RO had asked the people like **Ahsan Iqbal** to recite the Azan and approved his papers. *Ayaz Amir's* nomination papers were rejected by the RO Chakwal on the basis that he once in his writings had made an objection on the Two-nation Theory; next day his papers were approved in appeal.

**On 12th April 2013,** a full bench of the Lahore High Court, headed by Justice Ijazul Ahsan, admonished the ECP for not obeying the court's orders on provision of lists of defaulter candidates, and observed that the Commission's non-cooperation amounted to compelling the court to postpone the electoral process.

The 3-judge bench, comprising Justice Ijazul Ahsan, Mansoor Ali Shah and Justice Mazahar Ali Akbar Naqvi, had shown disappointment with the ECP for disobeying the court's repeated orders for producing defaulter's lists along with the reports, issued by national institutions like the SBP, FBR and the NAB etc. The court said that they wanted to devise some rules for the upcoming elections.

In fact the ECP was not providing the details of defaulter candidates deliberately despite various court orders. The ECP had failed to perform its duties as per the Constitution, it was argued. The court and the clients all agreed that the elections should be held on time, but a detailed review of the adverse reports of contestants was necessary before the elections. The ECP told the bench it was impossible for the commission to prepare the lists of nearly 27,000 candidates. The bench observed that as if the ECP wanted the court to stop the election process.

Amicus curie Advocates Babar Sattar and Bilal Hassan Minto assisted the bench by arguing that the office of RO was of administrative nature and it could not take action against any contestant whatsoever. The court was also told that *"the Returning Officers have no powers to interpret any article of the constitution;"* whereas the other lawyers in the court argued that *"the personal lives of the contestants should not be discussed on the basis of Article 62 and 63"*.

Purposefully a pseudo-consensus opinion was spread through media that only the public [voters] had the right of accountability of their representatives, not the Returning Officers. Finally, all agreed that the affidavits of candidates and their summary inquiry was enough for clearing their nomination papers instead of asking unnecessary questions from them.

The fact remained that the scrutiny of candidates was not held correctly and the FBR and SBP had not provided the ROs with the list of defaulters. About 1,000 appeals [out of more than 27,000 nomination papers] were filed. It was urged that the court should postpone the elections for two months so that strict scrutiny of the candidates could be held. The request was thrown away as per usual slogan of the plunderers that *'some forces want to derail the democratic system'*.

The bench, however, observed that how a RO would verify the credentials if false affidavits were submitted by a contestant. Justice Mansoor Ali Shah observed how transparency in the election could be maintained if no-objection had been filed against a loan or tax-defaulter contestant.

On the final day, over 14000 candidates survived with their nomination papers for 11th May 2013 election but details of tax defaulters had not been made public till then. *Over 4000 candidates did not posses National Tax Numbers [NTN].*

The court was urged that all mega schemes for jobs or plots announced by federal and provincial governments should be cancelled till the setting up of new governments, being a bribe to win votes at the expense of national exchequer. But ultimately this desire was also thrown in the dust bin.

The people were genuinely upset because the ECP did not have any authenticated mechanism to scrutinise the nomination papers of the contestants. Mostly the fake degree holders and defaulters were elected in the previous elections and made amendments in the Constitution for their own benefits; it was available on record.

In reality, all the election machinery was gradually bowing before demands of powerful traditional and dynastic politicians who during last five years had destroyed key institutions of the country and sunk its economy. People were demanding the care-taker government and the ECP to give no relaxation to candidates who were not fit to contest election; but their prayers and agitations were blown away in the air.

**On 13ᵗʰ April 2013**, the bench, however, issued a written order in the above case to ensure implementation of the Article 62 and 63 of the Constitution on nominees hoping to contest the coming general election; but at that particular moment, there was no likelihood that the honourable Court's orders would be considered by the governments or the ECP for implementation.

The bench, headed by Justice Ijazul Hasan, had also taken notice of the discrepancy in the data provided by the ECP and the National Accountability Bureau [NAB]. The ECP's representative had submitted a categorical written statement that *'the NAB, State Bank of Pakistan and FBR have not provided any record or list to the ECP regarding participating loan eaters or defaulters.'*

The court's six-page written order said the ECP had provided the court with data on 24,094 candidates whereas NAB had conveyed the details of 23,599 candidates. The court pointed out discrepancies between the information provided by the two departments over declaring 500 candidates and their family members as defaulters.

The LHC bench had also summoned details on the candidates whose names appeared in the list of defaulters from WAPDA, SNGPL, PTCL and other departments but the exercise went futile.

The bench, in its interim order, directed the FBR to add a column of defaulters in its records and to publish all the details on its website within three weeks but the orders were on deaf ears. On the same day, JUI(F)'s Chief Maulana Fazlur Rehman during a public address in his home town [DI Khan], urged that:

> *'The Articles 62 and 63 of the Constitution are essential to the electoral process. Those who have objections to the said articles should change it through the proper process and make necessary amendments. He would never give a returning officer the right to decide upon how patriotic he is for Pakistan.'*

The participating lawyers appreciated that the awakening process of the Pakistani nation in fact took start with the long march of Dr Tahirul

Qadri in mid January 2013 when he, in his 15th January's open public address to a million people crowd in Islamabad, enlightened them about the Articles 62 & 63 of the Constitution declaring the ECP unconstitutional, illegal, unauthorised, unlawful and un-democratic by all means.

[Though once, on 3rd July 2007; MQM had filed a reference against Imran Khan in the National Assembly under Articles 62-63 of the constitution. This was in reaction to Imran Khan accusing MQM's leader Altaf Hussain of terrorism after the murder of 43 people in Karachi on 12th May 2007 and preparing to file a case against him in the British courts. The matter, however, could not catch momentum in Islamabad or in London from either side.]

The MQM had presented a resolution against Imran Khan that 'these articles can only be applied to angels and not human beings'.

In the PM Gilani's disqualification case of March 2012, though the Supreme Court had not invoked Article 63(1)g directly and convicted the prime minister under Section 5 of the Contempt of Court Ordinance, but it did mention the said article in its verdict saying that 'the finding and the conviction are likely to entail some serious consequences in terms of this article which may be treated as a mitigating factor to the sentence they pass'.

The contesting members of the two outgoing governments kept the view that the terms like good character, good moral reputation, moral turpitude, practising obligatory duties prescribed by Islam, abstaining from major sins, Islamic injunctions, Ideology of Pakistan, bringing into ridicule the judiciary or the armed forces, etc were vague, immeasurable and hard to establish in a just way. They urged:

'For instance, in legal terms, public life is affected by crime and not sin. Morality is a relative concept and good reputation is highly subjective.

There was a two-nation theory when Pakistan was created. The Ideology of Pakistan became a usable term only after Gen Sher Ali Pataudi promoted it in 1969, soon to be desecrated in the eastern wing of the country.'

## DEMOCRACY ON RESTRAINT:

On 15th March 2013; for the first time, an elected government handed off power to another one after serving out its term in Pakistan.

The Pakistan Peoples Party (PPP) government, which came into power in February 2008, held a number of dubious distinctions – its massive corruption, its refusal to expand Pakistan's miniscule tax base by imposing industrial and agricultural taxes on parliamentarians and their legal patronage for terrorism networks, its inability to address the colossal power and gas shortages that had plagued the country, its weakness in addressing Pakistan's pervasive security problems, and its inability to stem intolerance against religious and ethnic minorities.

The PPP's achievements were more concentrated on savoury parliamentary legislation to safeguard their political family - kingdoms, from which of course, the PML(N), PML(Q), ANP and JU(I) brewed more advantage as side beneficiaries. 18$^{th}$ & 19$^{th}$ Constitutional Amendments were the glaring scenarios for which the PPP stalwarts still feel pride – and all that jugglery was manifested in the name of democracy. Amendment of Local Bodies Law in the Sindh Assembly is another example in which the PPP made drastic changes just to suit their candidates.

No law was focussed on the betterment of the general populace.

The foreign press was, however, happy that the government had gone a long way making considerable efforts to take responsibility for foreign and defence policy-making, which had been typically the domain of the army in Pakistan. They could realize that the room for such development was also provided by the sober attitude of the Army Chief Gen Kayani.

A positive development can be taken that President Zardari made unprecedented strides to pass power to the provinces, in order to mitigate the long-standing grievances of those in Balochistan, Sindh, and Khyber PK, as well as the tribal areas.

The PPP government, like the preceding civil and, military governments, did nothing to seriously reform how the FATA should be governed. The current codes date back to the colonial era and would remain a stigma on the face of democracy for which the Pakistani politicians have been dying since decades; FATA affairs has never been the priority of the ruling elite, both political and military, since 67 years.

The PPP government left numerous and daunting tasks for the next government; shortage of power and gas particularly in the industrial sector was on the top. The next government was left to bravely seek economic reforms against the wishes of their constituents and their own economic interests. This was a Herculean agenda. Although the PPP government propagated its movements by leaps and bounds during their regime but the actual depiction was totally different.

In Pakistan; the army shoulders most of the blame for failure of democracy; but it is also true that the army never came to power without reason. It remains hard fact that whenever the Generals seized power, they usually did so with the support of the people. Two cases which had escalated political crisis made army's interventions legitimate; 1957's take over by Gen Ayub Khan and 1977's Martial law of Gen Ziaul Haq can be placed in that list. After seizing power then, all the four army chiefs had declared themselves as the head of government, suspended the constitution, and dismissed the respective parliaments. The Superior Courts were made to swear an oath to the Chief Executive. Some of those with integrity had chosen not to do so and were retired or forced out, but they were easily replaced – a *'fine characteristics'* of Pakistan's typical judiciary.

In Pakistan, invariably all the in-coming Martial law Administrators announced general elections but three out of four got the elections engineered to produce a parliament that was amenable to their rule; because the army chief was not able to rule alone. This required creating a *"king's party,"* cobbled together by poaching those politicians from the existing parties who would rather serve the army than lose power altogether.

Pakistan's intelligence agencies also, at times, raised an *"opposition of choice,"* featuring Pakistan's various **Islamist & 'right handed'** parties found suitable at that given time. Country's history is replete with many such instances.

Usually after five/seven years or so the military Generals relinquished direct control and democracy re-established, but the two major political parties came up in succession – both proved in-competent. The politicians did not censured their colleagues who had collaborated with the army – in most cases they were welcomed and given much privileged slots in the cabinets. Similarly, the judiciary did not punish those justices who broke their oath to uphold the constitution –CJP Chaudhry himself twice took oath under the military directions.

Taking light from *Christine Fair's essay* of **14th March 2013**, appeared at **foreignaffairs** media site:

> '.....*worse, because the politicians feared that their time in power would be short, they focussed not on governance but rather on looting*

*what they could before they were forced either to flee the country again or tossed in jail. Whichever party landed in the opposition had often stalled the return to democracy by conniving with the army to bring about early elections.*

*In the 1990s, governments were lucky if they lasted three years. The prime minister's slot was volleyed back and forth between the inefficacious and corrupt prime ministers Benazir Bhutto and Nawaz Sharif. The army was always pleased to oblige; the chaos always made the people believe that the army saved the country while inept civilian dolts ran it into the ground – really in fiasco, disaster and shambles.'*

Gen Ziaul Haq & Gen Musharraf's military regimes over Pakistan brought negative effects on the armed forces and the population at large due to their controversial decision to cooperate with the United States in the deeply detested *"war on terror"*. More so perhaps the later General had agreed to permit US drones to operate in and from Pakistan to control Pakistan border with Afghanistan. This drone factor diminished the public support for the military, even though it remained acceptable due to its mentionable achievements in the economic fields.

Later, in ending 2013, the people had started realising that Gen Musharraf was right allowing the US drone attacks in FATA because of rising terror tides from the Taliban – Gen Raheel Sharif dealt with the same problem directly through Pakistan's own air force and military troops.

During 2008-13, the Pak-Army under Gen Kayani displayed little opposition toward the PPP government but the truth remained that the army was not in a position to abandon civilian authority. Despite several inconvenient decisions by the Zardari government, the army was unable to muster a coup.

Pakistanis were there to welcome another martial Law in an arena of corruption stories spread over all media concerns but it avoided for a simple hope that democratic system might prevail at last. *Furthermore, Gen Kayani was not from that greedy breed as the politicians were known for – a little shy, restrained and sober.*

The army was not all that helpless, especially since it still had backers in the Supreme Court. Even though the court had at times opposed the army, there was a tacit alliance between the men in khaki and the men in black when it came to managing the PPP in the given situation. CJP Chaudhury hated PPP's styles of governance – forget the old roots of enmity amongst the two. The NRO did not work for Gen Musharraf because Bhutto was killed in a suicide attack in December 2007 but it did pave the way for a PPP victory in the 2008 elections.

On the question of reinstatement of Justice Chaudhry's judiciary after PPP's take over in early 2008, the PML(N) had to pull out its ministerial component when the PPP resisted. PML(N) went on to launch massive protests against the PPP. It is believed that the months-long impasse was resolved by Gen Kayani, who, fearing that the standoff between the two parties would cause the country a colossal loss, persuaded Mr Zardari to reinstate the chief justice and its team. CJP Chaudhury, once reinstated, voided the NRO and ordered the government to reinstate all pending cases against Zardari and other PPP politicians.

Ironically, CJP Iftikhar Chaudhry behaved in a different way in Sindh. There were about 3800 NAB cases and references mostly against the members of the MQM. The CJP simply asked the government to make out an 'over-view committee' to look into all the files of all those NAB references. The committee was formed; the files were placed before it and after three days all the 3800 cases/references were consigned to record room – mysteriously declared finished and the CJP never bothered to call for details.

What a selective justice and what a quick disposal of NAB references it was. Not a single case was considered to be taken further. *The brave Chief Justice was so scared of the MQM's revenge recalling the fine treatment he was given by them on 12th May 2007 when he was simply kept confined up to the Karachi Airport lounge till evening and was un-ceremonially despatched back to Islamabad.*

The Supreme Court had apparently justified its commitment to the rule of law; had offered to the PPP government to get the NRO ratified by the Parliament within 120 days but the PPP failed to get vote of approval from within their own benches. But why the CJP Chaudhry had not okayed the formation of a similar committee here in Islamabad or Punjab as in Sindh.

Politicians notorious for corruption are abundantly available at all ranks of every Pakistani political party – including the religious ones; why Karachi or Sindh was declared highly innocent then.

Judicial activism against the PPP government touched its peak when the general populace found a viable alternative to the PPP – that was

Pakistan Tehreek e Insaaf [PTI]. The army was not at all moved when the only other option was PML(N), which had soured relationship with GHQ.

Notably, during 2011 and 2012, Supreme Court efforts to prosecute PPP politicians coincided with the sudden rise of Imran Khan, Chief of PTI. His term *'tsunami'* strengthened the electorate and mobilized them on the counter-themes of corruption, restoring Pakistani sovereignty, opposition to US drone strikes, and scaling back military cooperation with the US. When Khan's prospects dimmed, the apex court returned to its normal 'rule of law' feelings.

## *WINNERS & LOSERS IN 2013 ELECTIONS:*

Already given in detail above that in ending December 2013, Maulana Tahirul Qadri suddenly appeared on the scene. He was nonetheless able to marshal some of the largest crowds to protest against corruption. It appeared that his rapid rise, extensive funding, and access to Pakistan's media had the support of the army. His bomb - proof container, a fortified mobile residence, offered resistance to even high - velocity bullets and improvised explosive devices – even high profile Pakistani politicians were not able to afford such secure conveyances then.

Dr Qadri and his followers camped out in front of the parliament and insisted that the PPP government end its term early and form a caretaker government with his consultation. Although many of the clauses on his agenda were appealing, his methodology was shocking. Just a coincidence, that the Supreme Court in early January 2013, ordered arrest of the sitting Prime Minister Raja Ashraf in the Rental Power Cases. Dr Qadri projected it as his first winning step and his *'dharna'* in Islamabad extended.

In the end, the politicians succeeded in sidelining Dr Qadri and undercut a coup in the making. The critics termed it as a 'soft coup' through Dr Qadri but further developments around did not corroborate that fearful analysis.

Dr Qadri was able to dictate certain terms but could not achieve the real goal of *'improvements in the Election Commission rules'*, at least to make sure that the coming up Parliament would be comprised of representatives filtered through Articles of 62 & 63 of the Pakistan's Constitution.

Nevertheless, the challenges Pakistan faced were enormous: It required fiscal reforms, police reforms by changing Police rules of 1937, and a legislative overhaul – while throwing the Evidence Laws and CrPC of 1880s, Arms Act of 1965 and disgruntled Jail Manuals into the garbage bin - that would allow it to deal with the computer-era criminals and terrorist threats to the nation. The PPP's democratic government miserably failed to address such mega issues.

**Two months later;** the polling day was three weeks away but with the publication of the final list of candidates cleared by the ECP during the 3rd week of April 2013, it could be estimated that who would win and who would be disappointed. *Asif Ezdi,* in his article appeared in media *on 22nd April 2013* commented that:

> '.....*the winner is the same class of tax cheats, loan defaulters, looters of public money and other parasites which dominated the last parliament and whose foremost concern is to use their position to preserve the country's rotten political and socio-economic system which concentrates power and wealth in the hands of a small privileged class of hereditary politicians.*
>
> *And the losers are the millions of ordinary Pakistanis who have been hoping for a real political change through the ballot box that would rid the country of its predatory rulers.'*

After a 14-day period during which the eligibility of nearly 25,000 candidates was examined *under the criteria laid down in Articles 62 and 63 of the constitution, no one was disqualified for tax evasion, non-filing of tax returns, defaulting on payment of bank loans or for false declaration of assets and liabilities.* The fact that hundreds of those who had abused public trust to enrich themselves massively, cheated on the payment of their taxes or committed other misdeeds which should have disqualified them for election – but were cleared.

Doubts were raised about the ability AND the willingness of the ECP to implement Articles 62 and 63 in their true spirit. *ECP's earlier announcement on setting up of a permanent scrutiny cell comprising representatives of the ECP, the SBP, the FBR, the NAB and NADRA empowering to delve into the record of the candidates – all went into the air;* nothing moved.

As per ECP's announcement and plans, the new CELL was to be part of its political finance wing, tasked with inquiring into the annual assets declarations of members of the legislatures. That wing too, it transpired later, did not see the light of day; the ECP had buckled under the pressure of the entrenched political class based mainly in Sindh and Punjab.

Media criticism for the scrutiny process was shooting sky high. The FBR launched a belated probe into the tax matters of all the candidates to catch tax evaders. The NAB Chairman too declared that the bureau would hold another round of detailed scrutiny of successful candidates *after the elections*. But the general populace knew the dismal past record of the FBR and NAB so no one believed them.

- **Till this book going to the press in December 2015 at least, that process was not started – not on ECP cards even.**

Except some criticism from the PTI, all other political parties were delighted over the failure of ECP. Tax evaders, non-filers of tax returns and loan defaulters all were allowed to continue with their routine businesses of loot and plunder of the public money.

The two big parties, PPP & the PML[N], after gaining success through 18th Amendment **that the political parties were their family businesses –** seriously aimed at amendments to Articles 62 and 63 in order to do away with some of the disqualification clauses that they considered inconvenient.

Likewise, the PPP government did introduce a bill in the parliament seeking to remove the disqualification on holders of dual nationality and to nullify the judgement of the Supreme Court on the subject. An amended version of that bill was passed in December 2013 by the Senate but it was not introduced in the National Assembly because it lacked the necessary two-thirds majority.

In the wake of the debate over the new scrutiny process introduced for the 2013 elections, there was also a proposal from some of the politicians that Articles 62 and 63 should be restored in their original form as adopted in 1973. This effort was immediately discarded by the intelligentsia as it could open the doors to all kinds of manipulation and abuse by Pakistan's mostly tainted politicians.

In 1973's original Constitution, apart from the conditions of citizenship and age, it was left it to an act of parliament to determine the qualifications and disqualifications for election to the legislatures.

In other words, the federal government was free to add, delete or modify the said requirements at will if it had the support of a simple majority in the two houses of parliament or, failing that, through an ordinance. That power could easily be misused by the ruling party for weird political purposes. It was, therefore, kept intact that the conditions for membership placed incorporated in the constitution and could only be modified with the two-thirds majority needed for a constitutional amendment in both houses.

Some of the qualifications for membership introduced during military rules of Gen Zia and Gen Musharraf were changed through the 18th Amendment - no doubt bad laws and needed to be scrapped or modified. It should not be, for example, left to the returning officer – or some official or agency - to decide what level of knowledge about Islam would be adequate for a perspective candidate. Again in the words of **Asif Ezdi**, referred above:

> 'There was one clause of the constitution, namely Article 63 (2), which must be restored in its original form. This clause, as enacted in 1973, provided that all questions on the disqualification of a member of parliament would be referred to the Chief Election Commissioner [CEC] for decision.
>
> Under an amendment sneaked in through the 18th Amendment, the reference to the Election Commission can now be stopped by the Speaker of the assembly or the Chairman of the Senate.
>
> In other words, a member who is disqualified by the constitution can still retain his seat if the Speaker or the Chairman refuses to refer the question to the commission.'

Two well-known instances of the misuse of this power in 2012:

Firstly; the speaker refused to refer the question of former PM Mr Gilani's disqualification to the Election Commission after he was convicted of contempt of court. It was only after the intervention of the Supreme Court that he was made to quit his post.

Secondly; the Senate Chairman refused to refer the question of **disqualification of Rehman Malik** to the Election Commission despite the Supreme Court ruling that *'since he had made a false declaration on the question of dual nationality, he cannot be regarded as honest and ameen under Article 62'*. Because of the Senate Chairman's blatantly partisan ruling, the interior minister retained his seat in the upper house.

The amendment to Article 63(2) made secretly through the 18th Amendment was one instance of the many tricks - the Raza Rabbani

Committee resorted to in order to favour President Zardari. Together with other members of the Committee, **Rabbani was rewarded for such services with the grant of Nishan e Imtiaz,** although Article 259(2) of the constitution bans the conferment of any such honours on the citizens of the country.

In Pakistan, the Amendments and laws are tailored and framed as per individual needs of the ruling elite – that too in the name of democracy; after all it is Islamic Republic.

## DICTATORSHIP OF 'ELECTABLES'

Imran Khan's political start from Lahore was marvellous. He thought that so much gathering would take him in the sky and his PTI to the Parliament. Youngsters from all of the Punjab were there to listen him because he had announced for a change.

After a year, he developed thinking that to reach the Parliament, only youngsters would not be enough. He went out for *'elect-ables'*, Shah Mahmood Qureshi and Makhdoom Javed Hashmi and Jehangir Tareen joined him – it was a good gesture but the youth had taken a step back. Some people considered it as Imran Khan's mistake through which the confidence of the young generation was shaken a lot. Yet the coming elections were to prove if Imran Khan was wrong.

Imran Khan was rightly moving on Z A Bhutto's track. Bhutto's PPP had come with a slogan of change so he had swept margins from all the four provinces of [West] Pakistan in 1970's elections. In his Parliament there were every kind of people; from all walks of like, of all age, of all sects and clans, students and professors, *haris* [labour] and landlords, old and young.

Much before 1977 elections Bhutto had started depending upon *electables*; he recruited them in his PPP, given them tickets instead of poor persons who had links with masses – therefore, got a humiliating defeat and ultimately gallows, too.

Bhutto was hanged but those *elect-ables* continued to change horses with the time; as a result they were there and still there in power – earning hatred from the general populace, from all corners. *'They know which party's chips are up, you would find them there sooner or later',* was a businessman's loud thinking.

Referring to **'the Nation'** of 6th & 16th *March 2013*; a common Pakistani is skeptical given the reality of the contemporary political culture there.

It is an unsound impression that the populace in the rural areas of Pakistan is politically illiterate, conceptually uneducated and politically apathetic. Wrong – indeed, they have been powerless and oppressed for decades since the last 60 years. But now they have political consciousness and awareness of their democratic rights: they understand the underlying reasons for their deprivations, their poverty and their sufferings are now poised to fight back with adequate spirit, determination and political will.

Imran Khan's rise was witness to the above statement. He, in fact, has been instrumental in giving the nation an awareness and political consciousness of an anti-statusquo political movement. That in itself was a monumental achievement aimed to insure for the deprived people, their future dignity, self-reliance and self-determination, prosperity and survival.

Why this uprising? There were head lines in the media **on 6ᵗʰ March 2013; "PML(N) pockets Balochistan political gurus."** An analytical scrutiny of the background factors behind the said news reflected the typical mindset and the intrinsic political beliefs of the leadership involved.

Meaning thereby that inducting the traditional 'political elect-ables' into the party was the only way to ensure victory in the forthcoming general elections of 11ᵗʰ May 2013. This strategic political view also underlined that the PML(N) had no concerns with the economic and social issues related with the poor masses there – they were only interested in more seats through Sardars. The other parties like PPP or ANP followed the same pursuits.

Political agendas of any political party in Pakistan [they definitely announce during election days] are for election campaigns only. The PPP government had not bothered to see it again once the ministers took oaths nor the PML(N) government had any plan to read it again – their five years respective terms would go as per one top leader's personal whims, impulses, urges and wishful thinking.

There were, through the whole 2008-13 regime of the PPP, serious public apprehensions of the PML(N)'s role of a sham *"Muk-Muka"* democracy [give and take of wrongful gains]. The party leaders of both PPP & PML(N), behind closed doors, manipulated and collaborated on a number of national issues especially quick passing of 18ᵗʰ Amendment. The urban-rural divide in developmental schemes was also a bone of contention but solved through 'personal shares' basis.

By choosing the traditional politicians considered as *'elect-ables'* for the May 2013 national elections and exclusively promoting them and wholly depending on them for election victory, the PML(N) and the PPP both, dragged the nation backwards in time towards a political abyss – see Pakistan's Parliament & Senate. Referring to the *'Express Tribune'* of 7th **March 2013:**

> '......*the Hugo Chavez's economic and political legacy could be a model for Pakistan.... No harm in trying it....*
>
> *When Chavez came...Venezuela was one of the poorest and unequal societies in the world with around 50% of its population below the poverty line...(in 2013) extreme poverty is only visible in 3.5% of the population...Chavez's efforts meant several structural changes for Venezuela. He set up communal councils that handle local budgetary issues and legislation. The move helped improve poverty-stricken areas while empowering the people.'*

And here in Pakistan, the champions of democracy, both PPP & PML(N) had not allowed their local body elections since 2008 – *salute to Gen Musharaff who believed in decentralization of powers and budgetary allocations through local elections.*

Referring to another essay from Saad Rasool appeared in the *'Pakistan Today'* dated 17th **March 2013;**

> **The promise of democracy is larger than the simple idea of 'one man one vote'.** *The true spirit of democracy embodies the right of equal participation in all facets of the governance structure. It entails not only the right to have an opinion, but also to have the opinion be counted; not just the right to speak, but also to be heard; not only the right to vote, but the right to be counted; and, perhaps most importantly,* **not only the right to elect, but also (an equal) right to have a chance of being elected** *- [this last characteristic] must take the centre stage.'*

An appropriate question then: should the opportunity to contest for public office be the inheritance of only the very affluent and privileged? Or should the contours of democracy be extended to incorporate in its fold, those whose voices have been muted under unfortunate circumstances? Majority would agree that the doors of the electoral process must be opened to a larger fraction of the populace - surely the greatest impediment in this regard has been the forces of status quo.

Frequently, it is inherent and contained in the meanings of 'democracy' that it can be achieved only through *'education of masses'* and *'economic empowerment of the middle-class'*. Then why the PPP & the PML(N) failed to adopt that way – and when they had planned to take start – never in their five stints of rule together. Where was the starting mark?

It was possible through real **Land Reforms** [not of ZA Bhutto's in 1970s] and breaking of the *Jagirdar's role* in our politics. In a country still reeling from its history of colonial rule through a system of land revenues, hereditary power centres, and primarily an agro-based economy, the gates of democracy shall stay shut to the people at large so long as a few select families and individuals continue to own and control majority of the land.

An attempt to break this hegemony was made through Land Reform Regulation 1972, and the Land Reforms Act 1977, which introduced maximum caps on individual and family land-holdings. These reforms were challenged before the Federal Shariat Court (FSC) on the touchstone of being un-Islamic [*Hafiz Muhammad Ameen* case, PLD 1981 FSC 23 is referred], but the court dismissed the petition, holding that, firstly; the land reforms were not un-Islamic. Secondly; the FSC did not have jurisdiction to examine the validity of the land reforms, (the same being protected under Article 24 (Protection of Property Rights) and 253 (Maximum Limits as to Property) of the Constitution).

This judgment of the FSC was appealed before the Shariat Appellate Bench of the Supreme Court in the (in)famous [*Qazalbash Waqf* case **PLD 1990 SC 99**], in which a bench comprising three Supreme Court judges and two *Ulema* accepted the appeals, declaring the land reforms to be un-Islamic (despite the fact that the same, in effect, nullified other substantial provisions of the Pakistani Constitution).

Then in early 2013, as part of the larger electoral reforms challenge in the **Workers Party Pakistan** Case, Abid Hassan Minto and Bilal Minto, challenged the decision of the *Qazalbash Waqf* case, and asked for re-institution of Land Reforms, as an imperative precondition to the holding of free and fair elections. The petition argued, inter-alia, that land reforms must be introduced (and upheld as constitutional), not only as part of the constitutional mandate of Article 24 and 253 of the Constitution, but also as a necessary part of a democratic dispensation that required a 'level playing field' in the electoral process.

The Minto's Petition also emphasized how the existing feudal landholdings act as an instrument of subjugation, persistently affected the right to a 'better life' of a large proportion of our population. The petition correctly pointed out that those subjugated depend on their landowners for their livelihood and security. In such circumstances, these citizens cannot participate in the political process, as voters or candidates, in accordance with their own free will as visualized by the spirit of Article 17 of the same Pakistani Constitution.

The CJP Iftikhar Chaudhry's Supreme Court did not allocate required attention to that petition – the court's interest remained confined to the issuance of the notices to the concerned and nothing beyond. The general elections were ahead. The apex court kept on sleeping over that imperative issue which could have been the landmark of Pakistan's electoral process and its democratic hypothesis. A sarcastic saying:

*'Never mind our beloved countrymen! We'll be there once more in the Parliament; doesn't matter to which party you vote for.'*

# Scenario 120

## PRE-ELECTION POLITICAL PLAY

### *IMRAN KHAN's JALSA AT LAHORE - I:*

On 30ᵗʰ October 2011; Pakistan Tehreek e Insaf (PTI), held a rally in Lahore in which more than 200,000 supporters gathered as a show of strength against the ruling coalition as well as the PML(N) and explained the party manifesto addressing issues like welfare of minority & women's rights and corruption. It was PTI's first rally in Lahore at Minar e Pakistan, known as Iqbal Park too. This rally went 'marvellous' indicating a healthy change in Pakistani politics but the people remained sceptical of the turnout. In a city of rallies, where a singer Abrarul Haq held one on 27ᵗʰ October and PML(N) held one on 28ᵗʰ October, it was a big deal and risky also. Imran Khan, however, succeeded in making his way ahead.

Near Iqbal Park, the road was full of people; carrying flags of PTI, banners with Urdu phrases meaning thereby that: *'If not now, then when? if not us, then who?'*; posters of Imran Khan titled as *'Quaid-e-Inqilab'*, and much more. People were walking with a purpose, shouting slogans in favour of Imran Khan and against PML(N) & PPP's leadership especially naming Nawaz Sharif and Zardari.

The numbers were increasing fast but miraculously *the crowd was orderly*. Each section had three security checkpoints, where every purse and bag was checked after going through a metal detector. There were male and female police officers at each point and scattered around, enforcing security. Many of them looked shocked asking each other that where had all these people come from. A quick answer on most of the lips was that *'Lahore has woken up'*.

The stage looked huge even from distance. The backdrop was inspirational carrying the message for the people that: *'Tub Pakistan banaya tha, Ab Pakistan bachao gae'* (You had made Pakistan; now would you save Pakistan). A call for democracy indeed!

The rally finally started at 4pm. When Imran Khan appeared, the crowd went crazy: the sky was filled with flags and the shouts became louder.

Suddenly an announcement was made from the dice that 'now there are more than 2 lakh people and that 'ab cable bund kar diya gaya hai' (Cable TV has been shut down now); but the slogans mentioned above continued. The adoring crowd roared and the activity went on till the throats were sore; their arms became numb.

The fact was that over 200,000 people gathered in Iqbal Park on that Sunday afternoon had shown their frustration with the then administrators at Punjab and the capital. This kind of meeting, the enthusiasm, the excitement, the sheer numbers had not been seen before since 1967; PTI just proved that it was not one of the looting class political parties of pseudo industrialists or *jagirdars* who were exploiting the people in the name of democracy whereas they were civil dictators.

Omar Cheema, the Chief Information Officer of PTI, commented on rally's success saying that *'the youth of Pakistan has decided to take the future in their hands but it is yet to be seen whether or not we would be capable enough to translate this rally's outcome into an electoral success.'*

Imran Khan, amidst roaring shouts of beguiling slogan *'Agenda for Change'*, called for revolution to overthrow the corrupt and wrong doers and to replace them with dedicated people committed to save the country; while saying that:

> *'In 1940 at the same venue we passed Pakistan Resolution; today we have gathered here to save Pakistan from thieves, plunderers and corrupt politicians. Once for all get rid of corrupt politicians.*
>
> *Corrupt Zardari and Nawaz Sharif should learn lessons from Arab spring. We will revolutionize Pakistan and it will be a people's revolution. It's time for change; no more Sharifs and Zardaris will be tolerated. We will build a new Pakistan; corruption free Pakistan; Pakistan of Quaid-e-Azam and Pakistan of Allama Iqbal.'*

PTI's slogan was *"throw these governments out and save the country,"* but the party had no seats in Parliament and it was criticized for lacking grassroots support and the infrastructure needed to win an election.

The rally, seen as a show of strength, came two days after Shahbaz Sharif attracted some 30,000 people at an anti-Zardari protest held at *Bhati Gate & Data Darbar Lahore* where, it was said, that a crowd of that magnitude could otherwise be seen at the ending hours of each Friday prayer. Sharif's PML(N) held that rally tenaciously on *Friday dated 28th October 2011* to demand early elections in the country.

Shahzad Chaudhry, a former Deputy Chief of Pakistan Air Force, opined [referring to the 'Express Tribune' of 6th November 2011] and pointed out that, despite an un-precedented gathering of Pakistani educated and middle class people, Imran Khan would not be able to win majority in the Parliament because:

> 'He is not aware that **Pakistani politics resides in the mid-twentieth century** and the attitudes and ways of the political elite may be even more archaic. Patronage, tribalism and the **biradari** will determine who comes up atop the political pile. [In Pakistan] all that is needed is a compliant SHO, which their political clout, when in the assemblies, can easily contrive.
>
> So is the case with the district and provincial bureaucracy **where honesty is a disqualifier for mainstream** plum jobs. With an uninter-ruptible cycle of corruption now fully in place.... an overstaffed PIA; a sinking Steel Mill; broken Railways. When you input trash, what you get at the other end is unlikely to be anything savory – not different what you have pushed in.'

PAF's Deputy Chief was pleased and surprised at the number of people who attended Imran Khan's gathering at call; more importantly, they came of their own and were not pushed to or brought in Deputy Commissioner's arranged buses. They would definitely like to vote for Imran Khan but who would manage to get them or to lead them to the ballot boxes.

Secondly; what was the alternative? Vote for the status quo or don't vote and wait for yet another military General!

These two alternatives have been tested and retested in Pakistan but for sure none of them worked. They had their time more than once and the result had been a total disappointment. Let the people think and vote for a change; make an effort and try. *To those who say it's a 'one man show' but wasn't Z A Bhutto a 'one man show' as well? Bhutto's 'one man show' was so powerful that people are still voting for the promises in 1970s made by dead Bhutto in Pakistan.*

For Imran Khan to succeed PTI had to organize many such rallies throughout Pakistan; Karachi was tipped to convene a similar gathering

**on 25ᵗʰ December 2011.** Karachi, where people were still hanging in with Altaf Hussain; who had abandoned Pakistan but was controlling them through his telephonic addresses. And to Southern Punjab and Sindh where people were still basically voting for the promises made by the dead Bhuttos; and Lahore where the innocent poor junta were still **waiting for <u>Ameer ul Momineen</u>** who had once ran away from the country allegedly with their 21 boxes full of gold and dollars because the Attock Fort's cell was only equipped with one 40 watt dim bulb.

- An interesting blog on internet, placed by one Nadeem **on 7ᵗʰ November 2011** opined that: *'Imran Khan would not be able to change Pakistan for one simple reason: he was colluding with Army & ISI in his quest for power. How could a transformed Pakistan come up from someone who was receiving illegal help from the most anti-change institution?*

  *And the moment Khan pulled a Junejo on them (i.e. becomes assertive and independent) they would either fire him or perhaps ask him to make a speech at Liaqat Bagh (the Establishment's favorite spot for target killing practice).'*

The critics worried that how Imran Khan was able to gather so much crowd in Lahore unexpectedly; because the general populace wanted to exhibit their resentment towards the mainstream two political factions titled as PPP and the PML(N & Q) whose legislators in respective houses had always been interchangeable. *Barring few all were 'lotas',* the opportunists of the highest order. Most of the public had always been away from Pakistan's sham elections whether held in military regimes or in political era. To quote the exact figures:

*'During **elections of 1970**, the Awami League got 38.3% votes and the PPP got 19.5% votes whereas around 61% populace in remaining part of the West Pakistan went silent.*

*During **1977's elections** the PPP 'maneuvered' to get 77.5% votes which was immediately rejected by the people taking it as blatant fraud and the PNA agitation started which ended with Gen Ziaul Haq's martial law of 5ᵗʰ July 1977.*

*In **1988 election** the total turnout of voters was 43.1% telling that about 57% people went indifferent; in **1990 elections** the same turnout was 45.5%; in **1993 elections** the turnout was again 41%. In **1997 elections** the turnout went further low to 35.2% showing that the 64.8% people remained unconcerned.*

*In **2002** elections the turnout was 41.8% and during **2008** elections
the turnout remained 43.5%.*

*All the above figures have shown that majority of the Pakistan's
population remained aloof in general elections whereas the minority
groups getting total votes of less than 50% have been ruling the
country.'* (**Source: Daily 'Jang' of 5th August 2009**)

Imran Khan appealed to those non participant voters plus those
disgruntled voters of the main political parties in the main stream which
had contributed nothing to their voters except disappointment, despair,
misery and desolation.

## IK's LAHORE ADDRESS - II:

Several major events took place in Pakistan during elections of May
2013:

- The launch of TIP manifesto by Imran Khan on 23rd March 2013 at
  Lahore;

- Induction of 84 years old Justice Khoso as the caretaker Prime
  Minister;

- Return of Gen Musharraf to Pakistan on 24th March 2013;

- Return of Akhtar Mengal and othes just before the forthcoming
  elections. Their impact on the Pakistani politics was going to be
  unfolded over coming weeks.

Pakistan's election campaign kicked off during the last week of March
2013 with a impressive political gathering of about 1.5 million followers
for Imran Khan, a massive rally led by Dr Tahirul Qadri — plus the
surprise return of Gen Musharraf to the country after four years in self-
imposed exile, hazarding a journey expecting few political rewards —
but carried real risks to his life.

The *23rd March jalsa of TIP at Minar e Pakistan* was well attended as
expected but its leader Imran Khan did not give details of his party's
manifesto. Imran Khan decided to make his 'six promises' the focal point
of his speech – the voters knew that the main asset of the party was its
leader not its program.

The fact remained that Imran was attacking other parties as personality
cults and family businesses but in no other party except the MQM the

person of the leader was more important. He was relying almost entirely on his personal 'charisma' to win seats in the forthcoming elections. The enthusiasm of the youthful membership of PTI appeared to increase trust in himself and his program.

Referring to the *'TIME' of 25<sup>th</sup> March 2013*;

> *'The Khan's rally in Lahore was the closest Pakistani politics gets to a rock concert. The festive mood was apparent throughout the many clogged arteries that led to the venue, the landmark Minto Park in city's old quarter.*
>
> *Young men were crammed on top of brightly painted buses, whooping with joy, waving party flags and swaying to their blare of the music. A group of drummers roused pedestrians with quick-paced <u>bhangra</u> rhythms.'*

Imran Khan's admirers were drawn from all over the country through a well-financed and heavily advertised campaign. But they were also drawn by a simple yet nebulous message. *"We want change,"* echoed scores of other Khan supporters at the rally. The traditional politicians had failed their people. They were accused of being venal, inept and distant. By contrast, many supporters openly manifested that:

> *'Khan has an image of a clean politician committed to doing something for Pakistanis. People see Imran as a saviour; they don't really go much into what his policies are.'*

Gen Musharraf was unlikely to make an impact in the elections, partly because voters looking for an alternative had found Imran Khan a more attractive choice. There were concerns among some of Khan's supporters about his attitude to the Pakistani Taliban – Imran wanting to negotiate with them – and the decision to work with the *Jamaat e Islami* [JI], a hard-line religious party. But the mere fact that he represented a political force that had never compromised by power, worked in his favour. Most people held that: *'....he won us the Cricket World Cup, he built us a cancer hospital, and he's really good looking.'*

That appeal wasn't limited to women, who were more numerous at Khan's rallies than those of other parties. Young men walked around the park with T-shirts bearing a younger Khan's face on them, from his cricketing days. While other speakers shouted themselves rough on the stage, the crowd looked unmoved. The crowds chatted in small groups.

When the music played, they rose to dance. And when it came to Khan's turn to speak, the park quickly filled up. They sat down and waited intently for the closing act while saying for other speakers that:

*"We know what these opportunists are all about – these politicians have joined Khan's party over the past year, as his popularity has risen. We're only here for Imran."*

Khan relaxed about the focus on him and told **TIME's media team** that:

*"It's true all over South Asia that party leaders are important…but to achieve his ambition of coming to power, he'll have to build up a party, something that's eluded him.*

*Recent polls show that PML[N] is tipped to win the highest number of seats. While we were focused on holding internal elections, the PML[N] started propaganda against us that we had disappeared. Now, with this rally, we've shown our strength again."*

Since Khan emerged as a threat, the PML[N] has gone on the offensive. They built a mass-transit system in the city of Lahore that won wide praise, even among Khan's supporters. The PML[N]'s provincial government offered free laptops to promising students and solar panels for their homes. They also cobbled together an impressive string of electoral alliances. Since the province of Punjab held half of Parliament's seats, the main battle of the coming election was named between Sharif and Khan there – *PPP did not matter any where though they had finished their 5 years term about a week earlier.*

Media analysts had an opinion that PTI was to win about a dozen seats but PML[N]'s Kh Asif was a bit worried about Imran Khan's sweeping move. He had understanding that Khan was going to hold all PPP votes which were going to ditch their party because they had done nothing for Punjab.

Imran Khan's support, as the attendees at the rally demonstrated, was principally drawn from the urban middle classes. Better educated, more religious and more nationalistic than the rest of the country; they had praised Khan's criticism of US drone strikes in Pakistan; his stance against corruption and his own displays of religiosity. But they only represented a small, though influential, part of the electorate.

Imran Khan's educated followers were not so optimistic for his win in that election. They were seriously focussed on how best to cast their vote – a drastically positive change. But Khan was determined to win; speaking excitedly about his candidates from the youth' the people were worried that how Imran Khan could counter the money of the big and corrupt parties with an Internet - based fundraising drive of his own. Khan told the media:

> *"The party we have now is unbeatable; we're the only party that can hold big rallies in all of Pakistan's major cities, and 90% of the country wants change. The coming campaign will be like a tsunami."*

**Gen Musharraf** was courting the votes of people disenchanted with Pakistan's traditional parties. He landed in Karachi airport, vowing to *"save Pakistan."* In a sign of his limited appeal, however, only a few hundred people turned up to meet him. Gen Musharraf had dodged the threat of arrest by winning bail in cases against him. But a graver threat was the Taliban, who paraded a death squad on TV and threatened to kill him. <u>Gen Musharraf was taking an unnecessary risk for a political future which was just not there</u>, the intelligentsia and the media analysts held.

## *SC's CONTEMPT NOTICE TO IMRAN KHAN:*

**On 31st July 2013;** Chief Justice Iftikhar M Chaudhry issued a contempt notice to the PTI Chairman Imran Khan over his critical and derogatory remarks about the apex court; he was asked to appear before the court on 2nd August and explain as to why proceedings envisaged by the provisions of the Constitution and law might not be initiated against him.

The CJP took notice on the note of the Registrar SC based on press clippings of different newspapers containing the speech/remarks of Imran Khan. These remarks were fairly critical and very derogatory as regards the judiciary/judges of the Supreme Court. The notice stated that:

> '......*while holding a press conference on 26th July 2013, Imran Khan described the role of the judiciary and the Election Commission of Pakistan [ECP] during the general elections [of 2013] as shameful; that the elections were rigged, due to the role played by these two institutions.*'

Imran Khan added that the general elections of May 2013 were the worst in terms of rigging and mismanagement. Khan wanted to ensure that no such shameful elections would be held in the future adding that *'the PTI had accepted the election results but not election rigging.'*

Earlier, **on 29th July 2013**, Imran Khan had expressed a lack of trust in the judiciary and alleged that the **judiciary/*Supreme Court had a hand in rigging*** the recent elections. *On 30th July* he stated that judicial officers acting as returning officers (ROs) remained the most controversial in general elections. Khan also commented on the ***double standards of the judiciary***; he had come to the conclusion that his candidates were un-necessarily knocked down on technical grounds.

The note of the SC's registrar said:

> '....*it was hard to understand the outburst of the PTI Chairman for "unwarranted" criticism and making highly objectionable, indeed derogatory statements, against the judiciary and judges of the Supreme Court. Indeed, he used contemptuous and derogatory language against the Supreme Court and its judges.*
>
> *Fair comments could be made on judicial verdicts but it was impermissible to scandalise/ridicule the court or its judges.'*

The pro-judiciary figures held that Imran Khan's statements were aimed at *inter alia* shaking public faith and confidence in the administration of justice and undermining the prestige of the court, thereby tending to bring the court and judges into hatred, ridicule or contempt.

The Article 204 of the Constitution read with the Contempt of Court Ordinance 2003 provided for punishment for contempt of court. After going through the contents of the note of the SC's registrar, the CJP passed an order observing that:

> **"Prima facie, it seems that he (Imran Khan) has started a deliberate campaign to scandalise the court and bring judges into hatred, ridicule or contempt. Thus, his above acts call for action for contempt of court under Article 204 of the Constitution read with Section 3 of the Contempt of Court Ordinance, 2003."**

On **2nd August 2013**; the SC said the term "shameful" used by the PTI Chairman Imran Khan while referring to the judiciary was apparently abusive and not acceptable to the court. The SC rejected the rejoinder submitted by Imran Khan's legal team in the said contempt case and ordered to re-submit his detailed statement by 28th August. A 3-member bench of the apex court, headed by CJP Iftikhar M Chaudhry and comprising Justice Jawad S Khawaja and Justice Sh Azmat Saeed, heard the case and termed the reply as 'disappointing'.

The court had termed Khan's first response as 'insufficient'. In his first explanation, Hamid Khan Advocate submitted that Imran Khan had neither committed contempt of court under the law or the Constitution nor would even think of doing so. He also added that Imran Khan had not started any campaign either to scandalise the court or to bring judges into hatred, ridicule or contempt. He contended that Imran Khan believed in the rule of law, supremacy of the constitution and independence of judiciary and, for this reason he and his party were in the forefront of the movement for restoration of judiciary.

After the court's direction, Imran Khan along with his lawyer and party legislators including Javed Hashmi, Dr Sheeren Mazari and other provincial ministers went to the office of Pakistan Bar Council for consultation and later filed a second statement. In that, Hamid Khan submitted that the press statement was made in good faith on 26th July wherein reference to the judiciary was for the Returning Officers (ROs) and or District Returning Officers (DROs) who belong to subordinate judiciary. Also that Imran Khan had high esteem for the SC and had expectations from the apex court for redressal of the grievances of the PTI arising out of the general elections.

*"Restoration of the judiciary had been on my agenda. I had also spent eight days in jail for that,"* said Imran Khan in court.

The SC, however, rejected the PTI Chief's detailed response on using the word *"Sharamnak"* (shameful) for judiciary. Mr Khan's lawyer Hamid Khan insisted that it was meant for the ROs & DROs and not the Supreme Court. The court did not approve his second response as well and instructed his counsel to submit a third and more heartfelt written response by 28th August.

The court pointed out that perhaps correct facts have not been brought into Imran Khan's notice as his application was returned by the office on the same day by passing the order that it was not entertainable on the ground that instead of making this application in a pending review petition, the applicant should approach the appropriate forum and avail the proper remedy under the law.

In addition to these, the apex court ruled that learned counsel was told about 31 election petitions under section 52 of the Representation of People Act 1976, filed by the candidates of PTI before Election Tribunals requesting for, inter-alia, examining the thumb impressions of the voters through the process of biometric system, particularly, in respect of the four constituencies Mr Khan pointed out in open.

On 22ⁿᵈ **August 2013**, a three-member bench of the Supreme Court of Pakistan was constituted to hear the said contempt against PTI's Imran Khan. The bench comprised Justice Anwar Zaheer Jamali, Justice Ejaz Afzal Khan and Justice Khilji Arif Hussain, to resume hearing of the case on 28ᵗʰ August.

The PTI did not make the contempt issue as a matter of ego; whereas the party held that the SC was not attacked at all, but judiciary in general was criticised for which they had a number of cases to be mentioned as evidence. Secondly, about the comment regarding rigging in polls was not about the Supreme Court but about the 'judiciary'; the whole country was witness to the worst ever pre-poll rigging by returning officers in most places and all that was being continuously reported in media.

The PTI held before the media that criticizing any court's judgement was never a contempt of court. Rather one more objection about the judiciary that *suo moto* notices on very ordinary issues were taken by the apex court, but no *suo moto* action was taken regarding the huge bundle of complaints about rigging in polls. *PTI's petition for thumb verification only in four constituencies was not being taken up.*

PTI's MNA Shafqat Mehmood added three quick messages sent on Twitter and wrote:

- *Why contempt notice to IK when hordes of others including Faisal Abidi and Aitzaz Ahsan have questioned conduct of CJ and the SC. Why selective justice?*

- *Criticising judicial officers for bias and incompetence also does not constitute contempt as they were acting as officials of the EC and not judges.*

- *Making a fair comment on judicial decisions is not considered contempt of court in any democratic society - Notice to Imran Khan incomprehensible.*

The issues which the PTI wanted to bring to the court's notice included those of *no clear orders for ousting of tax evaders or fake degree holders, violators of law of filing mandatory income returns and not deciding issue long pendency of cases of loan defaulters.*

The said list of issues also included that the mechanism to oust any person convicted in corruption cases or who defaulted a loan was clear, but ROs and Election Commission [ECP] needed a clear direction from the Supreme Court on the issue. Former MPs refused to get their degrees verified; for some it was proved that politicians had defaulted loans as had also been verified by the SBP; some were hiding behind long stay orders from courts of law and especially when there was a list of 3.5 million citizens who were tax evaders according to joint investigations of Nadra and FBR – SC was expected to take notice of all.

PTI leaders held that when the apex court communicated an order to the ROs to provide copies of nomination papers to general public during the dates of submission for 11<sup>th</sup> May elections, *the ECP suddenly applied heavy fees on getting copies and despite this most ROs refused to issue copies.* The ECP uploaded nomination papers on web, but *only 3 or 4 percent nomination papers of non-important politicians were available on website till last date of filing objections.*

PTI leaders raised questions that the SC had ordered verification of degrees of some politicians who contested 2008 polls, lost then but again contested 2013 polls without verification. Why the SC had not ordered the verification of degrees of all such candidates *when Chairman HEC Javed Leghari was on record having said that HEC could verify any degree on the same day it is submitted*; in fact the courts went compromised, often coward and wilful criminal connivance.

Some candidates who submitted fake degrees in 2008 elections and barred but again contested 11<sup>th</sup> May 2013 polls; were allowed to go ahead - astonishing. This was something to be done by the SC and not by the ROs as it was out of their domain to order for verification of any document which was not attached with 2013 election nomination papers [as degree was not a condition in 2013 polls] and only superior judiciary could pass an order in this behalf. The records of past criminality were simply ignored by the Supreme Court and the ECP – what a justice and what fair elections.

The PTI leadership was also curious about tax and loan default cases of political elite coming pending since years, laughing at the judicial norms after getting STAY ORDERS from the higher courts. It is a common trait in Pakistan, but then why all such elements were allowed to contest polls - *Supreme Court and the ECP were wilful party to that kind of violations of Art 62 & 63 of the Constitution.*

PTI leaders also believed that members of the lower judiciary played negative role in the whole election process, and either it remained unnoticed or knowingly ignored. Evidences of rigging were mistreated.

PTI's request to verify thumb impressions of only four constituencies was ignored. PTI also believed that though ruling party had clear majority in the polls, but had all democratic forces been given the chance to run election campaign justly it could result in a better democratic process.

On 28th **August 2013;** the SC resumed hearing the contempt of court case against PTI's Imran Khan. A 2-member bench of the apex court comprising Justice Anwar Zaheer Jamali and Justice Ijaz Chaudhry heard the case. It was held that *'if the court decides that the word "Sharamnak" is not an abusive word, it will set an example; a dictionary could be consulted for the meanings. It is suggested to review the reply to take a respectable stance.'*

The reply comprising 21 pages submitted by Imran Khan through his counsels including M Anwar Qazi, Ahmed Awais, Shamsa Ali and M Waqar Rana requested the court to discharge the said contempt notice.

Mr Khan urged that the word *"Sharamnak"*, used by him was never meant to be an abuse to anyone, not even for the DROs and ROs. *"It was not used in its literal sense or connotation but it was rather used in the sense or context of unbecoming and it is humbly submitted that it may kindly be so construed."*

The PTI Chairman, in his detailed reply, once more contended that the criticism of ECP, DROs and ROs was directed at their performance which was in pursuance of their administrative duties. The counsels for Imran Khan contended and prayed that in view of the foregoing factual and legal position, no contempt was committed by Mr Khan and the said notice be discharged.

*The Supreme Court discharged the contempt of court notice.*

While speaking to the media after the notice was discharged, Imran reiterated that the word *"shameful"* was used against the conduct of presiding officers in 11th May elections only and not for the apex judiciary - the party's 2,500 - page long white paper documented the details of rigging. Khan held that the only objective of his comments was to have fair and free elections in the country. Those were the first elections to be held under judicial supervision and only the court could be called for justice.

# Scenario 121

## PRE-ELECTION ECONOMIC STAGE

### *LOAN DEFAULTERS OF PAKISTAN:*

On 16<sup>th</sup> December 2009, the CJ Iftikhar Chaudhry's Supreme Court of Pakistan had set aside the NRO for which the PPP suffered a lot and would continue to suffer for another decade or two; hats off to the PPP's advisors like Rehman Malik and Gilanis. Then PPP government's review petition on NRO was also declined in December 2011 by the apex court. The SC went vocal on the implementation of its judgment; more serious issue than the Memo-gate scandal of 2011 then.

Aitzaz Ahsan's assessment came true. The same happened as he had predicted. When the Supreme Court had dismissed the National Reconciliation Ordinance (NRO), the PPP and especially Mr Zardari & his close associates lost their credibility; the humiliation continued.

Let us see the other side of the coin:

Gen Musharraf's government had once launched an intensive drive against the loan eaters who were given one month ending in mid November 1999 to voluntarily return the loans. As per government's report, a recovery of Rs:8 billion [3% of the total defaulted amount then] was made out of Rs:146 billion. The then Governor SBP, Mukhtar Nabi Qureshi, had told that about 325 defaulters owe more than Rs:100 million each amounting to Rs:72 billion. *About 590 legislators were defaulters of Rs:9.64 billion mostly of Agricultural Development Bank of Pakistan (ADBP); 263 members were from those who were sent home immediately then.*

In November 1999, the National Accountability Bureau (NAB) was entrusted to recover the loans from the defaulters; they had arrested some of them mostly feudal, politicians, a few retired army officers and former bureaucrats. The list included Legharis, Saigols, Dreshaks, Khokhars, Kakars, Magsis, Mians, Rehmans and Farooquis. Jaffar Leghari [then a suspended senator] and Malik Asad Khan, two close relatives of former President Farooq Leghari were also among those who were nabbed by the NAB.

In the beginning, Gen Musharraf's team was impartial thus former CM Punjab Manzoor Wattoo and former federal ministers Anwar Saifullah & Faisal Saleh Hayat were also arrested along with one former Air Marshal Viqar Azim. It was perhaps the first time in Pakistan's history that such a forceful crackdown had been launched against willful loan defaulters but then the compromises, nepotism, deals and negotiations empowered; NAB became another FIA for friends and foes. Many arrested MNAs & MPAs were given ministerial slots and that NAB game continued for another eight years.

Referring to the *'Express Tribune' of 18th June 2010*, a three member bench of the Supreme Court headed by the CJP Iftikhar M Chaudry heard the loan defaulters case and remarked that *'the apex court wants to hear the case as it involves public money of Rs:256 billion'*. The Supreme Court sought the details of people who got their loans written off in the duration between 1971 and 2009.

The whole nation knew that the superior courts were never solemn in taking that case seriously throughout the last sixty years. During hearing of the NRO case in December 2009, the apex court was pointed out that it should also take cognizance of those corrupt politicians who had eaten up the poor people's savings worth billions in the name of bank loans then got waived off. *The SC had ordered then to produce the lists of loan defaulters* 'since 1971; .... we'll see'. *The court orders of 12th December 2009 are on record.*

May not be based on facts but the PPP had publicized on media that the judgment of **16th December 2009 on NRO** was hastily announced because it was mainly against the PPP and Mr Zardari in person. *The loan defaulter's list was placed before the apex Court on 22nd December 2009*, but deferred because CJP's dear sponsoring party members were named in the list; due to them the CJP Iftikhar Chaudhry was there in saddles.

The time proved it true as the facts are before everyone and has become a part of history now. The court, however, directed State Bank to provide details of all the loan cases being heard by the banking courts. *The Court adjourned the hearing till six months after [2nd August 2010] without recording any progress.*

In the **3rd week of October 2010** during another hearing, the CJP's serious warning was that *'those who had their loans written off have built empires. If they don't pay back the loans, their names should be* *put on the exit control list (ECL) and they be put behind bars.'* Nothing doing till today.

The State Bank's counsel, Iqbal Haider, produced a list of 50 defaulter companies and one Barrister MS Baqir apprised the court that Indus Sugar, a company owned by former MPA of the PML(Q) Nasrullah Dareshak, had Rs:820 million in loans written off through eight different banks upon which, the court summoned Mr Dareshak to the court on next hearing. The fact was that the State Bank had never become interested in getting the money back but always preferred to defend the loan defaulters. Not a single rupee from Dareshak's Rs:820 million could be recovered – he never attended any court.

A Senior lawyer [late] Hafeez Pirzada contended that the present *PPP government had written-off loans worth Rs:50 billion without any authority*, adding that the move was also endorsed by the executive director of the State Bank, Inayet Hussain declaring that it was part of an ongoing scheme. [*The State Bank had issued 33 circulars since 1972 to 2007 in that respect – but no one was found serious to implement them.*]

Astonishingly, the State Bank did not have the details of all companies and individuals concerned, the CJP went furious and remarked that if the banks concerned did not share the information, why their licenses should not be cancelled and the list containing names of defaulters should be published in newspapers. The CJP had also warned that if they did not pay their loans back, their properties should be confiscated and auctioned and they should be put behind bars in Adiala Jail; *but who bothers for court orders in Pakistan – stay orders are always ready* for those defaulters and then passed on to next generation.

The said *suo moto* case was initiated on the call of Altaf Hussain of the MQM who had urged that there was a need to give equal rights to everyone to improve the economy and that billions of rupees should not be given for personal benefits of some influential. According to Section 25 of the Banking Ordinance, a loan write off case should be sent to the Parliament but this section had continuously been ignored since decades.

The chief justice said that there was a need to enact new laws to give big loans against small securities. Knowingly that the whole Parliament was comprising of the *jageerdars, waderas* and such industrialists who are the proven loan eaters then who would make such laws. If *Parliament has not made the required laws in 67 years then the apex court should have made these laws much earlier.*

During the *2ⁿᵈ week of March 2011's* hearing, the Supreme Court approved the State Bank's request for constituting a commission for loan recovery and sought the opinion of banks and their customers and loan defaulters within four days. *The State Bank's governor agreed to form a 3-member commission headed by Justice (retd) Saleem Akhtar. It was proposed that:*

> 'The commission should be empowered to impose heavy financial penalties on loan defaulters and to send them behind bars because that is what they are afraid of.
>
> Only a powerful commission can ensure that the loans are recovered. Citing Circular 29, it was considered a viable document on banking laws but it has been misused. Banking rules need to be amended through legislation to stop misuse of loans and to increase the number of banking courts.
>
> People obtain loans to set up businesses and have their loans written off to install more firms. Loans waived off in Pakistan are far greater than anywhere else in the world. People don't pay taxes, why would they return their loans.'

**[In Pakistan it is very old and tested technique that if the government or the court wants to thin out some issue, or to detract people's attention from it, or to make the fools forget corruption; make out a commission or committee. The poor people will forget every thing soon.]**

Till the last day of 2011, not a single loan was recovered; not a single property confiscated, not a single man was jailed or convicted – it was CJP Chaudhry's Supreme Court. No one chased that NRO even, why the SC's decision has not been implemented yet.

On 14ᵗʰ March 2013, well before general elections of May 2013, the Supreme Court made public a report evolved by a 3-member judicial commission led by Justice Syed Jamshed Ali in respect of the persons who had got waived their loans since 1972. A 3-judge bench led by CJP Iftikhar M Chaudhry took up the case for hearing. With the opening of that report several names of important figures appeared and exposed - sword of disqualification was likely to hang over the heads of several politicians.

*Major defaulters among the politicians were Chaudhries of Gujrat who defaulted in payment of six loans worth Rs:109.66 million against*

*Phalia Sugar, Punjab Sugar and Sapco Limited; Ittefaq group Rs:83 million against Ittefaq Foundry, Saifullah's Rs:37.3 million while Zardari group was in default of Rs:7 million.*

*The total amount waived off as loans from 1972 to 1996 was over Rs:200 billion. Three lists of bad loans were published since 1993, the first by caretaker PM Moeen Qureshi, followed by two lists by Benazir Bhutto and caretaker government of Meraj Khalid in October 1996 and January 1997 respectively. The bad loans which were Rs:1,340 million when Z A Bhutto was removed in July 1977 swelled to Rs:80 billion in August 1993, Rs:126 billion in November 1996 and Rs:130 billion in January 1997.*

Some notable beneficiaries of loans written-off before August 1993 included New Era Textile (Rs:136.7m), Hashwani Hotels (Rs:120 m), Fancy (Rs:64.89m), Colony Group (Rs:51.4 m), Saifullahs (Rs:39.21m), Hyesons (Rs:35.7m), Habib group against RKD Sugar (Rs:17m), Saigol against Omaryar Limited and Kohinoor Textile Mills (Rs:17.1m), Mian Mansha (Rs:7.5m), Bibojee (Rs:4.2m), Packages (Rs:4.2m) and Bawany (Rs:2m).

*According to details, 244 loans were written-off amounting to Rs:4,724 million between March 1985 and August 1993 but the number of written-off loans increased to 942 in November 1996 valued at Rs:8,247 million. Thus during her second term, Benazir government wrote-off 698 loans worth Rs:3,550m.*

The 698 beneficiaries of written-off loans under Benazir included *Farooq A. Sheikh with five loans worth Rs:500 million* in Adamjee Industries, Dost Mohammad Textile Mills, United Exports and United Group of Industries were written-off. *Six loans worth Rs:131m of Jan Mohammad* relating to Charsada Sugar Mills were written-off. A few other beneficiaries were: Saifullahs, Hashwani, House of Habib, B.D Avari, Taufiq Sayed Saigol, MNA Shahid Nazir and former NA Speaker Gohar Ayub.

*Top Defaulter groups, concerns and persons [in Pak rupees (Rs)] till January 1997 remained Ittefaq 3,013m; Tawakkal 2,956m; Fazalsons 2,800m; Bela Chemicals 2,339m; Chaudri Shujaat 1,557m; Abdul Shakoor Koladia 1,254m; Fauzi Ali Kazim 1,159m; Saigol 1,086m; Naqvi 1,056m; Zahur 1,028m; Abdullah Al-Rajaih 1,031m; Ghani 903m; Habib 845m; Adamjee 832m; Hashwani 640m; Arabian Sea Enterprise 626m; Sargodha 581m; United 501m; Chakwal 441m;*

*Dawood 376m; Bawany-Alnoor 352m; Fateh 213m; Packages 166m and Colony 81m – Total Rs:25,389 million.*

**The Nation dated 23rd September 2010:** State Minister for Finance and Economic Affairs Hina Rabbani Khar said that during 2008-10 financial years approximately Rs:50.85 billion loans were waived off by banks; 252,114 people and companies were benefitted.

While Pakistan owed $31.16 billion to World Bank, Asian Developmental Bank [ADB] and the IMF including $3.63billion as added interest. Breakup remained as $11.49 billion to World Bank with an interest of $1.69 billion on these loans and Pakistan owed $11.58 billions to ADB that added $1.49 billions interest and loan of the IMF was at $8.7 billion.

Flood Tax was once imposed after its approval from the parliament. After prevailing flood devastations of 2010, the government had reviewed its expenditures to tackle flood wreckages in the country however the parliament's approval had not been sought. During 2009-10 fiscal year $2.20 billion investments were made in the industrial sector that was 40% less as compared to the investments made during the year 2008-09.

The Parliament was told that *till 30th June 2010* total value of foreign loans on Pakistan was $55 billion adding that waving of loans had not been an easy task because if loans were written off then in future the country would not be able to get loans due to its negative implications.

One could see the helplessness or the connivance of the then political elite with wrong doers that the State Minister for Finance and Economic Affairs **Hina Rabbani Khar was given the said portfolio to manage maximum relief for her own person and family.** See the details:

NIB Bank gave an *unprecedented relief to Galaxy Textile Mills*, owned by one Mr Feroz, husband of Hina Rabbani Khar; re-scheduled Galaxy's short and long terms loans of Rs:190 million for next 10 years and to put cherry on top of this deal, all of the markup was waived off. The loans were taken six years earlier. Moreover; all loan default cases in banking courts and Lahore High Court were also notified as withdrawn.

The loan of Rs:130 million was taken from Pakistan Industrial Credit Investment Corporation Limited [PICIC] on short term and long term basis. The borrowers included Hina Rabbani Khar's father in law Arif Gulzar, spouse Feroz Gulzar and brother in law Asad Gulzar. Rs:100

million of debt were taken from PCBL in different dates and for different time period. The debt had to be paid back till 31st July 2007, but was not paid.

If someone asks whether this rescheduled loan of Rs:190 million would ever be paid? It would be a stupid question to ask. After all, *'Who really cares and who will really remember after ten years?'*.

## MILLIONAIRES DOUBLED IN 2012:

As per information released by the State Bank of Pakistan [SBP] in the 2nd week of February 2012, top 24,000 millionaire account holders in Pakistan then owned Rs:2,118 Billion; 0.02% of Pakistani owned 40% of bank deposits. Interestingly, during 2008-12, presumed to be the worst years for Pakistan's Economy, the number of *crorepati* (multi-millionaires) in Pakistan increased by 50%; from 24,000 in 2008 to 36,500 in 2012.

The new 12,000 millionaires added about Rs:800 billion in bank deposits in the previous three years. Of course they were not depositing everything, there must be properties and other investments involved which were not included in this figure. 24,423 account holders, having an amount Rs:10 million and above, made a total deposit of Rs:1,323 billion at the end of December 2008. The figure of account holders rose to 36,509 by the end of December 2011, taking the total amount to Rs:2,118 billion.

The economic growth during the same four years registered an average of 2% only thus validly questioning about the source of income of these 12,000 people who mysteriously became multi-millionaires while Pakistan's economy was facing joblessness, security conditions, trade barriers and acute power shortage etc.

In that PPP's era, the key question with the SBP and the government was that what could be done with that kind of wealth? In such situations, the answer depends on who you're asking. Had those entire millionaires decided to acquire stake in companies listed in Karachi Stock Exchange - they could acquire KSE's top 30 companies at four times more price of each share. The companies could have included OGDC, Nestle, Unilever, PTCL, MCB Bank, United Bank, Habib Bank, Bank Alfalh, National Bank, Attock Refinery, National Refinery, Engro Corporation, Dawood Hercules and 17 other giants; OR all those top 30 companies with only 25% of their wealth.

Next question arose if that money was all illegal: very simple answer that *'given the economic conditions and tax evasion practices followed in Pakistan, this cannot be ruled out at all.'* It was 2012 – but the same is true today in ending 2015.

On 1st June 2012, the PPP regime read over their fifth annual budget of Pakistan once more painting a rosy picture for the poor populace of this *'beggar nuclear power state'*.

In an interview [*'the News dated 1st June 2012* is referred] with the Wall Street Journal, Yaseen Anwar, Governor State Bank of Pakistan [SBP], drew a sorry picture of why Pakistan's economy in the mess it was, not the least because of government borrowings from the central bank, were to the tune of $4.8 billion only in that financial year.

Governor SBP admitted that lending to the government was not only highly inflationary, it had also "crowded out" private investment, which was an important factor in fuelling economic growth. With the government borrowing so heavily from the market, investment in Pakistan was about 12.5% of the GDP, its lowest level in 60 years.

The biggest problem here was that *as SBP Governor, he didn't have the autonomy to turn away the government when it came calling to borrow more money.* The last governor who had tried to assert his autonomy was Shahid Kardar and after long running differences with the government over *borrowings and large allocations to the highly political Benazir Income Support Fund,* Kardar had to resign, unwilling to compromise on the autonomy of the State Bank.

Mr Kardar's successor had openly admitted that he had limited autonomy and was having difficulty convincing the government to fix its poor fiscal management habits.

After the SBP Governor's warning, the government's failure to get a massive budget and mounting trade deficit under control made it very difficult for it to meet more than $4 billion in IMF loans due in July 2012. The PPP government's solution to cover the deficit resulted in printing more money. Despite the fact that even the most basic economics teaches that hyperinflation results when a government prints money instead of collecting taxes to fund government activities. Indeed, printing notes in an environment of dismally low economic growth brought high inflation combined with high unemployment called stagflation.

The scenario made it clear that the real problem facing Pakistan's economy was not economic impediments – because promising fundamentals existed – but that it was in the hands of irresponsible managers. Pakistan had no option but to go knocking at the doors of IMF and World Bank once again.

In the past, whenever governments turned to the IMF, it was not to reform the economy but for new and ongoing development projects, supplemented by additional lending and debt relief by other international financial institutions and bilateral sources to meet their immediate foreign exchange requirements. But in this PPP regime, all such transactions were marked by a lack of genuine commitment to carry out the necessary policy reforms. And almost every time Pakistan had to compromise and agree to political, strategic or diplomatic interests of those remote controlling world bodies.

## *TAX RETURNS OF PAKISTANI LEGISLATORS:*

Referring to most *media reports dated 12ᵗʰ December 2012*, a study titled "**Represe-ntation without Taxation**" by investigative journalist Umar Cheema tried to take Pakistan's elected leaders to task for paying little or no tax despite an estimated average net wealth of $882,000. the report observed that:

> *"The problem starts at the top. Those who make revenue policies, run the government and collect taxes have not been able to set good examples for others. 62% of the members of the Cabinet have not filed their Tax Return this year, 36% of them have filed the returns whereas for the remaining 2% there is no basic data for tax information available."*

Till ending 2012, Pakistan had one of the lowest tax-to-GDP ratios in the world, estimated at 9.2%. Only 260,000 out of 180 million citizens had paid tax consecutively for the last three years, according to the Federal Board of Revenues (FBR) figures.

Pakistan's refusal to implement sweeping tax reform was instrumental in the collapse of a $11.3 billion IMF bailout programme in November 2010. The country was one of the biggest recipients of Western aid – payouts which US Secretary of State Hillary Clinton and British PM David Cameron said were difficult to increase when Pakistan's own elite did not pay tax.

The report, which marks the launch of the Centre for Investigative Reporting in Pakistan, based its findings on information from the FBR and lawmakers themselves. It urges politicians to disclose their tax returns voluntarily in future.

Discussing the party-wise position then, in the Pakistan peoples Party [PPP] only 52 Parliamentarians had filed their Tax Returns while 108 members had NOT, data for 8 members were not traceable. In the PML[N] only 33 members had filed their Tax Returns while 73 had NOT. In PML[Q] only 18 members had filed their Tax Return while 39 had NOT. In Mutehida Qaumi Mahaz [MQM] only 11 had filed their Tax Returns while 21 had NOT. In the Awami National Party [ANP] only 3 members had filed their Tax Returns while 21 had NOT. Amongst the Independents only 6 members had filed their Tax Returns whereas 24 had NOT considered it worth.

Amongst the non-filer leaders were Maulana Fazalur Rehman JUI[F]'s Chief, Makhdoom Faisal Saleh Hayat of the PPPP, Faisal Karim Kundi the Deputy Speaker National Assembly, Aftab Sherpao Chief of PPP[S], Pir Saddaruddin Rashdi of PML[F], Yaqoob Bazenjo of BNP[A] and Asfand yar Wali Khan Chief of the ANP.

The height of lawlessness was that the then *sitting President Asif Ali Zardari had not filed a tax return in 2011 and neither did 34 of the 55 Cabinet members including Interior Minister Rehman Malik.* Of the 20 cabinet ministers who did pay for 2011, most made only negligible contributions, including Prime Minister Raja Pervaiz Ashraf, with Rs:142,536 and Foreign Minister Hina Rabbani Khar with Rs:69,619 only.

The cabinet member who paid the most was Water and Power Minister Ahmad Mukhtar with Rs:1.09 million. Religious Affairs Minister Syed Khurshid Ahmed Shah paid the least with Rs:43,333.

The highest tax payer Parliamentarians in 2011 included Aitzaz Ahasan – Rs:12,975,996; Abbas Khan Afridi – Rs:11,228,592; Talha Mahmood – Rs:7603,719; Farogh Nasim – Rs:4565,137 and Osman Saifullah Khan – Rs:1795,874. Similarly the lowest amonts tax payer Parliamentarians were Mushahid Hussain Sayed – Rs:82; Kh Karim Ahmed – Rs:3636; Haji Saif Bangash – 4063; Naseema Ehsan – Rs:4280; Malik Salahuddin Dogar – Rs:8659.

Referring to *'the guardian' dated 4th April 2013;* a report from UK's Parliamentary Committee on International Development urged the Department for International Development (DfID) to focus more closely on supporting the rule of law and anti-corruption efforts while deciding financial aid for Pakistan. Malcolm Bruce, the Chairman of the Committee said:

> *"Many people in Pakistan who live below the poverty line gain from the projects supported by DfID's valuable programmes in education, health and governance. But Britain should increase aid to Pakistan only if there is clear evidence that the newly elected government will increase tax revenues.*
>
> *In particular, we cannot expect people in the UK to pay taxes to improve education and health in Pakistan if the Pakistani elite does not pay meaningful amounts of income tax."*

DfID was proposing to increase bilateral aid to Pakistan to £446m in 2014-15, from £267m in 2012-13, making this strategically important country the largest recipient of UK aid. *'Despite its status as a middle-income country, about one in three Pakistanis live on 30p a day or less, one in 11 children die before their fifth birthday, and half of all adults, including two-thirds of women, are illiterate, with 12 million children out of school'.*

Britain's MPs expressed particular concern at Pakistan's tax system, in a country notorious for corruption and tax evasion. Pakistan shamefully ranked low on **Transparency International's corruption perceptions index – coming joint 139th out of 176 countries** – and had weak auditing and budgeting procedures.

The report noted that for the past decade, tax in Pakistan as a proportion of GDP remained at or around 10%. This compared with tax collection rates of around 14% to 15% of GDP in countries with similar per capita incomes. Pakistan's VAT efficiency remained at 25%, the lowest in the world (Sri Lanka's is 45%).

According to the Pakistan's FBR, around 0.57% of Pakistanis – only 768,000 people – paid income tax during 2012, with only 270,000 paid something each year over the past three years. No one had ever been prosecuted for tax fraud for at least 25 years. The report observed that:

> *"Historically, Pakistan has been able to water down calls for longer-term internal reform, notably on taxation, because of short-term geopolitical concerns of western donor countries. This trend now has to end, and the UK must work alongside other donors and especially use its influence within the IMF to encourage urgent reform within Pakistan."*

However, the members of the Parliament knew that *'it's unlikely that this important conditionality [linking UK-aid to the effective Tax Collection] will have any teeth within the next two or three years when DfID's funding is set to rise so dramatically.'*

Education had been the DfID's largest programme in Pakistan, absorbing half of the bilateral aid programme. Other key areas were **governance, security and maternal health**, with smaller programmes on humanitarian assistance, wealth creation and vulnerability. In response to the development committee's report, and the apprehensions shown by the MPs, the DfID spokesman said:

*"We have made it clear to government and opposition politicians in Pakistan that it is not sustainable for British taxpayers to fund development spend if Pakistan is not building up its own stable tax take.*

*Following the election we will make available practical assistance to the incoming government to help deliver reform of the Pakistan tax system and work with the IMF, but tax and economic reform must take place."*

Umar Cheema had done a sort of miracle who triggered a public outcry when his organization published two reports showing that nearly 70% of Pakistani lawmakers did not file taxes in 2011 and around half did not file in 2012. Cheema told that:

*"Information is the first step towards change. Tax has become part of the mainstream debate and people are getting radicalised about tax evasion by the rich."*

The publication of the directory makes Pakistan the fourth country in the world – after Sweden, Finland and Norway – to publish the details of all individual and corporate tax payers. Citizens were asked to file any abjection within a month if they wanted to dispute the records.

Finance Minister Ishaq Dar held that the directory was a response to criticism by British and American donors who had questioned why they were sending development aid when wealthy Pakistani lawmakers refused to pay up. *'While Pakistani parliamentarians do not pay taxes ... why should we spend our tax payers' money?'* the Western donors had the valid question.

The directory contained the details of everyone paying tax in Pakistan and how much each paid. Authorities also had a much bigger database of 2.3 million wealthy tax defaulters; with details of their cars, foreign travel, mansions and bank accounts. That was not made public due to unknown reasons.

However, by publishing those figures, the job was not complete. The FBR could have pulled up its officers and staff, start an investigation and prosecute them; otherwise what was the purpose of publishing that list? It was just wasting time and stamping the bad governance on behalf of the sitting governments. Many judges, Generals and legislators were not on the 17,000 page list, thus the said list also needed improvements.

But Pakistan's problems were beyond just collecting more taxes – **the state officials still keep habits of wasting huge amounts of public funds on perks, ceremonies, state protocols, official cars and vehicles, residential plots and lands for themselves and VIP treatments in the name of security** coupled with tens of more luxuries.

Prominent candidates for National Assembly belonging to influential political and business families despite being very rich and holding huge assets paid only a meagre income tax in year 2012. The clearance certificates granted to them by the Federal Board of Revenue [FBR] divulged that they paid small amounts in taxes.

On 13ᵗʰ April 2013; some *details were released by the State Bank of Pakistan* [SBP], sent to the Election Commission of Pakistan [ECP] showing key politicians or their spouses' outstanding or written-off loans. These details, however, didn't cover the entire five-year period when they were sitting in the assemblies and Senate as lawmakers.

The certificates issued by the SBP only said: "*Details of overdue/written-off loans amounting to Rs:2 million or above for the last one-year reported by the financial institution as on Feb 28, 2013.*" This clearly indicated that any *loans written-off before the year 2012 were not covered in the documents – the poor populace was blatantly betrayed.*

Even the ECP had not asked information for the earlier periods – who had manoeuvred the ECP to make fool of the Pakistani nation; to whom the ECP intended to extend special relief and benefits; on whose instance the ECP asked so limited information; was that act of the ECP proved its independent nature of that body; was the question asked worthy of characters of those retired judges sitting there as members; had the ECP fulfilled their constitutional obligations for which the body had been made AND through such gimmicks how could the ECP ensure fair elections.

Despite such loopholes, some details still came out. One such example was that of former foreign minister **Hina Rabbani Khar** whose spouse, Feroze Gulzar, got a loan of a local bank amounting to Rs:56 million written off. Her father **Ghulam Rabbani Khar** also got a loan of Rs:109 million written off. He still had Rs:55.24 million overdue loans taken from three banks.

During the year 2012, Ms Hina Rabbani Khar paid Rs:145,142 tax although her income, declared by herself, was Rs:3.14 million in the year; in year 2011 she had paid her income tax as Rs:69619 only; meaning thereby that her income was exactly doubles within a year.

It remained a fact that in banking sectors '*overdue category of loans indicated that the loan had not been performing smoothly and it was possible that some amount had only been recently paid to get the outstanding loan out of "non-performing loan" category.*'

Among other people paying only a meagre tax included **Nawab M Yousuf Talpur** who paid Rs:57,064 tax in 2012 which was deducted at source from his salary as an MNA. But his declared income in the year was Rs:9.49 million as per documents on record.

**Munawar Ali Talpur** paid Rs:92,031 tax for a declared income of Rs:8.64 million in 2012. The statement of assets submitted to the ECP showed that Mr Talpur had more than 207 acres of agriculture land, Rs:1.5 million worth of farm animals and arms and ammunition worth Rs:747,000 apart from other assets and residential properties.

Similarly, his spouse, **Ms Faryal Talpur**, who is the sister of President Asif Ali Zardari, paid Rs:295,245 tax against Rs:22.42m income in 2012.

Another sister of President Asif Zardari, former MNA **Dr Azra Fazal Pechuho**, had an erratic income record, according of documents submitted in the ECP, her income was nil in 2010, but it suddenly increased to Rs:8.91 million in 2011 and in the year 2012 her income jacked up to Rs:11.18m. Out of this amount, she paid Rs:311,407 in tax.

**Mr Noor Khan of the PPP**, who himself acknowledged to be a multi-billionaire, paid only Rs:80,284 tax in 2012 as per certificate released by the FBR to the ECP.

- According to tax experts, on an average any person **LIKE AN MNA or SENATOR** getting a monthly salary of around Rs:120,000 pays around Rs:80,000 income tax, annually.

According to FBR, *Mr Noor Khan* paid Rs:67,479 tax in 2011. In his statement filed in the ECP, Mr Khan, who was *an MNA from NA-3 Peshawar*, himself told the net worth of his assets was more than *Rs:32 billion*; including 200 acres of agricultural land and commercial properties, a Prado, a Land Cruiser, 2.20 kg gold of his spouse etc.

PPP MNA from KPK and former federal minister *Dr Arbab Alamgir Khan* paid Rs:266,957 tax in 2012 out of Rs:1.90 million income. However, net worth of his assets was Rs:2 billion, including Rs:44m apartment in Dubai and agriculture & commercial lands.

*Mehboobullah Jan*, a former MNA from Kohistan, who was a candidate for NA-23 in up-coming polls, held assets *worth Rs:5.40 billion* - included real estate businesses, agricultural land worth Rs:1.9 billion, timber business worth Rs:2 billion and a construction company worth Rs:2.2 billion and two vehicles worth Rs:7 million. *However, he had no National Tax Number [NTN] and hence no tax filing record.*

*Ameer Muqam*, a PML[Q] candidate for NA-31, *paid no tax in 2012* despite earning *Rs:3.8 million* in the year because of adjustments made in the previous filing of his tax returns. In 2011, he paid Rs:28,094 tax and in 2010 he paid Rs:19,058 despite the fact that his income in those years was Rs:4.73 million and Rs:4.89 million, respectively. Mr Muqam stated in his statement that total worth of his businesses and other property, including agricultural land, was more than Rs:163 million. He had 17 vehicles, including a bulldozer, tractors and a bullet-proof Land Cruiser.

*Hamza Shahbaz Sharif* paid Rs:3.52 million tax in 2012. His income was Rs:12.5 million. PML[N] leader *Nawaz Sharif* paid Rs:2.20 million tax in the year 2012.

*Makhdoom Amin Fahim* paid Rs:1.35 million tax against his income of Rs:6.66 million in 2012. However, his spouse, *Ms Rizwana Amin,* owed Rs:16.91 million in terms of overdue bank loans.

Former MNA *Shahid Khaqan Abbasi* of PML[N] paid Rs:1.34 million in tax. He was the CEO of a private airline worth Rs:1.80 billion. The worth of his other assets, including property in Murree and Islamabad, was around Rs:300 million.

Former deputy prime minister *Ch Pervaiz Elahi* paid Rs:1.26 million tax and Rs:90,775 in terms of agricultural income. Former interior minister

*Aftab Khan Sherpao* paid Rs:58,882 in terms of taxes in 2012. His income was Rs:2.98 million in that year.

Former federal minister *Syed Khursheed Shah* paid Rs:97,190 tax in 2012 and he paid Rs:41,516 in tax in 2011.

PML[Q] leader and industrialist *Humayun Akhtar,* paid Rs:210,832 tax in 2012. His income in the year was Rs:1.59 million. PTI Vice Chairman *Shah Mehmood Qureshi* paid Rs:587,500 tax in 2012 out of an income of Rs:5.24 million.

In nut shell, most politicians and election candidates belonging to influential political and business families were found to be paying income tax even below the salaried executives. As many as *10,000 out of 24,000 candidates who have filed their nomination papers for National Assembly as well as four provincial assemblies and reserved seats do not have National Tax Numbers (NTN).* The certificates issued by the State Bank and other commercial banks provided a legal cover to their long standing clients.

<u>The exercise brought results.</u>

On 11<sup>th</sup> April 2015; the FBR issued the tax directory for the year 2014, which illustrated that 1,040 of total 1169 legislators, including all members of the Senate, the National Assembly and the provincial assemblies, had filed their income tax returns. The due process was underway for the remaining parliamentarians, who had failed to file income tax returns.

According to details, PM Nawaz Sharif paid Rs:2.61 million tax during 2014. Senate Chairman Raza Rabbai paid Rs:685,707; Finance Minister Ishaq Dar Rs:2.29 million; Interior Minister Ch Nisar Rs:641,284; Defence Minister Kh Asif Rs:311,638; Petroleum Minister Shahid Khaqan Abbasi Rs:2.21 million; Railways Minister Kh Saad Rafique Rs:2.04 million; Planning Minister Ahsan Iqbal Rs:130,749; Information Minister Pervaiz Rashid Rs:313,681 and National Assembly Speaker Ayaz Sadiq paid Rs:327,895 income tax during 2014.

Meanwhile, Opposition Leader in National Assembly Syed Khurshid Shah paid Rs:100,054 income tax; PTI Chairman Imran Khan Rs:218,237; JUI-F Amir Maulana Fazlur Rehman Rs:15,688; Awami Muslim League Chief Sh Rasheed Rs:303,893; Dr Farooq Sattar of MQM Rs:89,935; Shah Mahmood Qureshi Rs:1.5 million; Dr Shireen Mazari Rs:1.1 million; Pervaiz Elahi Rs:1.34 million; Ghulam Ahmad Bilour of ANP

Rs:17,271 and former Speaker National Assembly Dr Fehmida Mirza paid Rs:59,281.

MNA Hamza Shahbaz Sharif paid Rs:4.88 million tax, MNA Aftab Ahmad Khan Sherpao Rs:1.68 million; former KP Chief Minister Ameer Haider Khan Hoti Rs:31,377; MNA Omar Ayub Khan Rs:3.48 million, Prime Minister's Son in Law Cap (r) Mohammad Safdar Rs:39,900; PTI MNA Asad Omar Rs:489,457; Minister of State for Water and Power Abid Sher Ali paid Rs:112,415; PTI MNA Shafqat Mahmood Rs:72,095 and PPP MNA Faryal Talpur paid Rs:4.8 million.

Punjab Chief Minister Shahbaz Sharif paid Rs:5.13 million tax; Sindh CM Qaim Ali Shah Rs:111,772; KP CM Pervaiz Khattak Rs:660,619 and Balochistan CM Dr Malik paid Rs:63,443 income tax for the year 2014.

Leader of House in the Senate Raja Zafarul Haq paid Rs:99,446, Leader of Opposition in Senate Aitzaz Ahsan Rs:10.2 million, Senate Deputy Chairman Maulana Abdul Ghafoor Haideri Rs:30,169; PPP Senator Rehman Malik Rs:17,379; MQM Senator Farogh Naseem Rs:10.6 million; former Finance Minister Saleem Mandviwalla Rs:1.2 million and ANP Senator Shahi Syed paid Rs:622,569.

The senators who did not pay any tax last year were Gul Bushra, Mir Naimatullah Zehri, Muhammad Usman Khan Kakar, Sardar Muhammad Azam, Shahbaz Khan Durrani, Hilal-ur-Rehman, Iqbal Zafar Jhagra, Maulana Ataur Rehman, Muhammad Javed Abbasi, Sirajul Haq, Sittara Ayaz, Saleem Zia and Nighat Mirza.

The fact remained that for the first time tax directories have been published for the second consecutive year. The Finance Minister Mr Dar himself confirmed that the number of taxpayers in the country had gone beyond 0.8 million.

# Scenario 122

## NAB MALIGNED SUPREME COURT:

## *ADM'L BOKHARI's LETTER TO ZARDARI:*

**On 23rd January 2013,** NAB's Chairman Admiral (Rtd) Fasih Bokhari termed Pakistan's superior judiciary as the 'most corrupt institution'. *He told in a video conference with NAB staff on Kamran Faisal's death that the Supreme Court [SC] wanted its man appointed in NAB but he refused.*

The NAB officers were on pen-down strike throughout Pakistan to mourn and protest the mysterious suicidal death of their colleague, Kamran Faisal. A Deputy Director from NAB's provincial office of Khyber-PK Khawar Ilyas had questioned his Chairman that:

> *'Since the government is a party in Kamran Faisal case with PM among the key accused in RPPs scam, the [Justice Javed Iqbal's] Commission appointed by the government lacks credibility. We suggest that Kamran's murder should either be investigated by a serving judge of the Supreme Court or anybody notified by it.'*

NAB's Chairman started fuming and said:

> *'You should know that the judiciary is the most corrupt institution of Pakistan. I don't trust the present judiciary. The NAB would undertake its own probe in case the officers are dissatisfied with Javed Iqbal Commission report.*
>
> *Do you know why Supreme Court served me contempt notice thrice? Let me explain it today. Supreme Court wanted me to induct the (former prosecutor) Raja Amir in the NAB that I refused. Due to this reason, the Court has turned against me.'*

Adml Bokhari also turned his guns at the Jang Group, telling the audience of the video conference that *'they are the biggest tax defaulters. We are investigating against him therefore they have turned against us.'* Jang Group's spokesman, however, rebuffed NAB's claim vigorously; it was a routine denial.

NAB's Charmin had to face questions about the *'rejected coins'* surrounding him in the NAB; he, however, expressed his dismay over the officers' mistrust.

An issue was also discussed; the appointment of Kamran Faisal and other officials for RPPs scam despite the fact they did not have any investigation experience. Kamran Faisal, had IT background and did only a basic course of investigation, yet he was put on such a high profile case. Likewise, Raza Khan, the Additional Director, was made case officer in the RPPs scam investigation when he did not have any investigation experience though. Maj (R) Shehzad Saleem, Director Administration and Human Resource, was also assigned the same task despite no experience of investigations.

Admiral Bokhari simply ignored those questions.

**On 27th January 2013,** NAB's Chairman Adml Fasih Bokhari addressed a hard-hitting letter addressed to his appointing authority, the president Zardari. Adml Bokhari had cast serious doubts over the role of the SC that he said *"could be seen as pre-poll rigging."*

The said letter was dispatched from the Chairman's home address in Chak Shahzad Farms, Park Road, and later released to the media. Adml Bokhari directly accused members of the superior judiciary of trying to influence the outcome of the coming general election. Here is the text verbatim of that letter:

*Dear Mr President*

*Please accept my gratitude for supporting unhindered execution of my mandate. Large recoveries have been made (about Rs:25 Billion). The Prevention activity of focusing on the current procurements and projects of Rs:1.5 Trillion to eliminate possible corrupt practices, and the disclosure of heavy daily wastage of revenue and state owned resources indicative of decade's old systemic flaws is being addressed by the Government.*

*"However, I write to you at a critical juncture in the history of our country when our people anxiously await free and fair elections. At this juncture all political players appear unanimous and united to respond to the aspirations of their countrymen. There is broad consensus that non political players must not be allowed to derail the political process. The Military has made its position clear and firmly stands with the people.*

*"I am constrained to observe and bring to your notice that the position of the Honourable Supreme Court, on this issue, remains clouded by actions that are bearing heavily on my mandate to strictly abide by the NAO in both letter and spirit, as the time for elections approaches.*

*"The clear line between the recognized authority of the Supreme Court to monitor NAB investigations to the limited extent of ensuring fair investigation, and itself becoming involved in guiding investigations, appears to be becoming breached as a norm as the elections near. Contempt notices, verbal orders that differ from written orders, and insufficient time to prepare numerous progress reports, are placing extreme pressure on NAB personnel who appear before the Honourable Judges.*

*There is even a danger that NAB personnel could lose their independence and are unable to carry out their investigations in an independent manner due to the pressure being exerted on them by the Honourable Supreme Court to proceed along lines which seem to be desired by the SC. In relieving this pressure, to safeguard their jobs, and so as not to displease the Honourable Court, there is danger of unfair investigation being resorted to.*

*This phenomenon is observable in the investigation of very senior politicians of the government where orders, to even arrest them, have been issued on investigation reports of regional investigators that had yet to reach the Executive Board Meeting at NAB Headquarters that is chaired by me. This could be construed as a clear violation of the powers of the Chairman NAB, and to some degree circumventing the NAO which I am required by law to follow.*

*The NAO in my view as it remains law passed by Parliament represents the will of the people and as such I am bound to follow it. The National Accountability Ordinance mandates that no reference can be filed until I have been allowed to exercise my mind, and decide that a clear case of criminality has been made out. I would be failing in my statutory duty if I shirk from upholding the law that I am mandated to protect.*

*Let me assure you, Mr. President that I will not flinch from prosecuting whosoever may be identified as having committed a criminal act under the National Accountability Ordinance. All are equal before the law. The nation expects that there be no sacred cows, nor raging bulls.*

*I am constrained to also bring to your notice the revolt within NAB, clearly abetted by a certain section of the media that used the sad* demise of Mr. Kamran Faisal to vilify me and some senior NAB officers. This section of the media appears to be acting as an intelligence unit influencing the public, and possibly influencing certain members of the judiciary.

Long standing "stay" on taxes to be paid by this media house appears to be relevant also. This campaign, in which the role of the Honourable Supreme Court appears evident, is placing great pressure on me to please the Honourable Supreme Court in what could be seen as pre-poll rigging, and hurried unlawful action on my part.

Mr. President, I resigned my commission as Chief of the Naval Staff just prior to a Military coup rather than violate my oath to the Constitution. I was part of The Pakistan Ex Servicemen Association contingent that came on the streets protesting against the infamous 3rd November Emergency, and later for the movement for independence of the Judiciary. It is a sacred duty of every Pakistani to uphold, be guided by, and fiercely protect the Law and Constitution.

I fear that in the current direction that the Honourable Supreme Court appears to be taking, I will not be able to perform my independent statutory role. This situation needs to be addressed firmly in line with the aspirations of the people, and the clear mandatory provisions of the Law and the Constitution.

Although not directly within my mandate, as a citizen I am concerned about the current priority vital national interest (VNI) of achieving national cohesion before being able to address lower priority VNI such as HDI, Economic acceleration, infrastructure development, etc. Relevant state institutions must look carefully at the possible role of members of the judiciary, and a section of the media, in undermining state institutions, and the confidence of the people in the state itself.

The Ombudsman offices were established to also address human rights issues. The need to allow the Honourable SC to be diverted from its prime roles as the final Appellate and Constitutional Court may need to be addressed since ability to take Suo Moto notice of human rights cases can become an open license to undermine government, and may be taking time away from addressing the issues of judicial management of the current huge pendency of cases in our courts.

In the absence of timely justice the people are forced to take the law into their own hands and their anger becomes focused on their *governments. The essence of law is to provide a moral benchmark to society. That benchmark is sadly being lost by a judiciary that may be fast losing its own moral authority by relying on the contempt law, media, street power of lawyers, and unchecked violations of the Supreme Court Judges code of conduct.*

*For the well being of our people justice must be ensured, while protecting them from those who would callously allow "the heavens to fall".*

*Should these issues not be addressed expeditiously I will regretfully be forced to tender my resignation."*

The SC immediately took notice of that letter and initiated contempt of court proceedings against the NAB's Chairman Adml Bokhari.

## CONTEMPTS AND ALLEGATIONS:

**On 31st January 2013,** the SC issued a show-cause notice for contempt of court to NAB's Chairman Adml Fasih Bokhari over the above mentioned letter sent by him to President Zardari. The court summoned the Chairman to appear before it on 4th February instant as Adml Bokhari had accused the apex court of interfering in NAB investigations; particularly against politicians.

A 3-member bench of the apex court, comprising Chief Justice Iftikhar M Chaudhry, Justice Gulzar Ahmed and Justice Sh Azmat Saeed, heard the case concerning implementation of its March 2012 ruling in the rental power projects (RPP) case.

NAB's Prosecutor General [PG] K K Agha read out the text of the said letter while the Chief Justice inquired as to why such a letter was written and asked for the PG's advice on the matter as a lawyer; especially wherein the apex court had accused the court of colluding with a section of the media against NAB.

Once when PG Agha read out the words "pre-poll rigging" from the letter before the court, the CJP remarked [and reassured] that:

*'The executive, both civilian and military, shall not take any action or steps that are tantamount to deviation from the election. Deviation from the constitution or introducing any other system not recognised by the constitution shall not be acceptable.'*

The chief justice's words came amid widespread speculation that the military was working with the judiciary to force out a civilian [PPP's] leader and delay the elections. PPP's stalwart Raza Rabbani, had said earlier that week that *'a conspiracy was being hatched'* by certain elements to derail the democratic process and delay general election for two to three years; adding that *'A sword (of Damocles) is hanging over democracy and it would continue to be there till the election of prime minister after the polls.'*

The whole drama was being played in the backdrop of SC's directions dated 15th January 2013 through which the authorities were asked to **arrest Prime Minister Raja Pervaiz Ashraf** and 15 others accused in the RPP case. The PPP's prime minister had been accused of receiving kick-backs and commissions in RPP cases as minister for water and power.

The NAB Chairman had, however, informed the court that there was not yet enough evidence to arrest the premier and others accused in the case. In the original case, nine RPP firms were accused of receiving more than Rs:22 billion as a mobilisation advance from the government to commission the projects but most of them did not set up their plants and a few of them installed them but with inordinate delay. *In March 2012, the SC had held the RPP contracts non-transparent and ordered that the same be rescinded.*

After receiving the contempt of the court notice, the NAB's Chairman Adml Fasih Bokhari started making open attacks on the CJP Iftikhar M Chaudhry and the judiciary. Adml Bokhari's appointment was termed controversial by many, and on the count that he had converted NAB into a corruption-friendly institution and during his incumbency the national exchequer allegedly suffered losses of around Rs:2,000 billion because of closure of massive cases of loot and plunder against the top PPP leadership and the ruling elite of the country.

NAB Chairman was alleged to have ordered the bureau's prosecutors to remain silent in the cases reopened after the NRO judgment, which resulted in acquittals of all the accused in cases involving proven corruption of more than Rs:350 billion. Adml Bokhari allegedly ordered NAB prosecutors not to file any appeal against the closure of these cases in the high courts while it was a mandatory legal requirement.

In the Rs:9 billion Bank of Punjab (BoP) case, Adml Bokhari approved a controversial plea bargain to Sheikh Afzal and others despite the objections of the BoP. Sheikh Afzal etc had committed the biggest ever financial fraud of the country's banking history by using bogus collateral and fake NICs. Adml Fasih allegedly ensured that no action be taken against lawyers Sharifuddin Pirzada, Malik Qayyum, Ali Wasim and others who had taken money in the name of judges to get a verdict from the court in his favour and there were credible evidences against them.

Adml Bokhari did not approve reference against 21 accused, including the then incumbent PM, who were indicted in the Rental Power Plants (RPPs) inquiry report prepared by the deceased Kamran Faisal who was found dead in his room **on 18th January 2013** after sending a message to his close friend that he was being pressured to give a backdated affidavit against the Supreme Court by the top NAB management.

Adml Bokhari himself admitted before the media that Rs:12 billion corruption was being done in the country on daily basis, making Rs:360 billion corruption a month; then failed to respond to the questions how many looters were arrested by him for committing that Rs:4,380 billion annual corruption.

Adml Bokhari failed to initiate any action on the Rs:38 million wilful loan default of ex-PM Yousuf Raza Gilani's wife.

In his statement submitted before the Supreme Court here **on 7th February 2013,** NAB's investigation officer [IO] in the OGRA case Waqas Ahmad Khan informed the apex court how Kausar Malik had been interfering in this case and even giving the reference of Chairman Fasih Bukhari's meeting with the prime minister.

[*Waqas Ahmad Khan informed the SC that in October 2012 he was called by Kausar Malik in his office and told in presence of advocate Mehmood Mirza that the former should move an internal office note to the later suggesting that in the OGRA case one Ahmad Hayat Luk should be engaged on technical matters.*

*The IO refused to do so due to certain reservations with regard to Mr Luk but Kausar Malik had pressed him maximum. While doing so Kausar Malik said that in a meeting at the Prime Minister's House a day earlier, Mr Luk, Malik and Chairman NAB were all present to discuss the case. However, having disappointed from my side Kausar Malik got special letter issued from Deputy Director Operations.*]

Adml Bokhari once tore into pieces the arrest warrants of one of the biggest plunderers of the PPP's regime, Tauqeer Sadiq [of OGRA fame] and allegedly helped him flee the country. He did nothing to arrest Tauqeer from the UAE despite dozens of apex court orders. He further ensured that no action could be taken against the officers who helped Tauqeer Sadiq escape from the country.

Adml Bokhari also remained unmoved when SC ordered moving a reference against Prime Minister Raja Pervaiz Ashraf and ex-PM Gilani in Tauqeer Sadiq's appointment case.

Adml Fasih Bokhari, during his stay in NAB got a luxurious residential plot from the PPP government in return of his "outstanding" services in an expensive sector of Islamabad worth many millions over & above his entitlement.

## COMMISSION TO PROBE THE LETTER:

On 16th March 2013; less than an hour before it completed its five-year term; the PPP government formed a commission to probe allegations of *"persistent interference by outside institutions"* into the workings of NAB.

According to the notification issued late on 16th March by the Law and Justice Division, signed by Senior Joint Secretary Sohail Qadeer Siddiqui, a 2-member commission comprising former SC judges Mukhtar Junejo and Nawaz Abbasi was formed to look into the matter and submit a report in the next few weeks.

The commission had to start its probe within a week of the issuance of the notification, and had to submit its report within four weeks.

The terms of reference of the commission, listed in the notification, were to examine:

- Whether any outside institution or any individual in such institution other than NAB can act as investigator directly or indirectly in cases under the NAB Ordinance 1999.

- Whether it/he can "override provisions of the NAB Ordinance"... by assuming/arrogating powers of the chairman.

- Whether it/he "has overstepped their jurisdiction in violation of clause (2) of Article 175" of the Constitution.

Although the notification, did not name any government institution, it was believed the commission would be investigating allegations against the Supreme Court contained in the above given letter written by Adml Bokhari to the president.

Chief Justice of Pakistan Iftikhar M Chaudhry *on 19ᵗʰ March 2013* expressed annoyance over the formation of a commission by the government for protecting the National Accountability Bureau (NAB) from 'interference' by 'outside institutions'.

A 3-member SC bench headed by the CJP Iftikhar M Chaudhry [Justice Gulzar Ahmed and Justice Sh Azmat Saeed the other two members] heard a *suo motu* notice taken on the commission's formation. The court ordered that concerned documents be presented before it to determine who ordered the commission's formation.

NAB Chairman Admiral Bokhari was already facing contempt charges over his letter to President Zardari, and that the matter of the commission would also be analysed with the new charges. Joint Secretary Law told the apex court that the notification for the formation of the commission, comprising former SC judges Mukhtar Junejo and M Nawaz Abbasi, was issued following the presidential reference, *adding that the notification, however, had been withdrawn.*

The CJP observed that the said notification reflected that the judiciary was a subordinate body of the executive, which was unfortunate. PM Raja Pervaiz Ashraf had sought legal opinion on the letter and was asked to form a commission; thus the matter was seen as contempt of court.

**On 28ᵗʰ May 2013,** the Supreme Court of Pakistan declared the appointment of Adml Fasih Bokhari, Chairman NAB, as null & void. The ruling was issued by a 5-judges bench of the apex court headed by Justice Tassadduq Hussain Jilani saying that Mr Bokhari's appointment to the post was unconstitutional and unlawful, adding that it was in violation of Section 6 of the NAB Ordinance.

The judgment was passed on a petition filed in October 2011 by the former opposition leader Ch Nisar Ali Khan urging the Adml Bokhari's appointment [on 16ᵗʰ October 2011] was not made in consultation with the Leader of the House (prime minister) and Leader of the Opposition nor the Chief Justice of Pakistan. It was tainted with personal motivation on part of President Zardari. The petition had also insisted that President Zardari was not qualified to exercise power or perform function to appoint NAB's Chairman when he himself was an accused in more than a dozen cases of alleged corruption.

One can see the efficiency of Pakistan's superior courts that a simple question of law or regulatory nature, which the Chairman NAB's appointment was made through blatantly flouting the rules on the subject – the Leader of the Opposition was not consulted; *the petition could have been decided next day in one hearing. The Supreme Court took 19 months to decide it* and that too only because:

- Adml Bokhari's appointing PPP government had gone home in March 2013.

- Adml Bokhari had written a letter to the President accusing SC itself for interference.

Usman Khalid of RIFA opined that:

*'NAB has been used by all past governments to get their political opponents tamed. Diverse political pressures are exerted quite openly and very strongly. Admiral Bokhari was subjected to fierce pressures not only on behalf of influential accused but also the media and the courts.*

*During the incumbency of Admiral Bokhari as Chairman NAB, he was faced by the extraordinary situations; that persons under investigation included the President, sitting and past Prime Ministers and ministers, and the son of the Chief Justice. The conduct of Admiral Fasih Bokhari has been dignified, impartial and politically correct; he did not flinch from taking difficult decisions.'*

As detailed earlier, on 10th March 2011, SC's similar verdict had declared the appointment of Justice ® Deedar Hussain Shah as illegal, also on Ch Nisar's petition. In fact the PML(N) had been struggling in the last parliament for the constitution of an independent National Accountability Commission [NAC] for across the board accountability but the bill was kept pending for more than four years.

The bill proposing constitution of the NAC was moved in the parliament by the PPP government, seeking replacement of the Musharraf-era NAB with an independent NAC in line with the Charter of Democracy signed by Nawaz Sharif and Benazir Bhutto in May 2006 in London. But it became controversial and put on the back burner after certain clauses were opposed by the PML(N).

The proposed law had suggested the setting up of a 3-member NAC to be headed by a chairman who has been a judge of the Supreme Court or a federal government officer in BPS-22, a deputy chairman who has been a judge of a high court or a federal government officer in BPS-21 and a prosecutor general who is qualified to be appointed as a judge of the Supreme Court.

*[Part of this essay was published at Pakspectator.com as a 'Lead Story' on 19th October 2011]*

## POST SCRIPT:

Referring to *'Pakistan Today' dated 19th June 2013*, internal conflicts between two groups of NAB officers intensified to an alarming level, badly affecting the performance of the anti-corruption body as senior officials got entangled in legal battles against each other instead of preparing cases against criminals involved in massive corruption.

Both groups went locked horns for expelling each other from NAB through the Islamabad High Court [IHC]. The former military officers group challenged in the IHC the appointment of four new directors general in NAB while the other group of 11 officers also challenged the initial appointments of the former military officers in the same high court urging that their induction in NAB in 2003 and their subsequent promotion to next grade within three months was an illegal process.

According to documents, NAB had then appointed four DGs in BPS-21 on regular basis; namely Brig (R) Farooq Naser Awan as DG [HQ], M Altaf Bawany as DG [Finance], Zahir Shah as DG [Operations] and Hussain Ahmed as DG NAB Punjab. Their appointments were approved and notifications issued between 5 –15th April 2013 by the outgoing Chairman Adml Fasih Bokhari as a special case.

The group representing ex-military officials claimed that the PM had granted approval of the new recruitments of four DGs in violation of Sec 28-C of NAO 1999 in which the president of Pakistan was the only competent authority for such approvals.

On the other hand, these newly appointed DGs took stance that induction [in NAB] of ex-military officers' namely Col (R) Subah Sadiq, Col (R) Shahzad Anwar Bhatti, Maj (R) Burhan, Maj (R) Shahzad Saleem, Maj (R) Tariq Mehmood and other ex-military officers during Gen Musharraf regime was illegal.

Fact remained that serving military officers were permanently inducted in NAB without fulfilment of eligibility criteria i.e. academic qualification and experience in relevant field etc but were given key positions in NAB to manage all the affairs. They were then promoted illegally during 2003 and 2008 in higher ranks without considering seniority and prescribed promotion criteria. As a result, a large number of the officers went into litigation in higher courts.

## *CH QAMAR ZAMAN HEADS NAB:*

On 9th **October 2013;** the PML(N) government issued the notification for the formal appointment of Ch Qamar Zaman as the new Chairman of the National Accountability Bureau (NAB). The post for NAB's Chairman was lying vacant since 28th May that year when the Supreme Court had termed the appointment of Admiral (rtd) Fasih Bukhari as illegal. PM Nawaz Sharif, after consultation with Khursheed Shah, Leader of Opposition in the National Assembly, had nominated Mr Chaudhry as new Chief.

Under the NAB Ordinance, the Chairman cannot be removed from his office midway since he enjoys a tenure post of four years, from which he cannot be removed except under Article 209 through the Supreme Judicial Council. But, as the CJP Chaudhry was hands in gloves with the PML[N] and he knew that the new party when comes in power would need his own Chairman NAB, so he [the CJP Chaudhry] had kept all the backdoor arrangements ready to send Admiral Bukhari home.

The CJP Chaudhry had done that most hazardous job in utmost smooth way to keep Sharifs protected from NAB's clutches on the basis of their past records if the same were there in NAB till that day; AND if at all some hard moments were to come.

Meanwhile, Pakistan Tehreek e Insaf [PTI] decided to challenge appointment of the new NAB Chief, giving several reasons for going to the apex court against Qamar Zaman. Dr Shireen Mazari stated that the appointment served to undermine the letter and spirit of the law as Qamar Zaman had applied for retirement after his announcement was made and the process was hastily completed within 24 hours. It further revealed that there existed a contempt notice of the SC against Qamar Zaman stating:

> *"In order to meet the ends of justice, we find it necessary to issue notices under Section 17 (1) of the Contempt of Court (Ordinance V) of 2003, to Qamar Zaman Ch, Secretary, Ministry of Interior, Abdul Rauf Ch. Secretary, Establishment Division, and Khushnood Lashari,*

*Principal Secretary to the Prime Minister, for wilful defiance of the orders of this Court passed on 24.1.2011. This notice is still pending."*

On **22nd November 2013**; the SC ordered prosecution of NAB's new Chairman Mr Chaudhry for abusing his authority as a civil servant and also incriminated a whole bunch of top bureaucrats as well as a senior PPP politician responsible for the crime warranting cases against them. The indictment came in a 52-page detailed verdict in the Rs:1.68 billion NICL scam as well as contempt of court charges against senior government officials, including the NAB Chairman.

Authored by CJP Iftikhar M Chaudhry, the judgment said that the December 2009 appointment of Ayaz Khan Niazi as NICL Chairman was illegal, unwarranted and contrary to the Insurance Ordinance 2000. It also pointed finger, though prime facie, at former commerce minister Makhdoom Amin Fahim of the PPP, Qamar Zaman Chaudhry (then Additional Commerce Secretary), former Commerce Secretary Suleman Ghani, former Establishment Secretary Ismail Qureshi and former Acting Principal Secretary to the PM Nargis Sethi for their involvement in the scam. They were made liable to be tried under Section 9(a VI) of the National Accountability Ordinance 1999.

The appointment was challenged by PTI Chief Imran Khan in the SC but it has been the history. Earlier, former NAB Chief Nawid Ahsan had to resign after the apex court had on 16th December 2009, declared the controversial National Reconciliation Ordinance (NRO) illegal and expressed displeasure over the conduct and lack of proper and honest assistance and cooperation to the court.

*Former leader of opposition Ch Nisar Ali Khan had challenged the appointment of Justice Deedar Hussain Shah as well as Admiral Fasih Bokhari to the post. Deedar Shah's appointment was set aside by the SC on 10th March 2011 and that of Fasih Bokhari on 28th May 2013.*

*Referring to the day of 18th April 2011, transfer [as MD NPF] of the then Additional DG Capt Zafar Ahmed Qureshi, who was over-seeing the NICL investigation, the verdict implicated former DG FIA Malik M Iqbal, former Establishment Secretary Abdul Rauf Chaudhry, former Principal Secretary to the PM Khushnood Lashari and former FIA Director in Lahore Waqar Haider for creating hurdles and hampering the smooth and transparent investigation entrusted to Zafar Qureshi.*

Qamar Zaman, Abdul Rauf Chaudhry, Khushnood Lashari, Malik M Iqbal and former Interior Minister Rehman Malik faced contempt charges separately for interfering in the NICL investigation.

The verdict regretted that the FIA had failed to recover Rs:420 million from accused Mohsin Habib Warraich as well as Moonis Elahi, son of former CM Punjab Ch Pervaiz Elahi, for whom £1.138 million was deposited with EFG Private Bank Ltd, London, in the name of a company owned by him and another account in the name of Beenish Khan (wife of Mohsin Habib Warraich) in Barclays Bank London.

The court had directed the NAB Chairman to take necessary steps to recover the outstanding amount and also arrest Mohsin Habib Warraich and NICL officials Amin Qasim Dada and Khalid Anwar as early as possible.

*The full details of the said NICL Scam have already been given in 'Judges & Generals in Pakistan Vol-IV (Scenario 74).*

On 24th December 2013; The NAB saved its own Chairman Qamar Zaman Chaudhry in an inquiry into the Rs:6 billion NICL scam, while ordering a formal investigation against former prime minister Yousuf Raza Gilani. When his appointment had been challenged in the SC by the PTI, he went on a long leave while the court ordered investigation against him – a good gesture in a way to uphold rule of law. The NAB Chief was given a clean chit by the NAB's Executive Board at a meeting presided over by acting Chairman Rear Admiral Saeed Ahmed Sargana.

The NAB's spokesman told the media that the board had upgraded a separate inquiry against people accused of misusing authority in appointment of former NICL Chairman Ayaz Khan Niazi, including former prime minister Gilani and former Establishment Secretary Abdul Rauf Chaudhry who was then serving as the Federal Tax Ombudsman. Mr Gilani joined the investigation by sending his lawyer before NAB investigators next week.

On 26th December 2013, after getting a clean chit from the NAB, Mr Chaudhry was reinstated as the Chairman of Pakistan's top anti-corruption watchdog. He was dragged in controversies of an inquiry into the Rs:6 billion National Insurance Company (NICL) scam case for allegedly protecting Moonis Elahi involved as accused. For government officers such situations often become odd – here also, Mr Qamar Chaudhry had served under Moonis Elahi's father Ch Pervaiz Elahi when he was CM in Gen Musgarraf's regime.

## NAB's ANNUAL REPORT 2013:

The Annual Report of NAB for 2013 was released vide *PR 33/2014-NAB dated 20ᵗʰ May 2014;–* declaring it another challenging year in the history of Pakistan. On the Enforcement side of NAB activities, recovery through Voluntary Return (VR) and Plea Bargain (PB) remained Rs:3.125 billion. The Prosecution efforts resulted in 65 percent convictions in Courts.

During the year 2013, NAB received 18607 complaints. With addition of backlog of 1464, the number rose to a total of 20071 complaints. Out of these, 18,892 complaints were processed (converted into complaints verifications, inquiries, linked with cases, referred to other departments etc.) and 1179 complaints remained pending as on 31ˢᵗ December 2013.

A total of 284 fresh inquiries were authorized during the year 2013 thus including the backlog of 589 inquiries the total rose to 873. A total of 243 inquiries were finalized, whereas 630 inquiries remained under process. 463 individuals entered into VR and PB during the year 2013 and out of agreed amount of Rs:3149.985 million, Rs:3125.088 million (99.2%) were recovered. During the year 2013, NAB recommended placement of 157 accused on the Exit Control List (ECL) through the Ministry of Interior.

Awareness and Prevention Division of the Bureau processed 363 projects including procurements amounting to Rs:220 Billion; 18 Committees were established in all major areas of governance to improve performance. Despite upheavals during the year, NAB was able to perform satisfactorily under the Prevention Regime in the period from January to December 2013. NAB worked with bureaucracy for its restructuring and for renewal of rules to prevent corruption in planned procurements projects. Work on improvement of Legislative and Regulatory Structures of the State was under review to remove discretions and service anomalies, the annual report says.

NAB also established 14000 Character Building Societies (CBS) across the country in different Universities, Colleges and Schools. It is worth mentioning that substantial progress was achieved in the efforts for eradication of corruption as Pakistan's CPI index improved during year 2013. NAB expressed the hope that with continued efforts, the Bureau would achieve further noticeable improvements in the coming years.

The incumbent Chairman, Ch Qamar Zaman, took charge of his office in October 2013. Placed in an awkward situation by the Supreme

Court's decision to entrust an inquiry against his person to NAB, the Chairman decided to proceed on five week's leave until the inquiry was completed. However, the NAB remained functional during his absence, the Deputy Chairman with his powers acted on his behalf.

During the year 2013, NAB inducted 280 investigators through a merit-based and transparent recruitment process. They underwent seven months rigorous training conducted by local as well as foreign faculty. This training was arranged at COMSATS university campus Islamabad where state of the art facilities were made available and renowned professionals were invited to impart specialized training on various subjects.

NAB appreciated the Federal and Provincial governments for their cooperation and support in enabling it to perform its assigned functions. NAB believed that no process of accountability could be successfully undertaken without the cooperation of all citizens as well as the media. To this end the Media Wing of NAB had been instructed to take necessary initiatives so as to make that joint effort successful. Chairman Chaudhry held:

> "It is impossible for me or for the institution that I head, to succeed on its own. In this respect, NAB would need the active help and support of all the people of this country and all its institutions. Needless to say our efforts are tied by an umbilical cord to the judiciary. It is also important to acknowledge that our success or failure is also tied to the Media."

During the year 2013, after successful completion of training, 268 officers joined the field operations. This enhanced NAB's capacity and help brought down pendency; the bar for the year 2014 was raised further. NAB's goal for 2014 was to increase its role in contextualizing and setting the anti-corruption strategic agenda on behalf of the Government of Pakistan and the Political leadership of the country. Stronger emphasis will be placed on the far-reaching and often overlooked links between corruption and other serious risks.

International Anti-Corruption measures had been sub-divided under the headings of Enforcement, Prevention, and Education. More sensibly, Pakistan used the title Awareness instead of Education. In the past, NAB's main emphasis was on Enforcement. *"Out of empirical evidence it has came to light that Enforcement alone cannot succeed and it has to move hand in glove with Prevention and Awareness. NAB intended to pursue that internationally accepted model."*

In particular, Chairman Chaudhry's team focussed on connecting NAB with other anti graft organizations form emerging markets, linking the anti-corruption platform to broader messages on growth, competitiveness and risk resilience.

The Annual Report of the NAB for the year 2013 was duly presented to the President of Pakistan as required under section 33D of the National Accountability Ordinance 1999. Not only that it was a statutory requirement but also a reflection of NAB's contribution to the National efforts against corruption.

# Scenario 123

## GEN MUSHARRAF's COME BACK:

Former President Gen Pervez Musharraf returned to Pakistan on 24th March 2013 after more than four years in exile, seeking a possible political comeback in defiance of judicial probes and death threats from Taliban militants. He landed at Karachi Airport where only a few hundred people welcome him; a small turnout by any standard of Pakistani politics for any national leader.

Gen Musharraf struck a defiant tone while speaking to his supporters outside the airport terminal vowing that *'he was not cowed by a threat by the Pakistani Taliban to kill him'*. Gen Musharraf's come back could further complicate Pakistan's politics; was viewed as an enemy by many Islamic militants for his decision to side with America in response to the Nine Eleven terrorist attacks.

A day earlier, the Pakistani Taliban vowed to mobilize death squads to kill Gen Musharraf at appropriate time. As a token to that the militants launched a suicide car bomb attack against a military check post in the northwest tribal region, killing 17 soldiers therein.

Gen Musharraf was to face legal charges on certain big issues including assassination of former PM Benazir Bhutto on 27th December 2007; Nawab Akbar Bugti's killing in Balochistan, Judges Illegal Confinement Case and most importantly, the TREASON Case under Article six of the Constitution for imposing Emergency on 3rd November 2007.

## *NO WELCOME – UTTER DISTRESS:*

Gen Musharraf at last made to land in Pakistan after several failed promises to return previously. He tweeted that he was *"thrilled to be back home"* soon after his landing in Karachi. Moments after the security people whisked him away in a convoy of about a dozen vehicles, raising concerns he was being detained for the legal charges against him. His supporters, waiting over two hours for him, really got disappointed with the beginning of General's new political journey.

During his initial stay at a hotel in Karachi, he planned for the upcoming elections, and then travelled to Islamabad where his legal team was keen to see him to decide the best way to respond to the charges against him. A Pakistani court had granted him pre-emptive bail in three cases in which he was known to be implicated. He had 10 days to appear in court; albeit he had dismissed various charges as baseless in which he was named in absentia, without officially informing him.

A day earlier to his landing, the Pakistani Taliban [TTP] released a video threatening to unleash suicide bombers and snipers against Gen Musharraf if he comes back. One of the two people speaking in the video was Adnan Rashid, a former Pakistani air force officer convicted in an attack against the General. The Taliban had broken Rashid out of prison last year, along with nearly 400 other detainees from a jail in Khyber PK province. Adnan Rashid's video, in which he spoke in front of a group of about 20 militants holding rifles, said:

> *"The mujahedeen of Islam have prepared a death squad to send Pervez Musharraf to hell. We warn you to surrender yourself to us. Otherwise we will hit you from where you will never reckon."*

Gen Musharraf was expected to address supporters at a gathering in Karachi near the Qaid's mausoleum but police decided to cancel his permit because of a *"very serious threat"*. In addition, Gen Musharraf was provided an armoured vehicle to protect him. Banners and billboards welcoming Gen Musharraf back to Pakistan were, of course, lined the street from the airport to the Qaid's mausoleum.

In the aftermath of the 9/11 attacks, Gen Musharraf was pressurised by the US to back them in the then war in Afghanistan and cut off ties with the Taliban, which he did. For that, militants as well as many other Pakistanis saw him as carrying out the American agenda in Pakistan. He was also vilified by militants for ordering firing in Red Mosque episode of Islamabad in July 2007; the mosque had become a sanctuary for armed militants. At least 102 people were killed in the weeklong operation, most of them supporters of the Imams in-charge.

Militants tried to kill Gen Musharraf twice in December 2003 in Rawalpindi; firstly by placing a bomb intended to go off when his convoy passed by. When that didn't work, suicide attackers tried to ram his motorcade with explosives laden vehicles. The president was unhurt but 16 others had died.

In addition to the Benazir Bhutto killing case, Gen Musharraf had to face charges resulting from investigations into the killing of Nawab Akbar

Bugti, a Baloch nationalist leader who died on 26th August 2006 after a standoff with the Pakistani military. In another case, he was accused of illegally removing a number of judges including the CJP Iftikhar M Chaudhry.

Gen Musharraf's opponents had to pass remarks while he was in troubles. The media he muzzled delighted in replaying clips of his court attendances alongside frames of his old photos. Some former politicians thundered against him on television; others had quieter reactions. One PML[N] politician remarked that;

> *"It isn't nice for anyone to have to go through this - but I still remember how Musharraf forced me to see my mother and children in handcuffs. It filled their eyes with tears….."*

It is unclear why Gen Musharraf returned, given the controversies he had triggered. Last week, he confessed to CNN that he had entered a secret deal with the US to allow the CIA to operate drones in Pakistan. For years he had denied it and inexplicably chose the moment of his return to Pakistan to finally come clean. Some ascribed the decision to vanity - years of progressively quieter exile denied him the headlines he craved.

Next day, Khateeb Lal Masjid Maulana Abdul Aziz approached Supreme Court (SC) seeking placement of Gen Musharraf's name in Exit Control List (ECL) and registration of treason case against him.

The petitioner had taken the plea in the petition that Gen Musharraf was behind the killings of several innocent people and students in Lal Masjid incident. Therefore, such person should not only be proceeded against under law but his name be also placed in ECL. Gen Musharraf was facing several cases in courts and was on preventive bail; the SC was told. The interior minister and federal government were also made respondents in the *Lal Masjid* petition.

### GEN MUSH'F APPEARS IN COURT:

29th March 2013 was a rough day for Gen Musharraf when he appeared in the court in Karachi. A shoe was hurled at him as he was forced to appear in two murder cases to plead for bail. He secured bail but was barred from leaving the country. The embarrassment and humiliations kept on adding to the retired General's troubles since he arrived back in Pakistan about a week earlier. He tried to make another bid for power at the elections in May but had disappointed as when he landed at Karachi airport, fewer than 2,000 people were there to greet him.

The **TIME of 29th March 2013** described that day as:

*'Gen Musharraf had heralded his day in court with a tweet as he had claimed in interviews that his social media following demonstrated his popularity in Pakistan. His Facebook page had 825,000 Likes. "Leaving to appear in court today," he said, in the first time a former dictator has live-tweeted an audience with a judge.*

*The Twitter account shows the former commando in action: training at the gym ("Feel very energized"), tasting Pakistani food ("The best cuisine in the world"), posing with a dwindled crowd of fans and showing off his farouche looking armed bodyguard ("Taliban threat? NOT ON MY WATCH!!!").'*

As Gen Musharraf strode into court, with flashing cameras retreating in front of him, a shoe zipped over their heads. The assailant was a lawyer, a familiar type of opponent. In 2007, during his last year in power, Gen Musharraf had sacked Pakistan's Chief Justice Iftikhar M Chaudhry twice, sparking a lawyer-led movement that ultimately saw him resign as President of Pakistan the following year.

Like most shoe hurlers, the lawyer, Tajamal Lodhi, was a terrible shot and missed his target by some distance. Local news channels gleefully played the footage several times. They too have a gripe with Gen Musharraf: he had shut down a number of independent news channels when he imposed a state of emergency in 2007.

The lawyer Tajammal Lodhi was later released without charge. Gen Musharraf, however, managed to secure bail in the three cases he's charged with involvement in: the assassination of Benazir Bhutto, the death of Baloch leader Akbar Bugti and a case about his sacking of several judges and confining them home in 2007.

It was also the first time in Pakistan's history that a former military ruler was appearing in court. In his tweets, Gen Musharraf struck a deferential tone, referring to the judges as "honourable." But the Sindh High Court also ruled that Gen Musharraf would not be allowed to leave the country without their permission, placing his name on ECL.

During the next month, Gen Musharraf was forced to appear in courts of different parts of the country to extend his bail. It was unlikely, however, that he would end up convicted of his involvement in either the Bhutto or Bugti assassinations. He was widely accused of failing to give

Bhutto adequate security, including in a high-profile UN inquiry. In Bugti's case, Gen Musharraf had notoriously remarked on television that he would *"hit him from where he wouldn't see it coming."*

However, Gen Musharraf managed to attract considerable attention in media of Pakistan. Many news channels broadcast his press conference live from the luxury hotel in Karachi where he was residing. The familiar bluff rhetoric was on display, with Gen Musharraf controversially saying that Kargil — a military adventure he led as army chief in 1999 — was a success. But few believed that he would make a political impact. Another General, who was once close to Gen Musharraf, but a known media analyst opined:

> *"Despite a very poor performance by the democratic [PPP] govern-ment, people are not going to choose a former military ruler. He's fantasizing. He has highly exaggerated ideas about himself. He's out of touch with reality. He certainly has a grand vision, but it's about himself rather than the country."*

After having ruled Pakistan for nine years, it was not clear why Gen Musharraf wanted to be involved in politics again. Beyond the trouble with the courts, Gen Musharraf had realised hardships of campaigning. He insisted that he would hit the campaign trail, and was tipped to possibly win a couple of parliamentary seats, one in Karachi and one in Chitral but that was not his plan. He was going to sit as member in a Parliament headed by Nawaz Sharif, the former Prime Minister he ousted in the 1999 coup.

Amidst all these hopes; let us peep into more details for a while.

Like Z A Bhutto in an unprecedented way, Gen Musharraf was also booked for a criminal offence that could actually see him land in prison or his stay abroad into a permanent exile but surprisingly he came back. The Islamabad police registered an FIR (*No 131 dated 10-08-09 under section 344/34 PPC in Secretariat Police Station*) following the orders of a Sessions Court. It was done against him for illegal confinement of the country's top judges after his 3rd November 2007's dictatorial and tyrannical order of Emergency in Pakistan.

It was a point to note that on one side the intelligentsia and the civil society of Pakistan were adamant to set the path of democracy by block-ing the entry of the army in governments through back doors but at the same time the so-called democratic rulers, all the PPP stalwarts in the government boasting Gen Musharraf a Guard of Honour while see-ing him off from the government. Not only this, Pakistan High Commission in London was directed by Islamabad to give former dicta-tor full protocol of ex-president during his stay in London. Pakistan's High Commissioner to the UK Wajid Shamul-Hassan himself told the media that:

*"We are bound to act in line with the directions of Islamabad and we have been formally directed by the Foreign Office that Pervez Musharraf should be given the protocol of an ex-president, which we are giving to him.*

*The High Commission [HC] used to send a protocol car and a protocol officer to receive and see off Musharraf whenever he arrived or left the UK. The HC had been arranging a VIP lounge for Musharraf but the money was paid by the ex-dictator."*

Gen Musharraf had also kept at his disposal the services of about 12 (or more) regular officers of the Pakistan Army for his security in London. This deployment was made at Gen Musharraf's residence on Edgware Road London, for his security and for providing him daily services. Naturally this team was being paid a huge amount per month from the national exchequer of Pakistan.

On this news the former COAS Mirza Aslam Beg had given his candid opinion that according to the rules and regulations of the Pakistan Army, no such protocol was permissible for an ex-Army Chief. Beg disclosed that:

*"Some years back there was a rule of providing a batman, a PS, a driver and an Army telephone to an Army Chief on his retirement, but Benazir Bhutto, during her second tenure as prime minister, had ordered the then COAS Jahangir Karamat to withdraw these facilities from me. This rule of providing no facility to an ex-Army chief made on the orders of Benazir Bhutto still prevails."*

Now the key question: why Gen Musharraf decided to come back despite bags of bullying in the media and threats. Gen Musharraf had not returned to Pakistan from his self-exile to face legal battles, humili-ation, house arrests and imprisonments etc. What was the General's real agenda then? Who planned the General's return and with what specific political strategy? An important question in this context was: Why did the PML[N] remain absolutely non-vocal on the eve of the General's return – until he was arrested? Of course, Sharifs were told by friendly governments to maintain absolute silence over the matter.

Referring to the *'Nation dated 2nd May 2013'* Dr Haider Mehdi questioned that:

> '......... *why was the PML[N] leadership instructed to stay mum and mute – and by whom? These are the intricate puzzles and mysteries of Musharraf's return..... the Zardari regime had earlier sent off the General with a full guard of honor.*
>
> ....*all add a spice of political intrigue to Musharraf's return with a three-way collaboration of incumbent president [Mr Zardari], .... PML[N['s Sharifs, and the assertiveness of some foreign powers.'*

The subsequent developments: Ahmed Raza Kasuri, legal counsel for Gen Musharraf had threatened in the High Court and repeated himself several times on TV talk shows that *'Gen Musharraf's trial will be the Mother of all legal trials in this country'*. Kasuri had warned that about 500 people, including Parliamentarians, several Generals, provincial governors and high political figures and many members of the higher judiciary, would face legal actions in the prosecution of said case. Kasuri had also publicly proposed a Truth and Reconciliation Commission with the explicit purpose of "integrating" the nation.

The most intriguing and politically alarming part of this proposal was the suggested date of *31st July 2009, as the "cut-off date"* – Kasuri advocated that all irregularities [*financial, political, monetary, legal, constitutional as well as criminal*] be waived against all offenders prior to that proposed date, and only those offenders [*politicians, Parliamentarians, tax offenders, loan defaulters, members of the ruling elite, etc*] be dealt by law post 31st July 2009.

In other words, a second NRO was being proposed with public accountability of the ruling elite for only the previous 4 years – keeping decades of corruption and financial mismanagement aside to be dealt later.

Suddenly what happened was the unforeseen and unpredictable intervention of hidden variables – a judge of the superior judiciary had surprisingly taken Gen Musharraf to task. The game had changed its intended course of direction, though the original objective of a second NRO remained intact.

Referring to a letter from nationalist **M Abd al-Hameed, a Lahore - based media columnist,** had convincingly argued in a series of articles then that Gen Musharraf's return to Pakistan was organized by the US Pentagon: the State Department wanted a civilian government in Pakistan in 2013, while the Pentagon prevailed for Gen Musharraf's return as a strongman to Pakistan's political leadership who could unquestionably and effectively aid the American exodus from Afghanistan with the help of the Pak-Army and that *Muk Muka* setup. However, the humiliation Gen Musharraf faced then was not on cards.

Keeping aside the legal proceedings, the general populace believed the General should suffer for dragging the nation into a vicious and destructive war - the so-called war on terrorism. Gen Musharraf had no legal, political or moral authority to have made such a monumental decision unilaterally - he must face the music. But, *the PPP and PML[N] leadership dragged the whole nation into an anti-army campaign – it was not appropriate at all; the nation did not endorse it.*

The most important point was that had Gen Musharraf faced the music, so should all the loan defaulters, tax evaders, embezzlers of national assets, inefficient political managers, corrupt officials, account holders of unlawful deposits in Swiss banks, and so on and so forth.

## FACTS & ANALYSIS OF EVENTS:

Once he was flying so high and then lost his wings at last, lost in vacuum; then he fell down hitting the earth rock – he was Gen Musharraf.

In his nine years rule, the military dictator pushed his country into the crushing jaws of world players while raising loud slogans of *'Pakistan First'. He had handed over military air bases, naval harbours and his western borders to his American friends keeping his own commanders in dark.*

Then a moment came when Gen Musharraf was no more needed in the playing fields. The Americans got him replaced by similar civilian plunderers but had got their slave General departed with guard of honour. While declaring his base in London he had plenty of money bags with him gathered in the garb of *'lectures in foreign universities'.*

Suddenly after five years he landed at Karachi *on 24th March 2013*; with the same old passions that perhaps the general populace of Pakistan was waiting for him. The most shrewd General of his times was trapped in

Facebook & Twittered praises, might be his [evening] friends circle had made him to believe about his 'top-level popularity' or he was not able to forget the old fortune making days.

The same question again; why he came to Pakistan; who trapped him in such cruel way – no one really knows

**On 29th March 2013,** Gen Musharraf got fifteen days relief when the Sindh High Court [SHC] extended his bail in three separate cases but telling him NOT to leave Pakistan without permission. The bench further ordered: *'Let copy of this order be communicated to the Secretary, Ministry of Interior, as well as Director General of Immigration and Passports for strict compliance.'*

Gen Musharraf appeared in the SHC at <u>Karachi, the same city where **on 12th May 2007, 46 persons were slaughtered and 150 injured and the city**</u> remained besieged by containers; the ways to all hospitals were blocked; the court premises were engulfed by gunners but he was raising his fist at Islamabad declaring that massacre as *'Awam ki Taqat'* [the people's force].

*[On 26th May 2007; the Chief Justice Sabihuddin Ahmed [Sindh High Court (SHC)] had taken suo moto notice on a report of the In-charge Registrar of SHC submitted to him regarding the 12th May siege. The court converted the registrar's report into a petition and constituted a 7-member full bench for hearing it. The bench comprised Justice Sarmad Jalal Osmany, Justice Anwar Zaheer Jamali, Justice Mushir Alam, Justice Azizullah M Memon, Justice Khilji Arif Hussain, Justice Maqool Baqar and Justice Ali Sain Dino Metlo.*

*The In-charge Registrar of SHC, Abdul Malik Gaddi, had submitted in his report that at 7.45am on 12th May 2007 the entire High Court premises were surrounded by a mob and they were not allowing anybody, including advocates and members of the staff, to enter the court premises and the police were not helping in this regard.*

*The Registrar stated that when he proceeded towards the High Court for attending his duties, he found that all roads leading to the High Court were blocked by containers, buses and tankers, and he also could not find a way to enter the High Court premises. The police force deputed there was not taking any action against miscreants and it was sitting as a silent spectator.*

*The Registrar was informed by district and sessions judges Karachi West and South that the City Court premises had also been besieged*

*by miscreants, who were not allowing anybody to enter the City Court premises. All roads leading to the City Court premises were barricaded and blocked and 'the police were not taking action'.*

*The Registrar also submitted that miscreants had maltreated and thrashed advocates, including senior woman lawyer, Ismat Mehdi, and as a result a number of advocates had received injuries. When the SHC Chief Justice and members of the administration committee arrived at the High Court, they were also disturbed by the fact that access to the court had been blocked from various entry points, preventing the judges, court staff, advocates and litigant public from attending the court.*

*The CCPO and the **Town Police Officer concerned** appeared and offered their explanation, stating that they **had also arrived on foot** and they themselves were helpless. The **Sindh Home Secretary also appeared** and undertook to do his best but the 'situation remained the same'.*

*As all the roads were blocked, the CJP Iftikhar Chaudhry was not able to come to the High Court and he remained with Police at airport till about 8:00 pm till he boarded the plane back for Islamabad. The Police Head categorically admitted that when they returned from the airport at about 9:30 pm, the blockade was found to have been removed. The CJP was invited by the Sindh High Court Bar Association for addressing the concluding ceremony of the Supreme Court's 50th anniversary.]*

On 29th March 2013, the same 'Awam' was throwing empty water bottles on him; some one tossed his shoe on him; outside court his car was broken with stones and he himself was hearing the noisy shouts of *'dictator – hang him; traitor – kill him; seller – blacken his face'* but he kept on hearing helplessly. He kept on standing before the court powerlessly, combing his hair with fingers, eyes down when up – just seeing at walls.

Chief Justice Mushir Alam observed in his order:

*"Therefore in my humble opinion without adverting to merits, as rightly contended by the learned AAG Sindh, where the applicant has earnestly approached the court and prepared to surrender before the trial court for facing trial, this court in all fairness would give fair opportunity to the applicant, more particularly in view of Article 10-A of the Constitution, which has been recently introduced through 18th Constitutional Amendment, which guarantees to a person right for fair trial in any criminal charge against him."*

While walking from CJ's court to the other he asked some one to go through *'judges way'* in the name of security but was told that *'the said corridor was for judges not for accused ones'*.

Within the court premises and outside, angry lawyers protested and chanted slogans against ex-military ruler when he appeared in the court. A group of about 20 lawyers had gathered there to protest against Gen Musharraf while shouting *"he's a military dictator and he should be hanged"* before one of them hurled the shoe which, however, did not hit Musharraf. Shah Zain Bugti immediately announced Rs:200,000 reward for that shoe - advocate, named Tajammal.

The lawyer Tajammal was not detained by police because no charges were filed against him. Though the local TV channels showed video of the incident, but it was impossible to identify the shoe thrower because he was hidden behind part of the corridor. Well, one thing was evident that some one got courage to show the nation how **'some military dictators'** could be treated at times. That was mainly due to Pakistan's involvement in America's War on Terror [WOT] only due to his person.

Gen Musharraf was also directed to **visit in person** the respective courts of Rawalpindi and Sibi and Islamabad to get further 'fateful' orders. The real problem lied that before going in the respective courts for confirmation of his bail, he was required to stand before the *'pulsia'* investigation officers of those cased in which General Sahib had been named.

The President Rawalpindi Bar Association has already moved the Supreme Court to initiate proceedings under Article 6 of the Constitution against Gen Musharraf; this single move could turn all tables of Gen Musharraf's APML any moment.

In his press statements, Gen Musharraf tried to clarify that he was not at all involved in Nawab Akbar Bugti's killing or of Benazir Bhutto nor responsible for Red Mosque episode of July 2007; the respective courts would decide. But how one could forget the *brutal murder of Advocate Iqbal Ra'ad at Karachi who was assassinated* only for his fault that he was pleading Nawaz Sharif's 'hijacking case' in an Anti-Terrorist Court of Karachi.

Gen Musharraf, the 69-year old former president had availed pre-arrival protective bail for 10 and 15 days from two SHC benches respectively.

Though the SHC corridors echoed with pro- and anti-Musharraf slogans in a highly charged atmosphere, however, no untoward incident occurred as the number of both supporters and opponents of Gen Musharraf's APML did not exceed a dozen with sizeable contingent of Rangers and security guards in plain clothes. In two court rooms the General remained calm and quiet and heard the proceedings carefully and intently with clenched lips.

Gen Musharraf had demanded, through his council, five weeks' time to appear and surrender before the trial court in Islamabad and to obtain copies and other relevant material to defend himself in cases against him but the Prosecutor General Shahadat Awan opposed the bail application sternly.

Gen Musharraf ruled Pakistan from October 1999 to August 2008 after seizing power in a military coup and was intending to lead his party, the All Pakistan Muslim League [APML], in the general elections of May 2013. He was forced to step down in August 2008 by Mr Zardari's PPP but equally disliked by many lawyers throughout Pakistan because of his decision to suspend the CJP Justice Iftikhar M Chaudhry just for flimsy reasons.

It was a bad day for Gen Musharraf as another court of Sessions Judge served a notice upon him in a **'missing person case'**. He was asked to appear before the court **on 4th April 2013.**

## ANOTHER CASE IN ABBOTABAD:

In 2011, one M Siddique of Malikpura ward had filed an application under Section 22-A of the PPC seeking registration of a criminal case against Gen Musharraf. Therein it was alleged that his son Atiqur Rehman, an employee of Qadeer Khan Research Laboratory, was picked up by local police one evening of September 2005 – the very next morning of his wedding; was later taken into custody by the sleuths of intelligence agencies and never returned home since then.

On Siddique's application, the District & Sessions Judge had ordered the registration of a criminal case against Gen Musharraf at the city police station in Abbotabad. The accused [Gen Musharraf] had failed to appear before the court during the trial as he was in self-exile. The court had ordered the attachment of General's movable and immovable property and had declared him a proclaimed offender.

However, the case file was closed when the Supreme Court constituted a judicial commission on missing persons case headed by Justice (rtd)

Javed Iqbal Khan. Contrarily it was also on record that one Army Havaldar was hanged on the charge of conspiracy of killing Gen Musharraf and many of his associates were still undergoing prison sentences.

After the arrival of Gen Musharraf in Pakistan on 24th March 2013, the disgruntled lawyers again moved an application in the court of District Judge Arshad Khan seeking trial of the proclaimed offender in the said Atiqur Rehman case and all other cases that were pending against him. The court admitted the application for hearing and served notices to the prosecution and to Gen Musharraf for appearing before the court on 4th April.

Gen Musharraf has come to Pakistan to take another turn of ruthless rule but the general impression prevails that he had landed in self-called trouble; a booby trap of *thana-kuchehry* in Pakistan. For what? – just for one seat in the Parliament – his own seat, that too, if the MQM would like to repatriate his blessings of nine years. History would have called it a beggar's seat.

**On 5th April 2013;** in another blow to former President Gen Musharraf's bid for election, the Supreme Court accepted an application filed against the former military strongman, accusing him of committing treason under Article 6 of the Constitution. A 3-member bench of the apex court, headed by CJ Iftikhar M Chaudhry, was constituted to hear the case on, 8th April 2013. The application was filed by Ch Taufiq Asif, the president of the Lahore High Court's Rawalpindi bench bar association. He had asked the court to try Gen Musharraf for treason for imposing emergency rule in 2007, a move that ultimately paved the way for his downfall.

The former president's electoral future appeared to have gone bleaker as, a week earlier, the returning officer in Kasur, rejected his nomination papers for the elections. By law it was not fair because till then he was convicted.

A local lawyer, Javed Kasuri Advocate, had raised objections over the Gen Musharraf's candidacy for the NA-139 constituency, arguing that he did not qualify to contest elections under Article 62 & 63 of the Constitution. The Returning Officer, Mohammad Saleem, accepted the objections and rejected the former dictator's nomination paper. Gen Musharraf had filed papers to contest the general elections from four seats, including Karachi, Islamabad, Chitral and Kasur.

Meanwhile, a Supreme Court lawyer Barrister Zafarullah, on behalf of the PML[N] leader Ahsan Iqbal, filed an application before the Election

Commission seeking disqualification of Gen Musharraf. The applicant alleged that Gen Musharraf was not able to contest polls due to his involvement in four criminal cases: the Akbar Bugti killing case, the Lal Masjid case, the Benazir Bhutto killing case, and the Missing Persons case.

## JUDGES HOUSE ARREST CASE:

On 18th April 2013, Gen Musharraf, protected by his heavily armed security team, fled an Islamabad courtroom to evade his arrest after Justice Shaukat Aziz Siddiqui of Islamabad High Court ordered his immediate detention on criminal charges of wrongfully confining judges of the Supreme Court of Pakistan on 3rd November 2007 being the President of the country and the Army Chief in uniform.

One M Aslam Ghuman advocate had filed a petition with the Additional Sessions Judge Islamabad, Muhammad Akmal Khan in July 2009, that former president Gen Musharraf and others had detained judges of the Supreme Court of Pakistan and their families at their houses without lawful authority. Their children were neither allowed to attend their schools nor permitted to appear in examinations. District Attorney Mehfooz Paracha and S.I Shahid Mehmood were present in the court during the hearing.

The brief facts listed in the original petition were that on 3rd November 2007 the then COAS Gen Musharraf prevented all the judges of the Supreme Court and High Courts from functioning unless they took a new oath under his issued PCO. The same day seven judges of the Supreme Court headed by the Chief Justice [verification still needed] had declared the said action of Gen Musharraf as illegal and passed the judicial orders prohibiting the judges of the Supreme Court and High Courts from taking oath under the PCO. As a result they were sent home and the same day, orders were conveyed to the district authorities to keep them and their families in their houses till the next presidential orders.

History is cruel. Nawaz Sharif was sent to Attock Jail to bear life sentence in Plane Hijacking Case by the same Anti-Terrorist Court of Karachi which he had invented to take revenge from his political opponents. Similarly, it was an ironic fate of twist for a man who once boasted that he would never allow Nawaz Sharif and Benazir Bhutto to end their exile on their own and return to Pakistan.

In a dramatic move after the court unexpectedly revoked his bail in that case registered on 10th August 2009 with the Islamabad Police.

The retired General, surrounded by his guards, hustled past policeman and sped away in a black SUV to his home in Shahzad Town Islamabad, a compound protected by high walls, razor wire and watchtowers.

The police tried to reach the former military ruler but he was escorted by his personal security, fleeing in his bullet-proof black four-wheeler. In the written judgement, the IHC ordered that: *"He (Musharraf) be taken into custody and dealt with in accordance with law."* Later he was shown arrested by police on papers, kept him in his farm house in Chak Shahzad which was got declared as sub-jail. Judicial remand of 14 days used to be arranged there every time while confined in his residence.

*The lawyers were attacked with fists and shoes, while the officially deputed guards of the Gen Musharraf, turned their eyes back. The court did not take any notice of that attack, although when Ali Musa Gilani had been arrested by ANF from outside the court premises, in the notorious ephedrine case, the 'honourable' judges had jumped with shocks to claim that the sanctity of the court had been violated and they ordered the ANF to produce the accused before them in less than one hour. And of course when that order was obeyed, the accused was granted a bail within minutes.*

The detailed verdict issued by the **IHC *also ordered for sections of Anti-Terrorism Act to be added to the list of charges against the former military ruler*.** The order further said that Gen Musharraf's exit from the court earlier without giving arrest to the police warranted for separate charges to be filed against him.

The story was that Gen Musharraf's lawyers had approached the Supreme Court to file a pre-arrest bail application in order to avoid his surrender to the police. However, the SC returned the 14-page bail application as the timings for the Registrar's office had ended.

Putting a former army chief in jail was an unprecedented move in Pakistan, where the army, or army - backed politicians, had ruled for about 36 years. On administrative grounds, it was considered feasible to declare Gen Musharraf's spacious farmhouse, in an exclusive residential district of Islamabad, as *"a sub-jail where Mr Musharraf can be kept and would formally be declared as arrested"*, a form of de facto house arrest.

Such arrangements were permissible in law and had been in practice before to detain political elite and high-profile Pakistanis, rather than sending them to jail, such as some politicians including Mr Bhutto, Nawaz Sharif, Moonus Elahi and many more.

The matter of illegal confinement of judges in November 2007 and the similar related events were categorically narrated at pages of 599-601 of a book *Judges & Generals in Pakistan' Vol-II* published in 2012 in UK.

The high court's decision to revoke Gen Musharraf's bail reflected a bitter homecoming for the former Army Chief, who returned to Pakistan after about five years of self-exile in Dubai and London; claiming that he had returned to *'save the country'*.

Gen Musharraf's rallies and public appearance had generated negligible public enthusiasm while the four Returning Officers had disqualified him from contesting the polls, ruling mainly that he had imposed the army rule twice, in 1999 & 2007, in the country.

After 3rd November 2007's Emergency, the British media in March 2012 had once, while Gen Musharraf himself was in UK, published that event with concerns - the main paragraph contained that:

*'Most of the Supreme Court judges, including the Chief Justice of Pakistan, who was not called to take oath under the new Provisional Constitutional Order (PCO) of November 2007, were held incommunicado. No one, including newsmen and even the judge's own relatives or acquaintances, was allowed to enter the Judges Colony and meet any of those judges.'*

One (detainee) judge was quoted as saying that they had been isolated from the outside world:

*"......have we committed a robbery? We cannot get out of our residence and find heavy security conducting our surveillance and blocking our way out".*

The security officials who had met the (detained) judges found them in high morale but at a complete loss to understand why they had been detained and treated like criminals. Justice Javed Iqbal, who was offered to take oath as the Chief Justice of Pakistan under the PCO but had refused to do so, and being a heart patient, remained all alone in his official residence. Justice Javed Iqbal told afterwards that we were neither allowed to go out nor was anyone permitted to visit us. Adding that:

*"The judges do not get the newspapers while they also don't have any access to the private television channels; thanks to PEMRA (Pakistan*

*Electronic Media Regulatory Authority). The internet connections (DSL) were also removed from the residences of these so called defiant judges."*

In nut shell; Gen Musharraf was facing what he did with the judges and the judges had also not forgotten those painful days of their seniors. Most intelligentsia including retired CJ Saeeduzzaman Siddiqui, Justice (Rtd) Tariq Mahmood, Rtd AVM Shahzad Chaudhry and Gen (Rtd) Talat Masood in their TV interviews held that the authorities must obey the court orders and arrest Gen Musharraf. The Human Rights Watch observed that:

*"General Musharraf's act today underscores his disregard for due legal process and indicates his assumption that as a former army chief and military dictator he can evade accountability for abuses.*

*The continued military protection for Gen Musharraf will make a mockery of claims that Pakistan's armed forces support the rule of law and bring the military further disrepute that it can ill afford."*

In a poll conducted on the same evening by the **DAWN TV Channel**, conducted by Asma Shirazi, 86% of Pakistani populace voted that Gen Musharraf should be taken through a court trial to uphold the law in the country; 13% voted in favour of extending him pardon in the name of his association with the Pak-army and one percent abstained.

On another TV channel **ARY News of 18th April**, with Kashif Abbasi as host, two retired Generals including Gen Hamid Gul, openly opined that Gen Musharraf should be treated just as a normal citizen like others and should be taken through strict course of justice.

Moreover, lawyers in the capital chanted slogans and cheered the court's directive of bail cancellation whereas the decision was seen as a welcome development by political leaders.

Ironically enough, Gen Musharraf was in the hands of the same judiciary he had humiliated and punished in November 2007. When the IHC turned down his appeal for bail in that case, the former army chief's immediate flight from the court made him a laughing stock in the country and abroad. Two days earlier Gen Musharraf was produced before a magisterial court; a total disgrace because Pakistani president when happened to be the Army Chief too, had never walked up to a magisterial court at least. It was indeed a dramatic change in fortune – a twist of fate.

The All Pakistan Muslim League [APML] used to say he was ready to face justice. But the General himself was expecting special treatment; *perhaps he was looking towards Pak-Army for his rescue which was not moved at all. He had chosen, with typical arrogance, to ignore their advice of 'not to come back'.*

The final outcome of this drama is still awaited. It is in part a farce, in part a comedy, and in other ways a tragedy. Pakistan was witnessing the fall of a man who believed he was invincible and above the law - the message sent out was loud and clear.

The scenes witnessed over those two days were horrible; the lack of enthusiasm for the General from the people could demonstrate that his support was only extended to the number of 'likes' on his Facebook page or followers on his Twitter account.

A general perception prevailed that Pakistan Army should also forget about Gen Musharraf – as he had taken all criminal decisions as president, and not as COAS. *In fact he was guilty of dragging Army into many of his criminal activities un-necessarily and was instrumental in disgracing the good name of Pak-Army.*

Some people tried to paint the picture as if a row would be seen between the two institutions of Army and judiciary; not at all. Black sheep are every where; there may be more in judiciary. The intelligentsia, however, comprehended that the army would not put its own reputation at stake by owning certain wrong decisions taken by Gen Musharraf as the president. But instead of making it a media trial, let the law take its own course.

## *GEN MUSHARRAF ARRESTED:*

Gen Musharraf was also an accused in the Benzair Bhutto murder case and was granted interim bail till 24th April instant by the Lahore High Court Rawalpindi bench.

**On 25th April 2013;** the Federal Investigation Agency [FIA] formally arrested Gen Musharraf in the Benazir Bhutto assassination case after obtaining permission from the court of law to investigate him. Earlier, the ATC No 1, Rawalpindi Judge Ch Habibur Rehman issued orders for General's arrest. The court also granted permission to the FIA to formally investigate Gen Musharraf in the said case.

Gen Musharraf was already under arrest in the judges detention case, FIR No 131, dated 11th August 2009 with the Secretariat Police Station

Islamabad, under Section 344 PPC but *the Section 7 of the Anti-Terrorism Act (ATA) was added in the FIR on the order of the court.*

The jurists though could appreciate that it was un-called for but it was considered as tit for tat – the General had also extended the same treatment to Nawaz Sharif in Plane Hijacking Case in 1999. A JIT was asked to record statements, after which the court proceeding continued as per routine.

**On 9th October 2013;** Pakistan's Supreme Court granted bail to Gen Musharraf over the death of Baloch leader Akbar Bugti, bringing closer the former dictator's possible release after nearly six months of house arrest. His lawyer said the ruling meant he was a free man but he would remain under heavy guard at his residence where he remained under house arrest since April that year.

A 2-judges bench of the apex court, headed by Justice Nasirul Mulk, heard Gen Musharraf's appeal against the Balochistan High Court's rejection of his bail application in the Nawab Akbar Bugti murder case. The bench observed that substantial evidence was not available to involve the General in criminal conspiracy of Bugti's murder and granted bail to the former president.

**On 7th November 2013;** the Adiala Jail authorities formally released Gen Musharraf from his sub-jail, his farmhouse in Chak Shahzad near Islamabad, after he was granted bail by a court. The General remained confined for over seven months while he faced court trials.

Two days earlier, Additional District and Sessions Judge Wajid Ali granted Gen Musharrf bail with a solvent surety of Rs:100,000 against the alleged murder of former Lal Masjid cleric Ghazi Abdul Rasheed and his mother during the army operation on the mosque and the adjacent *madrassa* in July 2007. He had already been granted bail in three main cases discussed earlier in detail.

Even though the General had been granted bail in all cases, Gen Musharraf's name was still there on the Exit Control List [ECL]. The interior ministry had put his name on the ECL on the orders of the Sindh High Court [SHC] in March that year. A high treason case was still in pending against him as the FIA had not started formal proceedings till then. The Supreme Court had referred this case to the federal government to initiate the high treason case for twice holding the Constitution in abeyance.

**The dust settles Down:** After months of delay, Gen Musharraf appeared before a panel of three judges, which was named in November 2013 and had already met 22 times without the General's participation. Former military ruler was charged with treason for his decision of 3rd November 2007 to suspend the constitution.

Many previous appointments had been frustrated at the last minute; including on both Christmas Eve and New Year's Day, then due to suspicious discovery of explosives near his residence. Six weeks earlier, while he left his home for another court hearing, Gen Musharraf suddenly fell ill on the way; his car was swiftly diverted to a military hospital, where he remained for weeks under clinical tests and treatment.

The nature of Gen Musharraf's illness was directly related with his age – 70 years, which included hypertension, a clogged artery, a rickety knee, and some trouble with his spine etc. Once he left the courtroom after twenty minutes: his lawyers pleaded that the court first had to rule on whether a case against a former Army chief could be heard in a civilian rather than a military court. Among media reporters, the staggered court proceedings were likened to an interminable Turkish soap opera.

Gen Musharraf faced serious threats to his life from an array of dangerous militants, and he deserved adequate protection. According to many military analysts, they were deeply uncomfortable with one of their longest - serving chiefs being put on trial—raising the prospect of a possible clash between Pakistan's Generals and its elected civilian leaders if Gen Musharraf would be convicted.

Gen Musharraf's greatest misfortune was that Nawaz Sharif, the man he ousted when he seized power in a military coup in October 1999, had returned to government in June 2013. Soon after taking office, Sharif appeared in Parliament to announce that the government would try Gen Musharraf for "high treason."

After Gen Musharraf deposed him, Nawaz Sharif was hurled into a cell in a sixteenth-century fort along with some of his closest political lieutenants, and later dispatched into exile, to Saudia, where he remained for seven years. Critics argued that *Sharif was motivated solely by revenge and that, given the circumstances, Gen Musharraf was not able to get a fair trial.* But Musharraf's detractors were not only in the parliament: the judiciary was similarly ill-disposed toward the former military ruler due to the judges' confinement episode – quite un-warranted.

Salman Akram Raja, a leading lawyer and constitutional expert commented that *"it was a unique kind of constitutional subversion - a coup against his own government."* That evening, the policemen were scooping up troublesome lawyers and politicians; TV news channels went blank. There were no tanks on the street - only the police barriers around government buildings. In a blunt display of symbolism, Constitution Avenue was blocked.

Gen Musharraf was in fact propelled by the belief that he was still his country's savoir: there was no other explanation for his decision to return to Pakistan in March 2013 from his comfortable exile in London, despite the best advice of his erstwhile allies in both government and the Army. He had come to 'save Pakistan' but in the elections, his party won just one seat. The supporters who had once crowded around him at the height of his popularity fled to rival parties.

Referring to *'The New Yorker'* dated 20<sup>th</sup> February 2014:

*'The Pakistani Army had long urged Musharraf not to return. The former Army chief, Gen Kayani believed that his predecessor's plunge back into politics would invite legal troubles and damage the Army's image. He was correct: the Army is now trying to fend off a crisis it never wanted in the first place. However, it distanced itself from Musharraf's ruinous legacy; it nevertheless cannot abide one of its own former chiefs being convicted for treason.'*

Good luck for Gen Musharraf, the new Army Chief, Gen Raheel Sharif had a longstanding family connection to the General under trial. His brother, the war hero Major Shabbir Sharif, was a close friend of the man now in docks. To honour that bond Gen Sharif ordered the Army to take Gen Musharraf under its protection.

The situation went further complicated. The army under new commander Gen Raheel Sharif remained uneasy with the government's decision to pursue negotiations with the Pakistani Taliban, particularly when the militants were killing Pakistani troops. In January 2014, twenty soldiers were killed in Bannu town, Gen Sharif responded with immense force. Gen Sharif wanted to go offensive but the PML[N] government continued *'inviting the militants to the negotiating table'*. The Taliban have been quick to exploit the new space yielded to them.

The militants did not even bothered to meet PML[N]'s chosen interlocutors. Meanwhile, the bombings continued: in Peshawar, cinemas and pro-government tribal elders were attacked. In Karachi, eleven policemen were killed. Three different media organizations were either attacked by bombs or threatened; lastly the Taliban beheaded twenty-three soldiers in their custody. Beyond that the military's patience could not stand by PM Nawaz Sharif's government. A wider military offensive was launched that weakened Gen Musharraf's trial because the general populace started hailing Pak-Army and cursed the political elite as they deserved.

A much known maxim that *the soldiers cannot be expected to die for the country while their former chief is on trial for treason*. As the offensive against Taliban started the Army got tremendous backing from the people. The army had to come on one front otherwise a tense situation was likely to develop. PM Sharif's kitchen cabinet abstained to prolong Gen Musharraf's trial though they wanted a quick conviction for the record.

But it was not so easily possible.

# Scenario 124

## GEN MUSH'F IN TREASON etc CASES:

### *GEN MUSH'F IN TREASON CASE:*

On 8th **April 2013,** the Supreme Court of Pakistan summoned Gen Musharraf to appear before it next day in response to a petition claiming that his actions in toppling an elected government, suspending the constitution and sacking judges amount to treason; calling for the death penalty if found guilty. Justice Jawad Khawaja said *"...the state had a duty to take effective measures against Musharraf and others who subverted the constitution."*

It was the latest blow to Gen Musharraf's far from triumphal homecoming **on 24th March 2013** after about five years exile. Many of his former enemies were in powerful positions. His court appearance brought him face to face to those *'brother judges'* whom he sacked in 2007 and placed under house arrest.

A brief background: that before the general elections of **11th May 2013,** many political leaders addressed big rallies and public meetings urging in loud voices that *'Gen Musharraf should be taken through judicial process for sending an elected government home in October 1999'.* There were countless hands gesturing that the General should be tried for 3rd November 2007's emergency ONLY and should be chastised as per SC's judgment dated 31st July 2009 strictly.

While debating in favour of the later option the political elite actually wished for NOT opening that **'Pandora box of Treason'** which had been orchestrated on the apex court's floor time and again then. They wanted to finish this treason case in an artistic manner so that names of *'respectable stamping judges & parliamentarians',* could be avoided as co-culprits of treason; not a bad strategy anyway.

The main allegation raised was that Gen Musharraf had flouted and disobeyed Pakistan's sacred Constitution. Leave it aside for a while whether he did it once or twice; in 1999 and 2007. Just consider the golden words of Mr Justice Jawwad S Khwaja that *'Even parliament can't ratify dictator's action.....'* [*Top story of 'the News' dated 26th April 2013 is referred*]; from here we'll travel back.

In my humble opinion, the Constitution had already been defied and contravened before 1999 by the then Prime Minister Nawaz Sharif who, under the false interpretation of 'heavy mandate' had broken the limits imposed on the Chief Executive by the Constitution itself.

Sharif government introduced 13th Amendment to the Constitution, on 3rd **April 1997**, that did away with article 58 (2)(b) and deprived the President of the power to dissolve the National Assembly. One can condone it because this clause was 'misused' twice each on Nawaz Sharif and Benazir Bhutto but why, under the same 13th Amendment, the Prime Minister:

- Once again got that the governors of the respective provinces could only be appointed by the President 'ON THE ADVICE' of the prime minister.

- Once again acquired the powers to appoint the Services' Chiefs, which earlier were with the President.

Nawaz Sharif had sent President Farooq Leghari, Chief Justice Sajjad Ali Shah and COAS Gen Jahangir Karamat home; and the Armed Forces had to anticipate that he might attempt to remove another of their Services Chief Gen Musharraf any time.

Over-confident and more reckless, Nawaz Sharif, in late afternoon of 12th October 1999, thought it prudent and announced, the dismissal of Gen Musharraf as the COAS, precisely when the General was already on board a PIA aircraft on his return journey from Colombo where he had represented Pakistan. Nawaz Sharif appointed his handpicked and trusted man, Lt Gen Ziaud Din, then incumbent Chief of the ISI, as the COAS. The incumbent, DG ISI, failed and Nawaz Sharif fell prey to inability of the COAS designate.

The Corps Commander Karachi acted very swiftly to take the situation under his control, and Gen Musharraf landed safely at the Jinnah Terminal, Karachi. Within a few hours, it was announced on Radio and Television that the armed forces had seized power and Gen Musharraf was in command.

His taking over of 12th October 1999 was challenged in the then Supreme Court. After regular hearings of the constitutional petitions, the Supreme Court delivered its Short Order (Judgment) **on 12th May 2000**, the Supreme Court, *interalia*, stated:

*"With the repeal of Article 58 (2)(b) of the Constitution, there was no remedy provided in the Constitution to meet the situation like the present one with which the country was confronted, therefore, constitutional deviation made by the Chief of the Army Staff, General Pervez Musharraf, for the welfare of the people rather than abrogating the Constitution or imposing Martial Law by means of an extra-constitutional measure is validated for a transitional period on ground of State necessity and on the principle that it is in public interest to accord legal recognition to the present regime with a view to achieving his declared objectives and that it is in the interest of the community that order be preserved."*

*17. That having regard to all the relevant factors involved in the case . . . . three years period is allowed to the Chief Executive with effect from the date of the Army takeover i.e., 12th October, 1999 for achieving his declared objectives.*

*18. That the Chief Executive shall appoint a date, not later than 90-days before the expiry of the aforesaid period of three years, for holding of a general elections to the National Assembly and the Provincial Assemblies and the Senate of Pakistan.*

On 27th **April 2002**, the Supreme Court, **in Syed Zafar Ali Shah Case**, gave a short order validating the holding of the referendum. Significantly the Supreme Court's Order stated:

*"13. As regards the grounds of challenge to the consequences flowing from the holding of referendum under the Referendum Order, apparently these questions are purely academic, hypothetical and presumptive in nature and are not capable of being determined at this juncture. Accordingly, we would not like to go into these questions at this stage and leave the same to be determined at a proper forum at the appropriate time."*

Further; in the LFO challenge case on appeals of Lawyers Forum and others it was heard and decided by a larger bench comprised of CJP Nazim Hussain Siddiqui, J Iftikhar M Chaudhry, J Javed Iqbal, J Abdul Hameed Dogar and J Faqir M Khokhar, on 13th **April 2005**, *inter-alia*, holding; "**.....on facts, which are incontrovertible, there is no basis for initiating such a prosecution.**"

[Throughout that process the incumbent Honourable Chief Justice Supreme Court of Pakistan was at that time Chief Justice of the

Balochistan High Court (BHC), having been elevated on **22nd April 1999** and took oath along with four other High Court judges under **Order No. 1 of 2000, dated 25.1.2000 and was, after ten days i.e. 4th February, 2000 elevated as Judge of the Supreme Court and took oath of office under PCO.**]

*91. "The petitioners also submitted that it is imperative to* **take action against the President under Article 6** *of the Constitution Const. P. 12/2004 etc because under section 3 of the High Treason Act, 1973, no court can examine a charge on grounds of treason unless a reference is forwarded to the court by the President, which in this case is not possible. It is noted that section 3 ibid does not require a reference from the President but this duty has been assigned to the Federal Government. This provision remains in its original form since enacted. The petitioners' argument is misplaced.*

*The petitioners do not seek a striking down but virtually insist on re-writing the same and pray that after doing so, this Court may take cognizance of the matter and initiate a prosecution against the President. Suffice it to say that it is not the function of the courts of law.* **Even otherwise, on facts, which are incontrovertible, there is no basis for initiating such a prosecution."**

*"92. In consequence, the petitions are dismissed. Above are reasons for the short order announced* **on 13 April 2005."**

The 17th Amendment also gave indemnity to Gen Musharraf for subverting the Constitution and validated the referendum of 2002 as a substitute for presidential election which Gen Musharraf was declared to have won. Next, Gen Musharraf was duly sworn in for five years as 'elected' president.

## GEN MUSH's SELECTIVE TRIAL:

On **3rd November 2007;** Gen Musharraf in his capacity as Army Chief proclaimed a state of 'emergency' and issued Provisional Constitutional Order [PCO] which replaced the Constitution of 1973.

On **24 November 2007;** a larger bench of the PCO-Supreme Court under the Chief Justice, Justice Abdul Hameed Dogar, validated the Proclamation of Emergency of 3 November 2007 and the Provisional Constitutional Order of the same date. It also directed the Chief Election Commissioner [CEC] to announce the result of the presidential election.

However, it asked Gen Musharraf to relinquish the office of the Chief of Army Staff.

**On 28 November 2007;** Gen Musharraf resigned as the Army Chief and the following day he was sworn in as President for a second term. He lifted the 'emergency' on 15 December 2007 and revived the Constitution of 1973. A few months after the general elections of February 2008, he faced the threat of impeachment from the newly elected National and Provincial Assemblies and had to resign **on 18 August 2008.** He left the country in disgrace.

Once pre-PCO judiciary was restored in March 2009, the Supreme Court in its Short Order dated 31st July 2009 declared unconstitutional, *ultra-vires* of the Constitution and consequently illegal and of no legal effect, *inter alia* Proclamation of Emergency and PCO of 3rd November 2007 and the Oath of Office (Judges) Order issued in exercise of powers under the aforementioned and all other allied executive orders of the same day.

*The Parliament in PPP regime also declined to indemnify Gen Musharraf for his subversion of Constitution when it approved the 18th Amendment.* Instead, when Gen Musharraf declared that he would return to Pakistan in January 2012, the Senate had passed a resolution on 23rd January 2012 calling for his trial on the charges of high treason. Senator Raza Rabbani moved the resolution which was adopted unanimously. Rabbani moved the motion saying that: *'...that Musharraf twice abrogated the constitution, arrested the judges of superior judiciary and compromised the national interests.'*

It was only after the dissolution of the National and Provincial Assemblies in mid-March 2013 and formation of an interim government that Gen Musharraf returned to the country.

After Gen Musharraf's arrival in Pakistan, the Senate, **on 19th April 2013,** unanimously passed similar resolution again calling for General's trial under Article 6 of the Constitution for derailing democracy and abrogating the constitution. This time the resolution was tabled by PML[N]'s Senator Ishaq Dar and was approved by all members of the Senate.

In some quarters it was also debated that perhaps Gen Musharraf had secured guarantees from the military establishment and/or some Arab countries that he would not have to face a trial for high treason in

Pakistan. Certain legal minds had, however, held that *prima facie*, Gen Musharraf and those who abetted him in subverting the Constitution could be made guilty of high treason. The trial of Gen Musharraf for high treason was considered only a formality as his conviction was almost guaranteed in the light of the Supreme Court *Judgment dated 31ˢᵗ July 2009.*

But contrarily the PML[N] went for selective justice – only to penalize Gen Musharraf for November 2007 action but ignoring some other paragraphs of the SC's same decision dated 31ˢᵗ July 2009; see the next paragraphs:

*"Those high-ranking military officers, bureaucrats and politicians who abetted Musharraf in the commitment of a crime that had been categorically declared an act of high treason are also guilty. They were no fools and fully knew that Musharraf's sole aim was to remain entrenched in the presidency by hook or by crook.*

*The then corps commanders ignored the popular sentiments against Musharraf and supported a Chief who had become a burden on the institution of the armed forces. They were not bound to obey unlawful commands. They could have taken cue from the so-called ex-service men's society which was very vocal in condemning Musharraf for his policies and performance and demanded his resignation."*

During the last week of **June 2013;** the PML[N] government decided to prosecute only Gen Musharraf for his 3ʳᵈ November 2007's extra - constitutional actions. The top military brass was taken into confidence on the subject, **sarcastically emphasizing that the government would not open the issue of 12ᵗʰ October 1999 coup.** The government had also not found anything concrete to conclude that others, whether in the government or in the military on that occasion in 2007, had abetted the dictator in the abrogation of the Constitution. The *31ˢᵗ July 2009's SC order had settled the issue* by ruling:

*"The actions of General Pervez Musharraf dated 3rd November, 2007 were the result of his apprehensions regarding the decision of Wajihuddin Ahmed's case and his resultant disqualification to contest the election of president. Therefore, it could not be said that the said actions were taken for the welfare of the people. Clearly, the same were taken by him in his own interest and for illegal and unlawful personal gain of maneuvering another term in the office of president; therefore, the same were malafide as well.*

*The statement made in Proclamation of Emergency that the situation had been reviewed in meetings with the Prime Minister, Governors of all the four Provinces, and with Chairman, Joint Chiefs of Staff Committee, Chiefs of the Armed Forces, Vice Chief of Army Staff and Corps Commanders of the Pakistan Army, and emergency was proclaimed in pursuance of the deliberations and decisions of the said meetings, was incorrect.*

*The Proclamation of Emergency emanated from his person, which was apparent from the words 'I, General Pervez Musharraf.......' used in it."*

The PML[N] government held that the forces desirous of involving many like the then PM, his cabinet, services chiefs and some judges in the said case, wanted to create confusion between different state institutions merely to save Gen Musharraf. The government was conscious of the trial of Gen Musharraf in no manner should be interpreted as friction between the civil and military. That was why the PM had taken the top military leadership into confidence before unveiling his surprising move to proceed against the dictator.

The intelligentsia wondered that the *SC's order of 31ˢᵗ July 2009 was written by some of the same judges who had earlier declared the coup of 1999 against Nawaz Sharif as OK; then how can the state of emergency declared by the same person not OK in 2007* - did not make sense at all; both were doctrines of necessity.

However, most analysts argued that Gen Musharraf's trial for high treason would open a Pandora's Box. They correctly apprehended that the military establishment would not tolerate the prosecution of their former Chief and Corps Commanders in any way. The military establishment would exert covert pressure to suppress the trial. There were fears that if the Supreme Court ordered for the trial of Gen Musharraf, the military would be left with no choice other than to opt for constitutional deviation, although the chances of any such eventuality were quite remote then.

A midway course was to form a *Truth and Reconciliation Commission* before which all those who were involved in the unconstitutional act of 3ʳᵈ November 2007 could submit the whole truth, admit their fault, repent, seek forgiveness from the nation and pledge to respect the Constitution in future in letter and spirit. However, the Care Taker set up didn't have the courage or motivation to act like that – they preferred to wait for new political set-up to take reins of government affairs.

Coming to article 6, one may say that irrespective of the fact whether any such provision is there in a constitution or not, no constitution can legitimately be abrogated, subverted or put into abeyance by an individual or group of individuals at his/their personal whims.

Only in case of a popular revolution, like the one in Iran in 1979, or through the people at large, the constitution would be discarded or replaced or amended. Performance of the incumbent governments and public opinion seen in the highest order are the best safeguards against constitutional deviations.

## *JUSTICE OR PERSONAL VENDETTA*:

On 20th April 2013, a message titled [*The Fate of General Musharraf*] was circulated by an 'insider' on the Internet media 'revealing' the truth about Gen Musharraf while adding '*I see the media, the politicians and the judiciary asking for his head – the same people whose heads should also roll if the Constitution is applied to them! This is the irony*'. Some of the points mentioned therein were:

[Message begins]

"*Musharraf is in custody today; this is natural justice for the mistakes he committed during his rule.*

*Musharraf had chosen his allies and advisers very badly. He was destroyed by Shaukat Aziz, Tariq Aziz, Altaf Hussian and the PML(Q) which were his allies. Today, they have all abandoned him. This happened as he chose the corrupt, the Qadianis, the enemies of Pakistan and opportunists as advisers.*

*But his actions harmed Pakistan just as Zardari's actions and CJ's decisions are harming Pakistan today. Both Zardari and the CJ would also meet the same fate which Musharraf is facing today. [Both Mr Zardari and CJP Iftikhar M Chaudhry were in saddles then]*

*Musharraf is guilty of following crimes;* **indeed major crimes** *having lasting consequences.*

1. **NRO,** *which imposed upon hapless Pakistan this bunch of crooks in the name of democracy.* **Those who ruled Pakistan for the last five years were not only corrupt; they are traitors.**

2. He allowed the proliferation of electronic media [**foreign funded – mostly by Indo - Zionists**] without ensuring that control did not fall in foreign or hostile hands. Now the same media is skinning him alive.

3. He allowed the CIA to create TTP, offering Pakistan land to NATO unconditionally to supply weapons for terrorist and separatist groups like TTP, BLA and MQM. Thousands of "Raymond Davis" were allowed into Pakistan to wreck havoc with Pakistan's security.

[Rehman Malik's issuance of about 6000 visas to CIA agents, in the garb of security contractors, without scrutiny or security clearance by the ISI or IB, is referred. Some of them used their '**address of staying in Pakistan**' as President House Islamabad or Bilawal House Karachi.]

**But Musharraf is NOT guilty of following crimes:**

1. He or the army did NOT kill Akbar Bugti. That is a lie. Bugti was killed as the roof of the cave he was hiding in, collapsed. Details of the incident have already been discussed many times.

2. Musharraf did NOT kill Benazir Bhutto. That is a lie as well. BB was killed by the TTP. That has been confirmed by every investigation agency that looked into it.

3. The case of Lal Masjid is not so clear. It was confirmed that the TTP used it as a terrorist den. The use of force may have been excessive ...... but the rebellion – whatever its scale or form – has to be put down firmly with force.

Also, remember this:

- A case or FIR cannot be registered against the President on internal security duties or conducting an operation. ..... Are we registering FIR's against Zardari or the PM for all the violence going on in the country? NO! **Then how can FIR be registered against Musharraf for Bugti, Benazir or Lal masjid?**

- **Would that not be Target killing through the judiciary?**

**The present rulers including bureaucrats and judges should learn a lesson. Their fate is also going to be the same to the extent as they act as tools of foreign intelligence to destabilise Pakistan today."**

[Message ends]

The above message demanded a fair treatment and judicious handling of Gen Musharraf's affairs and certainly NOT tainted with personal vendetta of 'some' judges in line. Some segments of the media and the judiciary were, no doubt, complicit in this score balancing game while wrongly amalgamating Musharraf's affairs with the army as an institution.

The whole nation invariably and always hailed, more during the dark years of 2008-13, the statutory role of the army; especially when Asif Zardari allegedly acted deceitfully on two occasions. Firstly, when he put the nuclear arsenal of Pakistan on sale for just about 100 billion dollars; Israel had publicly recommended that the USA should accept the offer.

Secondly, when the Memo, Zardari sent through Hussain Haqqani to the USA, asking a deal for Pakistan's nuclear capabilities in the name of *'democratic civilian control'* over the armed forces including the ISI.

After Gen Musharraf's trial under Article 6 of the Constitution, the intelligentsia suggested to bring Zardari, some Justices, some Chaudhrys and some Maulanas in the same dock. *Over this message, <u>Maj Gen (rtd) Shafique Ahmed</u> tagged a much appealing note* that:

> '......let us not mix up...... Unlike ZIA whose neck was in danger, Musharraf is no threat to anybody. Let the law take its course. A fair trial even if prolonged is the need of the hour.
>
> Pakistan Army should also forget about it..... Musharraf took all criminal decisions as president, and not as COAS. In fact he is guilty of dragging Army into many of his criminal activities un-necessarily and is instrumental in disgracing the good name of Pak-Army.
>
> ......There is a long list of charges against ex COAS Musharraf like Kargil Operation, and as president......What was the need to employ commandoes to conquer JAMIA HAFSA, OR EVEN CAPTURE AKBAR BUGTI. He misused army as a personal property and not as per procedure IN AID TO CIVIL POWER. His unilateral decisions succumbing to the USA...... going for operations against FATA, giving Bases, allowing supply routes, removing Chief Justice of Pakistan, misconduct in organising 'mujras' etc etc have disgraced Pak-Army.
>
> Dealing with those who obeyed and assisted him in these disgraceful acts is a secondary issue and need not be touched now.
>
> There is a misconception of loyalty in many quarters. In Pak-Army we serve the state and not any individuals. We are promoted and

*given appointments on merit alone. [exceptions notwithstanding].*
*Paying respect to our elders is something different but, in state*
*affairs the national interest comes first. And the black sheep who are*
*instrumental in disgracing and causing COLLOSAL damage to the*
*NATIONAL POLICIES, NATIONAL AND MILITARY STRATE-*
*GIES, and governance and even to the Ideology of Pakistan must account*
*for their misdeeds.'*

Earlier; in a live **TV program of ARY News dated 27th June 2009,** the
veteran Army General of Pak-army and the ISI's former Chief Gen
Hamid Gul had said:

*'..... Shariat ko badnaam is [Gen Musharraf] ne karwaya, un logon*
*ko dehshat gard dikha ker, un logon ko jaan boojh ker bandooq se*
*muqabla karwa ker, unko askariat pasand dikhaya, aur Shariat pasand*
*logon ko shiddat pasand dikhaya. Is shakhs ki kabar me jo scene ho ga*
*- wo nakabile bardasht ho ga. General Musharraf,,, jo naam hai duniya*
*ke sab se ghaleez zehniat wale shakhs ka.!'*

[He (Gen Musharraf) had given bad name to the Islamic *Shariah.* He got
declared those Islamic people 'Terrorists' by showing them fighters and
gun-bearers. There would be extremely awful and distressed scene in
Gen Musharraf's grave; that would be un-bearable. Gen Musharraf is
the name of a person who keeps the dirtiest and filthy mindset.]

In another live TV program **'Jawab Deh' of 28th March 2010,** Gen
Hamid Gul had said the same thing in loud words that *'Gen Musharraf*
*should be court martialled for his sins and crimes disgracing the*
*Pakistan Army as an institution'.*

Both the said videos are still available on youtube.

For the past five years, Gen Kayani, the incumbent Army Chief, has been
keenly cultivating an image of a professional soldier who wanted
democracy to continue. In continuity he decided NOT to interfere with
the judicial process or to rescue Gen Musharraf from his legal miseries;
thus successfully avoided the possible backlash from the general
populace. Gen Talat Masood opined at that juncture that:

*"It is difficult for the army to defend Musharraf at this time. It would*
*be much worse than not defending him. The moment you start*
*defending, you are admitting your guilt and saying that you are part of*
*what Musharraf has done."*

Answering a similar question at the *GEO TV network* on the same day of Gen Musharraf's arrest, Gen Talat replied:

> "..... *While his arrest may exacerbate tensions between the army and the judiciary, public pressure to put him on trial may force military leaders to remain silent. This outcome is probably acceptable for the army, which is in an awkward situation, no doubt. If the army tries to protect him in any way, they will be heavily criticized.*"

## *SC ALSO ABETTED TREASON:*

The Supreme Court **on 25th April 2013,** while hearing identical petitions seeking initiation of treason case against Gen Musharraf, observed that **even parliament had no authority to ratify any act of a dictator.** That was another case that CJP Iftikhar M Chaudhry was not able to recall that he himself endorsed the same like acts of the same dictator thrice in the past; in 2000, 2002 & 2005.

Ibrahim Satti, Gen Musharraf's lawyer made special mention of the LFO, saying all the judges had taken oath under the PCO and the sitting Chief Justice Iftikhar M Chaudhry was also among them. *"The SC indemnified all the steps of November 3, 2007 in the Iqbal Tikka case and later the reinstated judges of SC nullified it."*

Ibrahim Satti also pointed out that the Supreme Court's verdict of 31st July 2009 in the judges case had not called for any treason proceedings against his client. He repeatedly contended that the court had no jurisdiction to take action in the treason matter, saying constitutionally the Federation was competent to launch a complaint and to take action under the treason charges. Thus the SC's verdict about treason in July 2009 judgment had no value.

On that point Justice Khilji Arif Hussain said, *"Do you intend that the current matter should be left between your client and the federal government and the apex court should not intervene in the matter."* The option was to leave the matter to the Federation, which would form a special tribunal to hear the case where he [Mr Satti] would present all the arguments to substantiate his client's stance.

Justice Khilji asked Satti to be focused on his contention rather than delivering arguments of the trial court level, adding that the bench was bound to give a decision on the current petitions before it.

Referring to **Ikram Sehgal's** analysis appeared in *'the news' dated 26th April 2013*; …. [if] Gen Musharraf violated Article 6 of the constitution, overthrowing an elected government in 1999, **the Supreme Court also became an abettor to the coup by default** when it gave him legal cover under the 'doctrine of necessity' **with some honourable judges taking fresh oath under the Provisional Constitutional Order.** Prosecution for the imposition of emergency in November 2007 is even murkier legally, restored by newly elected PM Gilani in April 2008. Why were legal proceedings not initiated through that time (in five years)?

The various allegations being levelled against Gen Musharraf included negligence leading to the assassination of Benazir Bhutto, Bugti's murder, the Lal Masjid episode, etc. Placed under house arrest, Gen Musharraf was charged with incarcerating judges after proclaiming emergency in November 2007. Looking at the speed with which he was being legally pursued, one could feel that Gen Musharraf was being hounded, negating the perception of a fair and impartial judiciary. **Certainly it was revenge.**

*No case or FIR can be registered against the army, the army chief or the president or the police on internal security duties or for conducting an operation.* Gen Musharraf was the president in November 2007, Zardari was the president in those days – were the FIRs registered against Zardari or the PM Gilani or PM Raja for all the killings and violence then going on in the country? How could an FIR then be registered against Gen Musharraf for Bugti, Benazir or Lal Masjid?

Issues of national importance and public interest, notwithstanding, settling of personal scores were the legal priority those days. The caretaker government sensibly decided that indicting Gen Musharraf in Article 6, the high treason, was beyond its limited mandate. **Bugti Case** - four army officers negotiating Bugti's surrender were also killed. They were killed along with Bugti when some explosives detonated bringing down the roof of the cave where the negotiations were on. If army wanted to murder Bugti, a rocket launcher fired into the cave would have been enough from a distance; could the army contingent attack the cave knowingly that their senior officers were inside.

Ikram Sehgal further opined that:

> *'What about Rehman Malik's rather bizarre behaviour in running off with the backup car abandoning his grievously injured leader, Benazir Bhutto, bleeding to death? Have the honourable judges gone through the findings of the UN Commission? Why should the buck stop at Musharraf's for failing to give Benazir adequate protection?*

*And was it deliberate? Why not prosecute the entire chain of command from the federal Interior Ministry to the local civil administration and the police?'*

*Justice Shaukat Aziz Siddiqui,* who cancelled Gen Musharraf's bail in a bail-able offence, *got 12,000 votes as the MMA candidate in the 2002 elections from NA-54.* This raises a question of conflict of interest and fair play. *J Siddiqui was Mullah Aziz's lawyer in the Lal Masjid case, did his choice meet the parameters of justice?* Intelligentsia could understand that J Siddiqui should have avoided hearing Gen Musharraf's bail matter because he had also on 'score balancing' spree and took revenge of Lal Masjid episode on behalf of Maulana Aziz.

See another tragedy with Gen Musharraf that his case was placed before an ATC judge named Kauser A Zaidi, who happened to be a brother of Capt (r) Mansur Zaidi, supposedly once court-martialled, on the charges of being a BlackWater-XE contractor, on the orders of Gen Musharraf being the Chief of the Army Staff. However, Mr Zaidi behaved in a routine manner while sending Gen Musharraf on judicial remand.

Gen Musharraf basically suffered due to his disillusions for expecting the streets to rise in protest, raising him high in politics. Unfortunately, he excelled in choosing his allies and advisers very badly. Benefiting from Gen Musharraf's generosity and compassion, many deserted him in the count-down to his forced resignation in 2008. No doubt a patriot but patronising western liberal secularism in the name of 'enlightened moderation', Gen Musharraf created extremism that polarised the society.

Gen Musharraf's hasty departure on extremely bad legal advice from the premises of the Islamabad High Court [IHC] was played up out of proportion by the media. This also complicated matters and eroded his stature in public perception – he could have faced that adversary with grace.

In Ingall Hall of the Pakistan Military Academy [PMA], it is carved:

*"It is not what happens to you that matters but how you behave while it is happening".*

## CH NISAR SPILLED BEANS:

On 22nd April 2013: the interim government refused to try former president, Gen Musharraf for treason under Article 6 of the Constitution.

In its reply to the apex court, the interim government said that considering, deliberating or commencing any legal proceedings under Article 6 of the Constitution would be a measure not in its mandate. The reply further said that the interim government was busy with the security of election candidates.

Justice Jawwad S Khawaja remarked that the court had been seeking an answer for the last eight days and [that day] the interim government said that nothing would be done.

Justice Khawaja further remarked that the interim government said it was not in its mandate to initiate proceedings and in the future it may say that FIR could not be lodged. The hearing of the case was deferred till 23rd April when the lawyers of Gen Musharraf would start their arguments.

**On 18th November 2013;** the Interior Minister Ch Nisar Ali Khan addressed an unscheduled news conference to let all and sundry know that Gen Musharraf was being put on trial under Article 6 of the Constitution, which might take the accused to the gallows in case the charge stood proved. He told the media that procedural formalities for the purpose would start soon as the government was writing a letter to the Chief Justice Inftikhar M Chaudhry – requesting him to nominate three judges of provincial high courts to conduct the trial; a public prosecutor was also nominated for assisting the court during trial.

The interior minister could not choose a better time to deflect public attention from the Rawalpindi's major terror incident. It was Gen Musharraf who was to remain in news in the days and weeks ahead while the killings in Rawalpindi gradually went into the background.

Might be just a coincidence that it was also Ch Nisar who had proposed the name of Gen Musharraf as army chief in 1998 when PM Nawaz Sharif had forced the then COAS Gen Jehangir Karamat to step down after he proposed the establishment of a National Security Council and criticised the accountability process as lopsided. Ch Nisar had to face tremendous embarrassment when Gen Musharraf overthrew the PML[N] government in October 1999.

The trial of Gen Musharraf was expected to bring many new facts to light. For example, the nation could know who were among the supporters of Gen Musharraf's plan to impose emergency; in the proclamation of emergency he had given many names of military and political leadership. All those leaders were going to prove that they were "not" on board in case they wanted to escape consequences. But if they couldn't, they were to be tied in the same rope that of Gen Musharraf. The trial was to open a new Pandora box with no one in position to predict its likely outcome.

Chief Justice Iftikhar M Chaudhry, who had to nominate the judges to try Gen Musharraf was an aggrieved party in the case. He was the one who was pulled by the hair – as recalled by the interior minister at his news conference. A cogent question was that whether an aggrieved CJP could show the moral authority to decline setting up a panel to try his perpetrators. All senior judges of the apex court were among the 'detainees' - and thus could be called aggrieved parties; that aspect had disturbed most think tanks in the government.

Another development cropped up; a resolution was passed by the Pakistan Bar Council [PBC] saying that since the CJP was about to retire, the Judicial Commission [JC] should suspend the process for the appointment of new judges. The question was: if the lawyers body didn't like new judges to be appointed till the retirement of the CJP Chaudhry, would it be fair for the government to ask him to nominate a panel of judges to try his 'adversary' who had called him *'scum of the earth'*?

The timing of opening the new trial was also important because during the next few days the prime minister was going to appoint a new army chief. And who so was to have the decoration was supposed to follow the government's policy against Gen Musharraf. In case he had reservations, a possibility could develop that it would be difficult for the army to have a cordial relationship with the PML[N] government. If tensions started immediately with a new COAS in the driving seat, the shape of the things to come was not expected to be pleasant.

It was more so important because the entire record of the matter on which Gen Musharraf's trial was based – was dumped with the GHQ. The FIA team investigating the matter was not provided with the documents being labelled as secret. Ch Nisar had once felt sorry for advising Sharifs to appoint Gen Musharraf as COAS - another embarrassment by putting the same General on trial was ahead then.

## GEN MUSH'F REFUSED TO LEAVE:

On 31st October 2013; a team comprising four senior PML[N] leaders and a former foreign minister in Gen Musharraf's tenure met him at his

Chak Shehzad residence during night times trying to convince him to leave the country voluntarily as he had got bail from Session's court, next day was fixed for announcement of the judgment reserved in *Lal Masjid* case.

However, Gen Musharraf told media that he had made up his mind not to volunteer into self-exile until and unless he would be exonerated in all cases. He was not ready even to pay visit to his ailing mother in Dubai had the administration offered him ground for leaving. Gen Musharraf was arrested that month on another murder charge regarding Ghazi Abdul Rashid of *Lal Masjid* during July 2007 operation in Islamabad.

*In September 2013,* Gen Musharraf was charged with the murder of cleric Ghazi Abdul Rashid in the *Lal Masjid* operation. The Islamabad High Court [IHC] had ordered a first information report (FIR) to be filed against Gen Musharraf on 12th July 2013 that year but it took the police nearly 50 days to do so.

The IHC passed the order after a writ petition was filed **on 7th July 2013** by GhazI Rashid's son Haroon demanding that the police should file a case of murder against Gen Musharraf who he said was responsible for the *Lal Masjid* operation which killed his father and grandmother. Despite the High Court's order of July 12, the station house officer (SHO) had not registered an FIR when they went to the Aabpara Police Station. Haroon had initially approached the Sessions for an FIR but failed; then he went to the IHC.

**On 10th July 2007,** admittedly 102 people were killed including many students of the *madrassa* in the storming of the Lal Masjid *Jamia Hafsa complex* after a 12-day battle between security forces and alleged militants inside. The *Lal Masjid* Commission in its final report in March 2013, held Gen Musharraf, the then PM Shaukat Aziz and others responsible for the operation and recommended murder cases to be filed against them.

It was generally perceived that Gen Musharraf, despite falling from the fame and power, had strong affiliations and connections in the right places who got relief for him in every case. In the final analysis the general was likely to go Scot free from all cases and PML[N] led government was going to get a stigma on its forehead for nothing – that was why the above cited meeting was considered appropriate.

Earlier, Gen Musharraf was bailed out by the Supreme Court which held that there was no substantial evidence about his involvement in the killing of Baloch nationalist leader Nawab Akbar Khan Bugti. He had also secured bail in two other cases including the Benazir Bhutto assassination case. The rumours of his leaving the country were rife after he got bail in the last case, which were, however, refuted.

Two weeks later, the media brought news that top mediators of the PML[N] government appeared to have succeeded in convincing Gen Musharraf to leave the country after the later was released from a six-month house arrest at his own residence. The first step was to move the Sindh High Court for removal of his name from the Exit Control List ECL, which the court had ordered on 29th March 2013, soon after his returning home from self exile. Although the General had made the ground for leaving the country to take care of his ailing mother, but in fact he was doing so on the advice of security agencies who had warned him of serious threats to his life if he stayed back.

It seemed the history was repeating itself and Gen Musharraf was tasting the same medicine which he had prescribed for the Sharif family 13 years ago on the advice of a friendly country, Saudi Arabia, which was also a guarantor for protecting him against incarceration/execution in the treason case. The media opined that:

> "It is now up to the PML-N government to put a stop on his planned exit from the country on the grounds that an inquiry is pending against him for trial for the abrogation of Constitution and slapping emergency in the country. It appears everything is going well about the government's plan to get rid of the General."

The Sindh High Court had put his name on the exit control list barring him from leaving the country till he was cleared of various court cases pending against him. In his application, Gen Musharraf had prayed that:

> "…..he wants to be with his mother after being released on bail in all the cases against him. His inclusion in the ECL is a violation of his fundamental rights. It was further prayed the court to modify an earlier order restraining him from leaving Pakistan without permission from courts hearing cases against him."

A division bench headed by Justice Sajjad Ali Shah had accordingly issued notices to the Deputy Attorney General and Sindh's Advocate General and Prosecutor General, asking them to respond to the application.

The days and weeks passed without any cogent development in General's trials. In the meantime, Gen Musharraf filed a petition before the IHC and the Special Court pleading that the said treason case be referred to the GHQ for the court martial as he had been an Army General. In the petition, Gen Musharraf through his lawyers had contended that:

> '....he [Gen Musharraf] imposed the emergency on 3rd November 2007 as Chief of Army Staff therefore the military court was the relevant forum for his trial for any alleged offence. Also that the government is trying to deprive me of my fundamental right to a fair trial as enshrined in Article 10-A and Article 25 of the constitution by not transferring his case to the military court.'

**On 23rd December 2013;** the IHC's single bench dismissed the petition. Justice Riaz Ahmed Khan held that the special court had taken cognizance of the matter and that Article 6 of the constitution under which the federal government had filed the complaint against Gen Musharraf had overriding effect on the Pakistan Army Act, 1952 hence the trial could not be transferred to the military court.

**On 21st February 2014;** a 3-members bench of the special court headed by Justice Faisal Arab of Sindh High Court [SHC] had rejected the plea for transferring the high treason case to the military court. Then the special court had said:

> "....the offences under the High Treason (Punishment) Act, 1973 are exclusively triable by the special court established under the Criminal Law Amendment (Special Court) Act, 1976 as its Section 3 (2) ousts the jurisdiction of all other courts."

**On 20th March 2014,** the registrar office of the Islamabad High Court [IHC] returned the petition of former president Gen Musharraf *he had filed before the court regarding his trial in high treason case under Army Act.* The registrar office held that since the special court, seized with his high treason trial, had earlier rejected an identical petition for transferring the said case to the military court therefore being the appellate forum such petition could only be filed in the Supreme Court.

**On 2nd April 2015,** Additional District and Sessions Judge Islamabad Wajid Ali issued warrants for Gen Musharaf over his repeated absence in the murder trial of *Lal Masjid* cleric Abdul Rasheed Ghazi. Two days later, Gen Musharraf challenged the said non-bailable warrants.

In that petition, filed through advocate Malik Tariq, Gen Musharraf contended that police had declared him innocent after a thorough investigation in the case and had placed his name in column 2 of the investigation report, prepared under section 173 of the CrPC and commonly known as the case challan. The petition requested the court to set aside the non-bailable arrest warrants. In October 2013, local police had already submitted the *challan* to the Session's court, declaring Gen Musharraf innocent and left him at the mercy of the court.

The petition also stated that on 2<sup>nd</sup> April 2015, Gen Musharraf had to appear before a medical board constituted to ascertain his health under the directions of a Quetta Anti-Terrorism Court (ATC), where the Nawab Bugti murder case was pending adjudication. Following the ATC's order, the Secretary Health Quetta constituted a nine-member medical board consisting of surgeons, cardiologists, ENT specialists and physicians to examine the former military ruler.

The medical board at Quetta was asked to ascertain whether Gen Musharaf was suffering from some disease and whether or not he was fit to travel. The nine-member medical board had advised Gen Musharraf not to travel out of the port city.

**On 19<sup>th</sup> June 2015;** District and Session Judge Islamabad Kamran Busharat Mufti again issued non-bailable arrest warrant against Gen Musharraf in the same *Lal Masjid* case. The court also rejected a plea requesting complete exemption for Gen Musharraf from appearing in the court. Police was ordered to arrest the General and bring him in court on 24<sup>th</sup> July 2015. The lawyers' panel of Gen Musharraf again approached the IHC to get that warrant vacated.

**On 28<sup>th</sup> July 2015,** Islamabad High Court [IHC] set aside the said non-bailable arrest warrants issued for Gen Musharraf in the murder case of *Lal Masjid*. IHC Justice Aamir Farooq referred the matter back to the Session's judge to decide on the plea for exemption of Gen Musharraf, on the basis of new medical report submitted by the counsel for former president.

Earlier, **on 7<sup>th</sup> July,** the IHC, while overlooking nine Doctors Board's report of April 2015, sought a fresh medical report from Gen Musharraf's counsel after an initial hearing on the petition. However, in the new medical report, the doctors once again advised the former military ruler not to travel outside Karachi. The report was placed before the special bench seized with the *'high treason trial'* of Gen Musharraf and the three members' bench considered it.

Even the ATC Islamabad considered the report and exempted Gen Musharraf from personal appearance in the judges' detention case.

**On 27<sup>th</sup> October 2015;** the special court expressed displeasure with the prosecution for not filing an amended complaint by nominating the co-accused of former president Pervez Musharraf in the high treason case. The case was adjourned till 27<sup>th</sup> November because the matter was sub-judice in the IHC. The IHC was considering the petitions filed by former PM Shaukat Aziz, former CJP Abdul Hameed Dogar and former federal minister Zahid Hamid against their implication in the treason case.

The trial in the treason case was stopped in December 2014 when the IHC admitted three identical petitions filed by Shaukat Aziz, Abdul Hameed Dogar and Zahid Hamid against the Special Court's order. The Special Court on 21<sup>st</sup> November 2014, had ordered the federal government to include these three persons in the treason case as they had allegedly facilitated the imposition of the 3<sup>rd</sup> November 2007 emergency for which Gen Musharraf was facing the treason trial.

Dr Tariq Hassan, the special prosecutor of the FIA, contended that the court could proceed with the trial of Gen Musharraf as there was no stay order. However, Justice Faisal Arab remarked that under the CrPC, there should be a joint trial of the main as well as the co-accused persons.

Moreover, the amended complainant had not been filed before the Special Court yet by the secretary interior after including the co-accused in it. The court was told that the IHC had reserved its verdict on the identical petitions of the co-accused; and the federal government had also expressed willingness before the IHC to proceed against the 'co-accused' persons.

**Ansar Abbasi,** through his essay in *'the News' of 20<sup>th</sup> November 2015* claimed that:

> *"Sh Akram the Special Prosecutor, had told him that he had received federal governments fresh instructions to proceed with the high trea-son case - also that the high-treason trial of Gen Musharraf was not welcomed by the military establishment. Though the government had initiated the former dictator's trial on the apex court's instructions yet it faced serious problems from what had been generally referred to as the remnants of Gen Musharraf.*

*The 2014 decision of the Special Court to include former PM Shaukat Aziz, ex-CJP Abdul Hameed Dogar and former Law Minister Zahid Hamid as abettors in the high-treason case had disappointed the government, which appeared to have lost interest in the case."*

In this nine-page judgment of the IHC, Justice Noorul Haq Qureshi and Justice Aamir Farooq severely admonished the federal government and the Federal Investigation Agency (FIA) for poor investigation and directed it for re-investigation.

The case was adjourned till 12th December 2015.

# Scenario 125

<u>**GENERAL ELECTIONS 2013-I:**</u>

<u>*ELECTION POLITICS STARTS:*</u>

Terrorism in Pakistan can be attributed to two main factors; primarily the Tehreek e Taliban Pakistan [TTP] & the other remained Lashkar e Jhangvi [LeJ]. TTP has been mainly operating on or near Pak-Afghan borders, FATA areas, Peshawar, Kohat, Hangu and DIK districts of Khyber PK province; and fighting against the Pakistan's foreign policies; its so-called friendly relations with America and the West; Pak-Army's intelligence agencies; its compromises with foreign forces etc.

Pak-Army wanted to take stand against the TTP but could not do without the support of the people and the green signal from the PPP's ruling government; both were not available to them; never in the five years 'alleged' democracy. The general populace of Pakistan was brought to favour the 'peace negotiations' with the TTP; considering that they were launching their attacks in Pakistan as a reaction of drone attacks from America. Certain groups' albeit maintained that the citizens were at fault in thinking so.

The general public kept on thinking that once the US forces would quit Afghanistan in 2014, the drone attacks would be ending so the TTP would behave in a better way; *Imran Khan's TPI and some media groups were waving the olive branch in this direction.* The intelligentsia took it other way round; based on their access to the international reports and analysis abundantly available on media under the head 'Taliban'.

LeJ mostly targeted the Shiite community. Initially they were operative in Punjab only but later targeted Gilgit, Karachi and Balochistan to the maximum. LeJ normally operated through suicide bombers; killing by firing was done twice in Balochistan and perhaps once in Gilgit; when they off loaded certain passengers from buses, checked their IDs and the firing squads killed them in a brutal way at the spot.

In a meeting *held on 23rd February 2013*, Chairman US Senate Foreign Committee, Senator Robert Menendez, with Nawaz Sharif, PML(N)'s

Leader of Opposition Ch Nisar Ali Khan and Punjab's CM Shahbaz Sharif, the future of both countries was discussed, particularly policies in the region. During the course of the generally warm and friendly meeting, the two sides had a comprehensive exchange on serious issues, as well. It was taken as *'indirect assurance'* to the US that *'nothing would change – we'll continue to be your slaves' after we won elections.*

This was the **pre-election US assurance** after which PML(N)'s spokesman Pervez Rasheed had told the media about the US-PML(N) meeting that *'the PML(N) will not go for seat adjustments [in the coming elections] with any extremist religious group or party. Moreover, the PML(N) is determined for a crackdown over LeJ in Punjab.'*

Strange enough that one of the top intellectuals of the PML(N), Ayaz Amir had categorically written in one of his essays that PML(N) was in constant contact with *Jam'at e Ahl e Sunnat* [the changed name of the LeJ] and were working out the proportional seats in the next general elections.

The intelligence reports were open till then that PML(N) was holding regular sessions with LeJ through Punjab's Law Minister Rana Sanaullah. The Federal Interior Minister Rehman Malik had told in a media conference that *'we can control the alleged terrorist activities any where if Rana Sanaullah dissociates himself from patronage of the LeJ'*. Nawaz Sharif had given a promise to the Saudi rulers that PML(N) would not nominate his candidates on 15 seats chosen or indicated by the that particular religious group.

Referring to Najam Sethi's analysis in daily the **'Jang dated 24ᵗʰ Feb 2013'**:

*'Malik Ishaq of LeJ was arrested by Punjab police in February 2013, when he was just back from Umra, where he had one to one meetings with kingpins of Saudi rulers. It was eye-wash operation, the media had declared. He had been accused for murder of seventy (70) people, has been in jail for fourteen (14) years but he has been leading the LeJ from jail. Rana Sanaullah got him bailed out after arranging acquittal orders in 34 cases.'*

Astonishingly, Malik Ishaq had no religious background nor had he studied in any big religious school yet he was widely respected by all *Ulemas* of Pakistan. Attack on Sri Lankan Cricket Team in Lahore was also attributed to the LeJ; they had admitted it too.

Since long, WikiLeaks was releasing 'intelligence reports' that Saudi Arabia had been patronizing certain religious groups for launching terrorist activities in Pakistan. However, *UK's daily 'Guardian'* was the first newspaper which openly placed written allegations, <u>declaring its rulers responsible, against the Saudi Arabia for terrorism in Pakistan</u>. After that all the electronic and print media started criticizing that holy land for those nefarious and wicked activities all around.

Not known that why Saudi Arabia had turned around from Pakistan since the last five years; may be due to its President Zardari and the then PM Mr Gilani being *Shia*. Nawaz Sharif had taken advantage of such feelings of Saudi rulers; perhaps that was why the *Shia* party members in the PML(N) were given so importance.

**On 27th February 2013;** PML(N) spokesman Pervaiz Rashid has said that Sharjeel Memon should disclose that

> – *It became a hot topic in media discussions that if LeJ was a terrorist faction linked with PML(N) then why the Sindh government had issued arms licenses to them. Moreover Punjab Chief Minister Shahbaz Sharif had never forgiven any culprit whereas the history keeps it on record that the PPP had struck an agreement with Maulana Azam Tariq, which also had the signatures of Asif Zardari.*

Mr Rashid also asked Memon that when the government would question those who were aiding criminal suspects in fleeing the country.

Earlier, the PPP had blamed the PML(N) of backing the terrorists who were responsible for the *Quetta blast of 16th February 2013*. It was alleged that the Punjab Law Minister Rana Sanaullah was harbouring and nurturing terrorists in Punjab, including those belonging to the LeJ which claimed responsibility for the then bombing in Quetta that killed 89 people, mostly Hazara Shias.

MNA Pervaiz Malik said in a press conference that:

> 'Rehman Malik cannot mislead the nation by levelling allegations against PML-N of having relations with sectarian organisations, neither could he evade blame for failure in protecting life and property of the people.
>
> ....... that Rehman Malik's disappearance from the scene at the time of attack on Benazir Bhutto Shaheed was highly meaningful and the

*nation asks him as to why did he go to Bilawal House instead of protecting and ensuring security of Benazir Bhutto.*

*Disappearance of Rehman Malik at the time of martyrdom of Benazir Bhutto was a secret which would ultimately be revealed by the time.'*

On the other side; **Imran Khan's political start** from Lahore was marvellous. He thought that so much gathering would take him and his PTI to the Parliament. Youngsters from all of the Punjab were there to listen him because he had announced for a change.

After a year he developed thinking that to reach the Parliament, only youngsters would not be enough. He went out for 'elect-ables', Shah Mahmood Qureshi and Makhdoom javed Hashmi and Jehangir Tareen joined him – it was a good gesture but the youth had taken a step back. Some people considered it as Imran Khan's mistake through which the confidence of the young generation was shaken a lot. Yet the next elections would prove if Imran Khan was wrong.

Imran Khan was rightly going on Z A Bhutto's track. Bhutto's PPP had come with a slogan of change so he had swept margins from all the four provinces of [West] Pakistan in 1970's elections. In his Parliament there were every kind of people; from all walks of like, of all age, of all sects and clans, students and professors, *haris* and land-lords, old and young etc.

Much before 1977 elections ZA Bhutto had started depending upon elect-ables; he recruited them in his PPP, given them tickets instead of poor persons who had links with masses – therefore, got a humiliating defeat and ultimately gallows, too.

Bhutto was hanged but those elect-ables continued to change horses with the time; as a result they are still there in power – earning hatred from the general populace, from all corners. They know which party's chips are up; you would find them there sooner or later.

So, never mind my countrymen! They would be there once more in the Parliament; doesn't matter to which party you vote for.

## GIMMICKS FOR OVERSEAS VOTERS:

On 14th February 2013; the Supreme Court of Pakistan ordered NADRA to issue NICOP [National Identity Card for Overseas Pakistanis] for overseas Pakistani's to all eligible voters, while also ordering the ministry for overseas Pakistani's as well as the Ministry for Law and NADRA to cooperate with the Election Commission of Pakistan [ECP] in that regard. It was ordered that overseas Pakistanis would be able to cast their vote via e-mail or by sending their ballot in a sealed envelope mentioning their constituency to the ECP by post.

The election process, in many ways, had take start several months back on a petition filed by Imran Khan's PTI, when the Supreme Court annulled millions of bogus votes that had been registered across Pakistan, primarily as a testament to the mysterious influence that forces of status quo held in Pakistani politics. Since then, an elaborate exercise was undertaken – involving NADRA, the Election Commission [ECP], the political parties, and individual aspirants of political office in different constituencies – to prepare fresh and accurate voter's lists.

An aspect of this exercise, an unending process – in fact never resolved, pertained to allowing Overseas Pakistanis to cast their ballot in the national and provincial elections. In this regard, two constitutional petitions, one by Nasir Iqbal, and another by Imran Khan, were filed before the Supreme Court. A final authoritative judgment had not been announced in the matter; nonetheless, **on 14ᵗʰ February 2013**, the apex court passed an important Order that outlined a tentative procedure for allowing all Overseas Pakistanis to exercise their fundamental right to adult franchise.

It remained a fact that no major political party in Pakistan, as an official stance, opposed the idea that Overseas Pakistanis should be allowed to vote in the general elections. In fact, almost all political parties expressed their desire to expand the right of adult franchise to include Overseas Pakistanis. However, based on popular perception, since the parties of status quo, PPP and the PML[N&Q] had more to lose than gain from Overseas Pakistanis voting in the elections, thus acted as unspoken inertia concerning the efforts to ensure that Overseas Pakistanis could conveniently and effectively cast their ballot.

Certain school of thought kept arguing against the very philosophy arguing that since most of the Overseas Pakistanis keep another citizenship sworn an oath of allegiance to another country than Pakistan, their vote was tainted. This was an inherently flawed argument that dual nationality, while being a disqualification in terms of getting elected to the Parliament, as per Article 63 of the Constitution, is not illegal for the voters to spell their opinion. Moreover, the Citizenship Act 1951 contained no provision disenfranchising a dual national from his or her right to vote.

The official stance of the government, thus far, remained that while it never resisted the principle of allowing Overseas Pakistanis to exercise their right to vote; the process concerning the same had to be formulated through a legislative instrument. This contention, while advocated by successive Attorneys General of the government, had been rejected by the Supreme Court, as evident from its order dated **14th February 2013**. The apex court, in laying down tentative methodology for allowing the Overseas Pakistanis to vote, had correctly observed that no legislation was necessary in this regard; and that the same could be done through a collaborative effort of NADRA, the ECP and the concerned ministry.

This contention gained force from the principle that since adult franchise was a fundamental right of every citizen, there was no need for a special legislation that allowed a portion of the citizenry to exercise their fundamental right. The right was already there – all that required was for a procedure to be adopted for its exercise, which could easily be done through administrative action.

On the administrative side, away from the process of allowing votes to be cast through mail or at Pakistani embassies or consulates, another issue needed to be addressed: Which overseas Pakistanis, under the law, had the right to cast their ballots? In this regard, Overseas Pakistanis could be placed into three broad categories:

- Pakistani nationals who were living abroad, but did not have foreign citizenship.

- Pakistani nationals who were living abroad and had a foreign citizenship.

- Foreign nationals of Pakistani origin who had subsequently sought the citizenship of Pakistan.

As per Section 6 of the Electoral Rolls Act 1974, *"a person shall be entitled to be enrolled as a voter"* if he/she is a) a citizen of Pakistan, b) not less than 18 years old, c) is not of unsound mind, and d) is a resident. To clarify the 'resident' requirement, Section 7 of the said Act states that resident is anyone who, inter-alia, *"owns or possesses a dwelling or other immovable property"* in any constituency in Pakistan. Consequently, in the light of this law, all the three categories of Overseas

Pakistani discussed above, to the extent that their requirements under the law could be ascertained, ought to be registered as a voter and be afforded a convenient opportunity to cast the ballot.

Hiding behind the shield of administrative difficulties or legislative tricks was nothing more than delaying tactics on the part of status quo political forces, resulting in frustration over 4.3 million Pakistanis living abroad. Neither the law, nor the Constitution, nor any standard of modern democracy allows for such evasion. The apex court had correctly dismissed the government's contention that a fresh legislation was required to bring the Overseas Pakistanis into the fold of our democracy, and pointed towards a plausible administrative path for the way forward.

**On 11th April 2013;** the ECP told the apex court that voting for Pakistanis abroad would be ensured; adding that home work had been completed to include overseas Pakistanis in the forthcoming general elections. The apex court was further told that at a meeting of the ECP and other functionaries of the government had already been held in that regard. The three member bench of the SC, comprising CJP Iftikhar M Chaudhry, Justice Gulzar Ahmed and Justice Sh Azmat Saeed, were told details of ECP's meetings on the matter.

Director General ECP Sher Afgan told the court that:

> "......as part of the first step Pakistanis residing in ten countries would be included. About 4.5 million registered voters are residing in other countries, out of which 3.5 million are in the Middle East and 2.9 million out of this figure are currently living only in two countries - Saudi Arabia and the United Arab Emirates.

> ......that the NADRA had made E-voting software for the expatriates and would be utilised during the coming elections. As per their plan in countries where the population of registered voters was over 100,000, two polling stations were to be set up. Any country with less than that number would get one polling station. The court was told that visas for the staff appointed in foreign missions were also under process.

**On 10th May 2013;** President Asif Zardari signed the **Electoral Laws (Amendment) Ordinance 2013,** [only a day before elections] facilitating overseas residents to cast their votes from abroad. Unfortunately this came so late for those overseas Pakistanis who looked forward to voting in this election since there was not enough time left to make the necessary arrangements. With the apex court unremittingly pressing the ECP to arrange for overseas vote, the plans remained up to long discussions and methodology.

At the initial stages, the ECP was much enthusiastic but later it had shown reluctance, stating that with the limited time available it was not possible for the electoral body to ensure that satisfactory arrangements could be made for the elections.

Following Supreme Court's directives the ECP drafted the text of an ordinance and sent it to the interim prime minister which was to be approved by the president. Since the national assembly was dissolved in March that year after completing its tenure, a presidential decree was the only way to amend the relevant law.

The **high joke** was that under the amended bill:

> '....the ECP will have at least 14 days before elections to establish polling stations in an embassy, a mission or a consulate, provided that the ministry of foreign affairs has obtained prior consent of the host country.
>
> .... overseas Pakistanis had to register themselves at the embassy, mission or consulate where they intend to cast their vote, no later than ten days before polling day."

It was clear that although the ordinance had been issued by the president, there were no chances of voting rights being extended to overseas residents for the elections scheduled on 11th May 2013. There was only one day left for the election and it was, of course, impossible to make all the arrangements needed to facilitate overseas voters to cast their ballots.

## *PPP COMPLETED 5 YEARS*:

Pakistan passed through a unique moment in its history during March 2013. In the past, the elected governments were thwarted by military coups or shunted aside due to their corrupt practices.

Five years ago, few would have predicted the achievement. During that period, Pakistan experienced political crises, Taliban insurgencies, a wave of terrorism, military offensives, dangerous standoffs with India, epic national floods and a breakdown of relations with the US after Osama bin Laden episode in Abbotabad. One media analyst said:

*"There's a lot of despair regarding the deteriorating security situation in Pakistan, continuing high levels of corruption and political kow-towing to extremist elements - but it's a true milestone that signals an emerging consensus that democracy is the right governing system for Pakistan. There's a long way yet to go."*

On 16<sup>th</sup> March 2013; the PPP government completed its full five-year term in office - a first for a civilian government in Pakistan's 66-year history. All indicators pointed that the country's first - ever civilian – to - civilian transfer of power would happen smoothly in May that year. Prime Minister Raja Pervez Ashraf said in his farewell address that:

*"It is an honour for me... to bring to the nation the tidings of democratic continuity. Pakistan has a long history of strife between the pro-democracy and anti-democracy forces, but now, with God's grace, the democratic forces have finally achieved victory."*

Since 2008, when PPP government came to power, the country had seen increased violence by Taliban and sectarian groups - both the economy and the energy situation got worsened. Political survival had been its chief concern.

Soon after the PM's address, TV carried live broadcasts from the streets of Lahore and Karachi, where the public mood was one of anger over corruption, the bad economy and faulty public services. The reaction of political analysts was mixed; with many holding massive corruption and nepotism as the reasons for the government's perceived failures. The absurd civil - military relationship did not matter because Gen Kayani was given three years extension by the PPP regime and most steps were taken with mutual consultation.

Even in his televised address on in last night in rule, while trumpeting the occasion, PM Raja Ashraf quietly conceded that his government had also been a source of disappointment.

Public resentment had been fed by an endless list of problems: enduring power shortages [up to 18 hours a day at the peak of summer]; the fail-ure to curb terrorist attacks, protect religious minorities and formulate a coherent antiterrorism strategy; a slow and weak response to the floods; sluggish economic growth, a bloated public sector, cresting infla-tion; and tales of legendary corruption, carving out private fortunes from a treasury to which they scandalously pay little in tax. Many Pakistanis, particularly among the urban middle classes, were looking to the next elections with relief.

The superior judiciary was, however, seen as having hounded former PM Gilani to make an official request to the Swiss government to re-open corruption cases against President Zardari. In 2012, Mr Gilani was symbolically convicted when he refused to comply, leading to his disqualification. Next PM Raja Ashraf sent that letter to Swiss authorities but till then the mandatory period had been lapsed; Zardari had managed to deceit and defeat the Supreme Court.

The Supreme Court continued to intervene in high - profile executive affairs through *suo-motu* jurisdiction - the power of the higher courts to oversee matters they deem to be of public interest; and continued to disrupt the normal functioning of the government throughout its tenure. The media's overwhelming support for judicial activism also kept nibbling away at PPP's credibility and legitimacy.

The military, traditionally suspicious of the PPP, embarked on a defiant course as early as July 2008 when it conveyed its bullied refusal to its Interior Minister Rehman Malik over a move to place the ISI under civilian control. A year later, it made the unprecedented move of publicly opposing a 5-year $7.5bn American aid [Kerry Lugar] bill because it was filled with filthy preconditions. Then a memo-gate Scandal of 2011 appeared in which the judiciary played a major role in highlighting it.

The said scandal revolved around accusations that the two men had written a memo asking US officials to prevent the Pakistani military from staging a coup against the civilian government – and moreover; America was requested to take over command of the Pak-Army through some mutually agreed mechanism.

There were more moments when it seemed the government wouldn't make it. Over a year ago, PM Gilani spoke of the hazards of having a *"state within a state,"* the Generals publicly reprimanded him. Once the PM Raja Ashraf narrowly evaded arrest in January 2013, after the court issued a warrant for his allegedly taking kickbacks in Rented Power Project scam. In the end, the court relented and allowed Ashraf to stay in office.

Under army chief Gen Kayani, the Generals were in no mood to snatch back direct control. From behind a thin veil, they continued to control much of foreign, defense and national security policy, leaving the day to day running of the country to the politicians. The religious right, chastened at the last elections, were expected to make some gains.

Dr Tahirul Qadri, a Sufi cleric from Canada, who led protests of tens of thousands in January 2013, was not taking part in the elections.

The government's failure to revive the economy was in large part due to its failure to curb militancy which was partially blamed on the political opposition. Pakistan continued to be racked by sectarian violence and a Taliban insurgency.

The PPP government had also claimed its achievements. With only marginal surplus seats in Parliament, the PPP managed to hold together an unruly coalition with junior partners. President Zardari proved to be a shrewd dealmaker while stitching together unlikely alliances with erstwhile enemies.

In a display of political maturity, the government and the opposition were able to collaborate and pass three constitutional amendments. In the past, Pakistan's politicians rarely let slip a chance to bring their opponents down, even if it meant opening the way for another return of military rule. Whatever strong disputes Sharifs had with Zardari's administration, both insisted they should be resolved within the fold of democracy. However, that maturity faded away, as the two parties squabbled over care taker slots – they had to refer the case to the Election Commission of Pakistan [ECP]

*The PPP government, through 18th amendment in the Constitution, abolished for ever, the elections within the political parties* – meaning thereby that PPP and the PML[N], the two big parties will remain the family properties of Zardari and Sharifs respectively. The MQM, ANP, PML[Q] and JUI also became indirect beneficiaries.

The PPP and its 'friendly opposition' PML[N] made fool of the whole Pakistani populace but never went for *'Local Body Elections'* since eight years – a constitutional requirement. However, during 2014-15 the local elections were successfully held.

## PPP GIMMICKS FOR ELECTIONS:

On 6th March 2013; when there were only nine days left with the PPP government in saddles; a meeting of the *Economic Coordination Committee [ECC]*, took some drastic decisions to push last nail into the country's coffin. The said decisions were taken to extend huge and recurring personal financial benefits to the ruling class – such like real democracy is often seen in Pakistan – apparently to attract the voters towards PPP.

The ECC of the Cabinet met under the chairmanship of Federal Minister for Finance and Economic Affairs, Senator Saleem H Mandviwalla to discuss various agenda items. The following decisions were taken in the meeting.

**Good Decision:** The ECC approved exemption of all foreign and local components of the Karachi Circular Railway [KCR] from imposition of general sales tax, customs duty and other federal levies in order to ensure financial viability of the project. To facilitate and accelerate the project of KCR, Ministry of Railways moved a summary to get the approval of the ECC for waiver of GST and customs duty on the loan component of the project.

The KCR was a mega project of national importance aimed to provide modern rail-based commuter service for the citizens of Karachi with a total cost of US $2.6 billion. ECC was informed that Japan International Cooperation Agency [JICA] would provide US $2.4 billion on a 0.2% mark up payable in 40 years, including 10 years of grace period.

**Bad Decision:** The ECC approved the request for grant of inland freight subsidy of Rs:1.75 per kg for 1.2 million MT of sugar allowed earlier for export by the ECC in view of *'the industry's thin liquidity position'*. Already the sugar mills owners were given inland freight subsidy of Rs:1.75 per kg which was then extended to the exporters.

All the sugars mills in Sindh are owned by the PPP' leadership, Zardari & Family; and of Punjab are owned by the PML's leaderships, Sharifs and Chaudhrys. Already they were given cash benefits of about Rs:8 billions on various counts and through this meeting another trash of Rs:2 billions were made pushed into their pockets.

The three top political families make a sugar mafia in Pakistan and had been selling sugar at Rs:130 per kg to the consumers being in an agriculturist country when the same commodity was sold in European countries at 43pence per kg in retail and since five years.

**Bad Decision:** The ECC approved a summary of Finance Division to solicit the approval for equity investment in Democratic Republic of Congo. The State Bank of Pakistan evaluated the proposal and recommended that M/s Lucky Cement Limited may be allowed to remit US $40 million on account of equity investment in connection with establishment of cement manufacturing plant through incorporation of Joint Venture Company with the condition that the company will manage foreign exchange requirements from the open market and the outflow will be coordinated with the State Bank of Pakistan.

In fact, it was a direct admission by the PPP government that they were unable to provide power supply as per industrial needs of the manufacturers so the investors were being allowed to take their money away. During PPP's this regime, 73% of Cloth manufacturers and Loom owners had already shifted their bases to Bangladesh and Indonesia.

**Good Decision:** In order to provide fiscal relief and to rehabilitate the economic life in Khyber PK, FATA and PATA, the ECC approved that the areas of *Hub* and *Hattar* may be included in the ambit of DTRE scheme available to ghee manufacturers and exporters based in KP and Balochistan. The ECC further approved withdrawal of the condition of export performance of last four years plus 20 percent enhancement. The ECC allowed the exporters of ghee to acquire the quantity of raw material for manufacture and export of 1000 MT of ghee only. The summary for subject approval was forwarded by Federal Board of Revenues.

**Good decision:** The ECC approved *"Framework for Power Co-generation 2013* (Bagasse/Biomass)" as an addendum to the Renewable Energy Policy 2006. This framework shall be effective for all high-pressure cogeneration projects utilizing bagasse/biomass. The ECC also approved extension of Renewable Energy Policy 2006 for an additional five years. The summary was moved by Ministry of Water and Power.

**ANOTHER INSTANCE:** During Pakistan's general elections of 2013, *Britain gave £300m of taxpayers' money* to PPP's Benazir Income Support Programme, a controversial programme of cash handouts. In evidence to a parliamentary inquiry, UK's leading development economist, Ehtisham Ahmad, told that the fund was being used to buy support for President Zardari, and his party. The said Economist at the London School of Economics, said:

> *"Britain's Department for International Development (DFID) was pouring money into a scheme driven by the mechanism to make friends and influence people. This is the re-election campaign of Mr Zardari - well done."*

The Select Committee on International Development was due to publish its report into aid to Pakistan next day. Britain had rapidly expanded its assistance in those years and Pakistan was then the biggest recipient of UK aid, receiving £450m per year by 2015.

The critics objected that *'Pakistan has one of the smallest tax bases in the world and two - thirds of its politicians pay no income tax at all, yet the country can still afford an expanding nuclear arsenal'*. Daily Telegraph dated 1st April 2013 is referred for details.

Cash handouts have been the buying technique of the PPP, later adopted by PML[N] also, and our political elite dragged the British aid into the same black hole. Half the £300m was named for the families to help lift them out of poverty, while the rest was used to encourage parents to send children to school. But the countrymen knew that all money goes to Swiss banks accounts of many – the lists of poor people are placed in the files since more than a decade. A copy of the same 'poor peoples list' was also handed over to the British authorities to get the aid.

The name of the [Benazir Income Support] program was enough to make the people believe that the money was coming from the **Bhutto family rather than the government** if al all it was distributed. Later, Mrs Bhutto's son Bilawal also used those lists of beneficiaries for follow-up visits in which families were told to remember where the cash had come from when they would go to the poling stations.

Imran Khan had also warned that Britain's surge in aid would not produce sustainable results - nothing less than a scam to "buy votes". PML[N] had promised to overhaul the BISP and rename it the **National Support Programme** to avoid the taint of politicking while openly criticizing that the programme was riddled with *"rampant corruption, nepotism and embezzlement"* – but nothing done practical; rather revitalised it with more money.

However, it was understandable that UK's development assistance should have been based on need and effectiveness - not politics.

### ELECTION CHALLENGES AHEAD:

The main charges cropped up were that Asif Zardari well-played by:

- *'Looting the treasury and appointing persons of ill repute to high executive and financial offices to keep the plunder under wraps;*

- *Going too far in patronizing the MQM, ANP and individuals like Asma Jehangir and Najam Sethi who were enemy agents in public eyes; may not be true.*

- *The 'religious extremists' were pushed into fight in Karachi, Gilgit and Balochistan.*

- *Falsely propagated that the armed forces and superior judiciary would create the situation like that in East Pakistan in 1971.*

- *On one side Gen Musharraf was given red carpet send-off; but at the same time Baloch nationals were covertly instigated to chase Gen Musharraf – just to get the Pak-Army maligned.'*

The PPP government ended on 16th March but Mr Zardari stayed there as President of Pakistan. His intrigues continued as a single PPP fighter.

President Zardari used delaying tactics as usual to buy time for inventing some remedy for his maladministration during his tenure in Presidency. He had used his position as PPP Chief for five years and maintained tight control over all levers of executive power. The provincial governors were his trusted appointees and he was sure that he would have similar control over the caretaker managers in the centre and also in the provinces.

President Zardari tried to follow footprints of President Ghulam Ishaq Khan to *'organize rigging of elections'* like in 1993 – but could not find a way. Imran Khan was right that with Asif Zardari as President, fair elections were unthinkable.

Mr Zardari played on the bad wicket. He wanted to recall his secret deals of 2005-07 with America forgetting that if they could abandon the Shahinshah of Iran, Saddam Hussain, Col Qazzafi and Hosni Mubarak; then Asif Zardari and Gen Musharraf were surely spent cartridges for Washington. The US played on their new bet – Nawaz Sharif.

The main concern was not what the contesting politicians were putting up; the anxiety was what Nawaz Sharif [NS] was up to – MFN for India, policy for dealing with Baloch dissidents and future of China – Russia - Iran relationships. He proposed Asma Jehangir as caretaker PM before media but abandoned her; got approved Najam Sethi as CM allegedly being India – favourite. Muslims in India, particularly in Jammu and Kashmir, were suffering with increased oppression thus the liberation of J & K region without an all out war was being thought and urgently needed.

Pakistan moved on back steps during Gen Musharraf's and of Mr Zardari rule to appease and please India on the premises that '*we cannot change our neighbours and it is in our national interest to keep good relations with India for the sake of regional peace and stability*'. To Pakistan's bad luck that India always defined it as enemy - ever since its creation in 1947. In fact, the 'natural alliance' of the USA with Israel and India has been there being as the enemies of Islam. Nawaz Sharif was being painted as in India's lap for his past inclinations.

*2nd NRO in Offing*: Let us put some simple facts on the table without bias, prejudice or partisan political affiliations. Let us be rational, logical and analytical with the core purpose of understanding what was happening in Pakistan at the given time.

It remained a hard fact that, in Pakistan, the civilian ruling elite and traditional politicians had failed the nation more than some military rulers had. The military dictators had abrogated the constitution – but they could not go beyond the amendments for their own safeguard – no amendment was ever introduced by them for the betterment of general populace. The civilian regimes simply followed the same dictatorial patterns but in the name of democracy.

Pakistan's civilian rulers had always been patronized, promoted and imposed upon by their foreign patrons - so the military rulers were, too – by the same foreign powers. The infamous NRO was an American sponsored compromise of mutual political interests between the PPP leadership and a military ruler. Similarly, the PML[N]'s Sharifs were protected by the same patron USA and vigorously charged by a friendly Muslim nation Saudi Arabia in addition.

Outside Pakistan both the above sponsors were inter-related and inter-locked - so a friendly opposition, PML[N], contributed much to the excesses of the PPP's political mismanagement and financial corruption in the last 5 years of a so-called democratic era by a *"Muk Muka"* coalition of mutual interests. These are some of the simple facts.

The front-men apologists on both sides of the divide went on fooling the nation by manipulating the facts and taking on a moral defense of their respective positions and claiming that democracy was at loggerheads with the threat of a military takeover. Those front men, from both parties belonging to the political factions and media, charged their full price in the form of secret funds and foreign contracts.

Thus no one could be held accountable for the massive corruption, financial embezzlements, mismanagement of national affairs, and flawed domestic and foreign policies. Nothing happened to those for whom Swiss Bank's Director had told the media that $97 billion owned by the politicians, bureaucrats and Pakistani Mafioso were stacked in Swiss banks. Loan defaulters and tax evaders and those who had repeatedly undermined national interests for personal gains and vested self-interests were let loose to get another chance of loot & plunder.

Pakistani nation was once again being taken for a ride. Traditional ruling elite was planned to remain there to maintain political - economic status-quo and pro-western foreign policy in the country. Gen Musharraf's return, and the PPP & PML[N]'s silence of *Muk Muka* democracy was part of the greater plan patronized by Washington, London and Saudia – and it prevailed; see the election results.

But alas; elections were held but no one voted for a change. Balochistan has been going through new political affiliations – Marri and Bugti tribes had since developed alternate leadership. Their discarded leaders were living abroad under the funding and protection of CIA and MI6 working for carving out *'Greater Balochistan'* from Baloch areas of Balochistan, Seistan province of Iran and southern Afghanistan. The weaponry and communication arsenal were being provided by India.

The Mengal [sub] tribe was confined to former Kalat State and was prominent in politics by aligning itself with other power centers; mainly with *Pashtuns* but sometimes others. After more than a decade in exile under Gen Zia rule, the Mengals made an alliance with the PML[N] and Akhter Mengal became the Chief Minister of Balochistan. However, the issue needed immediate political attention during and after elections.

PPP's Zardari was smart enough to evolve successful foreign policy based on good relations with China, Russia and Iran; simultaneously standing by the US. Nawaz Sharif opted to continue with the same but India was stuck with his person. Coming times had to define his true policy. Gen Kayani was apparently silent on the said issue and on PML[N]'s priorities.

The induction of 84 years old Justice Khoso as Caretaker PM was unpredictable. No one was sure whether he would endorse controversial orders and appointments from President Zardari or would resist pressure. He was in no position to make or change policy but he could implement orders of the Supreme Court which the earlier administration had ignored. It was only the judiciary that could rescue the country from wider bloodshed. But the Supreme Court could not accomplish the task without the support of the armed forces and CJP Chaudhry kept reviling the military persistently.

## NRO-2 IN OFFING:

Before general elections of 2013 in Pakistan, the media started talking about another NRO [National Reconciliation Ordinance] being imminent like the one promulgated by Gen Musharraf in 2007 which paved the way for Benazir Bhutto and Mian Nawaz Sharif to return to Pakistan and take part in 2008 Elections. There was nothing wrong with allowing the two leaders coming back to Pakistan; that was thought to be a pre-requisite for fair elections.

As per *Usman Khalid's analysis dated 7th March 2013* available on media:

*'This time, no Ordinance was needed; Pakistan had the 20th Amendment passed unanimously by the parliament to ensure that the election process could proceed through an impartial administration.*

*But the real string pullers were sitting far away in Washington DC and London and they had no concern with fairness of elections; they wanted any government in Pakistan but dependent on them; not on popular judiciary or the powerful military.'*

When NRO -1 was promulgated, no one - not even Gen Musharraf, had any idea that the end result would be the emergence of Asif Ali Zardari. The handlers of President Zardari – Altaf Hussain, Rehman Malik, Salman Farooqi and Hussain Haqqani etc- had been the real rulers of Pakistan over the five years of PPP regime. The judiciary and the security establishment both knew the handlers well but tolerated them in the name of democracy.

The same players, PPP + PML[N] & the US, coined **NRO-2 to ensure 'no change in policies'**; change of faces were tolerable. The main playing tools were the MQM, ANP, JUI (F) on Zardari side whereas 'ethnic nationalists' and religious parties were supporting PML(N). The stage was set for Nawaz Sharif to be the premier as the head of another 'coalition' and would **ensure 'no change in policy', particularly foreign policy; through NRO-2.**

The main players of NRO-2, PPP & PML[N] both, were not satisfied entirely because the judiciary and the military were enjoying considerable public support. The 'caretaker administration' had got huge importance in the development of alternative narratives. The three names for the caretaker PM given by PML(N) [Justice Nasir Aslam Zahid, Justice Shakirullah Jan & Rasool Bux Palijo] were obviously unacceptable to President Zardari. The perspective next PM Asma Jehangir, a likely choice of President Zardari, was also included in the short list of PML(N), thus her nomination by the PPP was going to make her a 'consensus candidate'.

Asma Jahangir was the favourite of both the PPP and the PML(N) because she had for decades demonized the Pakistan Army as the 'enemy' of the political culture; once accused the ISI for her assassination. But as she was not liked by the US so if she was appointed caretaker PM, there was every likelihood of her being assassinated.

Like the assassination of Benazir paved the way for the PPP to win the 2008 Elections and Asif Zardari becoming a despotic ruler of Pakistan to plunder the state with impunity, Asma Jehangir's assassination could have resulted in another military rule or the triumph of the PPP coalition that otherwise apparently had no chance to win the 2013 Elections. It would have been the 'end game' of the NRO-2, too.

Imran Khan of PTI had already declared that Asma Jehangir was not acceptable to them as the caretaker PM. PML(N) could also have rejected her right away and that was what they finally did. That cleared the way for PML(N) and its allies to win a clear victory and left Pakistan with a lesser problem – the problem of him being personal – being anti-Army which proved different this time. During the later months Nawaz Sharif went much well with the army – quite astonishingly.

The victims of violence in Pakistan, particularly the Shiite community, had already asked for the military to protect them. Under the PPP's rule, which was hostile to the military as evidenced by the 'memo-gate' affair, the military was constrained. Under an impartial 'caretaker administration' the military – without much direct intervention – was able to help deal with 'terrorism', reverse financial sanctions and to push the incumbent political elite to review their economy measures for welfare of the general populace.

## *MIR KHOSO AS C-TAKER PM:*

A bipartisan committee of PPP and PML[N], tasked with reaching consensus over the selection of a caretaker prime minister, had failed to reach consensus. The issue was handed over to Election Commission on Pakistan (ECP). The ECP had to finalise one name out of four, two each from the PPP's prime minister and the opposition leader from PML[N]. The Chief Election Commissioner [CEC] Fakhruddin G. Ebrahim left for Islamabad to head the meeting. It was unfortunate that politicians had not been able to reach a decision on the selection of a caretaker premier in three days consecutive meetings.

In its sessions over the last two days, the committee scrutinised the names of PML[N]'s nominees Rasul Bakhsh Palijo, Justice (rtd) Nasir Aslam Zahid and PPP nominees Justice (rtd) Mir Hazar Khan Khoso and Dr Ishrat Hussain. The members of the bipartisan committee included Sardar Mahtab Abbasi, Sardar Yaqoob Nasir, Pervez Rasheed, Saad Rafiq, Chaudhry Shujaat, Farooq Naek, Khurshid Shah and Ghulam Bilour. Panel members had denied that a deadlock existed between the two parties, saying the issue would be resolved at the committee level.

Some of the politicians' traits had rubbed off on the judges. A daylong meeting of the ECP on Saturday left the retired judges undecided on the name of the caretaker PM. With two votes each for two of the nominees, the vote of the fifth member — retired Justice Roshan Essani from Sindh — was to decide the fate.

The uncertainty over the name of the caretaker premier went into the last day as the CEC and members Riaz Kiani from Punjab, Shahzad Akbar Khan from Khyber PK and Fazlur Rahman from Balochistan failed to reach a consensus.

The CEC Justice Ebrahim and Justice Rahman found the PPP's nominee, retired Justice Mir Hazar Khoso, as the most suitable candidate, Justice Kiani and Justice Khan wanted the office to go to the PML[N]'s first nominee, retired Justice Nasir Aslam Zahid. PPP's first choice, Dr Ishrat Hussain, and the PML[N]'s second nominee, Rasool Bakhsh Palijo, were out of the race on the first day. During two rounds of deliberations on first day, the profiles of the nominees were debated. Two members of the ECP argued in favour of Justice Zahid, citing his integrity. It was pointed out that he had refused to meet the army chief when he was chief justice of the Sindh High Court.

The CEC and Justice Rahman, however, did not agree.

One of the four members of the parliamentary committee nominated by the PML[N], Sardar Yaqub Khan Nasir, had talked highly about the integrity of Justice Khoso. A third round of talks was to have taken place after the arrival of Justice Essani, but he did not arrive; his flight from Karachi had been delayed due to bad weather - the commission met next day on Sunday.

*The CEC Ebrahim announced the name of Justice (rtd) Mir Hazar Khan Khoso as caretaker prime minister for the upcoming elections.* The name for Justice Khoso was finalised after four members of the ECP voted for him.

The inability, if not failure, of the two major political parties, the PPP and the PML[N], to agree on a caretaker prime minister was the latest example how the political parties were taking up the issues of democratic politics as an ego competition and how they played tough with each other. This was meant to show to their supporters and voters that they had not allowed the other side to get away with its choice. This was a good example of the difference between the slogans of democracy and the actually delivered performance.

From the perspective of procedures and formalities, it was constitutional for the ECP to nominate a caretaker prime minister if the political leaders fail to do that. However, from the perspective of the quality and performance of democracy, it was poor politics that the political leaders and parties could not settle political issues and they approached non-elected institution for getting their problems resolved.

The ECP option was a conflict resolution method provided in the constitution that becomes operative when the ego-oriented politicians with feudal-tribal notion of political competition cannot solve the political problems which is their primary responsibility. One major challenge to democracy in Pakistan remained that political leaders always have a tendency to look towards non-elected institutions for settling their political scores. They may even discreetly cultivate the military to strengthen their political bargaining position. During tension between the civilian PPP and the military, the PML[N] had taken stand by the military at the expense of the civilian government - the Memo Issue of 2011 is referred.

Here, the ECP, a constitutional institution, nevertheless non-elected, settled the matter that the political leaders should have done it through mutual accommodation. Under the constitution, the caretakers PMs or CMs are not expected to make major policy changes – they come to ensure free and fair elections only. It also provides the necessary support to the ECP for holding transparent elections in addition to manage the day-to-day working of governments and to maintain law and order generally and for elections.

## A SALUTE TO JUSTICE JAN:

The critics held that PML[N] had put all their eggs in one basket; that was, in Justice Nasir Aslam Zahid's candidacy, and it suffered a big blow that their candidate wasn't picked by the ECP. PML[N] demonstrated a non-serious approach when they added Rasool Bakhsh Palejo's name as their second candidate; the inclusion of his name was just an effort to appease Sindhi nationalists; PML[N] knew that he wouldn't be picked.

PPP, on the other hand, nominated two individuals, Dr Ishrat and Justice Khoso, who could have a soft corner for the PPP but they weren't knowingly or apparently the PPP supporters.

When PPP raised an objection in the Parliamentary Committee that FIR of Justice Nizam, the brother-in-law of Justice Nasir, was registered against Zardari, it was obvious that Justice Nasir's name wouldn't be picked by an independent body, such as the ECP.

PML[N] had originally planned to include Justice Shakirullah Jan's name as their second choice instead of Mr Palejo but Ch Nisar dropped his name at the last moment amidst rumors that Justice Jan had met with Malik Riaz during those days; this news was later denied by Justice Jan - Ch Nisar needed to come out of his Malik Riaz phobia.

Later, PML[N] was stuck with Justice Khose who could have some hidden support for PPP but the 84 years old judge was not able to manoeuvre the things like shrewd politicians nor he was of the type.

In fact Mr Zardari had defeated the PML[N] in that first round of elections by getting Justice Khoso nominated as the caretaker PM. Justice Khoso had been the most favourite person of the PPP since the ZA Bhutto's days when he was in the Balochistan High Court. Mr Zardari had included names of Hafeez Sheikh and Dr Ishrat Hussain in the PPP's panel to please the American Pentagon, IMF and the World Bank etc otherwise he never seriously wished to get any of the two selected.

PML[N] had not done a mistake by nominating Nasir Aslam Zahid because he was very near to them since his decision at SC bench declaring PML[N]'s MNA Ch Munir and MPA Tariq Aziz and Shahbaz Goshi etc innocent in the 1997's notorious attack on the SC premises. But this fact was also known to the PPP that was why Mr Zardari had never agreed on this name through all the sessions of three days before referring the matter to the ECP.

Justice Shakirullah Jan was a very nice choice for all being dead honest – up to the madness level. PML[N] had initially included his name in the panel but then dropped due to their own internal fears for many known instances on record.

Justice Shakirullah Jan was the Chief Justice of the Peshawar High Court. Once his own son was detained and was not allowed to sit in the examination along with other twelve students. Justice Jan's wife and other family members asked him to do something for their son. Justice Jan refused to interfere and did not help his own son.

Justice Jan's son and other 12 twelve students approached the local Sessions Court to get permission to appear in the examination but Justice Jan instructed all the lower courts in person NOT to entertain his son's request. The then Sessions judge Jama'at Ali Shah had refused to admit the appeal of the CJ's son.

His own son plus the 12 students lost their one year of studies but the father CJ upheld the cannons of justice.

> *[One can compare Justice Shakirullah Jan's character with that of CJP Iftikhar Chaudhry who took his son Dr Arsalan Iftikhar through all the streams of corruption himself – now he is billionaire business tycoon of Pakistan.*
>
> For details see '**The Living History of Pakistan**' Vol-I; Scenarios 100-101. pp 1619-1650]

The then military ruler Gen Musharraf always remained angry with Justice Shakirullah Jan for his straight forward honest approach. The Establishment never liked him because he was one of the members of Supreme Court bench which had re-instated the Chief Justice Iftikhar M Chaudhry in July 2007 against the wish of Gen Musharraf.

Later when the matter regarding Gen Musharraf's eligibility came before the Supreme Court in September 2007, Justice Jan was also a member of the larger bench. Though the Supreme Court, with 6-3 decision, had allowed Gen Musharraf to contest presidential election while remaining in uniform but Justice Jan was one of those THREE judges who had given their dissenting notes; the other two judges were J Baghwandas and J Sardar M Raza Khan.

It was also on the record that when the discussion amongst the judges was held before the judgment was penned down; Justice Jan was the first judge to speak and to raise his hand against that permission for Gen Musharraf.

President Zardari never liked Justice Shakirullah Jaan because he was also there on Supreme Court's that bench which had, in December 2009, declared the NRO null and void.

Once Justice Shakirullah Jan was working as Acting Chief Election Commissioner in 2012; during those days PM Yusaf Raza Gilani was made dysfunctional by the Supreme Court in famous Contempt Case. When the matter was referred to the Election Commission, Justice Jan immediately issued the notification of PM Gilani's disqualification – and that was without any second thought, or ifs and buts.

During April 2012, there were supplementary elections in Multan at PP-194. PM Gilani from Multan had already been declared disqualified so President Zardari himself visited Multan to boost up electoral support for the PPP candidate. Justice Jan went there in the capacity of CEC to make sure that the federal government machinery should not be used for the PPP during elections because of President Zardari's presence. Of course, Mr Zardari was not happy for that kind of behaviour from the ECP.

Maulana Fazalur Rehman of JUI[F] also remained angry with Justice Shakirullah Jan because he was member of that bench also which had given its judgment against the *'Hasba' Bill* of the then MMA. After that Justice Jan always avoided those cases or writ petitions in which Mr Maulana or JUI[F] was a party from either side.

Nawaz Sharif wanted Justice Jan on the panel of Caretaker PM but President Zardari, as he was deadly against Justice Jan's person, started planned dis-information campaign against him. Zardari got fabricated certain fake documents alleging business partnership of Justice Jan with Malik Riaz; flimsy objections on the partnership papers, and secretly managed to be delivered the same to Ch Nisar of the PML[N].

One day Ch Nisar was found speaking to the media against their own candidate, the PML[N]'s nomination for the Caretaker PM's slot – so

# ⬇

justice Jan was out of the list. Justice Jan told later that he had seen Malik Riaz, the property tycoon, only once in life; that too in the court – never met him outside; what to speak of alleged partnership.

Certain media people later confirmed that Justice Jan was very upset over Ch Nisar's baseless allegations who had tried to tarnish the whole life clean image of him – for no apparent reason. Justice Jan had never consented the PML[N] to nominate him for that slot nor he knew before hand till that press conference.

PPP's intrigue and plan was successful; they laughed at Ch Nisar's innocense. That allegation against Justice Jan had also invited questions from his PML[N]'s colleagues over party's political insight and their ability to handle the hearsay things.

## GEN KAYANI TALKS ELECTIONS:

During the **last week of February 2013**, Gen Kayani, burst the bubble of hope of the anti-democracy elements for a military coup by supporting the continuation of the democratic process and transfer of power through impartial elections, besides emphasising the army's subservient role to a civilian government. He invited prominent print and electronic media men on lunch and **spoken out his heart during an off – the - record 4-hour briefing**. Gen Kayani said that:

'He fully supports the idea of holding a free, fair, and transparent election leading to a smooth transfer of power in the country. He had assured the Chief Election Commissioner of full cooperation on the matter.

The army has stood by the democratically elected government during the past five years as required under the constitution.

That everyone must respect the mandate of the people and for this the army will provide the maximum help, but only that much which is asked for by the civilians.'

Gen Kayani was successful to dispel the speculations about a possible delay in the polls and the installation of a caretaker set up for a longer period. Gen Kayani's statements, indeed, reflected a paradigm shift in the thinking of the military commanders in regard to role of the army in a state. Many media anchors recalled their Quaid who had, while reminding the army officers at Staff College Quetta *on 14th June 1948*, about the significance of oath of allegiance to the constitution, said:

*"I should like you to study the constitution, which is in force in Pakistan at present, and understand its true constitutional and legal implications when you say you will be faithful to the constitution."*

It has never been considered fair to chastise Pak-Army because of the recklessness of 'some' individual Generals; *Gen Kayani strengthened its credentials as supporter of the democratic system* and the government by resisting all temptations. Equally laudable were the efforts of the superior judiciary that repeatedly vowed not to allow any unconstitutional move from any quarter, adding unflinching faith in the democratic process. The end message seemed to be that:

*'No one should try to play games with the transparency and fairness of the elections and the results must be accepted but the army will not impose itself in any way and this job has to be done by the civilians themselves.'*

The bottom line Gen Kayani gave was that he wanted free and fair elections and a peaceful transfer of power and everyone must respect the mandate of the people.

In his briefing, Gen Kayani gave a long list of civilian failures during the last five years, almost a charge sheet against the politicians and the government and placed the blame of gigantic failures in many critical domains at the civilian doorstep. Not to intervene was constitutionally a constructive approach but in reality it brought the country to the verge of collapse; and Gen Kayani did not want to share the blame.

Examples of the civilians' failure that he quoted, in his own soft style were:

- The key issue of **war against terrorism**; do not blame the army as the civilians had not formulated a comprehensive anti-terrorism policy and they could not decide what to do.

- The army had not been consulted or taken on board about the political All Parties Conferences [APC] held on counter-terrorism.

- The civilians depend too much on ISI & MI and go scared of them too whereas the *tasks should have been done by their own civilian intelligence agencies like IB and Police's Special Branches in provinces.*

- Where are the civilian agencies? *Total failure of the Interior & Home ministries*; sometimes army guided the civilians to reform and take responsibility yet did not intervene to stop the decay.

- The army knew that these [incompetent] *politicians will not be able to handle the gigantic issues* like the war on terror, the Balochistan mess, the [religious] domestic extremism but they did not interfere so that the army may not be blamed.

For instance, on the key issue of **war against terrorism**, the civil government threw the ball in the court of army without giving them policy guidelines, the targets to be achieved and the way that was to be done.

Gen Kayani, in that context, quoted many examples and reminded the media men of the Swat situation where the President was persuaded by him to take a decision. He also took ANP leader Asfandyar Wali to the President and when the decision was taken to talk to Maulana Sufi Mohammed, the talks were held but when he violated the accord, an operation was launched. After the operation was concluded, the civilians had to take over the responsibility of running Swat in routine which they did not.

Gen Kayani specifically mentioned the arrests made in Swat and complained that:

'For more than five years, Pak-Army is holding those people; the establishment either violating laws by doing so or risks more terrorism if they are released. But if those arrested persons are not convicted because of lack of evidence, army cannot hold them forever.'

Gen Kayani said that an army operation could be launched in Balochistan had the civilians taken that decision and ordered the army to do so. *'But once the operation is done and people are arrested, they will have to be tried and convicted by the police and courts for which the civilians are not ready.'*

In short, Gen Kayani explained army's five years of non-interference and failure of the greedy politicians to cope with the disasters which could have been handled with good governance.

Gen Kayani and his colleagues knew the capacity of the civilians - that those politicians would not be able to handle such colossal issues like the war on terror, the Balochistan mess, the fight against domestic extremism and fanaticism but they left everything to those immature and inexperienced or incompetent politicians.

In fact, Gen Kayani had explained his army's wait & see attitude for five years while indicating failure of the civilians to cope with odd situations and the resulting disasters in that four-hour session and pointing to: *"Don't blame us. Do something if you can."*

There was no way the army could avoid the 2008 elections but the civilians could have improved many things. The popular perception was that:

> 'The PPP regime during 2008-13 could not maintain even that level of industrial production, inflation figure, foreign debt servicing, law & order situations, curbing sectarianism, holding local body elections and many other indicators that Gen Musharraf had left behind.'

Similar was the issue with 2013 elections. Gen Kayani was then saying that elections must be free, fair and transparent. Difficult it was because the political government had no set-up that could be seen in place – every institution and every policy - all controversial, weak and fragile, weakest at the top – that was PPP's rule.

Gen Kayani referred to **weakness of the ECP** in his own way by recalling the famous meeting between him and CEC Fakhru Bhai in which a briefing was given by the army to the CEC for over two hours and at the end Fakhru Bhai made a hand shake with Gen Kayani without recognizing him. Reading the question in CEC's eyes:

*"Yes I am General Kayani"* he told the ageing CEC but then also recalled the story of Alif Laila and the joke associated with it when after the whole night someone asked: *"Was Laila a man or a woman"*.

Referring to Fakhru Bhai, the 84 years old CEC and speaking about his age and his capacity, Gen Kayani indirectly expressed doubts that he could handle such a gigantic task of holding the elections. He also knew that *politicians had nominated the other four members of the ECP being their political nominees who always play games for their sponsors*. But it was plan of the two major parties PML[N] & PPP who had brought, through *'Muk Muka'* that management intentionally to play open.

When Gen Kayani said that elections must be fair and free, he was again shifting the blame to the civilians while knowing that they never meant a fair business and they would do the mischief in their own ways. He was not inclined to interfere but was only asking them not to try. Yet he walked out on question of providing army cover to the polls saying he would not spare 200,000 troops. Fakhru Bhai was left alone and dry; on his own.

Thus, if the politicians would not like to consult with their army chief, taking him from opposite theme of governance; or do not share things with him taking him as head of a key institution, the bottom line could go to the disappointments. Gen Kayani had already announced that he would retire later that year [2013], the politicians could even cut that period short by announcing his replacement three months ahead of the date; as had been once done in Gen Aslam Beg's case. So the politicians were ready to play around and the General was going, leaving the mess for the people to face.

Gen Kayani knew well that there had been Gen Musharraf's un-interrupted rule for complete eight years with complete dominance of the army including him; the persecution of selected politicians, the exploitation of the political system, physical threats to political leaders, their assassinations and mass murders, and importing WOT into this poor country at the cost of our meagre infra-structure were also equally responsible for leading Pakistan towards a failing state.

Shaheen Sehbai, in 'the News' of 1st March 2013, mentioned that:

'....... So there was no way the army could avoid an election [of 2008] but there was no way the civilians could correct everything messy that the Generals were leaving behind.

Similar is the issue with the present elections. Gen Kayani is now saying that elections must be free, fair and transparent but the set-up that has been put in place is controversial, weak and fragile, weakest at the top.'

# Scenario 126

## GENERAL ELECTIONS-II

Ahead of general elections of 11ᵗʰ May 2013, an article titled as
**'Sour grapes or an end foretold?'** written by _Ayaz Amir_
in the **'the News'** dated **20ᵗʰ April 2013**
is worth going through.

---------------------------------------------------------

'It is another matter that the Sharifs, never ones to proclaim
inconvenient truths, kept denying this deal [of going to Saudia for
ten years when Gen Musharraf had sent Sharifs to Attock Jail] until
Prince Muqrin, the Saudi intelligence chief, had to come to Islamabad
and (unprecedentedly) address a press conference where he waved the
paper with the deal on it. For anyone else this would have been a
knock-out blow. Not for our champions who promptly came back with
the rejoinder that the deal was only for five years, not ten, a
declaration of innocence which left most observers flabbergasted.

[For complete details of that deal _'Judges & Generals
in Pakistan Vol-II_ pages 555-562, [2012]
GHP Surrey UK is referred]

I lampooned, among other things, Nawaz Sharif's stand on Memogate,
considering him to be out of his depth and not understanding the
shaping of that particular episode. But I could not say what I thought
needed to be said regarding the Asghar Khan judgement by the Supreme
Court. Here was an open-and-shut case where a long line of politicians
headed by Nawaz Sharif and Shahbaz Sharif were caught with their
pants down receiving ISI money, from ISI officers, in the 1990 elections.
But no follow-up action, no prosecution, no accountability – the culprits
behaving as if they had been washed in holy water.

Imagine if the Asghar Khan case was about the PPP, and not the
N League. All hell would have broken loose, the declamations we
would have heard, the fire and thunder from the courts, the self-
righteous grandstanding. Pervaiz Ashraf, the former prime minister,
is disqualified on the basis of a CDA transaction, but the Asghar Khan
culprits wear suits of Teflon...nothing has stuck to them.

*There was more hilarity on parade. Bank defaulters, we were told, would be out of the elections. It is hard to think of any fat cat losing sleep over this. The Chaudhrys have been great ones for having their loans written off, everything in order on paper. But the Sharifs went one step further, not going to the trouble of getting anything written off and instead simply refusing to pay anything on the near – three - billion rupee loan taken by them from the National Bank and eight other banks in the 1990s.*

*All this was 'regularised' when Nawaz Sharif became prime minister in 1997 and he went on television and proudly declared that his family was clearing the loans by offering assets in lieu of them. Sharif suggested that this was an act of unrivalled sacrifice.*

*That the collateral offered was in the form of their most rundown assets is beside the point. The echoes of that announcement had hardly died down when a Sharif relative went to court saying he was a shareholder in the properties offered and that Sharif had no right to dispose them off. This matter is pending in the Lahore High Court, Allah be praised, for the last 15 years. The defaulters concerned are of course preparing to save the nation once more, as they announce the imminent birth of a new dawn.*

*Zardari was always Zardari, never pretending to be anything else. The Sharifs were who they were but through an optical illusion with few parallels in the nation's history we were also expected to take them as sole claimants to that hallowed space called the moral high ground. Loan artists of a kind, seldom witnessed before in the annals of Pakistani banking, at the same time high priests of morality: not an easy stunt to pull off.*

*The PPP has been a disaster thrice-over, not counting Zulfikar Ali Bhutto's stint in office. The N League has been an equal disaster, the recent performance of Punjab's little Hitler, Shahbaz Sharif, looking good only when compared to the PPP. Although on a dispassionate scale what he has to show for himself does not go beyond a line of expensive and directionless gimmicks: sasti roti, laptops, Daanish schools, etc. So there's not much to choose from here.*

*Einstein's definition of insanity: doing the same thing over and over again and expecting different results. From stale porridge we have tried before, we are expecting something new. There's no easy cure for such a malady.*

*Tailpiece: Musharraf's judicial hounding: in his position one gets what one deserves. But I wish our memories were not so selective. Everyone remembers, and waxes heroic about, November 3, 2007, completely ignoring October 12, 1999, when Musharraf and his generals committed their original sin. Is it because it suits us to forget some uncomfortable truths? The then judiciary, which includes present-day eminences, validated his coup not once but twice and there was no shortage of judges who took oath under Musharraf's PCO. Shouldn't this inculcate in everyone concerned a touch of humility?'*

---------------------------------------------------------------

## SUPREME COURT's INTERFERENCE:

In November 2012; in the course of a *suo moto* case relating to violence in Karachi, the Supreme Court of Pakistan [SC] directed the Election Commission of Pakistan [ECP] to devise a plan for a delimitation exercise in respect of Karachi. In making the order, the Court remarked that the exercise should be carried out in such a way that no political party would have complete control of the city.

The Muttahida Qaumi Movement (MQM), whose political stronghold was in Karachi, protested the ruling on the basis that by law, delimitation could only be carried out on the basis of a census, which had not been carried out. The Election Commission noted that the last census in Pakistan had been carried out in 1998 and that a fresh one was overdue.

In March 2013; the Supreme Court, criticising the ECP for its 'lethargy' on the matter, ordered that a fresh delimitation be carried out in the absence of up-to-date census data. The Commission then carried out a partial delimitation of three out of twenty National Assembly and eight out of forty-two Provincial Assembly constituencies.

Questions were asked as to why only some constituencies had been identified for delimitation. The MQM was unsuccessful in its legal attempts to halt the exercise.

The **Common-wealth Observer Mission** had also written in their report that in the run-up to elections, Chief Justice Iftikhar M Chaudhry travelled around the country addressing judicial officials who were to serve as Returning Officers [ROs] during the nominations and scrutiny process, to push them to uphold the judicial supervision of the elections; no good it was.

The role of the Chief Justice in this regard was criticised by some, who viewed it as undermining the role of the ECP. The excessively intrusive manner in which some ROs questioned candidates on religious knowl-edge and personal circumstances was subsequently attributed, by a number of commentators, to the earlier intervention by the Chief Justice.

The Supreme Court also ordered that overseas Pakistanis should be able to vote in the 2013 elections which were not administratively possible during short span of about sixty days.

## *ELECTIONS: ….STARTED MOVING*

General elections of 2013 in Pakistan were ahead; let us start a little earlier.

There were the days when PML(N), Imran Khan's PTI and even some sane persons like Najam Sethi [referring to daily the *'Jang' dated 24th February 2013*] were of the view that:

'**TTP is fighting against** the Pakistan's foreign policies; its (Pakistan's) friendly relations with America and the West; **Pak-Army's intelligence agencies; its compromises with foreign forces etc. – and not against the Pakistani people**'.

Later Mr Khan's eagerness was bitterly criticised and the vote bank had also suffered on that account considering that PTI had no acumen to peep into the future.

As the political parties finalised their list of candidates, the horse-trading and floor-crossing bargains were in full swing; one part of the electoral process was concluding. It was being felt that the Election Commission of Pakistan (ECP) was going to deliver a poor performance in terms of quality and content. The expectations were too high, the requirements of probity too ambitious and both needed adjustment, but the fact remained that the ECP had miserably failed to deliver in a number of significant areas.

Most glaring among those was the failure to net and eject from the opportunity of election any of the **'big fish' tax defaulters** - 70 percent of members of the last parliament were either tax defaulters, or had no tax number or paid improbably low levels of personal taxation – or a combination of all three. The Federal Board of Revenue (FBR) had communicated a list of 300 tax defaulters to the ECP but no name was barred from standing once again. In many cases, the sums involved were very large, multiple millions of rupees, but the ECP turned a blind eye and a deaf ear to evidence which was both damning and overwhelming.

Once again; a set of rules were framed for the rich to play by and a different set of rules for the less wealthy or influential to live within. It was the unequal application of the rule of law that once again institutionalised corruption at the highest level in Pakistan and made it more difficult to fight. Corrupt candidates were going to be voted in and to become lawmakers once more; their corruption sanctioned by the highest agency like ECP which had pledged to level playing fields and ensure transparency and accountability in the electoral process.

The entire scrutiny process was bogus which failed to disqualify, anywhere, any of the big political players who were manifestly playing mockery of law in terms of taxation. The ECP had shown zero interest in establishing a permanent scrutiny cell that would contribute to a more rigorous culture of honesty and fairness; and that even constitutional provisions of Articles 62-63 were twisted to maintain the status quo. The ECP had bowed before the vested interests of some and the general populace was sure that their next parliament would be as riddled with tax-defaulters as was the last one.

On 20th March 2013; Senior officials from the Election Commission of Pakistan (ECP), ministry of foreign affairs, ministry of interior and ministry of information at the foreign office briefed Islamabad - based foreign diplomats about the policies and procedures the government had crafted for *foreign election observers*. The government allowed foreign election observers after completing due formalities and took all steps within its means to facilitate those observers during their stay in Pakistan.

The foreign observers were the teams of **EU Election Mission for Pakistan** and **Common-wealth Observers Group** from United Kingdom. The election observers had the freedom to interact with political parties on issues related to polls; however, they were not permitted to interfere in the election process.

The Joint Chiefs of Staff Committee also extended *'all possible help'* to *the ECP* for holding free, fair and transparent polls in the country. Headed by Chairman Joint Chiefs of Staff Committee (JCSC) Gen

Khalid Shameem Wynne, the moot was also attended by Chief of the Army Staff Gen Ashfaq Parvez Kayani. As per statement issued by the Inter - Services Public Relations (ISPR), the meeting discussed the support of armed forces to the ECP during elections. The military leadership held that it was their 'national duty' to assist electoral authorities in holding free, fair and peaceful parliamentary polls due in May 2013.

Army's poll body had submitted its detailed security plan when the election schedule was announced. The Pak-Army leadership kept on reviewing after intervals issues related to the national security, regional geo-strategic environment, and internal security situation.

**On 26th March 2013,** the election schedule was announced for the voting to take place on 11th May 2013. The political period to be dominated during the election process for the next three months involved a lot more controversies, negative propaganda, character assassination of candidates and political leaders and court cases. There were side runners who had questioned the electoral process and attempted to make it difficult holding elections on time. Of course, they were right because in the absence of Art 62 & 63 of the Constitution, the free and fair elections were not expected coming up.

High trumpets blown for the outgoing assemblies while completing their terms were mockery of the so-called democracy. The world media simply laughed at slogans of that Pakistani style of **'strengthened democracy'** - the substance and quality of democracy was so poor. The PPP's government and PML[N] as opposition performed poorly and the political leaderships often found it difficult to rise above their narrow and biased approach.

The ECP gave a short margin of time for filing nomination papers from 24th – 29th March; how courts could take decisions on objections in so short span of time.

The new nomination papers required a lot of information; there was a widespread support for scrutinising the candidates minutely. Gen Musharraf thought before the 2002 elections that the people with the graduation degrees would make a better parliament. He imposed that condition but the political leadership invented to come out of that cage. Otherwise, the un-educated lot of voters seldom cared for the academic qualifications of the candidates.

The political opponents were getting ready to raise objections on each other's nomination papers. This was likely to open flood-gates of charges and counter charges. There were more controversies and court cases this time regarding the nomination papers than ever.

Imran Khan started his election campaign with a public meeting in Lahore on 23rd March 2013. His initial speech comprised highly religious and nationalist indications; however, the promises he made were secular in nature. There was music and dancing for the liberals and moderates, too. Imran Khan offered something to everybody, although his statements projected him more religious than the Jama'at e Islami [JI].

Referring to **Hasan Askari**'s essay in *'Pakistan Today' dated 28th March 2013; 'Pakistan was on the election ride and the political leaders were attempting to bridge the gap between rhetoric and reality, promise and delivery, as well as between the procedures and substance of democracy.'*

On 22nd March 2013; former federal minister and PPP founding member Dr Mobashir Hassan placed an application before the Supreme Court [SC] for early hearing of his pending petition, requesting an independent ECP and directions for free, fair and timely Elections, while stopping tax evaders, defaulters and bogus degree holders from participating in the upcoming elections.

Dr Mobashir Hassan urged the SC that due to the urgency of the matter to protect fundamental rights of the citizens, the main petition should be fixed for hearing on 26th March, so that the same may be decided on merit in view of enforcement of constitutional rights as guaranteed in the Constitution.

It was also advocated that since the filing of the constitutional petition, the media carried many reports with shocking disclosures of increasing abuse of power with the sole purpose of bribing the voters. Such tactics amounted to pre-poll rigging but the ECP had failed to take notice and act. Unless such actions of federal and provincial governments were declared illegal, the general election could not be held in a fair and transparent manner.

The credibility of caretaker set-ups formed in the provinces of Sindh and Balochistan were also questioned. The main point raised high was that the SC should issue directions to the ECP to stop politicians from contesting the then upcoming election who defied the principles set under Articles 62 and 63 of the Constitution.

In the main petition, Dr Hassan had requested that *'the ECP is declared an independent institution with the authority to frame rules, orders, regulations and pass any orders it may deem necessary for conducting elections fairly, justly, transparently and in accordance with law'*. For that purpose, he argued, **the ECP needed no approval, sanction and endorsement from the President of Pakistan.** Dr Hassan had suggested the formation of a special bench to ensure fair play throughout the election process.

Dr Hassan had rightly urged the SC to issue directions for the Chiefs of all political parties not to allow any person to contest the elections from his party platform unless it was confirmed that the candidate was paying tax and had genuine credentials. Heads of PML[F], PML[N], PTI, PPP, PML[Q], MQM, JUI (F), and ANP should have been made bound to file affidavit before the higher courts, confirming that their ticket holders were not tax evaders, loan defaulters or had indulged in any known event of corruption.

**On 1st March 2013;** Punjab's Chief Minister, Shahbaz Sharif, had made an announcement making 100,000 contractual employees permanent in government jobs. Dr Hassan wanted that all such steps should be declared as bribe to win the votes thus must be declared illegal.

## ELECTION RESULTS & ANALYSIS:

In Pakistan, the general elections held as usual **on 11th May 2013.** Till next day's morning most of the results were available with the media. The live TV programs continued; the commentators kept the show alive while going and coming back in shifts.

PML[N]'s Chief Nawaz Sharif played the first odd in that election game. Much before the scheduled ending time for poling, 5 PM that day but later extended an hour more in certain areas; Nawaz Sharif appeared before a select media team and announced his winning from the Lahore seat. Till that moment it was not practically possible that about 150 thousand votes could be collated, sorted out by the poling staff, counted and entered in ECP forms 14 or 15, communicated to the ECP through the Returning officer etc – but there were drum beats and *bhangras* and sweet bags in most streets all over Punjab.

*Not a case that Nawaz Sharif could have been lost the seat – no way.* But that move was especially made to convey a strong message to all the Returning Officers before starting counting that next head of the government would be Nawaz Sharif – so the counting in the marginal cases, winning could be manipulated by the poling agents of the PML[N] in collaboration with the poling staff – **and the trick worked.**

The Election Commission of Pakistan (ECP) announced that overall voter *turnout in the 2013* general elections was recorded at 55.02% — a much higher percentage than elections since the 80s. The previous record of the turnout remained as: 1988 – 43.07%; 1990 – 45.46%; 1993 – 40.28%; 1997 – 35.42%; 2002 – 41.08%; 2008 – 44.23% & for 2013 – 55.02%.

According to the ECP, the lowest turnout was recorded in NA-42 South Waziristan, where only 11.57% of registered voters came out to vote. The highest turnout was recorded at 84.77% in NA-191 Bahawalnagar. This year, over 46.2 million people exercised their right to vote in the elections. The PML[N] got the majority of votes (14.8 million) followed by the PTI (7.5 million), the PPP (6.8 million) and the MQM (2.4 million). Independent candidates picked up 5.8 million votes collectively.

For 266 seats **44859313** votes were caste; about 10% votes went to some parties which could not manage to get even a single seat. Number of seats won by each party along with the votes gained by them were as: PML[N] – 125 seats – 14794188; PTI – 27 – 7563504; PPP – 31 – 6822958; Independents – 32 – 5773494; MQM – 18 – 2422656; JUI [F] – 10 – 1454907; PML[Q] – 2 – 1405493; PML[F] – 5 – 1007761; JI – 3 – 949394; ANP – 1 – 450561; PK Milli Awami Party – 3 – 211989 and National Peoples Party – 2 – 196828. The other small parties like PML[Z], AML, Awami Jamhoori Ettihad Pakistan, BNP, APML, Qaumi Watan Party [Sherpao] all got ONE seat each in the National Assembly.

The results from the 2013 general elections surprised many candidates and political parties. The incumbent PPP government and its allies were all wiped out of the electoral map. PML(Q), the most significant ally of the outing PPP government, was reduced to a two-man party in the National Assembly. The ANP could not even afford that small dignity; their party had virtually disappeared. MQM, another ally of the former government, retained its hold on Karachi, for the most part.

PML(N) secured 125 seats in the National Assembly, and an incredible 214 seats in the Punjab Provincial Assembly. The fact remained that there was no dominant opposition party. PPP, the second largest party in the NA had less than one-third of PML(N)'s numbers, and PTI had nearly the same situation facing in the Punjab Assembly.

As usual in Pakistan; there was huge hue and cry about massive accounts of rigging. Specifically, the urban centres of Lahore and Karachi, where the privileged class had come out and voted, perhaps for the first time, were displeased that the candidates of their choice [PTI] were not declared the winners.

As an eye-wash, the ECP ordered to either recount the votes, or re-poll but only for few select poling stations. However, even if the rigging charges were all true, and even if the recounting or re-polling was ordered, it could bring maximum, changed results for 5 to 10 seats - PML(N)'s victory was going to stay there.

More deep analysis into the philosophies involved; this election revealed that in a contest between liberal voices [for PTI and even PPP] against the forces of conservatism [PML(N) and its religious allies], the conservatism comprehensively defeated the voices of moderation and liberal change. Regardless of the allegations of rigging, in an election with fairly high turnout, the nexus of Punjabi traders, rural farmers and a brand of conservative youth, had acquired sweeping victory.

An era of overhead bridges, underpasses, more *Jangla* buses and bullet-train was ahead while the majority had gone beyond Ramzan Ordinances, Blasphemy laws, or the Hudood Ordinance etc – the social media of twitters, facebook and Youtube had taken the nation at much higher pedestal though majority is illiterate.

This ideological divide was inbuilt in Pakistani design of democracy; was the command of our Constitution, too. The PML(N) leadership had got a clear and unchallenged mandate of the people; no hung parliament thus no real hindrances in the ability to deliver. And most importantly, as 55.02% was the exact turnover in the election, there was little room for anyone to complain that the **'silent-majority'** was not supportive of the government.

Whether one voted for PML(N) or not, nearly all Pakistanis were going to support PML[N] to meet the odd challenges which the previous government had left amidst mal-practices and intellectual & financial corruption.

Malik Zameer Hassan, *Bilawal Hose's media In-charge*, contributed a press note to the media on 16th May 2013 titled as: '*My party PPP lost because it forgot about the people*' giving details of their admissions, which said:

'.....however on May 11, the people's verdict not only wiped out PPP from three provinces, but also clearly rejected our manifesto and our *welfare programs. PPP's defeat was not merely a defeat of the party but a defeat of an ideology - defeat of **roti, kapra aur makaan** and of the policies we have been carrying since 2008.'*

PPP remained unbeatable in Sindh for the reason that of the Benazir Income Support Program [BISP] and more because Sindhis did not have an alternative to PPP. It was due to the sentimental song of Benazir Bhutto; not that PPP won Sindh because of the party's policies.

During the PPP's regime of five years, the CM Qaim Ali Shah was seen in public only once a year - during PPP's gathering in Naudero on 27ᵗʰ December. He, along with his cabinet, remained confined to the office and private parties. In this case, the PPP was thankful to the masses who remained Bhutto loyalists. They forgave PPP's mistakes and misgivings and blessed PPP with another chance to rule Sindh.

In Punjab, Khyber PK and Balochistan, PPP was ousted with a huge mandate. However, the consequences which led to PPP's defeat in Punjab should be considered; especially the persistent blow given to industrialists, labours, business concerns through power shortage.

All Pakistan Muslim League (APML) in Chitral, managed to grab one NA seat even though Gen Musharraf had announced an election boycott. People elected his candidate just because of the Lowary Tunnel which was General's gift to *Chitralis*.

PPP's leadership mostly sold their seats to feudal lords and rich, extracting money in the name of party fund. For instance, one of Manzoor Wattoo's daughter was made an ambassador for orphaned Pakistani children, while another daughter was made in-charge of the Pakistan Electronic Media Regularity Authority (PEMRA) Punjab. Manzoor Wattoo's son Jahangir was given an MNA seat to contest in the by-elections, which he managed to win.

The story of the Gillani family: his daughter was made an ambassador for women empowerment and his sons were granted provincial and national assembly tickets in by-elections. The elder one Qadir Gilani was MPA while the younger Musa Gilani was an MNA; even on 11ᵗʰ May, the entire family was contesting on PPP tickets.

In Karachi, no one had ever seen a PPP higher official attending the funeral prayers of a PPP worker who became a victim of target killing. This attitude resulted in the party losing two important seats, which had truly remained PPP domain since decades - the *Keemari* and *Malir* seats. Despite multiple developmental projects in Karachi's those two areas, PPP lost seats to PML[N] and MQM.

The discredit of PPP's demise could also be extended to their media & publicity wing. For five years of their rule, PPP vowed to keep a reconciliation [*mufahimat*] policy, whereas during election campaign the workers were made to think via TV programs & discussions that PML[N] and Sharifs were PPP's biggest rivals - they could have run a campaign for power projects, industries installed, GDP upheld, exports enhanced and schools opened and upgraded – nothing was with the PPP to bring forward. PPP kept playing the footage of Benazir Bhutto's assassination to clutch sympathy votes.

In 1997 elections, PPP was ousted from the national scene in Pakistan, but this time the party was rejected so miserably that one couldn't find a PPP candidate even in the third place. PTI candidates were mostly found in the second position with a massive mandate as well. In *Lyari*, a known PPP stronghold since 1967, a PTI candidate managed to collect 26,000 votes against PPP in NA and over 11,000 votes in PA.

## ELECTIONS 2013- MORE ANALYSIS:

The election was full of controversies – hundreds of petitions and appeals were placed before the election tribunals. However, one wondered that how **Gen Mirza Aslam Beg** had taken it as the 'most wonderful' elections in the country. See Gen Beg's essay **dated 14th May 2013** appeared in **'Opinion Makers'**.

> 'The 11th May 2013 verdict, in fact is the affirmation of the 1947 declaration of the Pakistan Movement, that **Pakistan will be a democratic state, with a just social order based on the principles of Islam.** The nation has rejected secularism, religious extremism and 'isms' of all kind. It has voted for Moderation as in 1947, expressing the 'true will' of the Pakistani nation.'

In Gen Beg's opinion, the verdict of 11th May 2013, by the Pakistani voters, had demolished several myths, emerging from the depths of sorrow and sacrifices of decades and the sufferings at the hands of a corrupt and incompetent government [of the PPP], which almost shook the very foundation of the country. The myth that the Pakistani nation, with 45% illiterates cannot nurture democracy had been shattered, by those voters, who rejected most of the corrupt and the incompetent, thus correcting the course of democracy.

Astonishing it was that being himself an Army Chief, Gen Beg wrote:

> '....*Our national institutions, **namely the Army and the Judiciary have mainly been responsible for the derailment of democracy** in the past. Now they stood wholeheartedly to determine the right course for the democratic order and have defeated all machinations and manipulations to sabotage the election process....And I may not be wrong in saying that the new leadership also has the 'fear of God' in their hearts......'.*

During elections of 2013, it was rather pathetic to see PPP and ANP rejected by the voters. ANP melted away conceding space to PTI which emerged as the majority in KPK. The PPP, battered and bruised, had receded to its base in interior Sindh, while MQM, as usual ruled urban Sindh, forcing a coalition government for the sake of political harmony. Surprisingly Imran Khan targeted Punjab, but hit the 'bull' in Khyber PK province – many analysts considered it a bad shot.

From the election results, it appeared that the PML(N) *jiyalas* were mobilized better than the rest. Overall, the results revealed two important conclusions. Firstly; the message of change by Imran Khan's PTI, had not fully penetrated through the rural masses that constitute the majority of Pakistan's population or it has failed to resonate with them. As usual, the votes across rural Pakistan were caste on ***Bradari, Qabeela & Clan*** basis and in favour of those who could get the ***thana kachehri*** [police & court jobs] work done for voters. PML(N)) was already in saddles in Punjab to do that work so it prevailed.

Secondly; the general populace preferred to caste their vote in terms of experience rather than hope. In view of PPP's abysmal performance over the past five years, PML(N) had comparatively showed signs of progress and forward momentum - Metro Bus, Danish Schools and lap-tops all conveyed a tangible message of reality at least - though criticism was there. Perhaps the PML[N] acted upon the lesson known well in the Urdu proverb: ***"Jo dikhta hai wo bikta hai."*** [What is visible is that sells.]

The PPP had nothing to place in their showcase. All this sounded rational; it could be justified and explained with reasons. The worrying part was the assessment of the projects – forget the intellect involved; the people wanted to feel the difference.

Pakistan's border areas with Afghanistan were inhabited by the tribal groups which had once defeated the Soviets and twenty years later the

Americans and their allies. From here also mounted the resistance against Pakistan - such was the muddle Imran Khan had to wade through. The PPP and ANP learnt the bitter lesson - while in power they should not have taken the masses for granted; it was the revenge for the betrayal.

The PPP regime had left the economy of the country in serious jeopardy; the nation had to fight back. Pakistan's agriculturists and industrialists had fought the curse of energy crisis maintaining the export level tolerable but they expected better situation to emerge in coming days. The American and NATO forces were on retreat in Afghanistan, who also had stakes in Pakistan. By political wisdom, Nawaz Sharif, Imran Khan and Maulana Fazlur Rahman were on the same page on the issue of dealing with the threat of terrorism, as had been declared by the All Parties Conference *on 28th February 2013,* subsequently endorsed by the parliament, too.

Gen Beg had rightly pointed out that Nawaz Sharif should not be in hurry to improve relation with India. Kashmir issue must be revisited in the context of changed geo-political realities of the 21st century – *particularly the 'Shift of the Strategic Pivot' to Asia Pacific;* withdrawal of occupation forces from Afghanistan; merging Russo-Chinese interests in the region; Indian hegemonic ambitions of regional primacy and the surge of Muslim Consciousness' and its impact on Pakistan. PML[N] was rightly expected to avail the opportunities to justify the trust reposed in them by the nation.

Contrary to Gen Beg's optimistic views, some analysts maintained that by the logic, rationale and history of events, the people's mandate was stolen once again. Going by media reports, the said election had been massively rigged by a meticulously organised pre-planned script authored by different forces, representing the traditional ruling elite in Pakistan and their foreign patrons; the England and America.

In the words of *Dr Haider Mehdi's,* referring to his article dated *16th May 2013* on media pages, elections of 2013 was the replica of 2nd NRO planned for the benefits of the traditional ruling elite and to maintain political - economic status quo on the western agenda.

As the election drew closer, the overall political dynamics, election campaigns and the magnitude of PTI's growing clout in the public had indicated visible signs of its success in elections. Thus the US and its western allies decided to lend full support to the two main parties in Pakistan, PML[N] and PPP, to ensure the political status quo was preserved. Hence, a script for the second NRO was planned.

**In February 2013,** the US Senate Committee on Foreign Relations met with the PML[N] Chief in Lahore. In March, a meeting was arranged between Gen Musharraf and Nawaz Sharif in Saudi Arabia to discuss the modalities of political action and political reconciliation and the General returned to Pakistan, with PML[N] and PPP leadership keeping dead silent on his return. Soon after, not by sheer coincidence, the PML[N] Chief and Pakistan's COAS were in Saudi Arabia at the same time to perform *Umrah* that year.

In April, the Army Chief met with the Afghan President and the US Secretary of State in Brussels. Earlier, Nawaz Sharif's long meeting with the British Foreign Minister prior to his trip to Saudi Arabia set the stage of the execution of the 2nd NRO in Pakistan.

The intelligentsia held that at least the Army Chief, Gen Kayani, should have avoided becoming party to America's that dirty game in Pakistani politics – the general populace didn't appreciate it.

Most historians termed the elections 2013 of Pakistan as US sponsored. The flurry of the then diplomacy and visits between London, Dubai, Qatar, Saudi Arabia, Bonn and Ankara indicated awareness to the fall-outs of the contemplated US exit from Afghanistan on Pakistan and by implication the composition of the future government. General question remained that would elections 2013 be a game changer or would they push Pakistan again into the sand grave of traditionally corrupt Pakistani politics?

In the given scenario, petitions in the ECP for re-polls in some areas would be inevitable but the parties with question marks would ultimately be cajoled and persuaded to accept the unavoidable and expected. However, even the influential army officers, more retired and less serving, did not wish to disrupt an era of effective parliamentary democracy and national reconstruction; fair elections were to be welcome.

Through Pakistan's scripted elections, 5 years of military dominated rule from 2002-2007 and subsequent 5 years of an NROed PPP regime failed to deliver on militancy and development. During the dark age of PPP government, the pliant nation did not succumb to economic hit men and turned out in large numbers to reject all characters that played havoc with the state; sweet revenge on a regime that termed democracy as the best revenge.

The 1990 elections that brought Nawaz Sharif led IJI to power is black marked by the Mehran Bank Scandal and Asghar Khan Case. Though the case was referred by the Supreme Court to the PPP's Government in 2012, the later showed no inclination to pursue it, nor did the ECP take cognizance under Articles 62-63 of the Constitution. It also appeared that the mutuality of the skeletons in the cupboard prevented most parties to pursue the ends of justice. 1990's IJI government could only last for two years.

1997 brought a landslide victory to PML[N] while PPP was reduced to miserly 18 seats in the National Assembly. Ultimately, in Pakistan's rogue system, the PML[N] turned on for its own benefits and brought down everything with it. The President, Chief Justice and COAS were all humbled till the Generals of fortune delivered the final blow. Gen Musharraf ruled for nine years but the history repeated itself with an ironic twist that the man who once held Nawaz Sharif in Attock jail himself faced the same fate at the hands of his once caged and pardoned person – Nawaz Sharif.

With PPP confined to Sindh, a favourable mandate once again awaited PML[N]. Pakistanis were to wait and watch whether PML[N] had grown in maturity or would again drag itself into pitfalls of corruption like their predecessors. On the other side, as reaction to the status quo, the people turned out in large numbers to make the choices. However, their vigour was marred by the endemic propensity of old actors to engineer results. ECP simply failed to deliver the things the people expected.

The election results implied that Imran Khan's slogans went high on emotionalism and short on substance. To its credit were the assembly of masses in unprecedented numbers and ability to convince the rich and poor to turn out and vote. As a new force to reckon with, the party had a sizable opposition in Punjab and the largest presence in KPK. Though not reflected in the number of seats, PTI laid claim to at least 18% of the urban vote bank in Karachi; some termed it as light at the end of tunnel.

Logically, the perception of free and fair elections would have kept this change energized. Anything to contrary could disillusion and discourage this segment of people from future participation. The ECP and the judiciary owe it to this massive additional turnout to prove their transparency. This was also going to cool political tempers and make way for co-existence in the larger interests of the country.

The fierce political and ideological rivalry between PML[N] and PTI put both on test in Khyber PK. Without a simple majority and a hostile centre, PTI was left to face the onerous task of governing KPK with odd allies – as both JI and QWP of Sherpao were profoundly failed parties representing status quo while PML[N] and JUI were in opposition to cut PTI's throat. The split mandate left no room for complacency; and herein was the challenge. PTI had to fight back from the corner of the ring, because Taliban around was another odd factor.

Post election grouping cornered PTI into KPK and expected it to deliver in extremely hostile and non-cooperative environments. PML[N] holding out an olive branch to PTI in KPK did well but then there was a familiar paradox. PML[N] leadership knew that if PTI failed in KPK, it might take down the whole system with it. Dream of a *Naya Pakistan* was put on practical testing – the people were waiting results.

## ELECTIONS - MOSTLY WELL DONE:

In the general elections of 2013, 4,670 candidates contested the 272 general seats for the National Assembly and 10,955 candidates contested the elections for the four Provincial Assemblies. Of the 4,670 candidates contesting the general seats in the National Assembly 161 (3.5%) were women as compared to 64 women contesting the General Seats in 2008.

The Electoral Roll was heavily criticised by stakeholders and observers in past elections. The 2002 roll was only partially computerised and as a consequence there was no way of accurately checking for duplicate entries or to search for unverified entries. The 2008 roll saw some improvements but was still criticised due to some one-third of the electorate being listed on a supplementary list rather than the main list and with many of the entries lacking unique ID numbers.

The Electoral Roll for the 2013 elections represented a major improvement and enjoyed widespread confidence. NADRA should be appreciated for that. It was fully computerised and reliant upon the unique CNIC numbers. The lists were easily used for cross-checking and verifying entries to maintain accuracy and reliability. On the election day it proved an accurate and a reliable document and the people had felt immense confidence.

Commonwealth Observer Mission for General Elections [2013] in Pakistan; had analysed the case of Gen Musharaf as an example of the inconsistencies in the nomination process. He returned to Pakistan on 24th March 2013, during the nomination process and submitted nomination papers in four constituencies. His documents were not accepted anywhere stating it was because of the high treason and murder charges brought against him.

The Mission observed that *'being charged with an offence does not preclude candidacy'*, rather it is being found guilty of an offence that precludes candidacy. In the end none of his applications for nomination went forward and he did not contest the polls and remained under house arrest during the election period.

During elections 2013, women represented just 1.8% of the ECP's 2,288 full time employees and there were no women in senior management positions. The ECP recognised this shortcoming and in its five-year Strategic Plan (2010-2014) it stated that *'it aims to increase the representation of eligible women within the ECP to at least 10%'*. No progress was however seen till May 2013.

Polling was scheduled to take place from 08.00 hours to 17.00 hrs in 69,729 polling stations across the country. In most instances polling stations were divided into male and female streams with multiple polling booths in some premises.

On Election Day of 11th May 2013; in majority of cases the opening and voting procedures were well conducted, although late opening was experienced in some remote places. Voters turned out in very large numbers, often from quite early in the day; especially the large turnout of women voters and youth deserve appreciation. Given the level of violence in the lead-up to the election, and some incidents on the day, this large turnout of voters was quite remarkable. Queues were formed at the polling stations and in most cases these were orderly and calm. Security was present around the polling stations and it was felt that officers had a positive effect on the process and were helpful where required.

However, the elections 2013 were affected by a significant level of violence, which impacted most dramatically in the city of Karachi, Balochistan and Khyber PK. While the violence in Karachi included inter-party violence, the bulk of the violence during the elections emanated from militant groups external to the elections. Three candidates were killed in targeted attacks, with well over a hundred party supporters killed and several hundreds injured.

The violence was largely, though not exclusively, due to and amongst three political parties, PPP, PML[N] and the MQM, seriously impeding their ability to campaign openly in many parts of the country and limiting their freedoms of movement and assembly. Affected parties were critical that more was not done to improve their security for the campaign and the integrity of the process in affected areas was compromised.

What was remarkable, though, was that *despite the level of violence against the process by militants, there was a determination by political parties to remain engaged in the process and ensures it was not derailed. Also, the high turnout of voters was in spite of threats of violence and reports of actual violence.* These two factors bode well for the further consolidation of democracy in the country.

The legal framework provided the basic conditions for credible, competitive elections and the 18th, 19th and 20th Constitutional Amendments and various electoral reforms strengthened the framework for the elections. Significantly the 18th Amendment provided for increased independence of the ECP and had increased the level of confidence in the Election Commission *except that the candidates were hand picked by the owners of the most political parties; nepotism was seen at the peak.*

It is significant that these were the first elections held under the full treaty obligations of the UN's **International Covenant on Civil and Political Rights** [ICCPR], following Pakistan's removal of its reservations in 2010. This further helped to improve the overall legal framework for the polls and the democratic process in the country.

There was a significant increase in the number of candidates and political parties contesting these elections compared to the previous general elections. However, the time was short for candidate nominations and inconsistencies among Returning Officers (ROs) in applying legal criteria in the confirmation of candidacies.

It was widely felt that most ROs reportedly went beyond their spheres of simply administering the process. The process for the nomination of candidates caused controversies in many areas because the DROs/ROs followed CJP Chaudhry's instructions and the ECP was seen often helpless.

One of the ECP's main successes was the much improved Electoral Rolls with the help of NADRA though the shortfall of registered women voters remained to be addressed. The use of NADRA's database to create the Electoral Roll and the use of CNIC's for the purpose of voter identification had created a far more reliable list of voters compared to previous elections. *The ECP's use of SMS to enable voters to verify their registration and identify their polling station was also an excellent innovation.*

The level of representation of women as candidates remains relatively low. For instance, while there were 60 reserved seats for women in the 342-seat National Assembly, women represented just over 3% of the total number of candidates contesting the general seats for the Assembly was 18. The level of women as registered voters also remained relatively low and despite some improvements in the number of women on the voter register and some positive initiatives by the ECP there remained, according to ECP data, a shortfall of about 10 million women compared to men on the Electoral Rolls.

The ECP issued a series of Codes of Conduct to help regulate the election campaign, media coverage, election observers and behaviour of election officials. Such an innovation is a helpful supplement to the Representation of the People Act.

On Election Day, the ECP was generally well prepared for the polls in most areas and the process was well administered. But delays and other problems were experienced in some locations, with Karachi particularly affected. There was a very large security deployment in support of the process throughout, and this was generally effective and helpful. Pak-Army and its Rangers deserved a full salute on that account.

Some polling stations struggled to deal with large numbers of assigned voters, particularly in places where the premises were too small for the task, but overall, faced with the high voter turnout; at polling station most officials worked diligently to administer the process and the new electoral roll proved to be reliable. In Karachi problems were also caused by the late delivery of materials, resulting in delays.

Towards the end of polling the ECP extended the hours of polling but this was not adequately communicated down to polling station level, leading some inconsistencies in managing this. The count at most polling stations was conducted in a transparent manner and polling agents were able to get a copy of the result at the completion of the count and the result was announced and posted. *Such measures help transparency and accountability.*

In selecting the sites for polling stations more stern efforts could have been made to find and search for good sized premises, number of voters assigned to that polling station, ease of access for persons with disability, the elderly and other persons for whom access remained a constant issue at most polling stations.

## *SUGGESTION FOR IMPROVEMENT:*

The following are the suggestions mainly addressed to the Parliament and the ECP. All branches of the state (the Parliament, executive offices and the judiciary) are required to work together within their constitutional competencies to support election reforms. Such reforms, based on consensus, mutual consultation, deliberation, implementation and immediate concentration - thus prompt attention was warranted.

Of the 39 recommendations made, 17 are assessed to require a change in the Constitution, laws and legislative procedures. For further 10 recommendations it would be desirable to have the suggested changes secured in the ECP's procedural framework; other state functionaries like NADRA, PEMRA and superior judiciary have also to play their roles.

It may not be out of place to mention that the **Common-wealth Observers** and the **EU Election Observation Mission,** who were here in Pakistan to overview the Elections 2013, had also made the same or similar recommendations to make the electoral system in Pakistan better.

### Recommendations For The Parliament:

1. Formation of a special Parliamentary Committee on elections/electoral reforms for timely review of legislation, based on international norms of democratic process and accountability.

2. The Freedom of Information Ordinance be amended to require State parties to proactively keep on ECP's internet site all the information of public interest. Federal Government's powers to decline disclosure be removed – let the ECP go independent to decide.

3. Presidential powers in regards to approval of rules, removal of difficulty, and approval of Appellate Tribunals etc are no more needed; - no unnecessary bottle necks. The ECP should go independent instead of wasting time.

   **[The fact remains that basically it is the prime minister which uses those powers because the President cannot sign the document unless it carries the PM's approval first.]**

4. There is constitutional provision for a judge of the Supreme Court to act as Commissioner in the absence of the Chief Election Commissioner [CEC]; it should be removed. Instead, the age of CEC and other members of the ECP be also limited to 65 years.

5. Parliament should review the system of reserved seats for women and minorities or professionals etc in the house. Every seat should come through ballot boxes – no special powers for winning party leaders. Separate electoral be designed for them each.

6. Consideration to be given to reviewing the system for allocating the reserved seats to the MINORITIES, so that they are directly elected by the voters and such representatives have a constituency to respond to.

7. Legislation for delimitation be reviewed to explicitly provide for nation-wide delimitation possibly using voter registration figures in the absence of updated census data. Timely de-limitation be undertaken, allowing for consultation and complaints.

8. Candidacy requirements be amended to remove vague moral conditions. ROs should not be left to interpret them differently. Provisions of Articles 62 & 63 be strictly implemented during nomination process.

9. Implementation of Articles 62 & 63, the process should be allowed to be completed within 90 days even after elections. No stay order of any sort. High courts will decide the merits within a week through summary procedures – appeals will be decided by the SC within three days. Amendments be made in the Constitution or the laws accordingly.

10. Law be made that only ONE candidate for one seat only. Candidates be limited to running in only one constituency, national OR provincial, in the given election. It is for clarity to voters and to remove the need for subsequent by-elections.

11. The financial limitation on election expenses of candidates be reviewed, together with the financing provisions for political parties, in order to enhance transparency and accountability. The financial monitoring and enforcement capacity of the ECP be developed.

12. Freedom of expression be subject to "necessary" rather than "any reasonable restrictions imposed by law" through amendment of article 19 of the Constitution.

13. The Pakistan Electronic Media Regulatory Authority (PEMRA) Ordinance 2007; Press, Newspapers, News Agencies and Books Registration Ordinance 2007; Defamation Ordinance and number of PEMRA regulations be amended in line with Pakistan's international commitments and best practices in journalism.

14. The mandate, functioning and neutrality of future caretaker governments be more clearly defined in law. Caretaker governments should be equipped with more powers with regard to election administration – their age should not go beyond 65 years as per judges of the SC.

15. 18th Amendment in the Constitution should be re-amended to the extent of *'regular elections within the political parties'* at least. Internal party democratisation processes are required and enforcement mechanisms be developed, to enhance participation and accountability in regards to candidate nomination.

16. *Party tickets should be given to perfectly deserving candidates in each party* and decision should be taken in respective party meetings at various levels.

17. Further constitutional reforms be undertaken to enable FATA residents to enjoy fundamental political freedoms and civil rights as other citizens of Pakistan do. The 12 Parliamentarians of FATA be given adequate powers to legislate for the FATA people collectively.

## Recommendations For The ECP:

18. The ECP should fully implement its Five Year Strategic Plan. In each upcoming by-election some better practice be included - regular reports be placed before the Parliament.

19. The ECP needs to ensure that on the polls-day, the election officials at all levels are able to communicate with their respective administrative officers. For instance, POs should be able to effectively communicate with ROs, possibly through an intermediary where necessary, in order to seek clarification on any matters of concern.

20. The ECP should promote voter engagement by undertaking voter education at appropriate times through regular media updates - including addressing administrative complaints, transparency and public apprehensions.

21. The ECP should take full management responsibility for the work of ROs; they should be guided from ECP and monitored - not be wholly drawn from the judiciary only. Some ROs should be at ECP's permanent strength as staff. By-elections should be done through them.

22. The ECP should work with full transparency, making all information of public interest immediately and easily accessible, including ECP decisions and notifications etc.

23. Procedures for checks on RO's assessment of candidate nominations be developed, so that all candidates are treated equally and fairly. Especially, computerised set procedure be developed to immediately scrutinize Forms 14, 15 & 16.

24. Every polling scheme be finalised as per law; any subsequent alterations due to court decisions or some dire necessity be made immediately public locally and on ECP website.

25. All ROs and polling staff be trained for consistent and correct implementation of procedures. Any last minute changes in polling staff be immediately notified and new staff be drawn from trained reserves. Counting, completion of forms and the results process training should be given priority.

26. The results management system should be further developed so that all polling station and constituency forms are swiftly transmitted to the ECP and are promptly displayed on the ECP website, as well as being displayed locally at the constituency level.

27. Special measures be taken to provide an effective electoral participation of the *'disable voters'*. Postal voting may be thought for the disables and special procedures be made to make this process fool-proof.

## Recommendations For The NADRA:

28. Special efforts be undertaken to secure CNIC registration for women; targeting rural and conservative areas to increase the number of women on the electoral roll. Photographs be included on all CNICs as an anti-fraud measure; awareness campaigns for the usefulness of having photographs on CNIC be enhanced. The information be published regularly and promptly on the websites of the ECP and NADRA.

## Recommendations For PEMRA:

29. In close cooperation with the ECP and Big Media Houses, PEMRA should establish efficient media monitoring units in all provinces meeting international standards, to seek legitimate and accurate information.

30. Jurisdiction and supervision over the state-owned media be transferred from Ministry of Information and Broadcasting to PEMRA. State-owned broadcasters' financial autonomy be sustained and editorial independence be further fostered by amending relevant legislation.

31. State media should develop a program to increase substantially the visibility of candidates from minority and vulnerable groups.

## Recommendations For Judiciary & Courts:

32. A clear *'Summary Procedure'* system for filing administrative complaints to the ECP and petitions to the Tribunals be laid down by the Higher courts, made it public to avoid overlapping jurisdictions and win the public confidence – no stay orders beyond a week. Information should be available on ECP's website that how, where and when to complain, and also on how and when decisions are expected; complaints tracking system be introduced.

33. The independence of Appellate and Election Tribunals be strengthened through making the judges apply their minds on admissible evidence; asking them to pen down exact reasons for reaching the conclusions and decisions through whatever evidence, electronic or documentary, placed before them.

34. The legislative framework for electoral offences and penalties be reviewed to remove any unwarranted clauses, such as boycotting or non availability of advocates etc. Processes of quick justice be encouraged by appointing *'Investigating Magistrates'* as in many European countries like France and Switzerland.

35. Strict actions should be taken against agreements that prohibit women from voting. Laws be amended to explicitly provide for the ECP and Tribunals to disqualify a returned candidate straightway through summary or show-cause if there comes evidence that the candidate, or their election agent or any other person with their

connivance, participated in an agreement banning women from voting or standing as candidates.

## Recommendations For Women NGOs:

37. Political parties' Women Wings and independent NGOs be required to design appropriate policies and provide information on women's participation within the party, and to take additional measures to promote women's involvement. Political parties be encouraged to nominate an increased number of women candidates for general seats.

38. State media should design special ads and programs to promote women's participation in the electoral process, such as including women candidates in their election programs, asking parties about their policies related to women's active role.

## Recommendations For Citizens NGOs:

39. Citizen observer groups, like 'Free and Fair Election Network' [FAFEN], should continue to develop in organisational capacity, advocate for electoral reforms, and undertake scrutiny of by-elections and local elections and take them to media.

# Scenario 127

## CABINET OF PML[N] IN 2013:

**On 7ᵗʰ June 2013**, a 25-member Federal Cabinet took oath in Islamabad; President Zardari administered the oath.

## *KASHMIRI CABINET SWORN IN:*

When Nawaz Sharif announced his cabinet for his 3ʳᵈ term in 2013, the people were concerned about knowing that most of his 27 members' cabinet comprised of his old friends from Lahore and Gujranwala Divisions. Not a single member was given representation in the federal cabinet from Faisalabad Division from where the PML(N) got 17 out of 20 seats [*the remaining three independent winners had also joined PML(N) later*].

Amongst the whole lot from Punjab consisted of **Rajpoots & Kashmiri** clans only with one from **Jats** whereas none from **Arain, Gujjar, Syed, Pathan, Awan or Moghals** were included to represent their communities.

Figures like <u>Khwaja Asif, Ahsan Iqbal, Zahid Hamid, Khurram Dastgir, Usman Ibrahim, Barjees Tahir, Khwaja Saad Rafiq, Rana Tanvir, Ishaq Dar and Pervez Rasheed</u> were all either from the said two Divisions [*nine ministers from Gujranwala while six from Lahore*] completely ignoring Dera Ghazi Khan, Bahawalpur, Sarghoda and Faisalabad Divisions. Obviously, there was a lot of cribbing among MNAs and heavy weights who were overlooked for the cabinet, but again, it was their chief's prerogative.

*From Multan Division Sikandar Bosan* was given a slot as federal minister; a member who had joined the PML(N) in the last moments with much hesitation and dithering sentiments otherwise he had spent his whole political career with Gen Musharraf and PML(Q).

There were few surprises in the cabinet line-up, with most being men, old loyalists of Nawaz Sharif from his previous stints in power, and overwhelmingly *[19 out of 25] from Punjab*, the PML(N)'s stronghold. It appeared natural, given the makeup and mandate of the party, but it raised questions about the new government's ability to take the other provinces along in crucial situations.

No woman was made full minister; the PM retained the Defence and Foreign Affairs ministries with himself, would of course use Sartaj Aziz's experience and Tariq Fatemi's connections to keep US & India on their right hand side. *Sanaullah Zehri*, perhaps to compensate him for the loss of his efforts for chief ministerial slot of Balochistan, was appointed a Special Assistant to the PM.

PM had successfully negotiated and guaranteed a deal between *Sanaullah Zehri and Dr Abdul Malik* to hold the chief ministry of Balochistan for half & half duration. Dr Malik held the term first in June 2013 and **on 12**th **December 2015**, Sanaullah Zehri took over the slot in turn.

**On 10**th **June 2013;** President Zardari addressed the joint session of the parliament, fulfilling a constitutional requirement, but he read out a speech given by the incumbent PML[N] government. The gesture was propagated as *'a sign of the institutional maturity'* but the general populace knew that from inside both party leaders were one and the same, two hands in one glove, taking care of each other's interests in the name of democracy and in an arena of *'meesaq e jamhooriat'*.

*Marvi Memon was given a special seat in 2013's* National Assembly by the PML(N). The people of Pakistan cannot forget a day of August 2008 when Gen Musharraf had quit the presidency. She was in Gujrat that day at the residence of her leader Ch Shuja'at Hussain and was continuously weeping and crying for the sad event. Gujrat had seen and realized her mighty presence during a supplementary election when she was making fiery speeches at each cross road gathering against the PML(N)'s candidate. Then she was openly repeating a long list of allegations against both the Sharifs of Lahore.

Then Marvi Memon suddenly appeared in Imran Khan's known big *jalsa* [political gathering] at Ghotki in Sukkar District of Sindh. There she announced that *'now I've reached the real political leadership of Pakistan and this was my destiny'*. However, when she was not seen in the next gatherings of the PTI, the people tended to forget her face.

Once more she surprised the people when the electronic media flashed her sitting besides Nawaz Sharif during a party meeting. The PML(N) had accepted her besides her long known associations with Gen Musharraf and the PML(Q). During her last tenure, Marvi Memon was given a women seat by the PML(Q) and that too from Punjab. It was her beauty and political wisdom that she had given her vote to Mr Zardari during the presidential elections of 2008 and made it known to the whole PPP. *It was her bad luck that she was not adequately paid by the PPP or the Presidency then.*

*PML(N)'s one third federal cabinet of 2013* was having the same faces which had been enjoying the blessings of Gen Musharraf during his nine years rule. Similarly exactly the same numbers of provincial ministers in the Punjab cabinet were the stalwart personalities who had been at the helm of affairs during the military rule of 1999 - 2007.

Throughout Gen Musharraf's military rule, Senator Zafar Ali Shah had been contesting Nawaz Sharif's cases in the lower and higher courts whereas one *Zahid Hamid*, being the Federal Law Minister of Gen Musharraf, had been openly opposing Nawaz Sharifs at all levels. During 2013's elections, Zahid Hamid not only got elected on PML(N)'s ticket but was also taken as the federal minister whereas *Zafar Ali Shah was pushed into the corner* when fruits of reward were distributed amongst the workers in new Nawaz Sharif's government.

[*On 30ᵗʰ November 2015; Zafar Ali Shah lost his local body election at Chairman Union Council's seat – he was aspiring for the post of the First Mayor of Islamabad. It was known to every one that Mr Shah was purposefully defeated at so small stake because the PML(N) workers were instructed from the high command - NOT to vote for him.*]

Sometimes, it becomes difficult to understand the real wisdom prevailing in the political corridors when one hears the news that people like *Engr Amir Muqam were also taken on Advisory Board of the PML(N) government*. Amir Muqam had been the right hand man of Gen Musharraf for the whole last decade. Then he was specially awarded PML(N)'s tickets in Khyber PK province for 2013 elections which he lost at the hands of Imran Khan's candidates.

*Even then Amir Muqam was preferred to be made Nawaz Sharif's Advisor whereas Saranjam Khan [known for laying his own CHADAR over Kalsoom Nawaz's head during hard days], Abdul Subhan Khan and Zafar Iqbal Jhagra like Leagui workers, who had been maltreated at numerous occasions for being with PML(N) during Nawaz Sharif's exile, were badly treated and totally ignored.*

Not only this; amongst the female representations in the assemblies, only those women were nominated who were recommended by Amir Muqam and Sardar Mehtab Abbasi whereas the real worker *ladies of the PML(N) like Shaheen Habibullah, Najma Noshirwan and Aasma*

*Zarrin were simply pushed into the dark shadows.* Six of the PML(N)'s ladies, who had represented their party in the National Assembly during the last troublesome tenure, including *Tasneem Siddiqui, Shirin Arshad, Nisar Tanvir and Qudsia Arshad were also shunted out* because the new relationships had won them over after 2013 elections.

Tasneem Siddiqui was the PML(N)'s member who had floated the famous bill of **'dual nationality'** over the parliament's floor which was successfully adopted and made to law subsequently.

Just on 2$^{nd}$ day of the oath ceremony, an English daily newspaper published story of a *turf battle between Sartaj Aziz and Tariq Fatemi* as there had been a history of hostility between the two gentlemen since good old days. The facts remained that:

> *'Fatemi and Aziz were in the opposing camps on the crucial issue of signing of the Comprehensive Test Ban Treaty (CTBT) in the 1998 nuclear tests. Sartaj Aziz was the foreign minister who wanted Nawaz Sharif to sign the treaty but Fatemi and his Foreign Office colleagues resisted it and eventually won. Till today, Pakistan has neither ratified nor signed the CTBT – but both were accommodated in the cabinet.*
>
> *Mr Fatemi was rewarded more as his wife was also given a seat in the National Assembly as MNA from reserve ladies quota of the PML[N]'*

Anjum Niaz in her essay appeared in *'the News' dated 17$^{th}$ June 2013* opined that *'why has Nawaz Sharif vacillated in naming a full-fledged foreign minister? Cutting up the most important portfolio to accommodate two of his party loyalists makes no sense. Worse still, was to corral the duo into a working relationship that reportedly has a history of ill feeling.'*

In his last two terms as the prime minister, Nawaz Sharif was misguided by his companions to choose some of the worst people to head embassies abroad and institutions at home; the history had witnessed.

## IPPs PAID RS:480 bn CASH:

On 28$^{th}$ June 2013; the newly saddled PML[N] government managed to get approval from the Economic Coordination Committee [ECC] of the cabinet worth of Rs:480 billion to clear dues of Independent Power Producers [IPPs]; ECC decided to release Rs:326 billion to IPPs in the first instance before 30$^{th}$ June 2013 – so were paid during that one night without AGPR's audit and recommendations/approval.

## Settlement on 28<sup>th</sup> June 2013

|                               | Rs: (Billion) |
| ----------------------------- | ------------- |
| Gross Transaction Amount      | 503.025       |
| Liquidated Damages            | (22.916)      |
| Total (Excluding LDs) (A)     | 480.109       |
| Gross Transaction (B)         | 341.958       |
| Dividend received             | 19.710        |
| **Total Net Transaction**     | **322.247**   |

**Payments Details**

| Cash IPPs       | 161.229 |
| --------------- | ------- |
| PIB OGDCL       | 56.322  |
| PIB PPL         | 23.363  |
| PSO Cash + PIB  | 81.333  |

**Settlement on 21 July 2013**

| WAPDA-Hydel      | 90.083      |
| ---------------- | ----------- |
| NTDC             | 10.216      |
| Gencos           | 14.888      |
| Nuclear Plants   | 22.964      |
| **TOTAL (C)**    | **138.151** |
| **GRAND TOTAL**  | 480.109     |

(Cash 33.217 + PIB 48.116)

## UPDATED ON 18<sup>th</sup> DECEMBER 2013
## PAYMENTS TO IPPS/ENERGY SECTOR OTHER ENTITIES

| Sr. No/Entity Name/Total Amount      | Rs. Billion |
| ------------------------------------ | ----------- |
| 1 HUBCO (RFO)                        | 75.000      |
| 2 KAPCO (GAS & RFO)                  | 41.354      |
| 3 AES (Pakgen) (RFO)                 | 6.982       |
| 4 AES (Lalpir) (RFo)                 | 4.546       |
| 5 KEL (RFO)                          | 3.504       |
| 6 SABA (RFO)                         | – –         |
| 7 LIBERTY (GAS)                      | 9.906       |
| 8 UCH (GAS)                          | 1.9261      |
| 9 ROUSCH (GAS)                       | 8.687       |
| 10 FAUJI (GAS)                       | 5.100       |
| 11 HABIBULLAH (GAS)                  | 2.540       |
| 12 ALTERN (GAS)                      | 0.270       |
| 13 AGL POWER (GAS)                   | 19.336      |
| 14 THE HUBCO NAROWAL (RFO)           | 17.397      |
| 15 ATLAS POWER (RFO)                 | 5.400       |

| | | |
|---|---|---|
| 16 | NISHAT POWER (RFO) | 7.080 |
| 17 | NISHATCHUNIAIN (RFO) | 6.860 |
| 18 | LIBERTY TECH (RFO) | 6.817 |
| 19 | ORIENT POWER (GAS/HSD) | 1.307 |
| 20 | SAIF POWER (GAS/HSD) | 4.902 |
| 21 | SAPPHIRE ELECTRIC (GAS/HSD) | 4.208 |
| 22 | HALMORE POWER (GAS/HSD) | 2.522 |
| 23 | ENGRO POWER (GAS) | 8.974 |
| 24 | FOUNDATION POWER (GAS) | 7.074 |
| 25 | SHYDO POWER (HYDEL) | 1.159 |
| 26 | LARAIB ENERGY (HYDEL) | 0.105 |
| | | **270.291** |
| 27 | SNGPL (Genco-II) | 18.996 |
| 28 | SSGC (Genco I&II) | 2.901 |
| | | 0.586 |
| 29 | Mari Gas (Genco-II) | 9.358 |
| 30 | PPL (Genco-II) | 13.843 |
| 31 | PSO (Genco-I & III) | 6.130 |
| | | 19.853 |
| | | **71.667** |
| | Sub-Total (28 June 2013) | **341.958** |
| 32 | WAPDA-Hydel | 90.083 |
| 33 | NTDC | 10.216 |
| 34 | Gencos | 14.888 |
| 35 | Nuclear Plants | 22.964 |
| | Sub-Total (21 July 2013) | **138.151** |
| | **GRAND TOTAL** | **480.109** |

**18 DECEMBER 2013**

**Payments to Ministry of Water & Power**
**For Settling Circular Debt**
**Summary of sources of financing**

| | |
|---|---|
| Pakistan Investment Bonds (PIBs) | Rs 128 billion |
| Expenditure savings | Rs 135 billion |
| (Fiscal deficit reduced from 8.8% to 8.2% for 2012-13) | |
| Dividends recovered from PSEs | Rs 20 billion |
| Cash paid from Federal Consolidated Fund | Rs 59 billion |
| Recovery of payables to Federal Government from PSEs | Rs 138 billion |
| **TOTAL** | **Rs 480 billion** |

[Names of beneficiaries for Rs:71.667 were not detailed completely; there were spaces in official statement of MoF released]

The ECC, which met under the chair of Federal Finance Minister Ishaq Dar, decided to eliminate the circular debt by clearing the Rs:480 billion to the IPPs. The government released Rs:326 billion in first instalment before 30th June for which it attached four conditions. The remaining dues were cleared next month.

The conditions included that IPPs would generate maximum power and bring 1700 megawatt [MW] to the national grid before start of the holy month of Ramazan; then to be started on 7th July 2013. Similarly, HUBCO and Pak Jin and other power plants would run through coal and PEPCO would provide oil on deferred payment for 60 days. The IPPs would not approach the courts in case of late payment.

The ECC had also **decided to revoke two LNG import** projects initiated by previous regime of PPP; instead it decided to initiate new bidding process for LNG import AND to contact with Qatar government also on priority basis. The ECC also decided to expedite the work on Nandipur project, as the same had been delayed by more than five years because of flimsy disputes and machinery worth billions of rupees imported for it had been rusting at Karachi port and incurring demurrage.

The ECC also gave approval to the Ramazan package worth of two billion rupees wherein subsidized commodities were to be made available at Utility Stores Corporations. The ECC also reviewed the economic situation of the country; mentioning PPP's lethargy during the past five years.

## CORRUPTION IN SWIFT PAYMENTS:

**The main issues were** that:

*a. After managing clearance from the ECC, Governor State bank of Pakistan [SBP] was straightaway ordered to release the said money. They released it to the Ministry of Finance [MoF] which on the same day transferred the whole amounts to Ministry of Water & Power [MoW&P] for onward distribution.*

*b. The IPP's files were not referred to AGPR for checking and report which was the constitutional requirement. Basically the whole set of payments should have been checked and cleared by AGPR.*

*c. The bills and invoices claimed by all recipients were mostly the photocopies which were not admissible for any payment method.*

*d. The then AGPR Akhtar Buland Rana had raised objections on the release of so huge funds without scrutiny; he was asked to transfer that officer who was chasing MoF and SBP for audits – the AGPR was immediately sent home.*

*e. The load shedding remained at such; the money paid went in vain apparently; the people could not get relief.*

*f. All the IPPs claimed their demurrages and late payment fines – which were admitted by the government and paid whereas the fines due on them due to less production were withdrawn.*

The IPPs earlier, in talks with the PPP government had offered a relief of 25% of the total arrears to the government but the PML[N] government paid all the arrears in one go. The payment also included Rs:31 billion penalty for not purchasing electricity from the IPPs [*verification needed as how the PPP government could refuse to buy power from them as there had been acute shortages of electricity throughout their tenure*].

On the other hand the PML[N] government relieved Rs:22.91 billion penalties against the IPPs – neither there was logic in it nor the demand was urged even.

Under an agreement signed in 1994 the government had to arrange the oil supplies for power generation in IPPs in exchange the company would have been paid the spending on costs. The agreement in year 2002 was amended and the companies were allowed to arrange oil supplies on their own with conditions of pre-audit, post-audit and inspection, which could not happen for even once since than.

On 24th July 2013; the MoF issued details of payment of Rs:480 billion to Independent Power Producers (IPPs); the payment had already been made before 30th June 2013. With voices growing against the lack of relief in load-shedding despite clearing of circular debt, the federal government had to release the details of those payments made to IPPs in a bid to address transparency concerns. The PML[N] government took the decision after the PPP alleged misappropriation in circular debt payments.

MoF undertook an exercise to clear Rs:503.1 billion in circular debt by May 31. Out of the total circular debt, the ministry paid Rs:480.1 billion in cash, bonds and book adjustments, while Rs:22.9 billion withheld on account of liquidated damages owed by IPPs to the government; which were also released later.

On 19th **August 2013;** PPP's Shehla Raza tweeted that Nawaz Sharif should tell the nation that out of Rs:480 bn how much had gone to Mian Mansha's Nishat Group. It was alleged that all the home work was kept ready by the PML[N] before taking oath for the new government and Mian Mansha's IPPs were to be compensated the most.

On 27th **September 2013;** The government ordered **a third party audit** of payments made to the IPPs, generation companies and fuel suppliers. Zargham Eshaq Khan, JS of the MoW&P, informed a sub-committee of the Senate headed by PPP's Maula Bakhsh Chandio that the third party audit by three chartered accountants had been ordered to address the perception of any wrong doing.

The Joint Secretary MoW&P also told that the circular debt had gone up again to Rs:240bn at the end of the current financial year because its major causes were still there. The causes included:

> '....increase in recoverable amounts of distribution companies of Wapda, more line losses than allowed by the regulator, delayed charging of fuel price adjustment, non-payment of GST refunds by the Federal Board of Revenue [FBR] and delayed receipt of tariff differential subsidy from the federal government.'

JS Khan told that out of the Rs:480bn circular debt, Rs:138bn was cleared through book adjustments in the accounts of public sector companies for clearing tax dues and debts. The sub-committee held that the money wasted to clear *the circular debt was more than enough to finance 4,300MW Dassu Hydropower project.*

The fact remained that *neither the audit of payments made to the IPPs had been conducted during the past five years nor any audit of National Electric Power Regulatory Authority [NEPRA] was carried out during the period.*

The National Transmission and Dispatch Company [NTDC] informed the sub-committee that the nation suffered a huge loss of over Rs:130 billion because of non-implementation of 425MW Nandipur project for more than five years.

On 11th **October 2013;** there were headlines in the print media - **CIRCULAR DEBT AGAIN PEAKS TO RS 157 BILLION AGAIN;** and some remarks were amusing that *'Mian Manshaa ki phir se mojein, Anjuman e Ghulamaan e Raiwind kya kehtein hain iss par.'* [Mian Mansha, being member of *'Raiwind Club'* would loot again]

Pakistan's energy sector circular debt had again peaked to Rs:157 billion three months after Rs:480 billion was settled by the MoF without audit of IPPs' claims. The government had reconciled an amount of Rs:561 billion in June 2013 of which Rs:480 billion was settled, which implied that only Rs:81 billion remained unsettled with the re-emergence of Rs:75 billion till September 2013. The NTDC argued that:

> '.....circular debt would not be eliminated without an increase in gas quota to thermal power plants, conversion of furnace oil fired power plants to coal, increase in hydel generation, fixation of tariff taking account of socio-economic conditions of consumers, improvement in recovery and eradication of power theft.'

An MOU was signed between the NTDC/CPPA and the IPPs on assurance of optimal utilization of available capacity. The IPPs were asked to ensure optimum of their available capacity which they did not comply with on the pretext that gas and oil supplies were not adequate. The MoU for conversion of four IPPs, i.e., Hub Power Company (Hubco), Lalpir, Pakgen and Saba Power to coal were also signed on 28th June 2013 between the concerned IPPs and NTDC.

The implementation of that MOU was being handled by the Private Power and Infrastructure Board (PPIB). Different IPPs approached PPIB for conveying the intentions and understanding of the GoP and power purchaser to Nepra in the light of which the IPPs may approach Nepra for revision in working capital component of the tariff to implement the proposed extension in payment time from 30 days to 60 days.

At the time of Rs:480 billion settlement, an undertaking was given by the IPPs to resolve disputes relating to liquidated damages and capacity payment deduction presently raised by the parties before the Supreme Court, in accordance with dispute resolution mechanism as provided in respective Power Purchase Agreements (PPAs). Of nine IPPs, eight served dispute notice under section 18.2(b) of the PPA and nominated former Justice Sair Ali as expert for resolution of the dispute between the IPPs and NTDC.

As per section 18.2(b) of the PPA, the notice receiving party has to notify the initiating party whether such person is acceptable or not within 15 days of receiving dispute notice or the responding party shall propose a person to be the expert. The MoW&P further stated that the case was under process for approval of the MD NTDC through General Manager (L&CA). The IPPs were to respond after MD's approval was received in CPPA.

On 1st **November 2013**; the Lahore High Court [LHC] ordered the audit of Rs:480 billion paid by the government to the IPPs and observed that the burden of the incompetence of the officials and politicians would not shift on the masses. Chief Justice Umar Ata Bandial also observed that equalisation surcharge would not be received from the consumers. The court was hearing petitions against electricity load - shedding, fuel adjustments and equalisation surcharge.

As hearing started, the court was told that load - shedding did not reduce despite payment of Rs:480 billion by the govt to the IPPs. Following court notices, JS MoW&P Zargham Khan appeared before the court and submitted that unannounced load - shedding had ended. Moreover, the companies had to bear line losses due to substandard transformers and supply lines. The Karachi Electric Supply Company [KESC] could not take electricity more than 650MW, but it drew 950MW from the national grid station.

At this, the CJ observed that the amounts of the line losses had to be paid by the poor masses. The companies could have adopted modern methods for distribution of the electricity so that nobody could get power more than its due share. The court ordered that all the appointments of officers in LESCO should be made on merit; the schedule of power load - shedding should be uploaded on the website. The court also summoned the record of equalisation surcharge imposed on the consumers besides ordering the audit of Rs:480 billion paid by the govt to IPPs.

## ISSUE RAISED IN PARLIAMENT:

On 19th **December 2013**; Dr Arif Alvi MNA raised questions in the National Assembly [NA] that:

(a) Whether it is a fact that Rs:480 billions have been paid to Independent Power Projects (IPPs) for settlement of circular debt;

(b) whether it is also a fact that the audit has been conducted and completed thereof; if so, the names of audit companies along with the details thereof;

(c) whether it is further a fact that excess payments were made to IPPs; if so, the details thereof;

(d) whether any tenders were called for grant of audit contracts there for;

(e) whether any of the said companies audited the said 23 IPPs in the past; and

*(f) whether bulk payments were made on June 29, 2013 till late at night; if so, the reasons thereof?*

Khwaja Asif, Minister for Water & Power replied that:

*The office of the Auditor General of Pakistan had completed the audit of cash payment [**which was a blatant lie, the payments were NOT made through AGPR**]; the audit report was awaited; whereas for the appointment of Chartered Auditor Firms the bidding process was completed. The bidding process had been initiated by the office of Director Finance of NTDC. No excess payment was made to the IPPs.*

*Top 14 audited firms listed in the country were hired by various entities and due care had been exercised to avoid any conflict of interest. Funds of Rs:341 billion were received from MoF on 28th June, 2013 and payment was made on the same day as per **Annex-II**.*

In reply to a question of MNA Shagufta Jumani, Kh Asif told that:

*(a) **Reconciled overdue payables to Power generators as on 31-05-2013 were Rs:561 billion [and not Rs:480 Bn]. Company-wise payment made in this regard is placed as Annex-I of the NA's record.**.*

*(b) **Total payments of Rs:787.447 billion [and not Rs:503.1 Bn] were made to Power generators from 01-06-2013 to 23-10-2013. Further, detail of outstanding payables as on 23-10-2013 attached at Annexure II of the NA's record.***

***MNA Nighat Perveen Mir asked Kh Asif** whether it is a fact that the electricity of Rs:1800 billions is being stolen annually in the country;....* Kh Asif went silent.

**During the 3rd week of May 2014;** the IPPs which had earlier been paid Rs:480 billion by the Nawaz Sharif government in June 2013 asked the government in plain words **to pay another Rs:300 billion or face 12-14 hours load - shedding.** A letter to the MoW&P, the Advisory Council of IPPs [IPPAC] sensitised the government and had held a meeting on 15th May 2014 to discuss the re-emergence of huge amount of circular debt.

The IPPs were then facing a huge liquidity crisis in the awake of re-emergence of the circular debt of Rs:300 billion owing to which they were not able to generate electricity at the required level. The letter said that the government took the bold step of clearing the outstanding amount of Rs:480 billion in June 2013 for electricity taken by Pepco during June 2012 - June 2013 but not paid for the electricity taken since then.

However, due to failing recoveries, the receivables of electric power distribution companies (Discos) had reached Rs:500 billion. This resulted in Rs:300 billion again re-accumulating as circular debt because the NTDC was unable to pay for the full amount for the electricity it was taking from the power generators.

The IPPs, individually and through IPPAC, had been agitating this issue with the relevant ministries in the Government of Pakistan in an effort to seek release of payments for electricity already supplied many months ago. Some payments made but were insufficient to keep the plants fully operational and as a result the receivables were escalating again.

In view of that serious liquidity crunch, the IPPs were not able to generate power at full capacity and due to huge increase in the summer demand, the shortfall substantially increased and as a result the load - shedding hit 12-14 hours a day during most part of the summer. Many companies, the letter disclosed, were likely to default on their bank loans, because of non-payment by NTDC. Moreover, the cost of power generation was further increasing the need for the subsidy due to non supply of gas to gas based IPPs as they were by and large being run on HSD (high speed diesel).

The fact remained that during 2012-13 when NTDC did not pay on time, and as a result IPPs were shutting down, NTDC imposed penalties as a violation of the agreement, and that matter was already being considered by the arbitrator. The imposition of more penalties resulted in serious legal complications and forced the IPPs to invoke their legal rights to protect themselves against being forced out of business. The situation was affecting the industry and economy both.

In the circumstances, IPPAC urged the government to realise the importance and urgency to take immediate action by clearing the overdue amount of all IPPs without any further delay and to keep retiring the circular debt frequently till the structural adjustments started by the present government start yielding results.

On 25th August 2015; *Security Exchange Corporation of Pakistan [SECP] expressed its inability to intervene* in the matters of IPPs in response to a letter of the MoW&P seeking the regulator's intervention in alleged financial irregularities in IPPs.

The SECP clarified Kh Asif, the concerned minister, that the entity was only the corporate regulator in case of the IPPs - it could not oversee their operations being not in their mandate; which were to be regulated by NEPRA. By law, NEPRA keeps the mandate to undertake inspection of these entities on a routine basis.

The high-handedness of the IPPs could be imagined that the SECP on several complaints had ordered the inspection of the accounts of those IPPs but the companies challenged the decision in courts and *got stay orders from high courts in Lahore and Islamabad. The IPPs who had managed stay orders from the courts since 2012* included Atlas Power, Liberty Power, Orient Power Company, Sephyr Electric Company, Safe Power Ltd, Mian Mansha's Lalpir Power Ltd and his son Hasan Mansha's Pak Gen Power.

It is pertinent to mention that the PML[N] government had paid staggering amount of Rs:480 billion in arrears to the IPPs including 60 billion rupees of Universal Service Fund [USF]. Payment of USF was ordered by a 3-member bench of the Supreme Court headed by Justice Jawwad S Khawaja - a verdict against spending the USF.

On 8th October 2015; Public Accounts Committee [PAC] of the Parliament directed the Auditor General of Pakistan [AGP] to present the audit report which raised objection on the Rs:480 billion payment to the IPPs. The Committee further directed the FBR to submit copies of all SROs withdrawn in past years and also directed to replace the legal team of FBR. The committee meeting was chaired by Syed Khurshid Shah which examined the FBR audit report for 2010-11.

> *[It was a mockery of the system that PPP's Syed Khurshid Shah, the Leader of Opposition in NA, was reviewing the audit report of 2010-11 which had the audit objections on 'irregular' spending during PPP's own government – just to clear it, shelve it and to make the Pakistani people fool once more in the name of democratic process.]*

The committee was informed that 90% legal cases pending in the courts of law were related to taxes. The panel of 1900 legal experts was curtailed to 700 legal experts. The Board was paying Rs:30,000 fee per case. One member remarked that big tax defaulters hired services of expensive legal experts to contest case in the court. In his ruling, Chairman Committee directed to dissolve the panel of legal experts of FBR and a new panel of lawyers having at least ten years experience of high courts practice would be constituted.

The audit official informed the committee that in 37 cases the audit department raised Rs:4.87 billion worth of audit paras. The recovery of Rs:1.89 billion was then pending in the courts of law, whereas Rs:2.47 billion had been recovered in various cases.

The case is still a rolling stone even after 30 months.

## CHAIRMAN SECP FIRED:

On 12th April 2013, a two-member bench of the Supreme Court set aside Muhammad Ali's appointment, saying that his selection failed to *"meet the requirements of the Securities and Exchange Commission of Pakistan Act 1997 (the SECP Act)."*

However, the skeletons in his cupboard continued to haunt Muhammad Ali despite his unceremonious exit from the SECP — this time through the FBR. Ali claimed in his written statement that he had sold his shares in the R.I. Enterprise to another person in April 2006 but further investigations falsified his claim. The Enquiry Officer held that the available documents had shown that his annual salary was Rs:380,000 only which did not commensurate with huge investment of Rs:52.5 million.

Many concerned people, however, believed that Mr Ali was an upright person who was keen to see the SECP in high profile with recognized transparent procedures.

On 26th September 2012, under his stern labour the SECP announced the formal launch of five manuals [for *Litigation Management, Adjudication & Supervision, Off-site Surveillance & Monitoring, Inspection & Enquiry and investigation*] which were hailed as a milestone in creating greater transparency and increasing market confidence. For him, the manuals were nothing short of a revolution. He had already set in motion plans to train all SECP officers along the lines prescribed in them. In less than a year, Mr Ali, with the support of his commissioners and senior management, had overhauled and uplifted the entire institution.

Time, however, was not on his side. On 12th April 2013, his appointment both as Chairman and as Commissioner was set aside by the court on the grounds that it had been made without due process. In fact he was made the scapegoat for the government's failure to create such processes otherwise he had the strength of character and ability to rise again with renewed vigor, keener insight and sharper focus. Some opined that the SECP had lost a gem and wondered if the institution would rise again.

In the 1st week of August 2013, Mr Ali strongly denied the contents of FBR's report about his non-filing of wealth tax and non-disclosure of any investment. It was in continuation with a planned media campaign against him because he had taken action against a certain brokerage house. 35 pages order by FBR confirming sale of Ali's stake in RI Enterprises in 2006 was available in FBR record but the Enquiry Officer had deliberately ignored it, it was urged.

In July 2013, Mr Ali wrote a detailed letter to the prime minister informing him of the pressure and black mailing tactics used by certain business and media groups to malign him and to stop him from coming back in SECP. The SECP had completed various high profile inquiries during Ali's tenure. The most important one was the criminal complaint in shares of Azgard Nine Limited, in which five companies of a major brokerage house were found to be involved in market manipulation.

This inquiry was started in 2008 but it was never taken to completion but during Ali's tenure the same were taken to their logical end. Despite tremendous pressure, the SECP went ahead and approved the criminal complaint in light of the law and filed the case. The Sindh High Court later stayed the proceedings.

On 1st August 2013; the Federal Board of Revenue [FBR] Pakistan ordered action against former *Chairman of the Securities & Exchange Commission of Pakistan [SECP]* Muhammad Ali for concealing personal investments and not filing wealth statements for the years 2010, 2011 and 2012 while serving as one of the country's top regulators. Commissioner IR Zone-II, RTO III Karachi, was asked to expedite proceedings against him under the relevant provisions of Income Tax Ordinance 2001.

Another more serious breach of law was that he had concealed his personal investment of about Rs:52.5 million in R.I. Enterprises in which he held 15% shares through the years 2006-11. The R.I. Enterprises — a land developing and construction company — had four other partners and all of them were stock market brokers. Holding shares in this company being the SECP Chairman was a direct clash of interest. Muhammad Ali was a former broker who was appointed the SECP Chairman in controversial circumstances in December 2010 due to his alleged closeness to a former adviser.

# Scenario 128

## UNDOCUMENTED PAK-ECONOMY:

What exactly is the black economy, or the informal or illegal economy, or even parallel economy as it is called? Not all of these terms truly define this phenomenon accurately. The black economy is not necessarily illegal. For example a cobbler who sits on the roadside peddling his trade probably pays no taxes, and keeps no records about his turnover, so he is a part of the informal economy, but he is by no means doing something illegal.

So, the parallel economy is not always a bad thing. A significant sector of the informal economy comprises entrepreneurs like the cobbler who operate out of the system but don't necessarily do it just to avoid taxes or rip off the government. This is especially true of the Third World. However, this is not to say that a very large part of the undocumented sector actually is illegal activity like drug trafficking, human smuggling and arms trade and even smuggling of non-contraband that absolutely needs to stop.

In Pakistan, one never hears of sending tax evaders to the prison for their illegal acts. This confirms extreme slackness on the part of tax administrators or their connivance with tax dodgers. Punishment of tax evaders is restricted to nominal fines or penalties, encouraging them to remain in the fold of underground economy, which is constantly expanding every day, at all levels and in all corners of Pakistan.

In a survey report *published in 'the News' for fiscal year ending June 2012;* the FBR estimated that the underground economy expanded at the rate of 9% from 1977 to 2000. The informal economy helped its sections make easy profits due to various reasons. *"Black economy grows along with corruption, speed money, consultations, smuggling, narcotics, government contracts and tax evasion,"* according to the FBR report.

The report also revealed that no government had shown nerves to tackle this problem. *"In 2000-01, Shaukat Aziz regime had launched a campaign for documentation of the economy but abandoned in the face of resistance of unregistered traders and factory owners."*

A study conducted by the Lahore University of Management Sciences [LUMS] in 2003 showed that out of Rs:100 due tax, the government received only Rs:38 and Rs:62 was pocketed by the taxpayer, tax collector and tax practitioner. *"It means that Rs:720 billion tax collection in 2005-06 was only 38% of around Rs:2 trillion, which should have been collected by the FBR."*

Applying the same calculation of LUMS, the expected revenue leakage in 2011-12 was Rs:3.132 trillion as the FBR collected around Rs:1,920 billion in that fiscal year against total potential of Rs:5,052 billion.

The FBR report also quoted a study prepared by the Social Policy and Development Centre (SPDC) that the black economy in Pakistan had reached its peak in the early 1960s, when the corporate income tax rate was 30% and super tax was 30%, the aggregated being 60%. This rate dropped to 40% during the late 1980s. Likewise, the maximum personal income tax rate was 75% during 1960-64, which was the reason for the black economy to remain well above 30% of the GDP in that period.

The black economy kept declining during 1965-75, until this rate came down within the 60-70% range. It was 56% in 1980-86 period and 39% in 1988 and subsequently 28% in 1993. The size of the informal economy increased from year 2000 onwards again.

> *"This is, perhaps, due to the reduction of rate of return on deposits, which declined by more than 30% in 2000-03 fiscal years. Despite the fact that the black economy as a percentage of the GDP decreased, its annual compound growth rate remained more than 11%."*

Talking about the tax revenue losses stemming from the underground economy – the FBR report said that the taxpayers do not register with the tax departments. *"One reason for this might be the activities they undertake, which are illegal or even criminal and another reason might be that taxpayers attempt to escape registration and interlope for the purpose of tax evasion, despite the legal nature of their businesses."*

A directed consequence of tax revenue losses is a reduction in the government's fiscal targets. The fiscal deficit could be substantially lowered or even zero had the state effectively tackled growth of the underground economy. In 2012, Pakistan's tax burden level was not very high vis-à-vis tax evaders; instead they availed tax amnesty schemes frequently to get their untaxed money whitened at a nominal rate, and the critical issue remained to reform the entire tax collection system preventing tax dodgers from going underground.

## PAK-WOT ECONOMY IN 2010-11:

Referring to *'the News' dated 29th October 2011*, Dr Shahid Siddiqui, Chairman of Research Institute of Islamic Banking and Finance, Karachi, said that *'Pakistan loses Rs:1,200 billion annually because of corruption and another Rs:1,900 billion because of tax evasion and non-imposition of taxes by the federal and provincial governments.'*

Also that **the large size of black economy,** lack of political will to unearth assets of billions of rupees acquired from concealed income though details of these assets were available in the government record, including bank deposits, amounts invested in National Saving Schemes, shares and stock exchange, real estate and vehicles, etc continued playing havoc with the poor populace of the country through decades.

As per details from Transparency International and World Bank, 40% of the development budget of the country was misappropriated; Rs:280 billion out of the total Rs:700 billion development expenditure. Only 1.8 million out of 180 million population were registered with income tax whereas there were innumerable corporate concerns that they earned millions but declared income of mere Rs:0.1 million. The export sector hardly contributed to the income tax revenues whereas the agriculture sector, whose share in the GDP was about Rs:3,620 billion, paid hardly a few millions as tax.

Then the stock exchange's market capitalisation was Rs:3,600 billion but had been taxed only in 2010 and that too half-heartedly. Referring to the 2007 economic survey, the official estimates disclosed that since there was no gain tax on stock exchange, so the country lost Rs:112 billion in one year. Pakistan's powerful cement, sugar and textile sectors hardly paid any income tax whereas properties and bank deposits were mostly not declared and thus no income tax. GST was paid by ordinary people but never fully deposited with the FBR by the business entities all over Pakistan.

Similarly, professionals like engineers, doctors, lawyers and architects never paid income tax on most of their income. The tax-to-GDP ratio in Pakistan remained around 9.5%, which was the lowest in the region as compared to between 14-18% in surrounding countries. Realistically speaking:

*'.....about 25% of the total exports and imports shown in Pakistan's official documentation were fictitious. Quoting official figures, the total rise in <u>exports recorded by the State Bank during the period</u>*

*2002 to 2007 was $7.8 billion, out of which $5.5 bn was bogus, the subsequent detailed investigations had revealed.'*

Besides internal corruption, Pakistan's economy continuously suffered on account of so-called **War on Terror [WOT]** - a daily loss of $33 million and an estimated monthly loss of more than $1 billion due to country's short sighted rulers. This loss caused an accumulated defeat during the last one decade and the successive rulers never bothered because they only visited Pakistan during their terms of government otherwise remained in London, Dubai, Saudia or America to look after their businesses.

The State Bank of Pakistan had calculated on account of WOT - a total loss of $68.9 billion till 30th June 2011 for the country's economy – escalated to $78 billion after seven month's re-assessment in February 2012. In return, Pakistan received directly or indirectly through NGOs and US-AID only $800 - 900 million annually.

On the whole, after November 2011's Salala incident the moneys due under the Coalition Support Fund [CSF], considered to be a disbursement of what Pakistan spent on WOT, were not paid or cleared thoroughly. *Out of bills worth $13 billion asked by the Pakistani government under CSF, the country received only $8.6 billion since 9/11 terror attacks in 2001.*

Official statistics *estimated Pakistan's economic losses caused by WOT at $28 billion* during about seven years post 9/11 tenure of Gen Musharraf but the cost of this war jumped to $78 billion during 46 month's tenure of the PPP regime till early 2012. The figures showed the WOT had put increasingly heavier financial burden on Pakistan's economy besides a phenomenal increase in the number of drone attacks breaching Pakistan's sovereignty.

The Pak-Army tried to clarify it to the US many times what it called a misperception about the CSF, which was usually termed as US aid by the American officials visiting Pakistan - the army got only $2 billion out of $8.6 bn in fact; $3.87 billion were deducted from the CSF by the US government for security assistance provided in kind, i.e. weapons, equipment, training, services, visits and pay of US trainers etc.

Additionally, the loss caused by the said WOT to Pakistan's economy till ending 2011 accounted for 8.5% of the country's GDP whereas the aid Pakistan received was merely 0.2 percent of its GDP. It meant that Pakistan sustained so big loss in its already meagre GDP merely to please the Americans – sufficient proof of being nationalists on the part of the successive rulers both civilians and the military Generals.

## STREET BUSINESS ECONOMY:

**Bloomberg Business Report dated 5<sup>th</sup> April 2012:** Pakistan's street businesses employ more than three quarters of the nation's 54 million workers and is worth as much as 50% of Pakistan's Rs:18 trillion ($200 billion) official gross domestic product [GDP]. While the documented economy had its smallest expansion in a decade at 2.4% in the year ended June 2011, soaring demand for cars, cement for houses, and other goods had shown that the underground market was OK if not thriving.

To narrow the budget gap, PM Yousuf Raza Gilani's government during 2010-12 had cut spending on roads, bridges, and other building projects but that didn't stop Lucky Cement, Pakistan's biggest publicly traded construction company, from posting record earnings that year on demand for new houses. The population was growing and there was a lot of potential on the domestic side; domestic demand for cement went up to 30 million tons from 24 million in the previous year.

The undocumented demand from Pakistan's 179 million people meant the nation's purchasing power was more than estimated; as per evaluations made by MD Karachi Stock Exchange. Rising crop prices had pumped an extra 1 trillion rupees into the rural economy during 2008-12, most of it undocumented. He estimated agriculture might account for as much as 35% of GDP, instead of the 21% reported by the FBR.

Evidence of consumer demand could be seen everywhere as new shopping malls and restaurants in Karachi were filled to capacity. Car sales rose 14% in February 2012 from corresponding month of 2011, as more people could afford Toyota Corolla than Suzuki Mehran 800cc. More than half a million motorbikes hit the road in the eight months ended February 2012 - a 5% increase.

Prime Minister Gilani pledged to increase the tax-to-GDP ratio to 15% by 2014, by collecting more taxes on farms and property, and curbing corruption among tax officials that then accounted for Rs:500 billion in uncollected taxes a year. Ashfaque Khan, dean of NUST Business School in Islamabad correctly pointed out that:

*"Bad governance promotes the underground economy. Undocumented activity leaves workers vulnerable, as employers aren't bound by labour laws."*

Parliament's support for a crackdown has never been possible in Pakistan. Different areas of the undocumented sector normally represent the constituencies of different political parties. The rural region and agriculturists represent one party [PPP]'s constituency so they won't touch it. Traders and retailers represent another party [PML(N)]'s vote bank so they won't touch that.

Earlier attempts to capture revenue from the undocumented economy had backfired. After the government imposed the first-ever sales tax at 16% on tractors in March 2011, the purchases of the vehicles hit a record low of just 369 units in next two months, from 5,673 a year earlier. Tractor makers Fiat and Massey Ferguson had to suspend local production, forcing the government to cut the tax to 5%.

The rhythms of life in the underground economy remain largely undisturbed in Pakistan. The taxi and rickshaw drivers, part of the flourishing local transport business, don't turn on the meters. Shops selling cooking oil, wheat flour, and sugar etc are officially non existent here. Out of about 1 million shops, about 40% are grocery stores, and most of them are not registered and don't pay taxes; though Markets Associations are there to protect their hidden interests. In the evenings, most labour watch Indian movies transmitted by local cable operators to whom a monthly fee is paid but in cash. A professor of economics held:

> *"Everything from auto parts to sports goods, knitwear, clinics, and beauty salons fall into the informal economy. All these make a significant contribution to employment and income, and that's one reason why the economy is still growing. Pakistan has one of the worst tax structures in the world, one should agree.*

> *Pakistan's tax-to-GDP ratio - that's taxes as a share of gross domestic product was 8.6% in June 2012, one of the world's lowest. Only 25% of the economy is taxed if the undocumented sector is taken into account. Developing economies usually have a tax-to-GDP ratio of from 13 – 18%."*

Former Finance Minister Shaukat Tarin said in 2010 that *'Pakistan loses Rs:800 billion a year in tax evasion: The government collected Rs:1.7 trillion in tax last fiscal year. That's not enough to close the budget gap, which is 6.3% of GDP.'*

A normal street shop pays Rs:400 a month to employees of the power company to overlook the illegal connection if it is there, and Rs:200 to the police to allow him to run his unregistered shop. Rs:300 rent to 'someone' is paid because the shops/*thelas* are illegally settled on the lands under his control. Then there are the occasional political contributions to local parties - protection money [*bhatta*], in other words, to keep the parties' criminal components at bay. *"We don't think paying taxes to the government would do any good to us - we are already paying taxes,"* the small shopkeepers held.

In 2012, only 1.5 million people, less than 1% of the population, filed tax returns, according to the Finance Ministry statistics - compared with 3% in India. A low tax-to-GDP ratio meant getting into a vicious cycle of high budget deficits financed by printing money or borrowing, which added to the debt burden and created inflationary pressures. Pakistan had, in 2011-12, the fastest inflation in Asia after Vietnam, and its budget gap expanded to 7% of GDP in the year ending in June 2012, according to an IMF release. In 2012, Pakistan paid about 48.5% of its revenues in debt servicing charges.

## *ECONOMY HIT BY WOT [2013]:*

Referring to *'Express Tribune'* dated 20th May 2013; needless to say, the informal sector needs to be roped into the system and documented if the economy is to grow exponentially. Again, this is even more important for Third World countries where the informal economy as a percentage of the documented sector is usually much larger.

There is not a lot of research on this because it is a difficult subject to investigate. But two researches of the recent past indicated that while on one hand documentation of the economy picked up pace, it was not possible to keep up with the growth in the undocumented trade that either originated in Pakistan or transited through Pakistan. Talking about untaxed shadow economy as a share of GDP during 2010-13; Russia was at the top with 44%; then Brazil – 39%; Pakistan – 36%; Egypt – 35%; Turkey – 31%; Greece – 28%; Italy – 22%; India – 16%; China – 13% and the US at 9%.

The research conducted by the Sustainable Development Policy Institute [SDPI] and UN Office on Drug and Crime [UNODC] estimated the size of Pakistan's illegal economy at between 20-30% of the formal economy. The following paragraphs deal mainly with the darker side of the informal economy, like human smuggling, drug trade, arms trade and other hardcore crimes. Another report generated by the Pakistan Institute of Development Economics [PIDE], released in 2012 suggested that size of the informal economy in Pakistan in 2008 ranged between 74-91% of the formal economy.

*[More citations are needed to verify the above figures as there lays much difference between the figures quoted by UNODC (20-30%) and by PIDE (74-91%); the economists should care about the diversity of figures.]*

Considering that the total size of Pakistan's GDP was about $180 billion, the above figures indicated that the informal economy was $160 billion; also implied that the total size of Pakistan's economy was almost $350 billion.

***Khaleej Times* dated 16th September 2013:** What used to shock foreign observers visiting Pakistan was that how economic activity of a common man resumed back to the normalcy within hours after frequent bombs blasts and suicide attacks in the markets and bazaars.

During those high days of War on Terror in Pakistan, the common man's economic survival was driven by a strong belief, which might not be fully understandable phenomenon for many economists. Mostly people linked losses to their life and properties to the **Will of Almighty Allah,** and continued their economic activities amidst all kinds of threats and fears in a country where virtually *"every day was a 9/11"* given the frequency of occurrences of terrorist attacks since late 2001.

It was hard to imagine that people in economically developed world, could demonstrate this level of resilience, flexibility and spirit - had there been even one 10th of violence of this scale in their countries. The 9/11 precipitated to expand, strengthened and camouflaged Pakistan's black and informal economies both. The economy of terrorist networks flourished with the rise in the incidents of kidnapping for ransom by the militants. The money supplied to those networks through informal channels from US, India, Saudia and Iran also expanded proportionately.

Islamabad, as per official figures, had suffered $68 billion economic losses since 9/11. The foreign direct investment had taken the nose dive given the surge in terrorist attacks. Similarly tourism industry almost ceased to exist. The north and northwest of the country once famous for tourists became notoriously epicentre of insurgency. The economic growth in formal sector slowed down with reduced demands for export and frequent travel advisory by the western countries to its businessmen to stay away visiting an insurgency hit country.

Even then Pakistan survived – astonishing it was.

## PML[N] BUDGET 2013-14:

Budget 2013-14 was made tolerable but not the whole delicious as per ambitions of the ruling party PML[N].

Once more poor Nawaz Sharif was misguided by the bureaucracy; Ishaq Dar was handed over a routinely tabulated budget file [for FY 2013-14] manufactured by the Finance Ministry's gurus which made the newly elected PM to taste the scepticism and criticism of nationalist economic experts and the mainstream media anchors.

By and large, the general populace rejected the budget proposals; the PML[N] government aimed to stabilise the country's battered economy through attempts of high growth that remained pegged at below 3% during the last five years of the PPP regime but the people got zero hope instead.

No doubt the team was charged with the nationalist approach to take Pakistan up in the air. PM Nawaz Sharif and the Finance Minister Ishaq Dar had all the aspirations to fulfil their dreams of leading the nation but in announcement of this budget they were betrayed; they were misguided by bureaucracy who had been announcing such budgets in routine since decades; all political and military regimes have been following the same practice.

However, Mr Dar's speech dealing with future plans of developing motorways, coastal ways and rail-links to Gwadar, and other plans to build the infrastructure were good – everyone appreciated it except that the maximum chunk of the development funds was earmarked to turn Lahore into Paris. The rest of the whole country was ignored as usual.

The economic wizards were doubtful about the government's capacity to achieve its proposed revenue collection target of Rs:3,420 billion – 21 % higher from the previous financial year. They went worried about meeting the fiscal deficit target of 6.3 % in 2013-14, too.

However, the following allocations were not at all needed in this budget at least. Those were 'welfare state measures', which we did not need at that moment. At present Pakistan could be more concerned with the 'survival issue'.

**Rs:75 billion for Benazir Income Support;** Rs:1200, given to one family as per fictitious files, brings nothing for the poor but Rs:75 billion collectively could have made a way.

*[Pl don't go after its cosmetic appeal that it was for poor people. It was for them no doubt, but in Rs:1200 what would a poor man get when 20kg Atta bag was @ Rs:750- those days.*

*Secondly, how much actually goes to the poor persons – is a question mark. Most people believe that the whole amount is consumed between bureaucracy and the concerned political office bearers. See if any authentic audit report for distribution of Rs:95 billion annually was available for the last 5 years.]*

High Voice: **needy youth will be given small business loans OR *Qarz e Hasna*.**

Again it was an aspiration leading to a false target – ultimately leading to the wastage of the whole money. Basically, it was a routine bureaucratic trick of plundering the state wealth. PML(N)'s MNAs and MPAs were asked to bring up the lists of their political workers and get the money allocated to them – not the actually needy persons.

Think; what was the business environment around when there was no electricity. The existing businesses & commercial concerns were gradually closing down due to massive load shedding then how the feasibility of new business would work. Some shrewd persons would get money, eat it up and next year would declare the loss due to shortage of power. All the money would be washed out ultimately.

The loan activity could have been avoided till the 100% supply of power was not ensured; let it be postponed for two years after; the economists urged.

High voice: **the distribution of lap tops amongst the students.**

Again was not required as a necessary need for some – it was done but invited undue criticism; described to be cheap goal; Nawaz Sharif should not have gone after bureaucracy's misleading advice to get abrupt praise; total wastage of money it was. Instead basic schooling was urgently required with Pakistan's literacy rate of 46% only – shameful for the whole nation; one of the lowest in the whole world.

Instead; Mr Dar could at least announce new schools or better environments in existing schools and colleges in and around Islamabad [Rawalpindi, though provincial area but could be included] to start with, their villages, in whole FATA, in Baluchistan's hard areas as a special case, in Gilgit and Baltistan areas TO ENSURE 100% literacy rate at least in federal areas to give boost to and example for the four provinces.

High voice: **the GST increase by 1%.**

A common man was worried about the inflationary impact of 1% increase in the GST and the absence of any cogent relief for the masses. Instead it could have been lowered by 1%, the national exchequer would have earned more.

Who else knew more than the PM and Mr Dar, being the most shrewd businessmen, that how much the manufacturers actually produce and how much they show on documents. Actually government would get only 5% more but the manufacturers would take out 95% for their own from the consumer's pocket.

It was because our tax & excise collection machinery was thoroughly corrupt. Unless the whole manufacturing and whole imports were genuinely documented, such measures like GST & VAT attack the poor consumer in streets only.

Lastly; **the power sector – the load shedding:**

17 IPPs were being paid Rs:501.23 billion within that week - capacity was again limited and the demand ever increasing.

Mr Dar could have announced for open import of GENERATORS of any size free of import duty and GST etc; it was likely to bring little more use of fuel but small units of productions would have come in operation – employment problems could have redressed, too.

The big industries could have allowed [rather forced] to generate their own electricity by whatever means [steam generation be more appreciated]; they could have been asked to distribute their excess power to the houses or commercial concerns around – let it be dealt with as a private business.

The government's aim for economic stabilisation was seen in doldrums since without boosting economic activity and growth achieving the goal of stability would remain elusive. The private sector needed incentives, confidence and encouragement to play its role, which was not possible without **Electricity First.** No new housing colony be allowed, no new industry be permitted unless they produce and consume their own generated power.

Mr Dar could have announced for more NUCLEAR GENERATED POWER plants to meet the future needs of the growing population – as in West most countries are generating their power through nuclear means or by using WINDMILLS.

Elimination of duty on hybrid vehicles up to 1200cc, soft loans for the youth and the controversial laptop scheme were the actual areas of concern. Top omissions included steps needed to expand direct taxation as the budget once more relied heavily on indirect taxes that hurt the lower and middle classes more than the higher-income group. The imposition of the much desired tax on agricultural income was completely ignored leaving it for the provinces to levy it; no word on the energy sector's reforms which raised eyebrows from many.

Restless but troubled PML(N)'s team was welcomed to the Pakistan of 2013 but without any honeymoon period. The people were not in a mood to give them any latitude as, in their opinion, they had made them believe since the beginning of the year that *'our home work is complete'*, - in fact it was not.

It was an endless subject – but that day it was enough for consumption. Everyone hoped that the new government of the PML[N] could rise up to the challenges left over by the two successive governments of the past decade.

## *ECONOMY - 100 DAY's LATER:*

Everyone knew that it was going to be a rough ride for the PML[N] government, but how soon the problems would start – no one had an idea.

The 100 days holiday period of the new PML[N] government was over; too many fronts were opened for them. The Taliban re-started their activities by *killing a PTI MPA in Kohat.* Karachi continued with its cycle of violence as several people were killed in daily routine turf wars. Punjab got enraged over the continued load – shedding; the *power riots in Faisalabad* being the first trailer of difficult times to come. Faisalabad was the district where PML[N] got almost all 13 seats of National Assembly and nearly all 23 seats of Punjab Assembly – but was not given a single slot in the Federal Cabinet.

However, *violence in Balochistan*, an *attack on the Quaid's Residency in Ziarat* left every thing behind; only one casualty but jolted the psyche of the whole nation with an irreparable loss of the Quaid's personal belongings and historical pictures. Terrorist activities in Quetta killing **14 female medical students, Deputy Commissioner Quetta, one senior doctor and four Punjabi nurses in Bolan Medical Hospital** was a harsh reminder from Balochistan's dissident forces.

Ishaq Dar's budget was being grilled in the Parliamentary debates **with thousands of civil servants on the streets** outside making demands for increase in their salaries. The PML[N] government, just on the fourth day on their lively protests, had to bow their heads before them with 10% increase even before the budget was given approval by the legislature.

The Supreme Court also marked its presence, during second week of June 2013, by taking a *suo moto* **notice on increase of petroleum prices** announced in the budget. Though this increase was quite nominal in comparison with that of PPP's era but Raza Rabbani had successfully manoeuvred in the Senate to make the new government uncomfortable; for him no more friendly opposition in the new Parliament.

*MQM's Farooq Sattar* had passed the most interesting remarks sarcastically pointing towards Nawaz Sharif:

*'Mr Prime Minister; for God's sake, Mian Sahib get out of this motorway syndrome in times of trouble. 'Yes, Sher Shah Suri is known for making G T Road, but Sher Shah did not have load - shedding in his time.*

*We are an agricultural country but why does its agriculture contribute only one percent taxes.'*

Farooq Sattar was talking about the big feudal lords who had their hostage and PML[N] continued to dish out sumptuous amounts of money to parliamentarians in the name of development schemes in the two previous terms of its rule. He had in mind that the PML[N] was indebted to the powerful lobbies of agriculture and big businesses and would not dare tax them during the new regime too.

Ishaque Dar's whole presentation of budget rested on the basic premise that the economy would pick up in a peaceful and stable environment but the Balochistan violence had tended to shatter that assumption. On the other hand only a little pressure followed by a threat of strike was enough to puncture the air out of Dar's gung-ho style. He was quick to compromise by announcing 10% increase in government employee's salaries. Additionally, almost the entire opposition, one by one, staged a walkout against 1% increase in General Sales Tax (GST) – an indirect tax on the poor populace.

Amidst the hot debate on the parliament's floor, Senator Saifullah Magsi from Balochistan raised his voice loudly but passionately urging that:

> '....*the House is discussing an issue of lesser importance while Balochistan is burning right now. We were always told that there was a vacuum in the earlier government; we have a new and the so-called truly representative government in place, so why can't they control the mayhem now?'*

The point raised by Senator Saif Magsi had much weight that the PML[N] had played partisan politics when it remained seated on opposition benches for five years; it never took a stronger position to combat terrorism in the whole country.

However, Senator Hasil Bizenjo was right to point out that the Balochistan government was hardly in place and could not be blamed for a decades old malaise. Balochistan's crisis was much deeper with multiple tiers - requiring a thorough analysis and action. Ch Nisar declared, *interalia*, that most *Lashkar e Jhangvi* [LeJ] miscreants targeting Hazaras were found to be Baloch; but still they were needed to be dealt with iron

## NATIONAL SECURITY POLICY [2013]:

After taking over by the new Army Chief Gen Raheel Sharif on 29th November 2013 the GHQ asked the newly installed PML[N]'s government to immediately formulate a national policy to fight the menace of deep rooted terrorism from the country.

On 19th December 2013; Prime Minister Nawaz Sharif chaired a meeting over the implementation of the decisions made by the Cabinet Committee on National Security [CCNS]. The meeting was attended by Chief of Army Staff Gen Raheel Sharif, Interior Minister Ch Nisar Ali Khan, CJCSC Gen Rashid Mahmood and DG ISI Lt Gen Zaheerul Islam. Amidst other things, talks with the Taliban and ensuring the execution of a security increase on the Pak-Afghan border, went hot on the agenda.

However, *the Taliban dismissed the idea of peace talks the same day* saying they had information that plans were already under way for a military operation, adding that the insurgents were ready for battle.

The first meeting of the CCNS, the Cabinet Committee on Defence, turned out to be a damp squib. After months of PML(N)'s tall claims about a new national security policy - what emerged was an exercise in illusion. *The official statement issued in that regard had ruled out military action against the Taliban and promised to pursue 'peace only through talks'.* Use of 'other options' was mentioned as the 'last resort' only. The CCNS focused on three issues:

- Formulation of a national security strategy.

- Internal security strategy.

- Good Relations with Afghanistan.

The CCNS deliberated upon the government's strategy to engage various discrete groups of the Taliban. It was confirmed that the government had already opened channels for dialogue with them. It was told that though the Tehreek e Taliban Pakistan [TTP] had immediately rejected any efforts by the government to hold talks but the things were moving headway.

Media reports had spoken about uncertain reaction from the newly appointed TTP leader, Mullah Fazlullah, who had cut short his stay in North Waziristan and returned across the border to his safe haven in Kunar province. The CCNS also seized of the security issue on the Pak-Afghan border; keeping vigilance was agreed on the expected attacks [as in the past] from Mullah Fazlullah's forces.

Despite all discussions on tactical strategies, it was generally confessed that the TTP would not negotiate and the path would thereby be cleared for a military operation. However, it was also felt that unrelenting emphasis in every statement by *the PML(N) & PTI's Imran Khan on peace through dialogue had affected the morale of the forces who were being slaughtered continuously in that region.* Here it went suspicious that if the government was serious in combating the menace of terrorism.

The Pak-Army, on the other hand, appeared to be shielding behind the contention that without political patronage, the army was not able to launch meaningful operations on the scale required against the terrorists.

*There has been a consensus in intelligentsia that the Taliban infection had travelled to within the ranks of the security services, which had made any struggle against them risky in terms of internal cohesion.*

Ponder about the ease with which two prisons of Khyber PK were broken in 2012 & 2013 and hundreds of dangerous prisoners were got released without a shot being fired. No follow up of those prisoners, no operation, no investigations into the collaborations between the jail crew and the attackers – not even remorse on the part of state administration.

In the backdrop of the given scenario of the National Security Policy, when the politicians were not willing, the military was reluctant for reasons of political patronage and internal issues, no military operation were tentatively found on cards; plans were not likely to succeed. In an arena of the TTP's vocal refusals to come to the table, the most likely situations were nothing beyond muddling through, hoping against hope, and getting bogged down in wishful thinking. Pakistanis were left to live in false anticipations.

On one side GOP was conveying instructions to the top brass of the Pak-army through the above detailed CCNS policy focussing on talks with Taliban but only a day earlier, *on 18th December 2013,* five soldiers were killed and 34 others wounded at a check post in Miranshah [Waziristan] while a girl and her mother in law died in a low intensity explosive attack near an *Imambargah* in Karachi.

> [*After that suicide attack, clashes between militants and Pak-Army erupted on that military checkpoint and at least 53 people were seen dead though not clear whether the individuals who were killed in that week's clashes were civilians or militants. Those events left the whole of North Waziristan under a curfew for four days.*]

Imran Khan, allegedly having a soft corner for the militants for proposing dialogue as the only way to bring peace, was also warned of dire consequences by the TTP. His ambition to fight polio in Khyber PK was also targeted by killing three including two police constables to shun that polio campaign.

> [*On 13th December 2013; unidentified gunmen shot dead two policemen named Ijaz Ali & Iftikhar Ali and a polio worker, identified as Yousuf, in two separate attacks in Swabi and Jamrud in northern Pakistan when they were on way to escort the anti-polio vaccinators. Both the cops were shot in the head; the anti-polio campaign was kicked away immediately in the two areas.*]

The TTP's attack on the praying soldiers in Miranshah was a story repeated by the militants many a times without yielding much change in the counter-terrorism strategy of the state. Check posts, the easiest targets to attack the security forces, remained as vulnerable as ever. No measures were taken to make them more secure. It was business as usual in overall Pakistani means and mechanisms to fight terrorism. The general populace were having no doubts about the Taliban's designs but the government continued selling the narrative of peace through talks; public opinion on this strategy was never measured.

Even the President of Pakistan believed that the country lacked the unity to fight terrorism. Once he addressed a tribal *jirga* in his presidency; they were the most affected people because of terrorism and were united to fight the menace. But when the president was hinting at the political discourse equivocating on the point of talks with militants, it was surely the failure of his own PML(N)'s government. The apathy, ineptness and ill will of country's intelligence agencies were adding fuel to the fire. The coordination required among the intelligence and law enforcement agencies has never been available in Pakistan; DI Khan and Bannu jailbreaks were the glaring examples of that flaw. The gulf kept on widening with the time and the political masters in succession never bothered to attend the issue.

The media continued to tell the stakeholders that the terrorists had developed their skills to the level of using rockets, mortar guns, anti-aircraft guns starting from AK47 American night vision rifles and remote controlled bombings but the police was kept confined to the use of batons and 303 mark rifles as per the Police Act of 1861 and the Police Rules of 1934. The successive rulers of the country, civil and military, could not develop acumen and insight to make new laws in their parliamentary sessions which could meet the day to day requirements for the security of the people.

The penetration of the terrorists into most parts of the country, from Khyber to Karachi, continued to gain strength. Karachi, being the most lucrative financial hub of Pakistan, provided them resources through *'bhatta'* [extortion] and kidnapping for ransom activities. Then those miscreants turned towards sectarian violence in the garb of various religious factions.

The country was engulfed in terrorism since two decades, in one form or the other, but the governments were not able to provide any cogent legislation to tackle this menace of terrorism; the businesses ruined, the innocent people massacred in suicide bombings, the army men slaughtered, doctors taken hostages and media persons gunned down but the parliaments only played blame games, walk outs, debates and resolutions – never bothered to amend their laws of 1861-88 what to speak for new legislations.

*On 21ˢᵗ December 2013;* just two days after the announcement of the 1ˢᵗ phase of National Security Policy, *the COAS Gen Raheel Sharif vowed not to tolerate any more terrorist attacks;* otherwise endorsing the ongoing PML(N) - led peace process with the Taliban. During his visit to the Corps HQ in Peshawar, he had emphasised that terrorist attacks would be responded effectively. Gen Sharif paid tribute to those five martyrs who sacrificed their lives for the country's defence. He appreciated the resolve displayed by the officers and men during fight against terrorism and bringing stability to the militancy-hit areas.

Ruling out military action against the TTP as its first preference, PM Nawaz Sharif had promised to persuade insurgents to lay down their weapons through peace negotiations while the use of force "was a last resort". The TTP, however, had dismissed the government's peace initiative saying they knew that plans were already under way for a military operation.

## BLUE PASSPORTS SCANDAL:

On 23ʳᵈ December 2013, National Accountability Bureau [NAB] Board decided to take up the inquiry of scandal regarding issuance of more than 2,000 blue passports [*blue passports are issued to the government officers to travel abroad for official job or duty only*] to unauthorized persons during the PPP regime of 2008-13. Interior Minister *Ch Nisar had already given directive on 5ᵗʰ October 2013 for cancellation of those blue passports* issued under Rehman Malik's hand in violation of rules.

Rehman Malik had issued those passports indiscreetly and illegally to sons and daughters of his beloved politicians including his own brother, two sons, and sisters in law, nephews and nieces; initially for ten years but then notified them valid for the whole life. However, NAB was more concerned about those government officials, who had issued fake documents to the private persons by showing them government officials after receiving hefty sums of money as bribe – opening another floodgate of corruption.

[*On 7ᵗʰ October 2013, the FIA Immigration arrested two persons at Islamabad Airport who were trying to proceed to Oslo on blue passports and gratis visas by using no objection certificates (NOC) of different federal ministries.*

*The two arrested persons were identified as Ahmad Ali bearing Blue Passport No: ML1808821 and Ghulam Murtaza carrying Blue Passport No: AF0973443, who were proceeding to Oslo by PIA's flight PK-771. When intercepted by the FIA on suspicion, they failed to satisfy immigration during questioning.*

*However, divulged that an agent, running a money changer shop at Blue Area, provided the Blue Passports and gratis visas against heavy amount, with the help of employees of the Passport Office and Ministry of Information as well as another ministry.*

*Later, the FIA conducted raid and detained that agent named as Abdul Qadeer, owner of Hamza Money Changer at the Blue Area, Islamabad.*]

**Blue passport has a background** – its holder can fly to 70 countries straightaway and will be given GRATIS [without visa fee whatsoever] visa at arrival on the airport along with a determined protocol and respect being considered as representative of government of Pakistan. They are normally exempted from personal searches and luggage checks, sometimes taken through special channels whereas the respectable with green passports are asked to stand in queue and sometimes are directed to get off all their clothing including shoes before passing through the immigration clearances.

The menace actually started in the last days of PM Shaukat Aziz. Some of the cabinet members requested the then Interior Minister Aftab Sherpao to issue them Blue Passports just as an honour which Mr Sherpao agreed. Consequently, *on 12th September 2007,* a notification was issued from the Ministry of Interior that *'all the federal ministers and state ministers will be issued blue passports for travel abroad.'*

Immediately after, an amendment to the said notification was released saying that *'all the FORMER federal and state ministers AND their wives will also be issued blue passports'.*

*On 19th October 2007,* on the specific instructions of the then PM Shaukat Aziz, another notification was issued that:

- *'All the RETIRED civil servants and RETIRED diplomats AND their wives will also be issued blue passports.*

- *The sons and daughters, parents of the retired civil servants and diplomats will also be issued blue passports.'*

One senior civil officer was blessed with a blue passport for his *daughter in law who was having the 'British Nationality'* – what a country, hurray. Subsequently the following people also got their names included in the lists because their wives and children upto the age of 28 years would be benefiting with that facility of blue passports for each.

- All provincial Governors, serving and retired.

- The members of Council of Islamic Ideology [CII] and their families.

- The RETIRED JUDGES and their family members

- RETIRED ARMY OFFICERS

On 9th September 2008, another notification was issued from the M/O Interior that *'the sons and daughters [up to the age of 28 years] of all the federal secretaries will be entitled to get blue passports'.*

*On 15th December 2011,* the Interior Minister Rehman Malik issued an office order that:

- *'The Interior Ministers, their wives, sons and daughters UP TO THE AGE OF 28 YEARS will be entitled for blue passports FOR THE WHOLE LIFE.*

- *All those people will be entitled to get blue passports for whom the Interior Minister will issue directions.'*

Getting encouragement, the Federal Interior Secretary availed an opportunity to include his wife and children up to the age of 28 years AND FOR THE WHOLE LIFE.

When the news went open that the loot sale of blue passports was on in the interior ministry, first lot of 75 high ranking businessmen approached the higher echelons of the said ministry with bags full of foreign currencies as a token of respect [*approximately equivalent to Rs: 1.5–2 million, as price of one blue passport was duly settled*] and got the things.

It was not at all a trade at loss for them because their blue passports were providing them the respectful landing rights at hundreds of international airports in 70 countries without searches and luggage checks. Some of them had multiplied their 'investment' in their first trip – many people might know it how.

Astonishingly, the PML(N)'s Interior Minister Ch Nisar told the media that *'had he made those 2000 names open, many people would hold their heads AND a Pandora Box would be opened'*.

The intelligentsia held that Ch Nisar should have divulged those names, should have provided another chance to people for holding their heads but he deliberately avoided doing so. Perhaps, nothing was at stake from his side as his family and children were allegedly enjoying benefits of the American passports – they didn't need the blue Pakistani passports anyway.

# Scenario 129

## *HYDERABAD JAIL BREAK PLAN:*

On **19ᵗʰ March 2012**, the Sindh Police claimed to have unearthed a brazen jailbreak plan by around 400 convicts at the Hyderabad Central Jail. The prison's Superintendent Pir Shabbir Ahmed Jan had compiled a report concluding that *"....the inmates might escape from the prison any time now."* Sindh's Inspector General and Hyderabad's district police were asked to prevent the fiasco.

Overcrowding might be one of the main reasons; nine or ten inmates were then confined in the 8 x 10 feet cells which were suitable for only a couple of prisoners. The report alleged that some influential criminals in incarceration were backed by political parties; that around 100 prisoners who were given death sentences and another 600 imprisoned for life refused to appear before the courts and misbehaved with judges conducting their trials. It was on record that the judges were avoiding hearings due to such misbehaviour of the inmates.

The report alleged that inmates used to invite women inside the prison at odd hours on the pretext of interviews; they had also established a network to procure and sell contrabands such as liquor and cannabis within the premises. The senior officials were constantly kept informed but no measures to prevent the menace could be implemented. The prison had not held any routine search for illegal items in the past few years. Some inmates possessed arms and use them to threaten authorities. The Superintendent Jail attributed that deplorable condition to the huge influx of prisoners beyond its accommodation capacity.

Sindh Police had also submitted a report to the National Assembly's Standing Committee on Human Rights in response to an incident occurred in 2011 in which seven prisoners had died and 40 were injured along with a policeman in a protest in the same jail. Hyderabad's DIG police, Samiullah, stressing on jail reforms told that: *"I have also given my recommendations to the Supreme Court."*

The NA Standing Committee's Chairperson Riaz Fatyana had directed the Sindh government to take notice of the deteriorating situation.

A paradigm shift was needed to revamp the police system and introduce jails reforms. Session Judge Fahim Siddiqui, who had visited the said jail a year earlier, wrote in his report that there were over 1,300 inmates in the said prison – much more than its capacity. Besides the presence of contraband items, an earlier search had recovered around 260 mobile phones from the possession of prisoners.

## BANNU JAIL BREAK 2012:

Between 14- 15th April 2012 [Sunday] night; more than 200 heavily armed Taliban militants travelling in several vehicles attacked the Central Jail in Bannu, Southern District of Khyber PK and got released 384 prisoners in a pre-dawn assault.

The Tehreek e Taliban [TTP] claimed responsibility for raiding the jail. TTP spokesperson Asimullah Mehsud told media from an undisclosed location that they [TTP] attacked the jail with hundreds of fighters; saying that: *"......the purpose was to free some of our men; we attacked with 150 Fidayeen (suicide bombers) and took over the area for more than two hours."*

Four police officials were injured in the attack; another policeman on guard at the police station told that: '....*dozens of the militants were in vehicles and <u>hundreds of them were on foot</u> carrying AK-47s and rocket launchers. The gate was rooted out after one fired a rocket at it. The militants had punctured the boundary wall to aid in their escape.*'

A large number of militants were then moved to the jail from neighbour-ing Kohat and Lakki Marwat prisons, which were being converted into centres to rehabilitate former insurgents. The FIR registered for that event said that hundreds of militants attacked the Bannu central jail around 1:15am and 384 prisoners were got released - *some of them were 'most wanted'*. Talking about the category of the militants that managed to escape, the official record contained that 20 men who were facing death sentences and were very dangerous also fled away.

Officials believed that the attacker's main aim was to release Adnan Rashid, a former employee of the Pakistan Air Force [PAF], allegedly involved in plotting the murder of Gen Musharraf. Inspector General of Police Khyber PK (IGP) Akbar Khan Hoti commented that the whole plan seemed to have been for the release of that top militant. An official from the Bannu Central Prison later told that:

*"..... the militants entered the premises of the jail after firing hand grenades and rockets and the only question they asked was - Where is Adnan? - they spoke different languages and their outfit was typical to the Taliban with boots, grown hair and loaded with arms."*

An investigative officer confirmed that there was *English and Arabic jihadi* literature recovered from the cell where Adnan was kept.

Adnan Rashid joined PAF as a junior technician in 1997. Security officials apprehended him from Balochistan in 2004 in connection with a plot to assassinate Musharraf. Sources said that he was shifted from Kohat to Bannu Jail some eight months ago. Amongst the prisoners was also one Aijaz, a militant who had previously managed to escape from the same jail. The names of the rest of the **'most wanted'** could not be ascertained immediately.

Federal Interior Minister Rehman Malik suspected the involvement of certain prison officials in the attack. Speaking to media in Islamabad, the interior minister added that the attack was due to security failure and that a high level enquiry would be conducted in this regard. Mr Malik added that:

*"We will find out about who had sent Adnan Rashid in Bannu jail......*
*that the cellular service providers would be asked to block their service*
*inside prisons. We got a mobile call traced to a Quetta jail which*
*revealed correspondence between banned outfits, Sipah e Sahaba and*
*Balochistan Liberation Army [BLA]."*

However, till a year after, till the end of the PPP's government on 15th March 2013 neither the sponsors of Adnan Rasheed could be identified nor the cellular phones were ever blocked in jails anywhere in Pakistan – no progress of the said jail break case was reported. The same Adnan commanded his contingent a year after to break the DIK prison.

The Khyber-PK government blamed 'intelligence failure' for that brazen jail break in Bannu city, however, intelligence reports claimed that the federal interior ministry was tipped about possible militant strikes three months earlier. **On 5th January 2012,** Commander Askari of the Tariq Geedar militant group was found plotting attacks on different targets, including on PAF base in Kohat, Kohat garrison and Lachi police station. The matter was brought on the record of Interior Ministry with the warning that the group could mount an assault on the Bannu prison to free Adnan Rasheed and other dangerous militants.

The National Crisis Management Cell [NCMC] of the interior ministry had sent the report to Khyber PK's home secretary, police chief and all others concerned officials, recommending necessary measures to foil such attacks – but nothing was moved.

The Khyber PK government announced a committee to investigate that serious incident which was also asked to find out whether the jailbreak, claimed by local Taliban, had any link to the coordinated attacks in Afghanistan. The committee, led by Director of Reform Management and Monitoring Unit, Dr Ehsanul Haq, was asked to complete its probe within 15 days but till today its findings have not been made public.

Home and Tribal Affairs Secretary Azam Khan, meanwhile, blamed the federal government for not heeding requests to mend loop-holes in security for the province. The paramilitary Frontier Corps [FC] was supposed to be deployed in the buffer zones between tribal and settled areas of Khyber PK whereas:

> *".... only 38% of FC troops are where they are actually required. The rest are deployed in Islamabad and elsewhere - we had communicated our concern to the federal government five months ago but no action – no improvement."*

Later investigations revealed that out of the 93 police officials who were supposed to be on guard, a whopping 63 were absent on that fateful day. Out of the remaining 30, only 10 were armed. Of the 20 FC officials who were supposed to be on duty, 14 were absent. Only six FC personnel were armed and on duty. In short, only 36 officials on duty were monitoring 946 inmates, when there should have been a total of 113 officials on duty. Up to 68% of those who were supposed to be on guard were absent. Of those who were present, only 16 were armed – figures highly contradictory to those provided by the authorities, who claimed that security strength was high on the day of the attack.

**Inside job?** a militant commander who helped plan the Bannu jailbreak divulged that his group had inside information. Reuters was told that:

> *"We had maps of the area and we had complete maps and plans of the jail as well. All I have to say is we have people who support us in Bannu. It was with their support that this operation was successful."*

DIG Bannu Iftikhar Ahmed also confirmed the media that there had been cell phone contact between the prisoners and the attackers.

The Khyber PK authorities had requested the federal government for the installation of mobile *jammers* in prisons much earlier than the event. The Pakistan Telecommunication Authority had not issued them *a 'No Objection Certificate'* [NOC] despite the fact that they had been in communication with them for four months.

The Inspector General for Prisons in Khyber-PK, Arshad Majeed, had not ruled out collusion of prison staff with the TTP; it was another agony. How such a big attack could be possible without collusion of the inner staff – the management knew it; it appeared.

## *JAIL BREAK; BUSINESS AS USUAL:*

While the attack was a classic manoeuvre, the guards inside the prison hardly put up even a token resistance and obeyed the orders of the attackers to stand aside. The Taliban's intelligence seemed to know exactly where Adnan Rashid was being held. The attackers operated at will for about two hours inside the prison, with nearly any sign of rein-forcements, although the prison authorities later claimed news of the attack had been relayed almost immediately. The police reinforcements arrived after the attackers had withdrawn.

As is usual in such matters, an inquiry was ordered to investigate the lack of response or resistance by the staff and guards of the prison, why the movement of such large numbers of armed terrorists riding vehicles went undetected, definitely the attackers had inside support, given their accurate intelligence, and last but not least, a probing of the massive intelligence and security failure.

As in many instances over the years since the TTP and affiliated groups took up arms against the state, it is by now obvious that no place in the country was adequately protected or safe, from north to south.

In their usual fashion, the authorities then set up check posts on all routes leading out of Bannu, particularly towards the tribal areas. This was a classic case of bolting the stable gate after the horse had long fled. Alarmingly, there were reports in the media that Adnan Rashid, whose appeals against his death sentence had been rejected by the High and Supreme Courts, enjoyed the 'facility' of a cellular phone in all the prisons he was kept in, and even had access to social networks on the internet, on which he regularly posted messages.

The cell phones, taken away at times were restored soon after, allowed Adnan Rashid to keep in touch with various journalists. None of those champions of the media thought it their duty to report the fact to the authorities, no doubt in the hope of exclusive information/stories from Adnan Rashid.

There were many serious problems with the manner in which Pakistani state agencies used to conduct the campaign against terrorists of various hues and shapes. Judicial system has never been equipped, either in law or prosecution capacity, to meet the challenge of putting terrorists away. In the then concluded International Judicial Conference in Islamabad, the Chief Justice of Pakistan had admitted that Pakistan's laws needed to be brought into conformity with international legal provisions against terrorism. Intelligence, security services and the police were woefully inadequately equipped, conceptually or in practice, to combat the most serious existential threat the state had faced in its entire history.

On *21ˢᵗ April 2012*; Khyber PK's IG Prisons said in the inter-provincial meeting held in Islamabad that:

*'Prisons Department of KPK is being run without resources and is facing shortage of staff. Rifles used in Bannu jail are so old that influential people of the area have been demanding them against heavy payments only to display them at home as unique items.*

*Since 1947, there were 26 jails in the province which reduced to 22 instead of increasing their number like that in other provinces. Prisons Department was also lacking staff since as within last about 65 years, only 36 new posts were created and induction was made against them. No training was being imparted to the jail staff due to which they have no capability to confront with any untoward situation like jail break last week.*

*The salary package of Prisons department of KPK was meagre; a warder of the Bannu jail as saying that he could not embrace martyrdom only for Rs:8,000 salary, when he was asked that why he and his colleagues did not retaliate when terrorists attacked Bannu jail.*

*No ammunition was purchased after 1947 and oldest rifles were being used for the security of jail; there were poor security conditions around the jail and power shortage was at peak and there was no alternate arrangement for the light in the jail.*

*No promotion system was there and officers and employees were working in the same grade for several years which was demoralising employees and officers. The Prisons authorities were repeatedly drawing attention of the rulers towards this situation but rulers remained unmoved and these deficiencies resulted in a big incident of jail break.'*

The Bannu jailbreak was only the latest demonstration of such hard facts. *Everything was 'business as usual'*; unfortunately, inertia soon returning to the usual laxity was what the terrorists relied on – and the menace continued as a routine matter.

**On 17th May 2012;** the TTP released a **propaganda video** that detailed the 15th April 2012 jailbreak in Bannu that freed 384 prisoners, including an estimated 200 Taliban members and Adnan Rasheed. The 34-minute-long video, which was produced by Umar Studio, the propaganda arm of the TTP, was originally being sold in all the markets of North and South Waziristan. The videotape was then published in three parts on YouTube by the Khyber News Channel [parts 1, 2 and 3].

Hakeemullah Mehsud, the Ameer TTP and Waliur Rehman Mehsud, the group's leader in South Waziristan, both appeared in the video. Both Mehsuds delivered speeches, and Hakeemullah vowed to fight the Pakistani government and military to *"the last bullet and the last man."* Hakeemullah and Waliur Rehman were routinely said to be in violent opposition to each other, and were even **wrongly reported to have killed each other** during a *shura* meeting in August 2009 to select Baitullah Mehsud's successor.

In the video, both Hakeemullah and Waliur Rehman were shown directing estimated 150-200 fighters who were gathering to conduct the attack. The Taliban leaders were organizing the large Taliban group in the daylight out in the open. The location of the meeting place is not clear. The Taliban appeared to have had good intelligence on the layout of the Bannu prison. A Taliban leader, whose face was digitally blurred, used a detailed hand-drawn map to brief the Taliban commanders and fighters on the plan of attack.

The fighters were then shown eating and praying before being put into vans and driven to the Bannu prison. The tape had shown the night time assault as the Taliban attacked the prison with rocket - propelled grenades, heavy machine-guns, and assault rifles. The Taliban were then shown opening the jail cells and releasing the prisoners.

The video also included interviews of the freed commanders and prisoners; Adnan Rasheed was among those interviewed. Rasheed had also supposedly worked for Amjad Farooqi, the Pakistani terrorist who engineered the two assassination attempts against Gen Musharraf in December 2003 at the behest of al Qaeda leader Abu Faraj al Libi; Farooqi was suspected of involvement in other terror attacks as well. Farooqi was a member of the *Sipah e Sahaba Pakistan;* the *Harkat ul Ansar* and its successor, the *Harkat ul Mujahideen* and *Jaish e Mohammed.*

Allegedly, Farooqi had also served as a close aide to Qari Saifullah Akhtar, the leader of the *Harkat ul Jihad al Islami.* In addition, he served as the group's representative to al Qaeda's International Islamic Front.

The message from the Chief of TTP Hakimullah Mehsud was recorded before the episode of Jail Brazen attack and in this message he had criticized the JI's leader, Qazi Hussain Ahmad, this message was just interlinked with the story.

The message from Waliur Rehman was genuine as the whole operation was planned by him. Adnan Rasheed was the main focus of the TTP fighters which they wanted to get released at any cost.

In the end of the video *three security forces personnel were also kidnapped by the fighters* as both the roads on the front and back of the jail were blocked by the fighters for all traffic and the security forces personnel driving on the road were captured and shifted to rugged region. The incident was not reported in media.

## DIK PRISON BREAK:

On 30th July 2013, over 100 militants came in vehicles and also on motorbikes to storm the Dera Ismail Khan [DIK]'s Central Prison from all the four sides simultaneously as one group opened fire on a security check-post near the jail. The militants helped 243 prisoners escape from the British-era prison [built in 1854] after killing 12 people, including six policemen, while five attackers were also killed.

A number of hardened militants were among the inmates of the DIK Central Prison; among them was Walid Akbar, who had been awarded 1,616 years jail sentence for his involvement in bombing of the Ashura procession in the city in 2012. The militants used a loud hailer to call prisoners out by name.

The six policemen killed were Mazhar Hussain, Saifullah, Rustam, Mir Zaman and Piao Sardar. Two prisoners from Multan; Sajid and

Juma Malang, who had been awarded death sentences, as well as two other inmates, Akhtar Abbas and Aslam were also killed inside their barracks. The three other people, including the watchman of a bakery, a passer-by and an unknown person, were also killed while 16 persons were wounded. Curfew was clamped in DIK and Tank districts after the attack and a massive search operation was launched by the security personnel.

Dozens of huge and minor explosions starting from 11:15pm on Monday that continued till 2:30am on Tuesday. Due to expansion of the city and increase in the population, the prison's location came in densely populated part and the bomb blasts could be heard in the nearby localities all night. It also scared the people and prompted them stay inside.

Dozens of improvised explosive devices [IEDs] and other explosives were defused during an operation to sweep the prison. The Bomb Disposal Unit [BDU] experts defused 28 time bombs, four remote control IEDs, a suicide jacket, five rockets and eight grenades during the search operation later. The inmates who escaped from the prison included around 30 militants. Five women prisoners were also among those who fled during the jailbreak.

Expressing anger over the jailbreak, Khyber PK Chief Minister Pervez Khattak termed it failure of the intelligence agencies. The Joint Inquiry Committee [JIC] that he constituted to probe the incident was asked to start work on immediate basis. The Committee comprised of Senior Member Board of Revenue Waqar Ayub, Special Secretary Home Department Syed Alamgir Shah, Additional Inspector General Police (Special Branch) Akhtar Ali Shah and representative of Pakistan Army (Headquarters 11 Corps).

Furthermore, 27 cops, including a Superintendent of Police (SP), were suspended for showing negligence during the whole episode. The authorities had reportedly got reports that the militants were planning to attack the prison. Ominously, a clash inside the DIK Prison a day earlier had resulted in injuries to two cops. The attackers also shot dead the watchman of a nearby bakery when he fired two shots in the air.

Reportedly the local police arrived too late as armed men had taken positions on all the four sides to counter them. The Commissioner's office confirmed that 242 prisoners had escaped during the attack. The residents around were told not to come out of homes as the police and army were clearing the area.

The proscribed Tehreek e Taliban Pakistan [TTP] claimed responsibility for that DIK prison break; over 100 militants, some wearing police uniforms, including suicide bombers took part in the said attack. However, the IGP Khyber PK Ihsan Ghani told that 60 to 70 men, were involved in the said attack. Meanwhile, the case of the jailbreak was registered against the unidentified attackers in the Chaowni Police Station; repair work was also kicked off at the DIK Central Prison.

TTP spokesman Shahidullah Shahid claimed that more than 250 prisoners escaped from the jail. *"Majority of our people along with the freed prisoners reached a secure place. Some of our very senior people also succeeded to escape,"* the spokesman claimed. Police sources claimed that 242 prisoners got escaped during that activity.

The IGP, Additional IGP along with Home Secretary visited the prison and heard the account of the incident from the cops. SP Elite Force Toheed and DSP Behram were among 27 cops suspended in that DIK event. An investigation team headed by SP Investigation DIK was also formed. JIC was already in place for parallel investigation; one Ijaz Ahmad was posted as DIG of DIK as the office was lying vacant due to routine transfer of the incumbent some days earlier to Mardan. Next day; local police claimed to have **arrested 45 of the over 242 prisoners who had escaped during that jailbreak** – thus relaxation in the curfew timings was also announced.

*Katherine Houreld*, a correspondent for **Reuters** news agency, **told the BBC:**

> *"Reports also suggested intelligence had warned of an impending attempt on the jail two weeks ago..... it had been a very sophisticated attack - they blew the electricity line, they breached the walls and they set ambushes for reinforcements; ....an ensuing gun battle raged for three or four hours.*
>
> *.... the shooting started, .....soon after, we heard an explosion and the main gate exploded......then the police started shooting towards the main gate from armed vehicle parked outside......during this time, may be either a rocket launcher or a mortar shell hit that armed vehicle. Two of the policemen were killed on the spot, and three of them injured....."*

The DIK prison was about century old and was not ever re-designed for high security inmates, but housed hundreds of Taliban fighters and militants from other banned groups. The Commissioner DIK later told that about *30 'hardened militants'*, who had been jailed for their involvement in major attacks or suicide bombings, were among those freed. Mr Jadoon told a local TV station that:

> *'....militants had taken away six women, five of them inmates and the other a lady police officer - that jail records along with other office essentials had also been torched.*

> *Among the inmates freed were two local Taliban commanders, Abdul Hakim and Haji Ilyas. The militants had booby-trapped the building with explosive devices, which had now been defused.'*

A Taliban spokesman told the foreign media that one of their commanders freed in an assault on a prison in Bannu in April 2012 played a key role in the latest jailbreak. He knew the security failures inside prisons so that was why the militants were able to stage a virtually identical attack here in DIK. That night's violence came hours before Pakistani politicians in the Parliament elected Mamnoon Hussain from the ruling PML[N] party as the country's new president; it hugely embarrassed the government, and once again highlighted the ability of the militants to strike at will.

The authorities had advance warning of the attack, but did not act on it, only made matters worse. The attack rekindled memories of the 2012 jailbreak in Bannu city in which 384 prisoners had escaped, including Adnan Rashid, who had also written an open letter to Malala Yousafzai justifying that why she was attacked by the Taliban.

The DIK jail attack came a month after the police said they had arrested a group of militants who were planning to launch a similar attack on Karachi Central Jail. This was indicative of an emerging Taliban strategy to break jails instead of negotiating the release of their prisoners by taking hostages, which they had successfully done in the past.

The *Awami National Party (ANP) leadership said Imran Khan's Tehreek e Insaf [PTI] had left the people of Khyber PK in the lurch –* it was a failure of the PTI-led government and they were unaware of the situation.

## ADNAN RASHEED's ACCOUNT:

Those investigating the **29th July 2013** midnight jailbreak operation in DIK concluded that the brazen assault was masterminded by Adnan

Rasheed, a dangerous *jehadi* and the mastermind of an assassination attempt on Gen Musharraf, who himself was freed in a jailbreak operation in Bannu, conducted on **15<sup>th</sup> April 2012** . Adnan Rasheed being the chief operational commander of a special unit of *fidayeen* attackers belonging to the TTP and the Islamic Movement of Uzbekistan [IMU] had planned it all.

Both the Waziristan based *jehadi* groups had joined hands to form *another jehadi unit called "Ansar Al Aseer"* (supporters of prisoners) whose prime aim was to secure freedom for the imprisoned *jehadis* by carrying out jailbreak operations across Pakistan. TTP's Ehsanullah Ehsan had said *on 20<sup>th</sup> April 2012* that the operation was chiefly meant to free Adnan Rasheed, a former officer of the Pakistan Air Force [PAF]. That the Taliban had been working on the jailbreak plan for the past several months and were in touch with Adnan and other prisoners in the Bannu Central Jail.

Referring to *'the News' dated 2<sup>nd</sup> August 2013*:

> *'Adnan Rasheed had claimed in an April 2013's rare interview that he was indoctrinated by a covert jehadi group which recruits officers from the three military services and utilizes them to wage jehad along with the Taliban. The interview was published in the first issue of an English-language* **jehadi magazine "Azan"** *which was launched by the Taliban elements, primarily to cater to the educated Muslims.*

> *Narrating in a first-hand witness account, Adnan Rasheed joined a clandestine jehadi group functioning in the PAF under the name* **'Idaratul Pakistan'**, *or the institution of Pakistan. Adnan Rasheed was led by senior military officers to believe that the Jaish e Mohammad [JeM] founder Maulana Masood Azhar was appointed the AMEER of the Pakistani Taliban by Mullah Mohammad Omar of the Afghan Taliban. Adnan got four months' leave to go home but joined Jaish training camp at Mansehra in Khyber PK.*

> *Interestingly, despite being an al-Qaeda linked convicted terrorist, Adnan was allowed to get married in the jail in 2010 and become father of a daughter. Coming from Chota Lahore village of the Swabi district, Adnan was arrested for his role in an attempt to assassinate Gen Musharraf in Rawalpindi on 14<sup>th</sup> December 2003. He was subsequently awarded death sentence by a Field General Court Martial [FGCM] on 3<sup>rd</sup> October 2005 at Chaklala Base of PAF along with six other Air Force men including Chief Technician Khalid Mahmood,*

*Senior Technician Karam Din, Corporal Mohammad Nawazish, and Junior Technicians Niaz Mohammad and Nasrullah.'*

Several interviews of Adnan, while he was in prison, were uploaded on the Facebook, wherein he had pleaded innocence besides urging the CJP Iftikhar Chaudhry to take notice of the issue. But in a video message released after his escape from the jail, Adnan Rasheed had confessed to his role in the 2003 assassination attempt on Gen Musharraf.

Adnan was finally made the Chief Operational Commander of *Ansar Al Aseer.* The formation of that *jehadi* unit was made public through a video which featured not only Adnan Rasheed, but also Yassin Chouka, one of the most wanted German commanders of the Waziristan-based Islamic Movement of Uzbekistan; and Abdul Hakeem, a Russian IMU member.

---------------------------------------------

**The Ending Lines**: the Taliban came to attack the DIK Central prison carrying their lives in their hands; they assaulted it with mortars and rocket - propelled grenades. Reportedly, the guards jumped into the nearest drain to save their lives, their instinct for self-preservation could be hailed. Not the investigators but the provincial Revenue Minister told later that:

> *'....the Taliban were not put to the necessity of blasting the jail main gate. Those on duty obligingly opened the gate for them.'*

But then why and how 13 persons were killed?

The attackers remained inside the jail for some time, using handy loud speakers to call their comrades by name whom they had come to set free. *They had time to literally slaughter some inmates, probably on account of their 'different' faith.* No police high-up came to the scene of action and when they appeared the attackers were far away.

## ON PRISONS IN PAKISTAN:

Referring to <u>*Sarmad Ali*</u>'s essay appeared in the 'Tribune' of 13th August 2013; there are 32 prisons in Punjab with an authorised capacity of 21,527 but till mid 2013 they housed 52,318 prisoners. Sindh has 22 prisons with a capacity of 10,285 but they housed 14,422 prisoners. Khyber-PK has 23 prisons with an authorised capacity of 7,982 and they housed 7,549 prisoners. Balochistan has 11 prisons with a capacity of 2,173 and the number detained was 2,946.

If prisons of Azad Kashmir and Gilgit-Baltistan are included, altogether there are 99 prisons in Pakistan. The authorised capacity of these prisons to detain prisoners was 42,670. However, 78,328 prisoners were housed in these prisons. Hence, the prisons in Pakistan were overcrowded and the prison system held 35,000 more prisoners than its designed capacity.

Thousands of prisoners were waiting for trial as the prison population had grown up owing to an increasing crime rate in Pakistan. Instead of reforming criminals, the prison system in the country proved a fertile ground for their further nurturing.

According to a research carried out by the **International Centre of Prison Studies (ICPS)** in 2012; this state of sorry affairs in Pakistan was compounded by a sluggish criminal justice system. There is only one prison staff training institute in the whole of Pakistan. According to a Punjab University report published in 2011, inefficiency and corruption marked the prison system like all other departments in Pakistan. While the prisons are plagued with administrative and financial problems, security devices are either not functioning or missing altogether.

An important step to reform the prison system and culture is to amend the rules and procedures. The Pakistan Prison Rules are 28 years old and need to be updated. Training of the prison staff at home and abroad is minimal.

The first prison reform programme was introduced in Pakistan in the 1950s under the chairmanship of Col Salamat Ullah, who was a former IG of Prisons for UP in pre-partition India. Later, different reform committees were constituted by the federal government to redress prisoners' grievances. The recommendations of those committees were invariably given official approval but hardly ever implemented, mainly because of financial constraints or lack of political will.

Referring to the 'Dawn' dated 7th September 2014: Punjab's IG Prisons Mian Farooq Nazeer told that:

> *"There are about 6,000 condemned prisoners in Punjab and the appeals of 60pc of these prisoners are pending with high courts, while the cases of 30pc of them are going on in the Supreme Court while there are 400 to 500 prisoners whose appeals have been rejected by the president.*
>
> *Such prisoners do develop psychological issues but most of them are not related to jails as they can't remain detached from the society and the problems that their families face once they are incarcerated."*

Most professionals in Criminal Justice Systems *maintain that a life sentence is harsher punishment as compared to a death sentence.* The countries which have abolished death sentence, like Turkey, have replaced it with **life imprisonment, jailed till death,** which is more severe form of torture. After about three year's time, the convicts started crying and urged the authorities to hang them if they were to remain in the cells till death – more cruel than death in fact.

In some countries where the death penalty stands abolished there the life imprisonment is limited to either 14 years or 25 years at the most. Remaining in jail till actual death is in-human by all means.

As per 2013's report of the Amnesty International, there were over 8,500 prisoners on death row in Pakistan, one of the largest death-row populations in the world, and the number was increasing by every passing day till December 2014 as the government had halted the process of executions.

Referring to *Kamran Khan's TV talk show* at **'Dunya News'** dated 25th **November 2015;** till that day only 290 persons could be taken to gallows for hanging till death after December 2014's government withdrawal of *'executions halted.'* With that pace of progress it would require another twenty years to clear the backlog of the death convicts in Pakistani prisons.

Since July 2013's DIK jailbreak, it became a routine practice to block the routes leading to the prison within a radius of around a kilometre and stop all vehicular movement during the night. Keeping the prison secure has been believed to be an uphill task since then as several of the localities in the outskirt turn into no-go areas after sunset.

Security arrangements in place for Khyber PK's three central prisons at Bannu, DI Khan and Haripur, known for housing the militants and other suspects charged under the Anti-Terrorism Act (ATA) had turned into a nightmare for the authorities after the two high profile jailbreaks at Bannu and DI Khan in April 2012 and July 2013, respectively.

Pakistan's existing jails are old and not meant for hardened militants. The country does not have any high security prison of international standards. The jailers have placed a three-layer security arrangement in their premises and keep closely coordinating with the army.

Militants arrested in various cases were lodged in different prisons. In Peshawar, only 35 suspects belonging to different outfits, such as TTP and religious factions, were kept during whole 2014; around 15 prisoners were shifted from Bannu Jail. In 2013, an ATC awarded life imprisonment to a prison doctor and a police official for abetting in escaping two prisoners.

The population in Pakistani prisons is almost five times more than the capacity with the prisoners in the barracks in the evenings at closing time not even being able to turn if they lie alongside each other in the tight space. So most just sit or squat on the floor until they can be let out in the morning. This goes against prison rule no: 745, which states that each inmate must get at least 18 square metres in a barrack and 31 square metres in a cell, if placed there.

Overcrowding in prisons leads to other serious problems such as hygiene, sanitation and the spreading of contagious diseases such as tuberculosis, Hepatitis C, HIV and skin infections.

Of the **17 prisons visited by a Survey & Study Group**, seven had detained under trial prisoners [UTP]s and convicted ones in the same barracks; five of the prisons had not segregated juvenile prisoners from the adult prisoners; 12 prisons in Sindh had not segregated repeat offenders from UTPs and four prisons had not segregated civil prisoners from persons imprisoned for a criminal offence. Fifteen UTPs were not segregated from prisoners suffering from infectious diseases, too.

However, women prisons are under – populated in Pakistan. After doing six months in prison here, the women, according to an amendment in the criminal laws, shall be released on bail. Meanwhile, **Youthful Offenders Industrial Schools (YOIS)** are most often just a barrack built near the adult prisoners' barracks leaving them vulnerable to bullying etc.

The **Badin Open Jail,** an idea conceived in 1958 for some 500 prisoners, was to have no walls, locks, bars or gates on 2,800 acres of farmland. It was a place to allow sufficient space to the **'good behaviour'** prisoners who had served one-third of their sentences there to prove to the authorities that they were capable of resisting temptations of running away and hence could be trusted. They were provided various job-related skills such as farming, bee-keeping, fishery, poultry, gardening etc, there under a stress free environment. There was also an option of calling over family members of the prisoners to allow them to spend time with them to make up for the lost time while they were in jail.

After Badin, open jails were to be set up in Thatta, Haripur, Multan, Jhang and Faisalabad but the pilot project itself failed due to lack of funds.

## *JAIL ECONOMY OF PAKITAN:*

There is an entire economy inside every big Jail; your happiness inside depends on how much money you have and whether you have any political association. *"You want drugs? Alcohol? Women? No problem, if you have money. The jail staff can arrange everything."*

Not paying money is not an option. When an inmate is both poor and without political association, jail staff tend to intimidate and break them down. *"There were people whose families took on loans, just so their loved ones would be spared the harassment."* All research studies led to the same conclusion.

Then there are those who willingly return to a prison, because they end up doing booming business from within. *Many inmates are hired for robbery or murder jobs, which they fulfil by greasing the guards' palms with a share of their earnings.* A hard fact that there is greater advantage in committing crime this way: on paper, they are physically in prison and cannot possibly have committed the crime in question.

> *"The entire jail knows what robbery or killing will be committed in the city the next day.*
>
> *Once, an inmate committed a robbery and returned back to the jail by evening. But a few weeks later, a newbie comes to the jail. When he tells what he had been charged with, the inmates laughed: it happens to be the same robbery that their fellow inmate had committed that day. The newbie was framed by the police to declare that robbery successfully investigated."*

Some inmates treat private hospitals as their jails. A former jailer [named Razzak Zuberi – but may not be his true name] told that:

> *"A political leader was charged with murder in mid 2014 — apparently he was drunk, and he shot someone. He was brought to Karachi from Hyderabad.*
>
> *But the man did not have to spend a night inside the prison. His paperwork showed that he needed medical treatment, and he was shifted to a private hospital. Two rooms were booked, one for the prisoner and another for the jail staff that had come with him. At night, the accused would often leave the hospital premises, go home or even for dinner.*

*Then there were some gangsters of Kala Pul. When they were first brought to the prisons, they brought a four-wheel drive with them and gave it to the jailer. Almost every night, they were allowed to return home, party all night and be back before morning."*

Some jailers were notorious for their cruelty. One legend is that of **Zulm ka Baadshah** (King of Oppression). *"But this man suffered a bad end. He was hit by a trailer near Sohrab Goth in a road traffic accident. His body was not found in a single piece."*

Another jailer whose tales ring around Central Jail is **Jin Chacha**: a flamboyant man, he would drink like a mule and would go around screaming and assaulting all whom he laid his eyes on. His trademark move was to bite people. One account held:

*"Everything that is available outside the prison is available inside as well: drugs, alcohol, women, even betting. Everything is happening out in the open.*

*The sad part is that the police are themselves involved in all these trades. Everyone is doing the same thing inside the prison, but some people are being punished for it. There is something wrong with the law, it has double standards."*

In ending 2013; walking into the Karachi Central Jail one didn't feel like it conformed to the stereotype image of what a jail was 'supposed' to look. Instead of plain white walls and bars, there were manicured lawns, murals painted on the walls, art studios, music rooms, a large mosque, a salon in the women's section, cells that resembled dormitories, inmates participating in recreational activities and a large open-air kitchen that served food tasting better than that sold at most popular *dhabas*.

An officer named Nusrat Manghan, the Inspector General Prisons (IGP) Sindh had introduced arts into the jail curriculum. There was a studio where inmates used to paint, while others found teaching, their work was often exhibited and sold as well.

The Karachi Central Jail also launched its own magazine, **'The Prison Review'**, in early 2014. They organised poetry recitals as well, in both Sindhi and Urdu. Then they were in the process of holding a drama for which rehearsals were underway; and they were also holding music lessons. Replying a hard question, the IGP held that:

*"It's impossible to completely eliminate drugs from entering the prison. Their job is to bring them; our job is to catch them. It's an on-going*

*process. The rate of confiscation is high but obviously it's not 100pc. That's not humanly possible."*

Much earlier, in March 2011; a major riot took place in Hyderabad's Central Jail resulting in death and injury to prisoners and prison staff. Inmates involved, who later appeared before a judicial commission, mentioned that drugs were sold to prisoners with the support of the prison authorities and prisoners claimed that cannabis was cultivated inside the prison. The main reason behind riots was mismanagement. If jailers keep everything properly managed, there would be no trouble.

In 2012, the Sindh Chief of Lashkar e Jhangvi [LeJ] Naeem Bukhari was caught with his companions. Hafiz Qasim Rasheed alias Ganja, who was also a high profile target killing suspect with over 100 murders to his credit was arrested and a hand grenade, Kalashnikov, pistol and a hit-list were recovered from his possession. The list contained names of police officers he had allegedly murdered because they created problems for his family when they used to come to visit him in jail during his incarceration. The IG Prisons stated that:

*"We have lost many of our people this way. This happens everywhere. Prison officials, guards are always under threat — by the mafia, gangs, terrorists — especially by those who belong to habitual and professional gangs. The pressure on the staff regarding this is always there."*

Parliament, Provincial Assemblies and higher courts are all sleeping since 67 years – let them sleep for good.

**Now the tailpiece,** repeating Ayaz Amir's words: the Taliban had clarity on their side; Pakistan's political elite had confusion. They had resolve and singleness of aim; Pakistanis were indecisive, and going round and round in circles – thus jailbreaks of the same pattern were bound to be repeated – analysis of both Bannu and DIK jailbreaks was leading the nation to ponder.

# Scenario 130

## PAK-ARMY: HARD TASK MASTERS

### PAK-ARMY: MYTHS & FACTS:

> *In and around December 2012, the relationship amongst superior judiciary, Pak-Army and the politicians had gone so tense that even JUI(F) leader , Maulana Fazal ur Rehman, had become the critic of the 'establishment' – its role and the defence budget.*

> *The press campaign to revile the armed forces was undermining the security and well being of the country more than murderous attacks by ethnic nationalists and sectarian militias.*

A think tank very rightly narrated that the army should not indulge in politics; definitely not. The army should not be buying off politicians; no question about it. Every citizen of Pakistan, whether an army General or a civilian minister, should be punished if found guilty by a court of law. Absolutely no debate about that one either. Pak-Army knew its limits - that a uni-dimensional national security strategy singularly focused on 'defence' would not prevail in the Pakistani nation-state. Country's future really depends on **three 'Ds' - defence, development and diplomacy;** other things come up later.

<u>Dr Farrukh Saleem</u>'s essay in media on **7th December 2012** is referred herein which he enlightens about myths and realities about the Pak-Army.

**Myth 1:** *Pakistan's military had eaten up the largest chunk of the annual budget.*

**Not true.** The *largest chunk went for servicing of debts* and the second largest chunk was eaten up by losses at public sector enterprises like the Pepco, PIA, Pakistan Steel and Pakistan Railways. The third largest chunk was routinely allocated for the Public Sector Development Program. In 2012-13, the fourth largest chunk, an amount of Rs:545 billion, was allocated for *'defence affairs and services'*.

**Myth 2:** *The military consumed a very high percentage of government expenditures.*

**Not true.** In 2012-13, *'Defence Affairs and Services'* consumed a meager 17% of all government expenditures. What that meant that remaining 83% of all government expenditures were non-defence related.

**Myth 3:** *Over the time, country's expenditures on the military had been on an increase.*

**Not true.** In the 90s, Pakistan's defence budget used to be 3.6 percent of the GDP. Since then there had been a steady decline. In 2012-13, allocation for defence was under 2.5 percent of the GDP – a 33 percent decline over a decade.

**Myth 4:** *Pakistan used to spend a very high percentage of the GDP on defence.*

**Not true.** There were at least fifty countries that spent a higher percentage of their GDP on defence. They included: India, Egypt, Sri Lanka, the United States, the United Kingdom, South Korea, France, Eritrea, Oman, Saudi Arabia, Israel, Jordan, Liberia, Brunei, Syria, Kuwait, Yemen, Angola, Singapore, Greece, Iran, Bahrain, Djibouti, Morocco, Chile, Lebanon, Russia, Colombia, Zimbabwe, Turkey, Georgia, Guinea-Bissau, Ethiopia, Namibia, Guinea, Turkmenistan, Kyrgyzstan, Algeria, Serbia and Montenegro, Armenia, Botswana, Ukraine, Uganda, Ecuador, Bulgaria, Lesotho and Sudan.

The above noted information from Dr Farrukh Saleem was true till ending 2012. The situaion has dramatically been changed since then. See thr following script:

*On 22nd November 2015, msn News* published interesting information on media pages titled as: "<u>Best defense – the countries that spend most on their militaries</u>".

Tim Graham published 25 slides with Annual Defence Budgets of respective countries with the following details:

USA – $569.3 billion; China – $190.9 billion; United Kingdom – $66.5 billion; Russia – $53.2 billion; France – $52.7 billion; India – $49.7 billion; Japan – $49.3 billion; Saudi Arabia – $46.3 billion; Germany – $43.8 billion; South Korea – $35.7 billion; Australia – $34.3 billion; Brazil – $30.7 billion; Italy – $29.0 billion; Canada – $17.2 billion;

Turkey – \$15.9 billion; Israel – \$15.6 billion; UAE – \$14.7 billion; Taiwan – \$14.5 bil-lion; Spain – \$13.9 billion; Algeria – \$12.4 billion; Poland – \$12.2 billion; Netherlands – \$10.6 billion; Singapore – \$10.4 billion; Pakistan – \$10.3 billion And Iraq – \$10.3 billion.

Pakistan was one of the two least spending countries on military budget – yet Pak-Army was worldly known for having the most professional army. Count the factors –.

One factor may be Pak-Army's *'internal system'* to rein the best norms of justice within. They don't mince words in the name of Pakistan's 165 years old legal procedures and admissible evidences – they are quick in delivering justice like of Qazis in Islamic history.

**Myth 5:** *The Pakistan Army received billions of dollars in the form of coalition support funds from America and the NATO.*

**Not true.** Of the \$10 billion that the US claimed to have reimbursed to the government of Pakistan, the army had received a total of \$1.8 billion, presumably the rest had gone into filling the deficit, training, Drone attacks Cgarges, weaponary, instrumentation and communication equipment. Remember; the \$1.8 billion was not additional funds for the army but mere reimbursements for expenses already incurred under the *'war on terror'*. Pakistan had demanded about \$76 bn as an accumulated loss.

**Myth 6:** *Commercial undertakings by the military have been a burden on Pakistan's economy.*

**Not true.** To begin with, commercial undertakings have literally nothing to do with active duty personnel – and everything to do with the welfare of retired soldiers. Defence Housing Societies are self-financing and popu-lar both among investors and residents (because of superior management and security of title). Fauji Fertilizer, a public limited company, for instance, contributed wholesome Rs:91 billion to the tax pot per year.

And then some facts:

**Fact 1:** Fiscal administrative losses during 2012-13 at Pakistan's public sector enterprises could pay for 100 percent of country's defence budget.

**Fact 2:** Pakistan's armed forces are the sixth largest but our expenses per soldier are the lowest. America spends nearly \$400,000 per soldier, India \$25,000 and Pakistan \$10,000.

**Fact 3:** Pakistan's armed forces undertook successful operations like Operation Rah-e-Haq (Swat), Operation Sherdil (Bajaur), Operation Zalzala (Spinkai), Operation Rah-e-Nijat (SWA) and Zarb e Azb in Sindh without any significant additional financial allocation.

**Fact 4:** Of all the armies in the world, Pak Army is the largest contributor of troops to the UN peacekeeping missions. Of all the armies in the world, Pak Army has received the highest number of UN medals.

## OSAMA BL: PAK-US JOINT OPERATION:

GEO News TV's live programs *'Aapis ki Baat with Najam Sethi'* of three consecutive days [*dated 3ʳᵈ - 5ᵗʰ May 2011*] had told the true story but the political leadership and military elite continued to make statements that Pakistan had not known about the American intentions of Osama's killing.

In the first *TV address of the American President Obama on 2ⁿᵈ May 2011,* immediately after Osama's killing, it was clear when he said that *'....the success was not possible without the cogent help of Pakistani intelligence agencies; they have led us to the right place and we have succeeded'.*

The US president had told his nation and the whole world proudly that the ISI's personnel had taken the SEAL team exactly upto Osama's residence and they made the marvellous achievement to keep the America and their global partners safe.

Secondly, it is still available on record that **President Obama rang Mr Zardari** immediately to convey congratulations over the success of the said Osama Operation. Same day the **US Secretary Hilary Clinton had talked PM Gilani** and the US **Commander Mike Mullen had told the Army Chief Gen Kayani** about the successful raid over Osama BL.

The most important factor was that the three top American figures had exchanged their good wishes and offered reciprocal congratulations to each other. Both parties were joyful and smiling amidst satisfaction over the development. None of the Pakistani statesmen took it as odd 'NEWS' or unexpected attack; none exclaimed with sorrow nor shown any worries whatsoever. The heads of both the countries talked just in normal way as it was a 'joint task' but accomplished by one party as had been worked out before.

An article in the *'Washington Post' dated 2ⁿᵈ May 2011* in the name of Mr Zardari [*said to be written by MNA Farahnaz Ispahani for Mr Zardari*] was sufficient to indicate that top Pakistani leadership knew about the operation; that was why the *'undated'* article was placed with the said newspaper in reserve to publish it when the *'Operation Giranimo'* would be successfully completed.

Hussain Haqqani, Pakistan's ambassador in Washington, and Wajid Shamsul Hassan, Pakistani High Commissioner at London, both on the very next day of Osama's killing on 2nd May 2011, had categorically answered media questions on TV that *'Pakistan knew about the operation and it has been carried out as a joint operation of intelligence agencies of both the countries.'*

One can also recall a live TV interview of the then US Secretary State Hillary Clinton in which she had clearly said that *'....many people in Pak-Army and ISI know that where are Osama and Mulla Omar hiding in Pakistan; we also know those people – but it is government of Pakistan's prerogative* [to do the next appropriate job]'.

In fact, after getting lead of a high value target's residence [*till then not sure of Osama Bin Laden's presence there*] in Abottabad, the American intelligence had started working on the proposition that:

- Why this lonely house, and so big, suddenly built after 2005 without Municipal Authority's approval for building plans etc. Then it was virtually constructed in open fields.

- So big house but no car or jeep going in or coming out; no telephone connection going in and no mobile registered at this home address; possibly no TV antenna on the roof.

- Why 18ft high walls outside; no windows towards the streets though there were two towards open fields.

- Within that big 18ft walled premises there was another house with 8 ft high walls [it was seen through satellite photography].

- No interaction of residents of that big house with anybody outside; seldom some person coming out or going in without any communication with anyone around.

The answers of above questions lead towards the conclusion that the residence was suspicious thus worth intensive surveillance. Then Doctor's testifying drama proved the DNA of Osama's presence [details are available in *'Judges & Generals in Pakistan Vol-IV*].

An important question that *'why Pak-Army was not made part of the operation'*. It was because the script was written so. This was the only American [intelligence] operation in Pakistan which was accomplished without the active participation of the Pak-army. *The Pak-army refrained and preferred to sit in the back to avoid the Taliban & Al Qaeda's possible revenge and strike backs* which they continued to inflict even otherwise – and with more intensity.

The frequent denials from the Pakistani government and military top-heads, pretending having no prior knowledge of the US operation, were the replica of Pak-US compromise over the 'Drone Attack Policy' [.....*that the Pakistan leadership would stick with issuing press statements for denunciation and disapproval of drone attacks BUT the US government would continue to go by its plans*].

Even when 369 Pakistanis were handed over to the US intelligence & interrogation agencies [*though there was no extradition treaty or diplomatic protocol existing between the two countries*] in the name of WOT [*Gen Musharraf's book is referred here*]; when they were taken to Bagram Base in Afghanistan or to Guantanamo Bay in Cuba; when most of them were killed at either place during interrogation; when the handed over lots also comprised of certain suspects who were ten years old – the Pak-army, ISI, IB & FIA and the American CIA and Pentagon were always seen hands in gloves. However, this time it was planned to be so, it was successfully played; it was termed a lonely operation by the US only.

Then the next question: *when the leaderships of the two countries, Pakistan & the US, planned to do this operation*. Simply check out the dates within two weeks prior to 2nd May 2011, when the two American war-lords, Gen Mike Mullen and Gen Petreas, were together in Pakistan; one coming directly from Washington and the other through Afghanistan, holding one to one meetings with top civil and military leadership of Pakistan – but then smilingly left for the US without leaving any 'bullshit' note for Pakistan having *'Do More'* instructions.

One more aspect be kept in mind that Pakistan's military elite knew about American tradition or strategy *that 'they never try to catch their high value target alive – they are trained to kill that'*. Whereas the Pak-army people are trained otherwise so they did not opt to be part of that killing game.

Another question: *'why the SEAL team preferred to put the dead body of Osama Bin Laden in the sea instead of burying it'*. Here one can believe that the suggestion might have come from the Pakistani leadership because they knew that Muslims and especially the Pakistanis are known for *'dead hero worship'*, little matters how much controversial one would have been in his life; ZA Bhutto & Gen Ziaul Haq can both be quoted as examples.

After Osama Bin Laden's killing in Abottabad, the world media started thinking that:

- Whether the US forces would quit from Afghanistan after declaring WoT over. OR

- The US would remain there, would intensify its operations, using Osama's presence in the region as an excuse.

The answer came immediately after as the very next day, the BBC released a list of 16 die-hard Al Qaeda members, all Arabic speaking, who were allegedly hiding themselves in the Pak-Afghan border region [North Waziristan] on whom similar operations were indicated.

It was conveyed to the world by the US very harshly that more severe attacks would be launched over the suspected places. The plans were acted upon. Consequently, dozens of suspected hide outs of Haqqani group and Al Qaeda were drone attacked but with no considerable success; civilian women and children were mostly killed.

## ISI OFFICE SUKKUR ATTACKED:

On 24th July 2013, suicide gunmen and car bombers mounted an unprecedented attack on the local office of the country's premier intelligence agency ISI in the otherwise sleepy town of Sukkur sparking a shootout that killed eight people and injured over three dozen. The gate and front walls were blown away; several vehicles and nearby buildings were damaged and it left a deep crater near the ISI premises.

There was no immediate claim of responsibility for that brazen attack on the ISI office in the Sukkur Barrage Colony but it revived fears that the reach of militants was spreading in the country. Next day, Tehreek e Taliban [TTP]'s *Jundullah group* claimed responsibility of that attack - saying that it was a revenge of Waliur Rehman's death and drone attacks because both the ISI and army were working with America. However, TTP's former spokesperson, Ehsanullah Ehsan, denied the association of *Jundullah* group with the Taliban.

The Sukkur Barrage Colony is a high security zone where offices of top government officials – including Commissioner House, DIG House, Sindh Rangers Headquarters and Judges Lodges – are situated. Four terrorists, armed with hand grenades, suicide vests and assault rifles, launched the organised attack just as local residents were busy in the *'maghrib'* prayers.

Apparently a suicide bomber first blew himself up in front of a police building and then a second bomber drove his explosive - laden vehicle into the main gate of the ISI office. Later investigations suggested that 30kg explosives were used in the car bomb blast while two suicide bombers had blown themselves up. Other terrorists started firing and throwing hand grenades at police. Eight fatalities were confirmed including four terrorist, three ISI officials and a civilian.

However, Edhi volunteers told that they shifted five bodies and 50 injured to different hospitals of Sukkur and Rohri. They added that the terrorists' bodies were lying at the site. The Commissioner House and the DIG House were partially damaged.

Police and Rangers sealed the entire area and disconnected the electricity supply to the building where the remaining two terrorists were held and then were killed in a shootout with police and Rangers. Media persons were not allowed near the site while the operation continued.

Later, it was estimated that one ISI officer Maj Zeeshan, had important documents containing details of terrorists. The officer was having evening meal after fast in his office when the terrorists mounted the attack - Maj Zeeshan was probably the main target and was killed. **On 26th July 2013;** a computerised national identity card (CNIC) recovered from a terrorist killed during the attack was discovered to be fake.

In May 2009, a suicide attack outside a police building next to the local ISI office in Lahore had killed 24 people. In November 2009 a powerful car bomb had ripped through ISI's HQ in Peshawar, killing 10 people and destroying part of the fortified building. A month later in Multan two suicide attackers had fired at soldiers while driving a truck past security checkpoints in an attempt to approach the local office of the ISI.

**On 26th October 2013:** An operative of al Qaeda possessing valuable information about the attack on Benazir Bhutto's convoy on 18th October 2007 and the ISI office blast in Sukkur was arrested from Baloch Colony. Shaikh Adil Azeem, who was also a Lashkar e Jhangvi [LeJ] activist, was a subordinate of al Qaeda's Sindh and Balochistan supervisor Talat Hussain. Talat Hussain was responsible for the attack on Benazir Bhutto's homecoming caravan and also sent militants to attack the ISI office in Sukkur.

Adil Azeem had disclosed during interrogation that he was asked by Talat Hussain to carry out the suicide attack on Benazir Bhutto's home-coming rally, but he had refused. Later, Talat Hussain convinced two other al Qaeda members, Rehan and Azeem, into attacking the convoy.

However, Azeem did not know whether Rehan had survived after the attack or not. Azeem also revealed that Talat Hussain had sent 15 militants to Sukkur to attack an ISI office. The attack was carried out to avenge the killing and arrest of al Qaeda members arrested by the ISI in Hyderabad, Sukkur, Nawabshah and Dera Ghazi Khan.

Adil Azeem admitted that he was trained in Afghanistan's Kunar province and he was an expert in making improvised explosive devices. He [Azeem] had brought explosives from Balochistan to Karachi to provide them to the militants - and was found in possession of a Kalashnikov and two grenades when arrested.

## PAK-ARMY'S GENERAL KILLED:

On 15th September 2013, a roadside bomb killed a Pakistani General, another officer and one JCO near Pak-Afghan border. They were visiting troop positions in the Upper Dir district of Khyber PK when their vehicle hit an explosive mine. Maj Gen Sanaullah, Lt Col Tauseef and a Sepoy Imran embraced martyrdom at the spot while two soldiers got injured in the blast. Taliban spokesman Shahidullah of Maulana Fazalullah faction claimed responsibility for the bombing.

Shahidullah had once welcomed the new government's move to begin peace talks, but maintained that it must show its sincerity. He reiterated:

*'First of all, troops in the entire tribal area should go back to barracks and then our prisoners should be released. The Pakistan government must take steps which can develop an atmosphere of trust. We cannot move forward unless the government accepts these two demands.'*

Shahidullah was speaking after the Taliban's *Shura* [decision-making Council] held three days of talks about the Pakistan government's offer of dialogue. *Shura* members from across the country took part in the meeting and stressed the need for confidence building measures.

*"The government has to announce the ceasefire if it is really sincere in peace talks,"* the Taliban Council held.

The said pre-conditions appeared as a meaningful jolt but Taliban's activities of attacks, killings and abduction continued. The more devastating news was that the seven Wapda employees, taken hostage while working for the Gomal Zam Dam project, were released by the Taliban not for love but a hefty ransom [Rs:25 million]. The same day as all this happened, there were other casualties, again from IEDs across Fata.

Contrarily, the All-Parties Conference [APC] was so shy and timid, that it did not mention the word Taliban but termed "<u>our people in the tribal areas…</u>" The PM's statement was not at all saying anything harsh about them thus the picture of appeasement and cravenness was boldly drawn by the APC.

Complying with the above demands appeared to be a non-starter since it meant surrender, not negotiation. As Taliban were aiming to get their fighters back and no military to hinder their training and organisation in FATA, they were likely to gain more strength and always ready to attack at will – as happened twice before. The policy strategists held that:

> *'Just because the state may favour talks with the TTP does not mean it should become suicidal and give the militants an opportunity to increase their influence in these important territories.*

> *Previous peace negotiations have shown the TTP to be a slippery and deceitful adversary. Combine that with their latest act [of killing the senior army officers] and you have an enemy that is not to be trusted at all. The memory of Maj Gen Sanaullah and others who died must not be besmirched.'*

The army in 2009 sent 30,000 troops to battle Taliban fighters controlled by cleric Maulana Fazlullah, who since 2007 had taken control of the scenic Swat valley and waged a campaign of beheadings, other violence and attacks on girls' schools. More than 20,000 troops remained in Swat and adjacent districts in Khyber PK province after the operation had concluded.

The Swat people had a general fear that Maulana Fazlullah and his loyalists, who had escaped into Eastern Afghanistan, could make a comeback in the event of a complete army pullout.

The Chief Minister of Khyber PK, Pervez Khattak, had approved the phased withdrawal of Army from Swat and Malakand Division just a day earlier. In the initial stage, 300 soldiers were to be withdrawn from neighbouring *Buner* and *Shangla* districts in October 2013.

On 16th September 2013, however, Pakistan's Army Chief Gen Ashfaq Kayani delivered a tough warning to terrorists, a day after the roadside bomb attack killing the two senior army officers. Reiterating the army's resolve and unflinching commitment in fighting terrorism, Gen Kayani vowed to spare no effort in bringing the terrorists to justice. While reaffirming army's support to a political process for peace, the COAS also said that *'terrorists will not be allowed to take advantage of it.'* He emphasized that:

> *"While it is understandable to give peace a chance through a political process but no one should have any misgivings that we would let terrorists coerce us into accepting their terms. Army has the ability and the will to take the fight to the terrorists."*

PPP's Mr Zardari joined the orchestra by conveying an open warning that: *"If there has been any doubt about the futility of appeasing the militants, these must be removed by the incident in Upper Dir."*

The highly trumpeted unconditional peace talks' offer by the APC soon met with a bizarrely violent response by the militant forces at war. Just a night before [14th September 2013] militants had attacked a patrol of tribal Khassadar police near the Bannu town killing one and injuring four. Next day morning, two army posts in Miranshah of North Waziristan tribal area were subjected to attacks, leaving two soldiers dead and two injured.

The militants continued to keep its pace of striking irrespective of peace-talks initiatives - rather preferred to fill their coffers with state funding. The print media, in their editorial comments, deplored that the civilian leadership was unable to even issue a strong condemnation of the TTP's group that claimed responsibility for the [Dir] attack. One pinching line from *'Dawn'* dated *16th September 2013* was that:

> *"With the kind of political leadership [PML(N)'s Rana Sanaullah in focus] on display in recent days, a fairly legitimate question would be — ought the country to fear the TTP more or its own elected leadership; surely the situation demands that the politicians rectify their pusillanimous approach."*

Most of the political leaders were justifying the offer of negotiations to TTP by stating that *'we have fought a war with TTP for years and have achieved nothing - we must give peace a chance'*.

Actually no one had fought any war with the Taliban; during South Waziristan operation hardly any terrorist was killed while most of them moved to other areas to re-group later. Unfortunately, Pakistani leadership, both PPP & PML(N), always went undecided during six years of suffering that how to deal with the terrorists – an utter confusion. In the words of Ayaz Amir [*'the NEWS' of 17th September 2013* is referred]:

> *'Wounds of Pakistani people are open and their leaders are pouring salt over them…. cups of humiliation are full and leaders want to add more to it. The leadership has no Plan B, no line of retreat, no other options - but have put all eggs in the appeasement basket.*
>
> *No surprise - the present rulers [Nawaz Sharif] were Gen Ziaul Haq's most loyal supporters back in the 1980s; they were jihad sympathisers then AND Taliban sympathisers later.'*

Nawaz Sharif of PML(N) and Imran Khan of PTI offered negotiations with terrorists from a point of utter weakness - they totally succumbed to them and accepted them as stake-holders. One could recall PML(N)'s call of three years back that *'their views were in line with the TTP and, as such, they should not carryout bombings in Punjab.'*

This time, though being in power, the PML(N) had again covertly conveyed to the TTP that *'they were in line with them but the Army was not.'*

At what cost? The Taliban were not hitting them; they spared Punjab. It was the army out there in the front, taking the most hits, and the luckless *khasadars*, poor police and the Frontier Corps. The academics of PPP & PML(N) had gone too far by saying that *'wasn't it the army – or the ISI – which nurtured the Taliban? So if the ghosts have come to haunt their creators there is poetic justice in that.'* It was self-punishment.

In the given situation [like killing of GOCs & Lt Cols], Pak-Army should have given a befitting response, massive retaliatory strikes on known Taliban hide-outs, but there were only statements; the people started raising fingers of martial status of Gen Kayani.

No cogent response came from the main political parties on that post - APC offensive by the militants except a futile resolution in the parliament.

Contrarily the retired military officers felt their Generals being killed badly and were dismayed at Pak-Army's response to the event – see some scripts:

- *'There should have been a massive air force strike and heavy artillery bombardment of known TTP positions to let them know that when they hit the Army and accept responsibility, there are consequences. Simply issuing a statement has no effect on them; that is disappointing. In the past immediate retaliation was the policy, now timidity is – not acceptable.*

- *.....the hare-brained idea of peace talks with Taliban, no body is sure about its success. This would soon give in to the same situation that arose before Swat operation in 2007. Dialogue's failure is already written large on the wall. Now they [the political leadership] will not make the Army a scapegoat for their failure.*

- *The recent killing of a General shows how much the TTP cares for niceties of negotiations. They see it as surrender negotiations offered by our cowardly politicians. They are talking and behaving as if we have lost and they are the victors. Will the Pak-Army accept the death of a valiant General with a whimper? Will his death go in vain? - Shame on all who surrendered at the APC moot to share the blame for cowardice.*

- *General Kayani should stand up and reject Nawaz Sharif's peace Plan, which is nothing but an outright surrender to the terrorists and thugs. Pakistan is more important than a motivated mandate to undermine the country.*

- *Killing of a popular General by TTP who had done so much for the people of Swat - may GOD show the right path to our political and military leadership and give them the courage to call a spade a spade and act with determination to eliminate this menace in supreme interest of Pakistan.*

- *Pakistan's history is littered with the carcasses of APCs. All governments have been wedded to the notion that "consensus" is the alternative to action. The media during this process has been on a long watch, each night presenting "theories" which have been fed to them by their "handlers". The deliberations of so-called experts, intellectuals, pundits, academics, and veterans went misleading. Peace talks and peace-making require blood and courage, not submission and inaction.'*

The nut shell of numerous letters to editors, editorials & opinions, and internet blogs conveyed that:

> *'If the Pak-Army or the state intelligence agencies have information about the hideouts of terrorists, they need to be struck from the air. Why does Pak-Army not use the most effective weapon they keep - helicopter gun-ships and Ground Attack aircrafts?*
>
> *The American drones and the TTP do not care about co-lateral damages – the Pakistan's troops should reply in the same way.'*

One Brig (rtd) Usman Khalid [of Rifah.org] told that:

> *'I was posted in Bannu in 1970 when **a lady doctor was abducted and taken to South Waziristan.** The response of the military was a warning to target villages followed by aerial bombing of those who had harboured fugitives. It was not known who had abducted the lady doctor but it was well known who harboured fugitives. No statement issued by the military or the Governor NWFP.*
>
> ***The lady doctor was driven back to Bannu the very next day.*** *The life and honour of the lady doctor was endangered but no one waited for negotiating a ransom; prompt and strong response was more important.*
>
> ***Actions speak louder than words.'***

Here, the army chief Gen Kayani had responded firmly saying that the army would not be arm-twisted into accepting the terms set by the Taliban for a truce. He had vowed to bring the perpetrators of the attacks on the security forces to justice – but no practical move was seen from the army side.

Army Chief's deliberation was a pointed reference to the PML(N) government, hinting that unconditional peace talks without naming the adversaries or militants in this battle for the survival of the nation were not the best choice. The intelligentsia had also felt that though the two highest ranking army officers were there in the APC but the political leadership and the military establishment were not on one page.

Rana Sanaullah group of the PML(N), of course with the able consent of Shahbaz Sharif, suggested the APC to forward their demands, three at least, before commencing negotiations with Taliban. The hard group, however, took it a strategy to mild the military minds – the death event of senior army officers would fade away with time and Gen Kayani's retirement would come closer to make the matter diluted. The three points were:

- *A ceasefire, the renouncing of arms, and stopping the infiltration of militants from across the Pak-Afghan borders.*

- *The militants should hand over all the prisoners that were whisked away by the Taliban to safe havens in the remote tribal hideouts from D I Khan and Bannu jails as those convicts and under-trials were locked up as part of due judicial process.*

- *The militants have to agree to negotiate within the constitutional and legal framework of Pakistan which they have been denying since a decade.*

The serious minds could understand that TTP would not be admitting even one part clause of that offer – but they would definitely get more time to gain more strength. Referring to Tariq Khosa's essay on the subject appeared in the *'DAWN' dated 18th September 2013*:

'*Maj Gen Sanaullah Niazi's sacrifice should not be in vain like that of IG Police Sibghat Ghayur, Commandant of Frontier Constabulary, who was targeted in Peshawar by the Taliban in 2010.*

*There comes a time in the history of a nation when its character is tested; Pakistan faces that moment today.*'

## GEN KAYANI RETIRED:

Gen Kayani had an eventful tenure - had inherited a highly demoralized army while taking over from Gen Musharraf in ending 2007. Among a number of other such incidents, 207 soldiers under a Lt Col had surrendered to a handful of Taliban in August the same year – perhaps the officer and his troops were not convinced of the morality of that war due to Gen Musharraf's flawed policies. During Gen Musharraf's times, the army could not succeed in Kurram, Orakzai and Khyber as it did in Swat within months,

Gen Kayani, on assuming charge, had switched his divisional commanders, addressed all garrisons, and announced the return of all serving officers employed on non-military duties. He had also convinced his troops that WOT was Pakistan's war – a morally justified one.

Gen Kayani knew that an unconventional war would not be won through the strategy and tactics of a conventional war. *Rejecting American advice, he demonstrated his superior understanding of this new generation warfare during the Malakand and Swat operations in 2009, stunned his American counterparts with his success in less than six weeks from commencement.*

Pakistan's Prime Minister Yousaf Raza Gilani once visited India for the India-Pakistan cricket semi-final after the visit was cleared by the Army. He would not have been able to board the flight had Gen Kayani not smiled. Gen Kayani, while in command, retained the support of the soldiers; largely because he stayed away from the media. He was never interested in publicity unlike his predecessor Gen Musharraf and had shown little interest in becoming the politician in uniform. This all went to his credit ensuring only with one extension as Army Chief.

During Gen Kayani in chair, the politicians were able to focus on the civilian institutions of state and went for strengthening democracy in Pakistan. This policy also allowed the Army to consolidate its hold on matters of strategic importance. Gen Kayani went successful in improving relations with Afghan President Hamid Karzai from freezing to almost warm levels and ensured a level of cooperation between the two.

Gen Kayani's clearest warning was on the economy and time and again he blamed the civilian rulers entirely for the failure. He recounted so many instances and asked –

'......... *do you blame the army for this, for that and for everything*'? *He, however, tolerated the corrupt civilians to do the damage before his own eyes.*

The media did not disagree with him on that count. Politicians always held that the piles of dirt and filth were left behind by the army after 'nine years of misrule', thus could not be cleared – but the history keeps all facts and figures in tact. *Why the PPP had not published his achievements during their five years rule making comparison with those of Gen Musharraf's era* - simply because there was none to mention with.

Gen Kayani's South Waziristan operation was less successful – mainly because *the US troops had mysteriously vacated six posts on the Durand Line* just as the operation began, permitting Hakimullah Mehsud and his supporters to escape.

Gen Kayani once accompanied President Zardari during a *visit to Siachen*. Within a year of taking over he had, not only restored morale in his force, but had also won it back the respect and support of the people of Pakistan. However, his second, extended tenure of another three years undid most of what he had done during his original tenure. *Gen Kayani's second term was a period of innumerable controversies.*

Raymond Davis could have been interfered to be kept and tried in Pakistan – putting behind the vicious planning of Rehman Malik, the CIA agent in Pakistan. Osama Bin Laden's execution by US Marines alone in Abbotabad was another negative point. The *'Memo-gate Scandal'* followed soon thereafter. The Salala attack by NATO troops, followed by a prolonged closure of the routs to Afghanistan – all events happened in quick succession.

Referring to *the 'Friday Times'* of 18th October 2013:

> *'The army [under Gen Kayani's command] was not succeeding in its anti-guerrilla operations as it had been earlier – its leadership was not as confident as it was in 2009. Gen Kayani seemed to have lost some of the confidence that of his troops. Perhaps the mere fact that Kayani was given an unprecedented additional three years....... making too many compromises.*

> *I [Najam Sethi – the Editor] can certainly state unequivocally that the antics of his siblings which have made them rich beyond their wildest dreams did not help....Gen Ashfaq Kayani might not be a direct beneficiary of their schemes but he was guilty of turning a (not-so) blind eye to them.'*

Moreover, the intelligentsia held that Gen Kayani retired as *another Gorbachev in South Asian region* – he could do a lot more to make institutions better without army's direct interference but he avoided – saying it was not his domain.

On 25th November 2013: 'the News' dared to publish a story about alleged corruption done by his brothers especially of Amjad Kayani, a retired Brigadier of the Infantry Division of the Army, second oldest after Gen Kayani and retired in 2005. Kamran Kayani, the youngest brother, is in business thus the richest among all the brothers.

Brig Amjad categorically denied while talking to media correspondent Azaz Syed that none of the four brothers ever used Gen Kayani's name in business circles. The facts appeared that:

- Brig Amjad Kayani had once hired a plaza in Rawalpindi to start a restaurant. The people talked about that *'this is the plaza of Gen Kayani's brother'* – it was never my plaza.

- Gen Kayani's other younger brother Maj (R) Babur Kayani, lived in an ISI apartment allotted to his doctor wife who used to serve the agency. He installed stone-crushing machines in Hattar district of the Khyber PK. Babur developed some issues with his landlord in Hattar. The landlord violated the agreement with Babur and not only ordered him out, *but also started giving applications here and there. The matter was in the court.* Babur was depositing the rent with the court; the issue is going on.

- Gen. Kayani's youngest brother Kamran Kayani is the CEO of JKB Constructions which once handled the Ring Road Project in Lahore. Kamran Kayani came into the media glare in 2009-10 when Ch Nisar Ali Khan once told media reporters outside Parliament House that Gen Kayani's brother had not done good work in Punjab – a deliberate move to defame Kayani family.

- Kamran Kayani had won that contract in an open bidding; it was around 2004. After that project Kamran stopped doing contracts with some departments. However, his construction business always went good - a BMW was in Kamran's use in 2004. Kamran's company had been a no-limit company since 2005. No-limit company is the one that can get a project of any cost. *"We rose from the ashes to the skies; why would we use the influence of our brother?"* Brig Amjad told proudly.

The nutshell remained that the stories of corruption regarding Gen Kayani's brothers were seemingly baseless – spread by certain angry media anchors.

**Kamran Khan, in Geo News Live TV talk show of 30th June 2014** said that former spokesman for the Army, Maj Gen (R) Athar Abbas, in an interview to the British media, acknowledged that due to Gen Kayani's reluctance and weak decision making, the Pakistan Army, despite having made up its mind, could not launch an operation against the terrorists in North Waziristan in 2011.

The former Army Chief had not been willing to rid North Waziristan of terrorist hideouts despite the willingness of some key commanders of the Army to do so. All the preparations for an operation had been completed then and final briefing had also been given to the concerned commanders at the Military Operations HQ. It had been estimated that if a comprehensive military operation was launched, the centres of terror would be destroyed within three weeks; but Gen Kayani could not make up his mind.

Kamran Khan said that former president Zardari had also communicated his 'No Objection' but Gen Kayani had not only been unwilling to go with the decision of his corps commanders but he also kept telling the political leadership that the chances of success of the operation had been quite remote. Gen Kayani had shared his point of view with Nawaz Sharif and told him that there had been only 40 percent chances of success of an operation in North Waziristan.

Gen Kayani's thoughts on the matter were incorrect. Later, Gen Raheel Sharif's decision to go after the terrorists and to eliminate them was praised by everyone in Pakistan and equally by foreign powers.

*However, it also remains a fact that the former DG ISPR Maj Gen Athar Abbas was not promoted by Gen Kayani.*

There were other issues also over which Gen Kayani remained reluctant. His most controversial decision was the one in which he accepted extension in the tenure of the post of Chief of the Army Staff - the speech of the then prime minister Mr Gilani in which he had announced the extension in the COAS's tenure was sent to the Army House by PM Gilani for prior approval.

However, his younger brother Brig (rtd) Amjad Kayani once told the media that *'almost every family member was against the extension'*.

Yet another incident during the tenure of Gen Kayani had been the attack on the GHQ – the COAS was himself present in his office which was close to where the terrorists had attacked rendering the Army HQ operationally inactive.

Regardless of all the points which were raised by Gen Kayani's critics be kept aside and let the nation praise him that despite the utter disappointing performance of the PPP government, the General never tempted to interfere in the democratic process. In Pakistan's chequered history Gen Kayani's that stance deserved a big credit note.

www.ingramcontent.com/pod-product-compliance
Lightning Source LLC
Chambersburg PA
CBHW031143270326
41931CB00006B/125

9 781781 489550